POWER
AND
SOCIETY
An Introduction to the Social Sciences
Second Edition

Thomas R. Dye
Florida State University

Duxbury Press, North Scituate, Massachusetts

Power and Society: An Introduction to the Social Sciences, second edition was edited and prepared for composition by *Sarah Evans*. Interior design was provided by *Margaret Tsao*. The cover was designed by *Nancy Gardner*.

Duxbury Press
A Division of Wadsworth, Inc.

Library of Congress Cataloging in Publication Data

Dye, Thomas R
  Power and society.

  Includes bibliographies and index.
  1. Social sciences.   I. Title.
H61.D95   1979   300   79-612
ISBN 0-87872-064-2

Printed in the United States of America
4   5   6   7   8   9 — 83   82

In memory of James C. "Jeff" Dye

Contents

vii Contents

ix Contents

Preface

Power and Society: An Introduction to the Social Sciences is designed as a basic text for an introductory, interdisciplinary social science course. It is written specifically for freshman and sophomore students at community and junior colleges and at four-year colleges and universities that offer a basic studies program.

Power and Society introduces students to central concepts in

anthropology	psychology
sociology	political science
economics	history

But, more importantly, it does so by focusing these disciplinary perspectives on a central integrative theme—the nature and uses of power in society. In this way, students are made aware of the *interdependence* of the social sciences. Compartmentalization is avoided and students are shown how each social science discipline contributes to an understanding of power.

Power and Society also introduces students to some of the central challenges facing American society:

ideological conflict	crime and violence
racism and sexism	energy and the environment
poverty and powerlessness	defense and arms limitations

Each of these national challenges is approached from an interdisciplinary viewpoint, with power as the integrating concept.

Power has been defined as the capacity to modify the conduct of individuals through the real or threatened use of rewards and punishments. Doubtlessly there are other central concepts or ideas in the social sciences that might be employed to develop an integrated framework for an introduction to social science. But certainly *power* is a universal phenomenon that is reflected in virtually all forms of human interaction. Power is intimately related to many other key concepts and ideas in the social sciences—personality, behavior, aggression, role, class, mobility, wealth, income distribution, markets, culture, ideology, change, evolution, authority, oligarchy, elites.

xi

Power is also a universal instrument in approaching the various crises that afflict human beings and their societies—racism, sexism, poverty, violence, crime, pollution, energy, urban decay, ideological and international conflict.

Several special features are designed to assist the student in understanding the meaning of various concepts. The first is the identification of specific *masters of social thought* and the clear, concise presentation of their central contributions to social science. Specific attention is given to the contributions of:

Bertrand Russell	Charles Beard
Sigmund Freud	John Locke
B. F. Skinner	Martin Luther King, Jr.
Adam Smith	Ruth Benedict
John M. Keynes	Karl Marx
C. Wright Mills	

The second special feature is the presentation of *timely, relevant case studies* at the ends of chapters to illustrate important concepts:

Social Science in Action: The Busing Controversy
Sociobiology: It's All in Your Genes
The Power Elite
Inflation: The Silent Thief
Authority and Obedience: The "Shocking" Experiments
A Tale of Two Presidents: Watergate and Its Aftermath
Reconstruction and Black History
Marxism-Leninism in the Soviet Union
The *Bakke* Case: Affirmative Action or Reverse Discrimination?
Welfare Reform and the Work Ethic
The Ghetto Riots
Power, Energy, and the Environment: The Competing Interests
The Balance of Forces: U.S. and U.S.S.R.

The second edition of *Power and Society* grows out of our experience in developing an introductory, interdisciplinary social science text with power as a unifying theme. Instructors throughout the nation assisted in this difficult task: developing interesting, timely, stimulating material, while avoiding the compartmentalization that is frequently encountered in social science texts. This second edition is extensively revised, updated, and rewritten. Specific changes include:

A new chapter "How Scientific Are the Social Sciences?" with explanations of the scientific method and scientific research designs, exploration of problems in applying the scientific method to the social sciences, discussion of social indicators, and a particularly interesting case study of the busing controversy, which illustrates social science research in action.

A new section on the growing field of sociobiology.

An expanded discussion of microeconomics to complement our treatment of macroeconomics, and a new, relevant case study on the subject of inflation.

A new discussion of the work of humanistic psychologist Abraham Maslow to complement our presentations of psychoanalytic, behavioral, and social psychology, as well as a stimulating new case study on the relationship between authority and obedience.

An expanded case study on the relationship of the president to the "establishment," which includes new material on Jimmy Carter's rapid rise to power.

An expanded chapter on inequality and discrimination, which, in addition to presenting material on racism, includes discussions of "Sexual Inequality and Discrimination," "The Power of Women's Protest Movements," and "Abortion and the Law."

Intensive treatment of the controversial *Bakke* case, illustrating the conflict between affirmative action and equality of opportunity.

A new case study on the competing interests that affect the management of energy and the environment.

A new chapter, "Power and the International System," which includes material on international relations, peace and deterrence, the balance of terror, the SALT agreements, and a case study on the balance of forces maintained by the U.S. and the U.S.S.R.

A new appendix on "social indicators" for the United States, showing trends in family life, marriage, and divorce; life expectancy; education, income, and occupation; crime; poverty; inflation; racial and sexual differences in socioeconomic conditions; and public attitudes toward national priorities and the quality of life.

I am particularly grateful for the many constructive comments and criticisms made at various stages of this work by Merlin G. Cox, University of Florida; Leonard J. Mills, Northern Virginia Community College; Matthew H. Epstein, Michigan State University; Richard D. Humphrey, City Colleges of Chicago (The Loop College); Donald L. Uppendahl, Portland Community College; Ruth Gruenberg, Montgomery Community College; R. Bruce Donlan, Brevard Community College; Charlton D. Keen, Jr., Chipola Junior College; Steven W. Valavanis, Brevard Community College; William Scalapino,

College of Marin (California); James Dale, Youngstown State University; Sandra B. Damico, University of Florida; Danney Goble, Tulsa Junior College; Kirk Johnson, Fisk University; and James McElyea, Tulsa Junior College. I am also indebted to Sarah Evans and Virginia Lakehomer of Duxbury Press for their valuable editorial assistance, and Pat Fitzgerald for his encouragement in this project.

Thomas R. Dye

PART I

THE NATURE AND STUDY OF POWER

The purpose of this book is to introduce you to the social sciences. Because power in society is a theme that pervades each of the social sciences, as well as the problems they study, we have chosen this theme as the focal point for our presentation. Part I is designed to familiarize you with the notion of power, with the nature of each of the social sciences, with the scientific methods they employ, and with the framework of this book. You will find that chapter 1 reflects the structure of the entire text. Like the book as a whole, its first part focuses on the nature of power, its second part on the individual social sciences and the particular ways in which they contribute to our understanding of power, and its third and final part on the problems with which the social sciences are concerned. Chapter 2 is devoted to a discussion of the methods used in social science research.

Photo from Stock, Boston by Cary Wolinsky

Photo from Stock, Boston by David A. Krathwohl

Chapter 1
Power, Society, and Social Science

Power in society is not just an abstract concept, or a convenient focus for academic exercise. Nor is power something that is located exclusively in the nation's capitals. Power is very much a real factor that affects the lives of every one of us. We experience it in some form in our own families, in school, and at work; we feel its effects in the grocery store and on the highway. And we each react to it in characteristic ways. Our aim in this chapter is to understand just what power *is*. We will also see why it provides us with a useful perspective from which to gain a unified view of the social sciences and the social problems that concern us all.

After you have read this chapter, you should be able to:

- define power in society and describe its characteristics.
- define the area of study of each of the social sciences, as well as their common focus, and discuss how each relates to power in society.
- identify the major social problems that the social sciences study and explain why they are interdisciplinary in nature and how they relate to power.

THE NATURE OF POWER

Ordinary men and women are driven by forces in society that they neither understand nor control. These forces are embodied in governmental authorities, economic organizations, social values and ideologies, accepted ways of life, and learned patterns of behavior. However diverse the nature of these forces, they have in common the ability to modify the conduct of individuals, to control their behavior, to shape their lives.

Power is the capacity to modify the conduct of individuals through the real or threatened use of rewards and punishments. Power is exercised over individuals or groups by offering them some things they value or by threatening to deprive them of these things. These values are the *power base*, and they may include: physical safety, health, and well-being; wealth and material possessions; jobs and means to a livelihood; knowledge and skills; social recognition, status, and prestige; love, affection, and acceptance by others; a satisfactory self-image and self-respect. To exercise power, then, control must be exercised over the things that are valued in society.

Power can rest on various power bases. The exercise of power assumes many different forms—the giving or withholding of many different values. Yet power bases are usually *interdependent*—individuals who control certain base values are likely to control other base values as well. Wealth, economic power, prestige, recognition, political influence, education, respect, and so on, all tend to "go together" in society.

Power is never equally distributed. "There is no power where power is equal." For power to be exercised, the "power holder" must control some base values. By *control* we mean that the power holder is in a position to offer these values as rewards to others, or to threaten to deprive others of these values.

Power is a relationship between individuals, groups, and institutions in society. Power is not really a "thing" that an individual possesses. Instead power is a relationship in which some individuals or groups have control over certain base values.

The elite are the few who have power; the masses are the many who do not. The elites are the few who control what is valued in society and use that control to shape the lives of all of us. The masses are the many whose lives are shaped by institutions, events, and leaders over which they have little control. Political scientist Harold Lasswell writes, "The division of society into elites and masses is universal," and even in a democracy "a few exercise a relatively great weight of power, and the many exercise comparatively little."[1]

Power is exercised in interpersonal relations. Psychologist Rollo May writes that "power means the ability to affect, to influence, and to change other persons." He argues that power is essential to one's "sense of significance"—one's conviction that one counts for something in the world, that one has an effect on others, and that one can get recognition of one's existence from others. Power is essential to the development of personality. An infant who is denied the experience of influencing others or of drawing their attention to its existence withdraws to a corner of its bed, does not talk or develop in any way, and withers away physiologically and psychologically. Thus power is essential to *being*. Political scientist Robert Dahl also defines power in terms of *individual interaction*: "A has power over B to the extent that he can get B to do something he would not otherwise do." He argues that every exercise of power depends upon interpersonal relations between the power holder and the responder. Since there are many different aspects of power in interpersonal situations, Dahl thinks it unlikely that there will ever be two cases in which power is exercised in precisely the same fashion.

Power is exercised in large institutions—governmental, corporate, educational, military, religious, professional, occupational. Power that stems from positions in the social structure of society is stable and far-reaching. Sociologist C. Wright Mills observes: "No one can be truly powerful unless he has access to the command of major institutions, for it is over these institutional means of power that the truly powerful are, in the first instance, powerful."[2] Not all power, it is true, is anchored in or exercised through institutions. But institutional positions in society provide a continuous and important base of power. As Mills explains:

> If we took the one hundred most powerful men in America, the one hundred wealthiest, and the one hundred most celebrated away from the institutional positions they now occupy, away from their resources of men and women and money, away from the media of mass communication that are now focused upon them—then they would be powerless and poor and uncelebrated. For power is not of a man. Wealth does not center in the person of the wealthy. . . . to have power requires access to major institutions, for the institutional positions men occupy determine in large part their chances to have and to hold these valued experiences.[3]

BERTRAND RUSSELL
Power Is to the Social Sciences
What Energy Is to Physics

Bertrand Russell (1872–1970), English philosopher and mathematician, is regarded as one of the twentieth century's greatest thinkers, mainly because of his contributions to mathematics and symbolic logic. However, Russell possessed a great breadth of interest that included history, economics, and political science as well as education, morals, and social problems. He received the Nobel Prize in literature "in recognition of his many-sided and significant authorship, in which he has constantly figured as a defender of humanity and freedom of thought." He summarized his views about the importance of power in society in a book significantly entitled *Power: A New Social Analysis.**

First of all, power is fundamental to the social sciences:

> The fundamental concept in the social sciences is power, in the same sense in which energy is the fundamental concept in physics.

Secondly, the desire for power as well as wealth motivates people:

> The orthodox economists, as well as Marx, who in this respect agreed with them, were mistaken in supposing that economic self-interest could be taken as the fundamental motive in the social sciences. The desire for commodities, when separated from power and glory, is finite, and can be fully satisfied by a moderate competence. The really expensive desires are not dictated by a love of material comfort. Such commodities as a legislature rendered subservient by corruption, or a private picture gallery of Old Masters selected by experts, are sought for the sake of power or glory, not as affording comfortable places in which to sit. When a moderate degree of comfort is assured, both individuals and communities will pursue power rather than wealth: they may seek wealth as a means to power, or they may forgo an increase of wealth in order to secure an increase of power, but in the former case as in the latter their fundamental motive is not economic. . . .

Thirdly, power takes many forms:

> Like energy, power has many forms, such as wealth, armaments, civil authority, influence on opinion. No one of these can be regarded as subordinate to any other, and there is no one form from which the others are derivative. The attempt to treat one form of power, say wealth, in isolation can only be partially successful, just as the study of one form of energy will be defective at certain points, unless other forms are taken into account. Wealth may result from military power or from influence over opinion, just as either of these may result from wealth. The laws of social dynamics are laws which can only be stated in terms of power, not in terms of this or that form of power. In former times, military power was isolated, with the consequence that victory or defeat appeared to depend upon the accidental qualities of commanders. In our day, it is common to treat economic power as the source from which all other kinds are derived: this, I shall contend, is just as great an error as that of the

---

*Selection is reprinted from *Power: A New Social Analysis* by Bertrand Russell, with the permission of W. W. Norton & Company, Inc. Copyright 1938 by Bertrand Russell. Copyright renewed 1966 by Bertrand Russell.

purely military historians whom it has caused to seem out of date. Again, there are those who regard propaganda as the fundamental form of power . . . It has about the same measure of truth and falsehood as the military view or the economic view. Propaganda, if it can create an almost unanimous opinion, can generate an irresistible power; but those who have military or economic control can, if they choose, use it for the purpose of propaganda. To revert to the analogy of physics: power, like energy, must be regarded as continually passing from any one of its forms into any other, and it should be the business of social science to seek the laws of such transformations. The attempt to isolate any one form of power, more especially, in our day, the economic form, has been, and still is, a source of errors of great practical importance. . . .

Finally, power produces social change:

Those whose love of power is not strong are unlikely to have much influence on the course of events. The men who cause social changes are, as a rule, men who strongly desire to do so. Love of power, therefore, is a characteristic of the men who are causally important. We should, of course, be mistaken if we regarded it as the sole human motive, but this mistake would not lead us so much astray as might be expected in the search for causal laws in social science, since love of power is the chief motive producing the changes which social science has to study.

POWER AND THE SOCIAL SCIENCES

Social science is the study of human behavior. Actually, there are several social sciences, each specializing in a particular aspect of human behavior and each using different concepts, methods, and data in its studies. Anthropology, sociology, psychology, economics, history, and political science have developed into separate "disciplines," but each shares an interest in human behavior.

Power is *not* the central concern of the social sciences, yet all of the social sciences deal with power in one form or another. Each of the social sciences contributes to an understanding of the forces that modify the conduct of individuals, control their behavior, and shape their lives. Thus, to fully understand power in society, we must approach this topic in an *interdisciplinary* fashion—using ideas, methods, data, and findings from all the social sciences.

An interdisciplinary approach to studying power

Anthropology   Anthropology is the study of people and their ways of life. Because it is concerned with culture, it is the most comprehensive of the social sciences. *Culture* is all of the common patterns and ways of living that characterize a society. The anthropologist tries to describe and explain a great many things: child rearing and education; family arrangements; language and communication; technology; ways of making a living; the distribution of work; religious beliefs and virtues; social life; leadership patterns; and power structures.

Power and culture

Power is part of the culture or the way of life of a people. Power is exercised in all societies, because all societies have systems of sanctions designed to control the behavior of their members. Perhaps the most enduring structure of power in society is the family: power is exercised within the family when patterns of dominance and submission are established between male and female and parents and children. Societies also develop structures of power outside the family to maintain peace and order among their members; to organize individuals to accomplish large-scale tasks; to defend themselves against attack; and even to wage war and exploit other peoples.

In our study of power and culture we will examine how cultural patterns determine power relationships. We will examine patterns of authority in traditional and modern families and the changing power role of women in society. We will examine the origins and development of power relationships, illustrating this development with examples of societies in which power is organized by family and kinship group (polar Eskimos), by tribe (Crow Indians), and by the state (the

Aztec Empire). Finally, as a case study, we will look at the controversy over "sociobiology"—that is, the extent to which genetics or culture determines behaviors.

Sociology   Sociology is the study of relationships among individuals and groups. Sociologists describe the structure of formal and informal groups, their functions and purposes, and how they change over time. They study social institutions (such as, families, schools, churches), social processes (for example, conflict, competition, assimilation, change), and social problems (crime, race relations, poverty, and so forth). They also study social classes.

All societies have some system of classifying and ranking their members—a system of *stratification*. In modern industrial societies, social status is associated with the different roles that individuals play in the economic system. Individuals are ranked according to how they make their living and the control they exercise over the living of others. Stratification into social classes is determined largely on the basis of occupation and control of economic resources.

Power and social stratification

Power derives from social status, prestige, and respect, as well as control of economic resources. Thus, the stratification system involves, among other things, the unequal distribution of power.

In our study of power and social class, we will describe the stratification system in America and explore popular beliefs about "getting ahead." We will discuss the differential lifestyles of upper, middle, and lower classes in America and the extent of class conflict. We will examine the ideas of Karl Marx about the struggle for power among social classes. We will describe the differential in political power among social classes in America. Finally, we will explore the ideas of sociologist C. Wright Mills about a top "power elite" in America that occupies powerful positions in the governmental, corporate, and military bureaucracies of the nation.

Economics   Economics is the study of the production, distribution, and consumption of goods and services. There are never enough goods and services to satisfy everyone's demands, and because of this, choices must be made. Economists study how individuals, firms, and nations make these choices about goods and services.

Power and economic decisions

Economic power is the power to decide what will be produced, how much it will cost, how many people will be employed, what their wages will be, what the price of goods and services will be, what profits will be made, how these profits will be distributed, and how fast the economy will grow. Control over these decisions is a major source of power in society.

Capitalist societies rely heavily on the market mechanism to determine who gets what—what is to be produced, how much it will cost, and who will be able to buy it. In our study of economic power, we will explore both the strengths and weaknesses of this market system, as well as the ideas of economic philosophers Adam Smith and John M. Keynes. In addition, we will consider the role of government in the economy, which has increased over the years. We will then turn to an examination of America's vast wealth—how it is measured, where it comes from, and where it goes. We will examine the relationship between wealth and the quality of life, which are not always equivalent things. We will also examine the concentration of private wealth and corporate power in America. Finally, in our case study, we will consider that silent thief in our economy: inflation.

Psychology   Psychology may be defined as the study of the behavior of people and animals. This simple definition fails, however, to convey the richness and diversity of psychological inquiry. For example, *behavioral psychologists* study the learning process—the way in which people and animals learn to respond to stimuli. They frequently study in laboratory, experimental situations, with the hope that the knowledge gained can be useful in understanding more complex human behavior outside of the laboratory. *Social psychologists*, on the other hand, study interpersonal behavior—the way in which social interactions shape an individual's beliefs, perceptions, motivations, attitudes, and behavior. They generally study the whole person in relation to the total environment. *Freudian psychologists* study the impact of unconscious feelings and emotions and of early childhood experiences on the behavior of adults. *Humanistic psychologists* are concerned with the human being's innate potential for growth and development. Many other psychologists combine theories and methods in different ways in their attempts to achieve a better understanding of behavior.

Personality is all of the enduring, organized ways of behavior that characterize an individual. Psychologists differ over how personality characteristics are determined—whether they are learned habits acquired through the process of reinforcement and conditioning (behavioral psychology), or products of the individual's interaction with the significant people and groups in his life (social psychology), or manifestations of the continuous process of positive growth toward "self-actualization" (humanistic psychology), or the results of unconscious drives and long-repressed emotions stemming from early childhood experiences (Freudian psychology), or some combination of all these.

Power and personality

The study of personality is essential in understanding how individuals react toward power and authority. Power is a personal experience. Everyone is subject to one form of power or another during all the waking hours of life. And everyone has exercised some power, if only in microscopic degree, at some time. Individuals react toward these experiences with power in different and characteristic ways. Some individuals seek power for personal fulfillment. Philosopher Bertrand Russell writes, "Of the infinite desires of man, the chief are the desires for power and glory."[4] Other individuals are submissive to authority, while still others are habitually rebellious. It is said that "power corrupts, and absolute power corrupts absolutely." However, there is ample psychological evidence that lack of power also corrupts. The feelings that one cannot influence anyone else, that one counts for little, and that one has no control over one's own life all contribute to a loss of personal identity.

In our study of power and personality, we will examine various theories of personality determination—specifically, those of behavioral psychology, social psychology, humanistic psychology, and Freudian psychology—in an effort to understand the forces shaping the individual's reaction to power. Using a Freudian perspective, we will study the "authoritarian personality"—the individual who is habitually dominant and aggressive toward others over whom he exercises power, yet submissive and weak toward others who have power over him; the individual who is extremely prejudiced, rigid, intolerant, cynical, and power-oriented. We will explore the power implications of B. F. Skinner's ideas of behavioral conditioning for the control of human behavior. We will also examine David Riesman's notion of the "other-directed" person and the effect of individual powerlessness in mass society. To gain an understanding of humanistic psychology's approach to power relationships, we will explore Rollo May's formulation of the functions of power for the individual and Abraham Maslow's theory of a "hierarchy of needs." Finally, in our case study, we will describe the startling results of an experiment designed to test the relationship between authority and obedience.

Governmental power: legitimate authority

Political Science   Political science is the study of government and politics. Governments possess a particular form of power: the legitimate use of physical force (*authority*). By *legitimate* we mean that people generally consent to the government's use of this power. Of course, other individuals and organizations in society—muggers, street gangs, the Mafia, violent revolutionaries—use force. But only government can legitimately threaten people with the loss of freedom and well-being to modify their behavior. Moreover, governments exercise power over all individuals, institutions, and individuals in

"To the Housing Authority, Port Authority, Tunnel Authority, Transit Authority, Bridge Authority—to *authority*!"

Drawing by Dana Fradon; © 1976 The New Yorker Magazine, Inc.

society—corporations, families, schools, and so forth. Obviously the power of government in modern society is very great, extending to nearly every aspect of modern life—"from the womb to the tomb."

Political scientists, from Aristotle to the present, have been concerned with the dangers of unlimited and unchecked governmental power. We will examine the American experience with limited, constitutional government; the philosophical legacy of English political thought; and the meaning of democracy in modern society. We will observe how the United States Constitution divides power, first between states and the national government, and second among the legislative, executive, and judicial branches of government. We will examine the growth of power in Washington and the struggle for power among the different branches. We will also explore competition between political parties and interest groups and popular participation in decision making through elections. Finally, in our case study, "A Tale of Two Presidents: Watergate and Its Aftermath " we will look at the relationship between the president and the nation's "establishment," at what happens when political elites in America fail to abide by "the rules of the game," and at the tactics that embattled elites may employ to recoup their losses.

History   History is the recording, narrating, and interpreting of human experience. The historian recreates the past by collecting recorded facts, organizing them into a narrative, and interpreting their meaning. History is also concerned with change over time. It provides a perspective on the present by informing us of the way people lived in the past. It helps us to understand how society developed into what it is today.

Power relationships and the historical perspective

The foundations of power vary from age to age. As these power bases shift, new groups and individuals acquire control over them. Thus, power relationships are continually developing and changing over time. An understanding of power in society requires an understanding of the historical development of power relationships.

In our consideration of the historical development of power relationships, we will look at the changing sources of power in American history and the characteristics of the individuals and groups who have acquired power. We will describe the men of power in the early days of the Republic and their shaping of the Constitution and the government that it established. We will discuss Charles Beard's interpretation of the Constitution as a document designed to protect the economic interests of these early power holders. We will also discuss historian Frederick Jackson Turner's ideas about how western expansion and settlement created new bases of power and new power holders. We will explore the power struggle between Northern commercial and industrial interests and Southern planters and slave-owners for control of western land, and the Civil War that resulted from that struggle. In addition, we will explore the development of an industrial elite in America after the Civil War, the impact on that elite of the Depression, and the resulting growth of New Deal liberal reform. Finally, in our brief study "Reconstruction and Black History," we will examine how history occasionally overlooks the experiences of powerless minorities and later reinterprets their contributions to society.

SOCIAL SCIENCES AND SOCIAL PROBLEMS

Social problems, the major challenges confronting society, include ideological conflict, racism, sexism, poverty, crime, violence, pollution, urban decay, and international conflict. These problems do

*The interdisciplinary nature
of social problems*

not confine themselves to one or another of the disciplines of social science. They spill over the boundaries of anthropology, economics, sociology, political science, psychology, and history—they are *interdisciplinary* in character. Each of these problems has its *historical* antecedents, its *social* and *psychological* roots, its *cultural* manifestations, its *economic* consequences, and its impact on *government* and public policy. The origins of these social problems, as well as the various solutions proposed, involve complex power relationships.

Ideological Conflict   Ideas have power. Indeed, whole societies are shaped by systems of ideas that we call *ideologies*. The study of ideologies—liberalism, conservatism, socialism, communism, fascism, radicalism—is *not* a separate social science. Rather, the study of ideology spans all of the social sciences, and it is closely related to philosophy. Ideologies are integrated systems of ideas that rationalize a way of life, establish standards of "rightness" and "wrongness," and provide emotional impulses to action. Ideologies usually include economic, political, social, psychological, and cultural ideas, as well as interpretations of history.

Ideology and power

   Ideologies rationalize and justify power in society. By providing a justification for the exercise of power, the ideology itself becomes a base of power in society. Ideology "legitimizes" power, making the exercise of power acceptable to the masses and thereby adding to the power of the elite. However, ideologies also affect the behavior of the elites, because once an ideology is deeply rooted in society, power holders themselves are bound by it.

   In our study of power and ideology, we will first explore the ideology of *classical liberalism*—an ideology that attacked the established power of a hereditary, feudal system and asserted the dignity, worth, and freedom of the individual. Classical liberalism and capitalism justify the power of private enterprise and the market system. While classical liberalism limits the powers of government, *modern liberalism* accepts governmental power as a positive force in freeing men from poverty, ignorance, discrimination, and ill health. It justifies the exercise of governmental power over private enterprise and the establishment of the welfare state. In contrast, *modern conservatism* doubts the ability of the governmental planners to solve society's problems; conservatism urges greater reliance on family, church, and individual initiative and effort.

   We will then look at ideologies that have influenced other societies. *Fascism* is a power-oriented ideology that asserts the supremacy of the nation or race over the interests of individuals, groups, and other social institutions. *Marxism* attacks the market system, free enterprise, and individualism; it justifies revolutionary power in overthrowing liberal, capitalist systems and the establishment of a "dictatorship of the proletariat." *Socialism* calls for the evolutionary, democratic replacement of the private enterprise system with government ownership of industry.

We will also examine the ideology of the *New Left* in America and the meaning of contemporary radicalism. In our study of "Marxism-Leninism in the Soviet Union," we will see how an ideology justified the exercise of unlimited political and economic power by a totalitarian communist party.

Power and protest

Racial and Sexual Inequality   In our discussion of racial and sexual discrimination in American society, we will briefly describe the history of the civil rights movement and the response of the national government in the Civil Rights Acts. We will examine the *power of protest activities* and the strategies available to powerless groups to affect social change. Of course, other groups in America—Chicanos, Indians, and Puerto Ricans, for example—face similar problems of powerlessness. But we will try to understand these problems by studying America's black urban ghettos and the discrimination practiced against women. We will trace the development of the black power movement and of women's protest movements. Finally, we will explore the controversy over "affirmative action" and "reverse discrimination," and its implications for how America is to achieve real equality.

Various definitions of poverty

Poverty and Powerlessness   The American economy has produced the highest standard of living in the world, and yet a significant number of Americans live in poverty. We will observe that poverty can be defined as *economic hardship* or as *economic inequality*, and that each definition implies a different governmental approach to this problem. Poverty can also be defined as *powerlessness*—a social-psychological condition of hopelessness, indifference, lack of motivation, distrust, and cynicism. We will discuss whether or not there is a culture of poverty—a way of life of the poor that is passed on to future generations—and what its implications for government policy are. We will describe government efforts to cope with poverty, including the "War on Poverty" and the current welfare programs. Finally, we will discuss the problems involved in "welfare reform and the work ethic."

Social power vs. individual freedom

Crime and Violence   *Social power* must be balanced against *individual freedom*. A democratic society must exercise police powers to protect its citizens, yet it must not unduly restrict individual liberty. We will explore the problem of crime in society, the constitutional rights of defendants, the role of the courts, the wisdom of capital punishment, and the difficult tasks of the police. We will also describe briefly the history of violence in American society and the continuous role that violence has played in American struggles for power. We will summarize social-psychological explanations of violence; violence as a form of political activity; and violence as an aspect of lower-class culture. Finally, we will try to describe and explain urban violence and "the ghetto riots" of the 1960s.

Power struggles and environmental problems

The Quality of Life   There are a variety of social problems that affect the quality of life in America. The solution to these problems, if there is any solution, depends in great part on how government chooses to exercise its powers. We will look first at the problem of environmental pollution. Then we will turn to an examination of the causes of the "energy crises" and the conflict between the regulatory agencies that deal with it and those that deal with the problems of pollution. Next we will explore the growth of urban and suburban populations in America. We will also explore the social patterns of urban life—the characteristic forms of social interaction and organization that typically emerge in a large metropolis—and the socioeconomic conflicts between cities and suburbs. Finally, we will present a case study: "Power, Energy, and the Environment: The Competing Interests."

Power and sovereignty

International Conflict   The struggle for power is global—it involves all the nations and peoples of the world, whatever their goals or ideals. Nearly two hundred nations in the world claim *sovereignty: legal power over their internal affairs, freedom from outside intervention, and political and legal recognition by other nations.* But sovereignty is a legal fiction; it requires power to make sovereignty a reality. Over the years nations have struggled for power through wars and diplomacy. The struggle has led to attempts at maintaining a fragile balance of power among large and small nations, as well as to attempts at achieving collective security through the United Nations and other alliances. Today the balance of power between the two "superpowers"—the U.S. and the U.S.S.R.—requires a delicate balance of strategic nuclear power. In our discussion of the international system, we will describe this "balance of terror," or mutual assured destruction (MAD). We will briefly examine the weapons that maintain this balance, as well as the efforts of the Strategic Arms Limitation Talks (SALT) to slow the arms race. Finally, as a case study in national power and military force, we will consider the current balance of forces maintained by the U.S. and the U.S.S.R.

NOTES

1. Harold Lasswell and Abraham Kaplan, *Power and Society* (New Haven, Conn.: Yale University Press, 1950), p. 219.
2. C. Wright Mills, *The Power Elite* (New York: Oxford University Press, 1956), p. 9.
3. Ibid., p. 10.
4. Bertrand Russell, *Power: A New Social Analysis* (New York: W. W. Norton, 1938), p. 11.

DISCUSSION QUESTIONS

1. If you were assigned the task of describing the concept of power to a group of students, how would you define power? What characteristics of power would you discuss?
2. Consider the power relationships that directly and indirectly affect your life. On the basis of your experiences and observations, assess the validity of these statements by Bertrand Russell: "The fundamental concept in the social sciences is power, in the same sense in which energy is the fundamental concept in physics. . . . When a moderate degree of comfort is assured, both individuals and communities will pursue power rather than wealth. . . . love of power is the chief motive producing the changes which social science has to study."
3. Identify and briefly define the area of study of each of the social sciences. Discuss how you would study power from the perspective of each of these disciplines.
4. Define ideology and discuss the purposes of ideology in society. Briefly discuss the approach to governmental power of three of the following ideologies: (a) classical liberalism, (b) modern liberalism, (c) modern conservatism, (d) fascism, (e) Marxism, (f) socialism.
5. Choose two of the following social problems and briefly explain how they involve power: (a) racial and sexual inequality, (b) poverty, (c) crime and violence, (d) the quality of life, (e) international conflict.

SUGGESTED READINGS

Bernard Berelson, ed., *The Behavioral Sciences Today* (New York: Basic Books, 1963).

Frank J. Bruno, *The Story of Psychology* (New York: Holt, Rinehart and Winston, 1972).

Henry Steele Commager, *The Study of History* (Columbus, Ohio: Merrill, 1966).

Seymour Martin Lipset, *Politics and the Social Sciences* (New York: Oxford University Press, 1969).

Richard S. Martin and Reuben G. Miller, *Prologue to Economic Understanding* (Columbus, Ohio: Merrill, 1966).

Pertti J. Pelto, *The Nature of Anthropology* (Columbus, Ohio: Merrill, 1966).

Caroline B. Rose, *The Study of Sociology* (Columbus, Ohio: Merrill, 1966).

Frank J. Sorauf, *Perspectives on Political Science* (Columbus, Ohio: Merrill, 1966).

Photo from Stock, Boston by Cary Wolinsky

Photo from Stock, Boston by W. B. Finch

Chapter 2
How Scientific Are the Social Sciences?

How can the subject matter of the social sciences actually be measured and identified? How, for example, can a psychologist accurately and objectively measure a person's reaction to authority, or a sociologist identify someone's social status? How can a political scientist be sure that a reduction in crime is the result of a governmental program and not the incidental effect of some other factor? Social scientists are often accused of being not truly scientific. Are they guilty as charged and, if so, why? What are the problems, the promise, and the sometimes paradoxical effects of social science research?

These are the questions that chapter 2 addresses. After you have read it, you should be able to:

- define science and describe the scientific method.
- describe the classic research design and discuss some of the problems that social scientists have in applying this design and the scientific method to their research.
- define social indicators and discuss their utilization.

SCIENCE AND THE SCIENTIFIC METHOD

A *science* may be broadly defined as any organized *body of knowledge*, or it may be more narrowly defined as a discipline that employs the *scientific method*. If we use the broad definition, we can safely say that all the social sciences are indeed sciences. However, if we narrow our definition to only those disciplines that employ the scientific method, then some questions arise about whether the social sciences are really scientific. In other words, if science is defined as a *method of study*, rather than a *body of knowledge*, then not all studies in the social sciences are truly scientific.

The scientific method is a method of explanation that develops and tests theories about how real-world, observable phenomena are related. What does this definition really mean? How is this method of study actually applied in the social sciences? To answer these questions, let us examine each aspect of the scientific method separately.

Explaining Relationships *The goal of the scientific method is ex-*
planation. When using this method, we seek to answer the question
"why." Any scientific inquiry must begin by observing and classifying
things. Just as biology begins with the careful observation, description, and classification of thousands upon thousands of different
forms of life, the social sciences also must begin with the careful observation, description, and classification of various forms of human
behavior. But the goal is explanation, not just description. Just as
biology seeks to develop theories of evolution and genetics to explain
the various forms of life upon earth, the social sciences seek to
develop theories to explain why human beings behave as they do.

To answer the question of "why," the scientific method searches
for *relationships.* All scientific hypotheses assert some relationship
between phenomena—that is, observable facts or events. The social
sciences seek to find relationships that explain human behavior. The
first question is whether two or more events or behaviors are related
in any way—that is, do they occur together consistently? The second
question is whether either event or behavior is the *cause* of the other.
Social scientists first try to learn whether human events have occurred together merely by chance or accident, or whether they occur
together so consistently that their relationship cannot be a mere coin-
cidence. A relationship that is not likely to have occurred by chance
is said to be *significant.* After observing a significant relationship,
social scientists next ask whether there is a *causal relationship* between the phenomena (that is, whether the phenomena occurred
together because one is the cause of the other), or whether both
phenomena are being caused by some third factor.

Significant and causal
relationships

Developing and Testing Hypotheses *The scientific method seeks to*
develop statements ("hypotheses") about how events or behaviors
might be related and then to determine the validity of these state-
ments by careful, systematic, and logical tests. Scientific tests are
really exercises in logic. For example, if we want to find out
something about the relationship between race and party voters, we
might collect and record data from a national sample of black and
white voters chosen at random. (*Random* means that the sample was
chosen in such a fashion that every voter had an equal chance of
getting into the sample, and therefore the sample should—if it is large
enough—be an accurate reflection of all the voters.) If our data
showed that all blacks voted Democratic and all whites Republican, it
would be obvious that there was a perfect relationship between race
and voting. If both blacks and whites had voted Republican and
Democratic in the same proportions, then it would be obvious that

Random sample

there was *no* relationship. But in the social sciences we rarely have such obvious, clear-cut results. Generally our data will show a mixed pattern. For example, in the 1976 presidential election between Democrat Jimmy Carter and Republican Gerald Ford, 85 percent of blacks voted Democratic and only 15 percent voted Republican. In that same election, 52 percent of whites voted Republican and only 48 percent of whites voted Democratic. If there had been *no* relationship between race and voting, then blacks and whites would have voted Democratic and Republican in roughly the *same* proportions. But as we have just noted, blacks voted Democratic in far heavier proportions (85 percent) than whites (48 percent). This difference is not likely to have occurred by chance—it is "significant." So we can make the *inference* that blackness is related to Democratic voting.

Inference

However, the existence of a statistically significant relationship does not prove cause and effect. We must employ additional logic to find out which phenomenon caused the other, or whether both were caused by a third phenomenon. We can eliminate the possibility that voting Democratic causes one to become black as illogical; being black comes first in life and voting Democratic comes later. That leaves us with two possibilities: Blackness may cause Democratic voting, or blackness and Democratic voting may both be caused by some third condition. For example, the real causal relationship may be between low incomes and Democratic voting: low-income groups, which would include most blacks, tend to identify with the Democratic party. We can test this new hypothesis by looking at the voting behavior of other low-income groups to see if they voted Democratic in the same proportions as blacks. (It turns out that blacks vote more heavily Democratic than white low-income groups, so we can reject the low-income explanation. Race must therefore be independently related to voting behavior.) There are many other possible alternatives to our explanation of the relationship between race and voting behavior. Social scientists must test as many alternative explanations as possible before asserting a causal relationship.

Every time we can reject an alternative explanation for the relationship that we have observed, we increase our confidence that the relationship (as between race and voting behavior) is a causal one. Of course, in the areas of interest to social scientists someone can always think of new alternative explanations, so it is generally impossible to establish for certain that a causal relationship exists. Some social scientists react to the difficulties of proving "cause" by refusing to say that the relationships they find are anything more than *correlations*, or simply statistical relationships. The decision whether or not to call a relationship "causal" is a difficult one. Statistical tech-

Correlations

niques cannot guarantee that a relationship is causal. Social scientists must rely, finally, on the "feel" that comes from their familiarity with the details of the phenomena they are studying; and they must be prepared to deal with probabilities rather than absolutes.

Dealing with Observable Phenomena   *The scientific method deals only with observable—"empirical"—phenomena.* In other words, the scientific method deals with *facts*; it deals with what *is*, rather than what *should be*. It cannot test the validity of values, or norms, or feelings, except insofar as it can test for their existence in a society, or group, or individual. For example, the scientific method can be employed to determine whether voting behavior *is* related to race, but it cannot determine whether voting behavior *should be* related to race. The latter question is a *normative*, or *prescriptive*, one (dealing with "oughts" and "shoulds"), rather than an empirical one (dealing with "is's"). The scientific method is *descriptive* and *explanatory*, but not *prescriptive*. The social sciences can explain many aspects of human behavior but cannot tell human beings how they ought to behave. For guidance in values and norms—for prescriptions about how people should live—we must turn to ethics, religion, or philosophy.

Developing Theory   *The scientific method strives to develop a systematic body of theory.* Science is more than crude empiricism—the listing of facts without any statement of relationships among them. Of course, especially in the early stages of a science, research may consist largely of collecting data; but the ultimate goal of the scientific method is the development of verifiable statements about relationships among phenomena. It is the task of social scientists to find patterns and regularities in human behavior, just as it is the task of physicists and chemists to find patterns and regularities in the behavior of matter and energy. The social scientist's use of the scientific method, then, assumes that human behavior is not random, but rather that it is regular and predictable.

Theories are developed at different *levels of generality.* Theories with low levels of generality explain only a small or narrow range of behaviors. For example, the statement that blacks tend to vote Democratic is a fairly low-level generality about political behavior. Theories with higher levels of generality explain a greater or wider range of behavior. For example, the statement that racial differences cause political conflict has a higher level of generality. Strictly speaking, a *theory is a set of interrelated concepts at a fairly high level of generality.* Some social scientists concentrate on theory building rather than empirical research; they try to develop sweeping social theories to explain all, or a large part of, human behavior. Still other social theorists provide merely insights, hunches, or vague notions that serve to suggest possible explanations of human behavior, thus developing new hypotheses for empirical research.

Maintaining a Scientific Attitude   Perhaps more than anything else, *the scientific method is an attitude of doubt or skepticism*. It is an insistence upon careful collection of data and systematic testing of ideas, a commitment to keep bias out of one's work, to collect and record all relevant facts, and to interpret them rationally regardless of one's own feelings. For the social scientist, it is the determination to test explanations of human behavior by careful observations of real-world experiences. It is a recognition that any explanation is tentative and may be modified or disproved by careful investigation. Even the scientific theories that constitute the core knowledge in any discipline are not regarded as absolutes by the true social scientist; rather they are regarded as probabilities or generalizations developed from what is known so far.

WHY THE SOCIAL SCIENCES AREN'T ALWAYS "SCIENTIFIC"

Not all of the knowledge in social science is derived scientifically. A great deal of knowledge about human behavior comes to us through insight, intuition, random observation, folklore, and common sense rather than by careful scientific investigation. The scientific method that we have just described was devised in the physical and biological sciences. There are many difficulties in applying this method to the study of individuals, groups, economies, classes, governments, nations, or whole societies. Let us examine some of the obstacles to the development of truly *scientific* social sciences.

Personal Bias   *Social science deals with very subjective topics and must rely on interpretation of results.* Social scientists are part of what they investigate—they belong to a family, class, political party, interest group, profession, nation; they earn money and consume goods like everybody else. If the topic is an emotional one, the social scientist may find it much harder to suppress personal bias than does the investigator in the physical sciences: It is easier to conduct an unbiased study of migratory birds than of migrant workers.

It is difficult to conduct "value-free" research. Even the selection of a topic reveals the values of the researcher. Researchers study what they think is important in society, and what they think is important is affected by their personal values. If it were only in the selection of the topic that researchers' values were reflected, there would be no great problem in social science research. But researchers' values are also frequently reflected in their perceptions of the data itself, in their statement of the hypotheses, in their design of the test for the hypotheses, and in their interpretation of the findings. "Value intrusion" can occur in many stages of the research process, which is why social scientists studying the same problems and using the same methods frequently end up with contradictory results. Perhaps it is impossible to separate facts and values in social science research. As sociologist Louis Wirth explains:

> The distinctive character of social science discourse is to be sought in the fact that every assertion, no matter how objective it may be, has ramifications extending beyond the limits of science itself. Since every assertion of a "fact" about the social world touches the interests of some individual or group, one cannot even call attention to the existence of certain "facts" without quoting the objections of those whose very raison d'etre in society rests upon a divergent interpretation of the "factual" situation.[1]

Public Attitudes   *Another problem in the scientific study of human behavior centers on public attitudes toward social science.* Few laypersons would consider arguing with atomic physicists or biochemists about their respective fields, but most people believe they know something about social problems. Many people seemingly know exactly what should be done about juvenile delinquency, unwed mothers, expanding welfare rolls, and race relations. Very often their information is limited and their view of the problem is a simplistic one. When a social scientist suggests that a problem is very complex, that it has many causes, and that information on the problem is incomplete, the layperson believes that the social scientist is simply obscuring matters that seem obvious.

Social science sometimes develops explanations of human behavior that contradict established ideas. Of course, the physical and biological sciences have long faced this same problem: Galileo faced the opposition of the established church when he suggested that the earth revolved around the sun, and the theory of evolution continues to be a public issue. But social science generates even more intense feelings when it deals with poverty, crime, sexual behavior, race relations, and other heated topics.

Limitations and Design of Social Science Research   *Another set of problems in social science centers on the limitations and design of social science research.* It is not really possible to conduct some forms of controlled experiments on human beings. For example, we cannot subject people to poverty and deprivation just to see if it makes them violent. Instead, social researchers must conduct their research in situations that have been produced naturally. They must, therefore, find situations of poverty and deprivation to make the necessary observations about causes of violence. In a laboratory we can control all or most of the factors that go into the experimental situation. But in real-world observations, we cannot control factors, which makes it difficult to pinpoint precisely what it is that causes the behavior we are studying. Moreover, even where some experimentation is permitted, human beings frequently modify their behavior simply because they know they are being observed in a social science experiment. This phenomenon, which is known as the *Hawthorne effect*, makes it difficult to determine whether the behavior observed is a product of the stimulus being introduced, or merely a product of the experimental situation itself.

Hawthorne effect

Complexity of Human Behavior   *Perhaps the most serious reservation about social science research is that human behavior is shaped by so many different forces that it resists scientific explanation.* A complete understanding of such a complex system as human society is beyond our current capabilities. At present human behavior can be as well understood through art, literature, and music as through scientific research.

WHAT IS A "FACT?"

In the social sciences there are very few statements that can be made that apply to *every* circumstance. We cannot say, for example, that "all blacks vote Democratic." This is a *universal statement* covering every black person, and universal statements are seldom true in the social sciences. Moreover, it would be difficult to examine the voting behavior of every black person in the past and in the future to prove that our statement is true.

Universal statement

A more accurate statement might be: "Most blacks vote Democratic." This is a *probabilistic statement* covering "most" blacks, but it does not exclude the possibility that some blacks vote Republican. An even more accurate statement would be that "85 percent of blacks cast their ballots for Democratic candidate Jimmy Carter in the

Probabilistic statement

1976 presidential elections." This means that there was an 85 percent *probability* of a black voter casting his ballot for Democrat Jimmy Carter.

A probabilistic statement is a fact, just like a universal statement. Students in the physical sciences deal with many universal statements—for example, "Water boils at 100° centigrade." Water always does this. But students of the social sciences must be prepared to deal with probabilistic statements—for example, "Blacks are three times more likely to experience poverty than whites." Social science students must learn to think in probabilities rather than in absolute terms.

Social scientists must also beware of substituting individual cases for statements of probability. They must be careful about reasoning from one or two observed cases. A statement such as "I know a black family that always votes Republican" may be true, but it would be very dangerous to generalize about the voting habits of all black voters on the basis of this one case.

Representative samples of the universe

We always build up tentative generalizations from our own world of experiences. However, as social scientists, we must insure that our own experiences are typical. To do so, we must study the behavior of *representative samples* of the groups we are investigating. This means using careful methods to insure that the sample of cases observed is truly representative of the *universe* about which we wish to make some statements. It is impossible here to go into statistics and statistical inferences, with all of their rules and methods for determining when a sample is likely to be representative of the universe. But we should keep in mind that the "facts" of the social sciences are seldom absolute—they rarely cover the complexity of any aspect of human behavior. So we must be prepared to study probabilities.

THE CLASSIC SCIENTIFIC RESEARCH DESIGN

The *classic scientific research design* involves the comparison of specific changes in two or more carefully selected groups, both of which are identical in every way, except that one has been given the program or treatment under study while the other has not.

This design involves the following:

1. Identification of the goals of the study and the selection of specific hypotheses to be tested.
2. Selection of the groups to be compared—the *experimental group,* which will participate in the program or undergo the treatment being studied, and the *control group,* which is similar to the experimental

group in every way except that it will *not* participate in the program or undergo the treatment being studied.

3. Measurement of the characteristics of both the experimental and control groups before participation in the experiment.

4. Application of the program or treatment to the experimental group, but not to the control group. (The control group may be given a *placebo*—some activity or program known to have no effect—to make them believe they are participating in the experiment. Indeed, the scientific staff administering the experiment may not know which group is the real experimental group and which group is the control group. When neither the staff nor the groups themselves know who is really receiving the treatment, the experiment is called a *double-blind experiment*.)

5. Measurement of the postprogram or posttreatment condition or performance of both the experimental and control groups. If there are measurable differences between the experimental and control groups, the scientist can begin to infer that the program or treatment has a specific effect. If there are *no* measureable differences, then the scientist must accept the *null hypothesis*—the statement that the program or treatment has no effect.

6. Comparison of the preprogram/pretreatment status versus the post-program/posttreatment status in both groups. This is a check to see if the difference between the experimental and control groups occurred during the experiment. This method, used alone, is sometimes called a "before-after" study.

7. A search for plausible explanations for differences after treatment between the control and experimental groups that might be due to factors other than the treatment itself.

Let us consider a specific example of the classic scientific research design being applied to social science research. A local government is considering the installation of street lighting in residential neighborhoods to combat neighborhood crime. The hypothesis is that increased lighting will reduce crime rates. Before spending large sums of money to light up the entire city without knowing whether the plan will work, the city council decides to put the program to a scientific test. The council selects several neighborhoods that have identical characteristics (same crime rates, land use, population density, unemployment, population ages, incomes, racial balances, and so forth). Some of these areas are randomly selected for the installation of new street lighting. The remainder of these identical areas are not given new lighting. Crime rates are carefully measured before and after the installation of street lights in those neighborhoods that received new lighting, as well as in those neighborhoods that did not. After several months of new lighting, crime rates are again carefully measured in the experimental neighborhoods (which received lights) and the control neighborhoods (which did not). The results are compared. If a significant reduction in crime occurred in the neighborhoods with new lights, but did not occur in the neighborhoods without lights, and no other changes in the neighborhoods that might account for the differences can be identified, then the city can have some confidence that lighting reduces crime. An expansion of lighting to the rest of the city would then seem appropriate.

Special Problems   The classic research design is not without its problems. Social scientists must be aware of the more difficult problems in applying this research design to social science research and must be prepared on occasion to change their procedures accordingly. These problems include the following:

1. As noted earlier, members of the experimental group may respond differently to a program if they know it is an experiment. Because of this "Hawthorne effect," members of a control group are often told they are participating in an experiment, even though nothing is really being done to the control group.

2. If the experimental group is only one part of a larger city, state, or nation, the response to the experiment may be different from what it would have been had all parts of the city, state, or nation been receiving the program. For example, if only one part of a city receives street lights, criminals may move to the unlighted streets. But if the whole city is given street lights, criminals may simply operate as usual (even with the lights), and total crime rates will be unaffected.

3. If persons are allowed to *volunteer* for the experiment, then experimental and control groups may not be representative of the population as a whole.

4. In some situations, political pressures may make it impossible to provide one neighborhood or group with certain services, while denying these same services to the rest of the city, state, or nation. If everyone *thinks* the program is beneficial before the experiment begins, no one will want to be in the control group.

5. It may also be considered morally wrong to provide some groups or persons with services, benefits, or treatment, while denying the same to other groups or persons (control groups) who are identical in their needs or problems.

6. Careful research is costly and time-consuming. Public officials often need to make immediate decisions. They cannot spend time or money on research even if they understand the long-term benefits of careful investigation. Too often politicians must operate on "short-run" rather than "long-run" considerations.

SOCIAL SCIENCE AND SOCIAL INDICATORS

The scientific method requires accurate measurement. In recent years a number of social scientists have advocated the development of a set of indicators to measure social progress (or retrogression). They have urged the preparation of an annual "Social Report" designed to assess the social condition of the nation. Most Americans can agree on the values of a healthy, well-educated, adequately housed, and affluent population, even if they cannot agree on public policies to achieve these values. Perhaps a general assessment of the nation's progress toward these goals would be helpful in an overall evaluation of the effectiveness of public policy. *Social indicators* are defined simply as *quantitative data that serve as measures of socially important conditions in a society.*

Presumably a set of social indicators and a social report would accomplish two things. First, by focusing attention on certain social conditions, they would promote more informed judgments about national priorities; and second, by showing how different measures of social well-being change over time, they would help evaluate the success of public programs.

As an example, let us consider progress in education as a social indicator. Table 2–1 shows how the college-age population increased

Table 2–1   College Enrollments, 1950–1975, by Sex and Race

College-Age Persons in Population	1950	1955	1960	1965	1970	1975
All	18.2%	19.1%	27.4%	35.0%	37.3%	36.7%
Male	20.7	24.4	33.0	40.1	40.2	36.7
Female	15.9	14.7	22.5	30.3	34.6	36.7
White	NA	21.0	29.4	37.2	39.3	38.1
Black	NA	6.1	14.5	16.5	21.8	25.3

Source: U.S. Bureau of the Census, *Social Indicators 1976* (Washington, D.C.: Government Printing Office, 1977), p. 301.

its college enrollments over twenty-five years (1950–1975). In 1950, only 18.2 percent of college-age people were enrolled in college; this figure rose to 36.7 percent in 1975. Moreover, we can also see that by 1975 women's enrollment in college caught up with men's enrollment. In 1950, only 15.9 percent of young women were in college, compared to 20.7 percent of young men; but by 1975, the figures for men and women were the same—36.7 percent. (Note also a slight decline in male enrollment from 1970 to 1975. Does this mean that college enrollments are now going to level out? Does it mean that the end of the military draft allowed males to drop out of college without fear of being drafted?) The progress of blacks in higher education is also recorded in this particular "social indicator." Only 6.1 percent of college-age blacks were enrolled in college in 1955, but by 1975 this figure had risen to 25.3 percent—still below the comparable white percentage, but a marked improvement (see also appendix, figure A).

Other examples of useful social indicators appear in the appendix. The tables and figures there show trends in the United States in family life, marriage and divorce; life expectancy; education, income, and occupation; poverty; crime; inflation; racial and sexual differences in socioeconomic conditions; and public attitudes toward national priorities and the quality of life.

CASE STUDY
Social Science in Action: The Busing Controversy

One of the most interesting and controversial uses of social science in recent years has centered on equal educational opportunity and how to achieve it. The first influential report on equal opportunity in American education was sociologist James S. Coleman's *Equality of Educational Opportunity*, frequently referred to as the "Coleman report."[2] Although Coleman's study was not without its critics, it was nonetheless the most comprehensive analysis of the American public school system ever made.[3] The Coleman report included data on 600,000 children in 4,000 schools. This report, and the reaction to it, can help us to understand the problems, as well as the possibilities, of social science research. .

Coleman began his study with the conventional hypotheses that factors such as the number of pupils in the classroom, the amount of money spent on each pupil, library and laboratory facilities, teachers' salaries, the quality of the curriculum, and other characteristics of the school affected student achievement levels. However, scientific testing revealed that these factors had *no* significant effect on student learning or achievement. Moreover, Coleman found that student achievement was *not* affected by the presence or absence of a "track system," grouping by ability, guidance counseling, or other standard educational programs. Even the size of the class was found to be unrelated to learning, although educators had asserted the importance of this factor for decades. In short, the things that "everybody knew" about education turned out not to be so.

The only factors that were found to affect a student's learning to any significant degree were the student's family class background and the family class background of the student's classmates. Family class background affected the child's verbal abilities and attitudes toward education, and these factors correlated very closely with scholastic achievement. Of secondary but considerable significance were the verbal abilities and attitudes toward education of the child's classmates.

Coleman made no recommendations about what should be done in American education. However, his research was quickly taken up by the U.S. Commission on Civil Rights, which was concerned with equality of education for black students throughout the country. The commission asked another sociologist, Thomas F. Pettigrew, to reanalyze Coleman's data to focus on *racial* inequalities rather than *class* inequalities.

Pettigrew found that black students attending predominantly black schools had lower achievement scores than black students *with comparable family backgrounds* who attended predominantly white schools.[4] When black students attending predominantly white schools were compared with black students attending predominantly black schools, the average difference in levels of achievement amounted to more than *two grade levels*. Moreover, special programs to raise achievement levels in predominantly black schools were found to have no lasting effect.

The U.S. Commission on Civil Rights used the Coleman report to buttress its policy proposals to end racial imbalance in public schools in both the North and the South. Inasmuch as money, facilities, and compensatory programs have little effect on student learning, and inasmuch as the class background of the student's classmates does affect the student's learning, it seemed reasonable to argue that the assignment of lower-class black students to predominantly middle-class white schools would be the only way to improve educational opportunities for ghetto children. Hence, the commission called for an end to neighborhood schools and for the *busing* of black and white children to racially balanced schools.

The Coleman report and the report of the U.S. Commission on Civil Rights have been frequently cited by proponents of busing—those urging deliberate governmental action to achieve racial balance in public schools. Courts and school officials in northern and southern cities have cited the Coleman report as evidence that racial imbalance denies equality of educational opportunity to black children, and as evidence that deliberate racial balancing in the schools, or busing, is required to achieve "the equal protection of the laws" that is guaranteed by the Fourteenth Amendment.

However, James S. Coleman conducted a second study, published in 1975, which analyzed the success of busing in achieving racial integration in the schools of large cities. This new report, *Trends in School Desegregation*, appeared to counter earlier implications about busing as a means to achieving equality of educational opportunity.[5] In examining changes in segregation over time in twenty-two large cities and forty-six medium-sized cities, Coleman found that an increase in desegregation was associated with a loss of white pupils—"white flight." This response to desegregation was greatest in large cities with large proportions of black pupils, and with surrounding, predominantly white, independent, suburban school districts. The long-run effect of white pupil loss in these cities was predicted to offset governmental efforts to desegregate public schools and to contribute to *greater*, rather than less, racial imbalance.

In short, governmental effort to guarantee equality of educational opportunity by busing large numbers of students within school systems in large cities was not working out. According to Coleman's second study, busing was creating "white flight" and causing racial segregation in big cities to increase.

The point of this brief case study is that social science research sometimes produces unexpected and even embarrassing findings, that public policies do not always "work" as intended, and that different political interests will interpret the findings of social science research differently—accepting, rejecting, or using these findings as they fit their own purposes.

NOTES

1. Louis Wirth, preface to *Ideology and Utopia: An Introduction to the Sociology of Knowledge,* by Karl Mannheim (New York: Harcourt Brace Jovanovich, 1936).

2. James S. Coleman, *Equality of Educational Opportunity* (Washington, D.C.: Government Printing Office, 1966).

3. For reviews of the Coleman report, see Robert A. Dentler, "Equality of Educational Opportunity: A Special Review," *The Urban Review,* December 1966; Christopher Jenks, "Education: The Racial Gap," *The New Republic* 1 October 1966; James K. Kent, "The Coleman Report: Opening Pandora's Box," *Phi Delta Kappan,* January 1968; James S. Coleman, "Educational Dilemmas: Equal Schools or Equal Students," *The Public Interest,* Summer 1966; James S. Coleman, "Toward Open Schools," *The Public Interest,* Fall 1967; and a special issue devoted to educational opportunity of *Harvard Educational Review* 38, Winter 1968.

4. U.S. Commission on Civil Rights, *Racial Isolation in the Public Schools,* 2 vols. (Washington, D.C.: Government Printing Office, 1967).

5. James S. Coleman et al., *Trends in School Desegregation 1968–1973* (Washington, D.C.: Urban Institute, 1975).

DISCUSSION QUESTIONS

1. You are about to begin a social science research project, and you want it to be "scientific" rather than normative, or prescriptive. Describe the method you would choose, explaining how it works and what its goals are. Using this method, will you be able to prove cause and effect? Why or why not?

2. Discuss some of the difficulties the social scientist has in applying the scientific method to the study of social problems.

3. Suppose you are a school psychologist who wishes to determine if students learn more when television is used in the classroom than when only conventional teaching methods are used. Construct a classic research design for this purpose. Describe some of the problems you might encounter in applying this design.

4. Define *social indicators*. Using a specific example of a social indicator, discuss how it might be used in combating a social problem.

5. Referring to the Coleman report as an illustration, explain how social science research sometimes produces unexpected results and how different political interests may use these results.

SUGGESTED READINGS

Thomas R. Dye, *Understanding Public Policy* (Englewood Cliffs, N.J.: Prentice-Hall, 1972).

Harry Hatry, Richard E. Winnie, and Donald M. Fish, *Practical Program Evaluation for State and Local Government Officials* (Washington, D.C.: Urban Institute, 1973).

Philip M. Hauser, *Social Statistics in Use* (New York: Russell Sage Foundation, 1975).

Seymour Martin Lipset, *Politics and the Social Science* (New York: Oxford University Press, 1969).

Alice M. Rivlin, *Systematic Thinking for Social Action* (Washington, D.C.: Brookings, 1971).

U.S. Department of Health, Education, and Welfare, *Toward A Social Report* (Ann Arbor: University of Michigan Press, 1970).

U.S. Department of Commerce, *Social Indicators 1976* (Washington, D.C.: Government Printing Office, 1977).

PART II

POWER AND THE SOCIAL SCIENCES

In part II we will take a close look at the ways in which each of the social sciences contributes to our understanding of power in society. In so doing, we hope to gain some feel not only for the different areas of interest, methods, and data of each of the social sciences, but also for the goal that they share in common—that is, an improved understanding of human behavior.

In chapter 3 we will focus on what *anthropology*, with its concern for culture, has to tell us about the growth of power relationships in societies. In chapter 4 we will examine the *sociology* of relationships between power and social class, particularly as evidenced by stratification in American society. Control of economic resources is an important base of power in any society, and in chapter 5 we will turn our attention to *economics*. In chapter 6 we will attempt to determine how and why it is that individuals react in characteristic and different ways to power and authority. Here we will turn to the theories of personality determination offered by various schools of *psychology*. In chapter 7 we will examine government and power from the point of view of *political science*. Finally in chapter 8 we will look at how the perspective of *history* can increase our understanding of power in society.

Photo from Magnum by Richard Kalvar

Photo from Anthro-Photo by R. Lee

Chapter 3
Power and Culture

"No-no" is one of the first phrases that most of us have ever spoken. This mimicking of a parental reprimand is evidence that by age two most of us have had our first encounter with power and authority. Even earlier as helpless infants, we have, with our insistent cries, had the power to control the behavior of our parents. When we are older and our parents assign us household chores, we experience yet another instance of power being exercised within the family.

Anthropologists, in their study of human culture, have been able to document that the exercise of power and the division of labor within the family constitute the most basic power relationship, the one from which true political power structures develop. What causes these structures to develop? Why should we need to control each other's behavior and how do we manage to do it? How do anthropologists document the growth of power relationships? How, in fact, do they approach the study of something as diverse as human culture?

These questions are the focus of chapter 3. After you have read it, you should be able to:

- describe how power in society is exercised and for what purposes.
- discuss how and why it is that the family is the fundamental social unit in which power relationships originate.
- discuss the stages of development of power relationships and the factors that influence this development.
- discuss anthropological approaches to the study of culture.

THE ORIGINS OF POWER

Sanctions

Power is exercised in all societies. Every society has a system of *sanctions*, whether formal or informal, designed to control the behavior of its members. Informal sanctions may include expressions of disapproval, ridicule, or fear of supernatural punishments. Formal sanctions involve recognized ways of censoring behavior—for example, ostracism or exile from the group, loss of freedom, physical punishment, mutilation or death, or retribution visited upon the offender by a member of the family or group that has been wronged.

Power in society is exercised for four broad purposes:

Purposes

1. To maintain peace within the society.
2. To organize and direct community enterprises.
3. To conduct warfare, both defensive and aggressive, against other societies.
4. To rule and exploit subject peoples.

Even in the most primitive societies, power relationships emerge for the purposes of maintaining order, organizing economic enterprise, conducting offensive and defensive warfare, and ruling subject peoples.

At the base of power relationships in society is the family or kinship group. Power is exercised, first of all, within the family, when work is divided between male and female and parents and children, and when patterns of dominance and submission are established between male and female and parents and children. In the simplest societies, power relationships are found partially or wholly *within* family and kinship groups. True political (power) organizations begin

Development of power relationships

with the *development* of power relationships *between* family and kinship groups. As long as kinship units are relatively self-sufficient economically and require no aid in defending themselves against hostile outsiders, political organization has little opportunity to develop. But the habitual association of human beings in communities or local groups generally leads to the introduction of some form of political (power) organization. The basic power structures are voluntary alliances of families and clans who acknowledge the same leaders, habitually work together in economic enterprises, agree to certain ways of conduct for the maintenance of peace among themselves, and cooperate in the conduct of offensive and defensive warfare. Thus, power structures begin with the development of cooperation between families and kinship groups.

Effect of warfare

Warfare frequently leads to another purpose for power structures—ruling and exploiting peoples who have been conquered in war. Frequently primitive societies that have been successful in war learn that they can do more than simply kill or drive off enemy groups. Well-organized and militarily successful tribes learn to subjugate other peoples for purposes of political and economic exploitation, retaining them as subjects. The power structure of the conquering tribe takes on another function—that of maintaining control over and exploiting conquered peoples.

CULTURE: WAYS OF LIFE

Culture and generalizations

The ways of life that are common to a society make up its *culture*. The culture of any society represents *generalizations* about the behavior of many members of that society; culture does not describe the personal habits of any one individual. Common ways of behaving in different societies vary enormously. For example, some societies view dogmeat as a delicacy, while others find the idea of dogmeat nauseating. Some people paint their entire bodies with intricate designs, while others paint only the faces of the females. In some cultures a man is required to support, educate, and discipline his children, while in others these functions belong to the children's uncle.

The concept of culture is basic to what *anthropology* is all about. One could say that anthropology is the study of culture. Anthropologist Clyde Kluckhohn has defined culture as all the "historically created designs for living, explicit and implicit, rational, irrational, and nonrational which may exist at any given time as potential guides for the behavior of man."[1] In contrast to psychologists, who are interested primarily in describing and explaining individual behavior, anthropologists tend to make *generalizations about behavior in a whole society.* Of course, generalizations about behavior in a whole society do not describe the personal habits of any one individual. Some of them apply only to a portion of that society's membership. In other words, there may be *variations* in ways of life among different groups within one society, variations frequently referred to as *subcultures.*

Subcultures

Actually the term *culture* encompasses two major types of behavioral patterns: the ideal and the real. *Ideal cultural patterns* are what the people of a society would do or say if they conformed completely to the standards of their culture. *Real behavioral patterns,* on the other hand, are derived from observations of how people actually behave. For example, anthropologist Morris Opler reports that when an Apache husband discovers that his wife has been unfaithful he is supposed to mutilate or kill her and then find and kill her lover. However, affronted husbands do not always take such extreme steps. In one account, the husband simply "didn't care. He married right away to a Comanche."[2] Thus, the ideal patterns of a culture represent the "musts" and "shoulds," but these patterns may differ to a greater or lesser extent from actual behavior patterns.

Most anthropologists believe that various aspects of culture are interrelated—that the religious rituals, the work habits, the beliefs and ideologies, the marriage relationships, and so forth, form a whole system whose parts are related to one another and affect one another. Anthropologists frequently attempt to analyze each aspect of culture in terms of its relationship to other aspects and to the functioning of the total system. Thus, for example, religious rituals will be associated with agricultural activities in a society that relies upon farming for its food; but religious activities will center about hunting in a society that hunts for its food. Anthropologists frequently search for underlying themes that give unity to a culture. Only recently has anthropology departed from this *holistic* approach. Some anthropologists now believe that many cultures, perhaps even a majority, are not dominated by a single unifying idea, but instead encompass a number of general themes, which may not be interrelated at all. Nevertheless, most anthropologists still hold that culture is systematically related, its parts influencing one another.

Anthropologists believe that culture is learned. They believe that culture is transferred from one generation to another, but that it is *not* genetically transmitted. Culture is passed down through the generations because people are brought up differently. Individuals learn from other people how to speak, think, and act in certain ways.

Symbolism plays a key role in culture, for it is the ability to create and use symbols—including words, pictures, and writing—that distinguishes human beings from other animals. A symbol is anything that has meaning bestowed upon it by those who use it. Words are symbols, and language is symbolic communication. Objects or artifacts can also be used as symbols: A cross may be a symbol of Christianity. The color red may stand for danger or it may be a symbol of revolution. Mathematics is symbolic. It is the creation and use of such symbols that enable human beings to transmit their learned ways of behaving to each new generation. Children are not limited to knowledge acquired through their own experiences and observations; they can learn about the ways of behaving in society through symbolic communication, receiving, in a relatively short time, the result of centuries of experience and observation. Human beings therefore can learn more rapidly than other animals, and they can employ symbols to solve increasingly complex problems. Because of symbolic communication, human beings can transmit a body of learned ways of life accumulated by many people over many generations.

It is possible to divide culture into several categories. Anthropologists commonly use the following divisions:

Cultural categories

1. *Technology:* the ways in which people create and use tools and other material artifacts.
2. *Economics:* the patterns of behaving relative to the production, distribution, and consumption of goods and services.
3. *Social organization:* characteristic relations among individuals within a society including the division of labor and the social and political organization; and the relationships between a society and other societies.
4. *Religion:* ways of life relative to the human concern for the unknown.
5. *Symbolic culture:* systems of symbols (such as language, art, music, literature) used to acquire, order, and transfer knowledge.

THE FUNCTIONS OF CULTURE

Culture assists people in adapting to the conditions in which they live. Even ways of life that at first glance appear to be quaint or curious may play an important role in helping individuals or societies cope with problems. Many anthropologists approach the study of culture by asking what function a particular institution or practice performs for a society. How does the institution or practice serve individual or societal needs? Does it work? How does it work? Why does it work? This approach is known as *functionalism*.[3]

Functionalism

Functionalism assumes that there are certain minimum *biological needs* that must be satisfied if individuals and society are to survive, as well as *social and psychological needs*. The biological needs are fairly well defined: food, shelter, bodily comfort, reproduction, health maintenance, physical movement, and defense. Despite great variety in the way these needs are met in different cultures, we can still ask how a culture goes about fulfilling them and how well it does so. Social and psychological needs are less well defined, but they probably include affection, communication, education in the ways of the culture, material satisfaction, leadership, social control, security, and a sense of unity and belongingness. Functionalists tend to examine every custom, material object, idea, belief, and institution in terms of the task or function it performs.

To understand a culture functionally, we have to find out how a particular institution or practice relates to biological, social, or psychological needs, and how it relates to other cultural institutions and practices. For example, a society that fulfills its biological needs by hunting may fulfill its psychological needs by worshipping animals. Similarly, we may find an agricultural society worshipping a sun-god or a rain-god. The function of magic is to give human beings courage to face the unknown; myth preserves social traditions; religion fosters individual security and social solidarity; and so forth.

Technology, with its tools, weapons, and artifacts, underlies nearly all these human activities. Variations in ways of life reflect different attempts by human beings to adjust or adapt to their environment. Technology can be viewed as a cultural screen that people set up between themselves and their environment. While most animals simply utilize the environment for food and shelter, changing it very little in the process, human beings alter or transform their environment. As a result, human beings, who probably originated as tropical animals, can live almost anywhere on the earth's surface. Of course, peoples differ widely in the degree to which they exploit environmental resources. A society without means of transportation is restricted to a single area and depends on that area's resources. The technologies of "primitive" societies are not necessarily simple; the products of Eskimo technology, for example, are often ingenious and complex and require great skill in their manufacture. Societies with more advanced technologies exploit their environment more fully. Indeed, the technological advance of Western societies threatens to exhaust environmental resources.

RUTH BENEDICT
Patterns of Culture

The concept of culture helps us to understand ourselves by allowing us to see ourselves in relation to individuals in other societies and other cultures. Not only does culture explain many of the regularized behaviors of people—for example, eating, sleeping, dress, or sex habits—but perhaps more importantly it helps us to gain a wider perspective on our own behavior. Through the study of diverse cultures we realize that there are many different ways of living—

many different ways in which people can satisfy their social and psychological needs as well as their biological requirements; that our own culture is not the only possible way of life. Awareness of other cultures provides us with some perspective on the conscious and unconscious values and assumptions of our own culture. The realization that there are other ways of life besides our own may make us more tolerant, even appreciative, of alien cultures. Thus, we not only learn more of the variety of human experience, but also become more sensitive to the values and lifestyles of others.

Perhaps this perception of the diversity of human existence was the really important contribution of cultural anthropologist Ruth Benedict in her widely read *Patterns of Culture*. As professor of anthropology at Columbia University, Ruth Benedict (1887–1947) popularized the notion that different cultures can be organized around characteristic purposes or themes. "A culture, like an individual, is a more or less consistent pattern of thought and action. Within each culture there come into being characteristic purposes not necessarily shared by other types of societies."[4] According to Benedict, each culture has its own patterns of thought, action, and expression dominated by a certain theme that is expressed in social relations, art, and religion.

For example, Benedict identified the characteristic theme of life among Zuñi Pueblo Indians as moderation, sobriety, and cooperation. There was little competition, contention, or violence among tribal members. In contrast, the Kwakiutls of the northwestern United States engaged in fierce and violent competition for prestige and self-glorification. Kwakiutls were distrustful of one another, emotionally volatile, and paranoid. Members of the Dobu tribe of New Guinea, too, were suspicious, aggressive, and paranoid:

> Life in Dobu fosters extreme forms of animosity and malignancy which most societies have minimized by their institutions. Dobuan institutions, on the other hand, exalt them to the highest degree. The Dobuan lives out without repression man's worst nightmares of the ill-will of the universe, and according to his view of life virtue consists in selecting a victim upon whom he can vent the malignancy he attributes alike to human society and to the powers of nature. All existence appears to him as a cut-throat struggle in which deadly antagonists are pitted against one another in a contest for each one of the goods of life. Suspicion and cruelty are his trusted weapons in the strife and he gives no mercy, as he asks for none.[5]

Yet Benedict was convinced that *abnormality* and *normality* were relative terms. What is "normal" in Dobuan society would be regarded as "abnormal" in Zuñi society, and vice versa. She believed that there is hardly a form of abnormal behavior in any society that would not be regarded as normal in some other society. Hence, Benedict helped social scientists realize the great variability in the patterns of human existence. Men can live in competitive as well as cooperative societies, in peaceful as well as aggressive societies, in trusting as well as suspicious societies.

Configurationism

Today many anthropologists have reservations about Benedict's idea that the culture of a society reflects a single dominant theme. This idea is now known as *configurationism*, and it includes the notion that societies, like individuals, have characteristic personalities. However, it is doubtful that societies can really be as well integrated as individuals. There are probably a multiplicity of themes in any society, and some societies may be poorly integrated indeed. Moreover, Benedict may have underestimated the fact that, regardless of the importance of culture in shaping individual behavior, even within a single culture wide variations of individual behavior exist.

AUTHORITY IN THE FAMILY

The family is the principal agent of socialization into society. It is the most intimate and most important of all social groups. Of course, the family can assume different shapes in different cultures, and it can perform a variety of functions and meet a variety of needs. But in *all* societies the family relationship centers on sexual and child-rearing functions. A cross-cultural comparison reveals that in all societies the family possesses these common characteristics:[6]

Characteristics of the family

1. Sexual mating.
2. Childbearing and child rearing.
3. A system of names and a method of determining kinship.
4. A common habitation.
5. Socialization and education of the young.
6. A system of roles and expectations based on family membership.

These common characteristics indicate why the family is so important in human societies. It replenishes the population and rears each new generation. It is within the family that the individual personality is formed. The family transmits and carries forward the culture of the society. It establishes the primary system of roles with differential rights, duties, and behaviors. And it is within the family that the child first encounters *authority*.

Variations in family arrangements

Family arrangements vary. First of all, the marriage relationship may take on such institutional forms as monogamy, polygyny, and polyandry. *Monogamy* is the union of one husband and one wife; *polygyny*, the union of one husband and two or more wives; *polyandry*, the union of one wife and two or more husbands. (Throughout the world, monogamy is the most widespread marriage form, probably because the *sex ratio* [number of males per 100 females] is near 100 in all societies, meaning there is about an equal number of men and women.)

Second, marriage mates may be selected by *parents*, or by the *elders* of the community, or by the *individuals concerned*.

Third, the reckoning of descent may be through the male line (*patrilineal*), through the female line (*matrilineal*), or through both (*bilineal*).

Fourth, the newlyweds may reside with the family of the husband (*patrilocal* residence), or with the family of the wife (*matrilocal*), or in a new residence of their own (*neolocal*).

Fifth, the family may be dominated by the husband-father

(*patriarchal*), or the wife-mother (*matriarchal*), or the dominance pattern may be diffused so that both parents (and in some instances even the children) have considerable authority (*democratic or equalitarian*).

As we have noted, the child's first experience with authority in all societies is within the family. Indeed, the entire culture first appears to children as something their fathers or mothers want them to do. Differences in the type of authority exercised, and whether or not the authority is exercised primarily by the mother or father, can shape the character and personality of the growing individual.

The Family in Agricultural Societies   In most agricultural societies the family is *patriarchal* and *patrilineal*: the male is the dominant authority and kinship is determined through the male line. The family is an economic institution, as well as a sexual and child-rearing one; it owns land, produces many artifacts, and cares for its old as well as its young. Male family heads exercise power in the wider community; patriarchs may govern the village or tribe. Male authority frequently means the subjection of both women and children. This family arrangement is buttressed by traditional moral values and religious teachings that emphasize discipline, self-sacrifice, and the sanctity of the family unit.

Women face a lifetime of childbearing, child rearing, and household work. Families of ten or fifteen children are not uncommon. The property rights of a woman are vested in her husband. Women are taught to serve and obey their husbands. Women are not considered as mentally competent as men. The husband owns and manages the family's economic enterprise. Tasks are divided: Men raise crops, tend animals, and perform heavy work; women make clothes, prepare food, tend the sick, and perform endless household services.

The Family in Industrialized Societies   Industrialization alters the economic functions of the family and brings about changes in the traditional patterns of authority. In industrialized societies the household is no longer an important unit of production, even though it retains an economic role as a consumer unit. Work is to be found outside of the home, and industrial technology provides gainful employment for women as well as for men. This means an increase in opportunities for women outside of the family unit and the possibility of economic independence. The number of women in the labor force increases; today in the United States nearly 40 percent of adult women are employed outside of the home.

The patriarchal authority structure that typifies the family in an agricultural economy is altered by the new opportunities for women in an advanced industrial nation. Not only do women acquire employment alternatives, but their opportunities for education also expand. This independence permits them to modify many of the more oppressive features of patriarchy. Women in an advanced industrialized society have fewer children (and closer together) and generally stop bearing children by age thirty. Divorce becomes a realistic alternative for an unhappy marriage. The trend in divorce rates in industrialized societies is upward.

At the same time, governments in industrialized societies assume many of the traditional functions of the family, further increasing opportunities for women. The government steps into the field of formal education—not just in the instruction of reading, writing, and arithmetic, but in support of home economics, driver training, health care, and perhaps even sex education, all areas that were once the province of the family. Government welfare programs provide assistance to mothers of dependent children when a family breadwinner is absent or unable to provide for the children. The government undertakes to care for the aged, the sick, and others incapable of supporting themselves, thus relieving families of still another traditional function.

The authority of the male also may be threatened by unemployment. The failure of the male to find gainful and respectable employment in an industrialized society can seriously undermine his self-esteem, status, and role as the family breadwinner. The problem is compounded if the female can find employment while the male cannot, or if the female can obtain public assistance and the male is an obstacle to her receiving it. The result can be the emergence of the female-dominated family.

Despite these characteristics of industrial society, however, the family remains the fundamental social unit. The family is not disappearing; marriage and family life are as popular as ever. But the father-dominated authority structure, with its traditional duties and rigid sex roles, is changing. The family is becoming an institution in which both husband and wife seek individual happiness, rather than the perpetuation of the species and economic efficiency. A majority of women still choose to seek fulfillment in marriage and child rearing rather than in outside employment. The important point is that now this is a *choice* and not a cultural requirement.

The American Family   Although its decline is frequently predicted by newsmen, commentators, and scholars, the American family

"We'll call you back after nine. We're in the middle of the Family Hour."

Drawing by Geo. Price; © 1975 The New Yorker Magazine, Inc.

somehow endures. Its nature may change, but the family unit is none-theless the fundamental unit of society.

Today there are over 56 million families in America, and 191 million of the nation's 215 million people live in these family units.[7] Only about 10 percent of the population lives outside of family units. These "unrelated individuals," as the U.S. Census Bureau calls them, have *not* been increasing over time.

However, the nature of the family unit has indeed been changing. The "traditional" American family, with a working husband, and a wife who stays home to care for two or more children, *is* declining.

Today only about 22 percent of all families fit this "traditional" pattern. Husband-wife families compose 84 percent of all families, but fully 16 percent of all families have only a single adult. Of all husband-wife families, 47 percent have no children. The birth rate has declined from 3.7 births per woman of childbearing age in the 1950s, to 2.6 in the 1960s, to only 1.8 in the 1970s (see appendix, figure B). This last figure for the 1970s is *below* the projected zero population growth rate (2.1 children per female of childbearing age).

Divorce figures have shown some tendency toward leveling off over the last few years. However, 38 percent of all first marriages will end in divorce. Of these divorces, 79 percent will remarry; but 44 percent of second marriages will end in divorce. (Figures C and D in the appendix show statistics of first marriages, divorces, and remarriages of women from 1921 to 1974.)

It is not really clear what factors are contributing to these changes in the American family. Certainly new opportunities for women in the occupational world have increased the number of women in the work force and altered the "traditional" patterns of family life. Only about half of today's mothers stay at home and devote full time to child rearing. The availability of preschools and public child-care centers has also helped to increase the number of mothers in the work force. Inflation may be an even more important factor: As inflation spreads, a middle-class family must increasingly depend on the incomes of both husband and wife to support itself.

The relative ease of state laws and social customs regarding divorce has also contributed to changes in the American family. Certainly in contrast to years past, divorce and remarriage are more readily available as options to unhappy spouses. (See appendix, table A for statistics on attitudes toward marital happiness.) What used to be called a "broken home" is now widely accepted as a style of life: Approximately 40 percent of children born in the 1970s will spend part of their lives in a single-parent family, usually with the mother as the head of the household.

A problem of considerable concern is the decline in the husband-wife family among the poor, and especially among the poor and black. Years ago, U.S. Senator Daniel Patrick Moynihan (D., N.Y.) argued that one of the worst effects of slavery and segregation was its impact on black family life.[8] At the time that Moynihan made his statement (the mid-1960s), about 25 percent of all black families were headed by women. Some scholars argued that there is nothing "pathological" about the female-headed black family. However, fully 38 percent of all black children are currently receiving federal AFDC (welfare) payments. Many people attribute this statistic to the workings of the welfare system itself, which they believe is antifamily.

These people argue that because it is easier to obtain AFDC aid, medicaid, food stamps, public housing, and so forth, if there is no employable male in the family, the welfare system itself provides an incentive for men to leave their families.

STAGES OF DEVELOPMENT OF POWER RELATIONSHIPS

As a general guide to the study of the development of power relationships in society, we can identify the following stages:

1. Societies in which there is no separate power organization outside of the family or kinship group. In these societies there is no continuous or well-defined system of leaders over or above those who head the individual families. These societies do not have any clear-cut division of labor or economic organization outside of the family, and there is no structured method for resolving differences and maintaining peace among members of the group. These societies do not engage in organized offensive or defensive warfare. They tend to be small and widely dispersed, to have economies that yield only a bare subsistence, and to lack any form of organized defense. Power relationships are present, but they are closely tied to family and kinship.

2. Societies where families are organized in larger bands, tribes, or confederacies that have organized sets of power arrangements extending beyond family ties. In these societies population tends to be somewhat more concentrated; the economy yields a richer subsistence but no real surplus; and warfare, although frequent and often of great importance, is usually a matter of raiding between neighboring societies. When wars are decisive, they result in the killing or driving off of enemy tribes, rather than their conquest for exploitation.

3. Societies that are organized as permanent states and that have a more or less well-defined territory and a recognized organization to make and enforce rules of conduct. In these societies populations are large and highly concentrated; the economy produces a surplus; and there are recognized rules of conduct for the members of the society with positive and negative sanctions. These societies have an organized military establishment for offensive and defensive wars. In war, conquered people are not usually destroyed, but instead held as tributaries or incorporated as inferior classes into the state. In the vast majority of these societies, power is centered in a small, hereditary elite.

These stages of development of power relationships in societies certainly do not exhaust the variety of current and past power arrangements. They represent only broad divisions, each of which can be subdivided. (For example, states can be classified in Aristotelian fashion as *monarchy*, *aristocracy*, or *democracy*—rule by the one, the few, or the many.) Sharp lines cannot be drawn among these three stages; each stage shades into the next, and there are many transitional forms.

Let us consider three examples of societies in which power is organized by these broad divisions: (1) family and kinship group (polar Eskimos); (2) tribe (Crow Indians); and (3) state (the Aztec Empire).

POWER AMONG THE POLAR ESKIMOS

Environment

Societies lacking formal power organizations are found today only in the very marginal areas of the world. These societies, with no formal power structures outside of *family and kinship groups*, exist only in the most difficult environments where physical hardship and a lack of adequate food resources keep the human population small and thinly scattered. Among the polar Eskimos of northern Greenland, for example, a harsh environment and a limited food supply, together with a limited technology, force families to wander great distances to maintain themselves. Inadequate food resources make it physically impossible for these Eskimos to maintain, except temporarily, any groupings larger than one or two families. As a result, there is little in the way of power organization outside of the family. No leadership system develops, and social control is vested in the family.

Economic patterns

Anthropologists who have observed Eskimo culture note that it has just two social units: the primary family, a small but autonomous kinship group; and the winter village, an unstable association of primary families who are not necessarily linked by kinship ties. The winter village is only partially a power grouping. Its member families do not stay together long enough or undertake the common enterprises necessary for the development of a stable leadership system. Ordinarily the families in a winter village, though temporarily united by common residence, act independently of each other. Their technology, whether in food gathering or house building, requires no high degree of cooperative labor. In times of stress, when a storm or lack of game reduces food stores to the danger point, a *shaman*, respected for his supernatural powers, may call the families together to participate in a ceremony intended to restore the food supply. But the

*Leadership and the absence
of warfare*

shaman's authority is limited to such occasions; at other times he has no right to direct or command.

A strong and aggressive hunter may gain the esteem and respect of his fellows, but there are few occasions when he may capitalize on this prestige to assume a position of leadership. In short, the winter village has little need for leadership outside of the family. There is not even the occasion of warfare to call for the organization of families for offensive or defensive action. Leadership resides only within the primary family, where it is shared by husband and wife, each in his or her sphere of activity. The family maintains itself largely through its own efforts. It is linked to other families through intermarriage, remote kinship, or ties of mutual affection and regard. Conflicts are often resolved by song sessions in which the disputants lampoon each other in songs that they sing before an audience of their neighbors. More aggressive behavior is inhibited by fear of retaliation by kinsmen of the victims. Protracted disputes may be resolved among some Eskimos by one party's moving to another winter village, although an overbearing and abusive individual may be speared while on a hunt.

Among these Eskimos, then, there is no structure of power outside of the family group. Cooperation among families in joint enterprises is rare. Leadership outside of the family is seldom evidenced, usually only during a crisis when some particularly able member of the community takes charge. Ecological circumstances prohibit large permanent groupings of people, and the technology of the society is so simple that it utilizes individual rather than group effort. Variations on this fundamental type of power system that exists solely within the family group are also found among other primitive peoples living in harsh environments.

POWER AMONG THE CROW INDIANS

Population groupings

Perhaps the simplest form of power arrangement outside of the family is a *band* or *clan* or *tribe*. Although its members may be linked by kinship, such a group is generally made up of many family units, not all of which need to be related by marriage. These groups form the next stage of development in power relationships above that of the family or kinship groups. The band or clan or tribe consists of numbers of individuals and families who (1) live and travel together; (2) regularly engage in one or more large community enterprises—for example, an organized hunt; (3) regulate conflict and maintain order among themselves; and (4) organize to protect themselves from their enemies and wage war against them.

Leadership

Within the band there is as a rule an acknowledged leader—a chief—together with other respected individuals who assist in implementing authority. This authority may be backed by force, but more often it rests upon the ability of the leadership to *persuade* and *influence* its followers. The leaders generally owe their status to their personal achievements as hunters or warriors. Members of the band or tribe share a common language and culture.

Antropological research on the American Crow Indians in the early nineteenth century provides an example of the development of power relationships at the tribal level. The Crows were more or less continually hostile to their neighbors. Any non-Crow was automat-

Warfare

ically an enemy. Warfare, however, was largely a matter of small-scale raiding, either to steal horses or to avenge the death of a tribesman. Horse-stealing parties tried to take as many horses as they could without disturbing the enemy camp; they fought only when necessary to defend themselves. When revenge was the object of a war party, however, they tried to surprise the enemy and to kill as many as possible without losing any of their own men. A war leader, whether he set out to capture horses or to get revenge, was not considered successful unless he brought his own party home intact.

Success in warfare was very important. Crow men achieved reputation and prestige through the slow accumulation of war honors. War honors were clearly defined. They were awarded for (1) leading a successful war party, (2) capturing an enemy's weapon in actual combat, (3) being first to strike an enemy in the course of a fight, and (4) driving off a horse tethered in an enemy encampment. A man who performed all these deeds became, in Crow terms, a "good and valiant man," and his status increased as the number of his earned war honors increased. A Crow who had not yet attained the minimum four honors was regarded as not yet a man, but only an untried youth.

The warriors formed a kind of military aristocracy that made up the band council. One of their number, usually an older man with many war honors, was recognized as chief. He decided when the band was to move or settle down in its yearly wanderings in search of

Economic patterns

food and when war parties were to be sent out. He directed the annual buffalo hunt, a cooperative endeavor in which the whole band united to secure a store of winter food.

However, the chief's authority was by no means absolute; he was "neither a ruler nor a judge." In effect, the chief was a leader rather than a ruler; it was his function to persuade and influence rather than to command. This point is illustrated by the procedure employed among the Crows to settle disputes. When quarrels and violence occurred between members of the same clan, these were resolved by the older kin, acting as clan heads. But when a feud threatened between clans, the chief, his council, and influential warriors belonging to neutral clans exerted their powers to prevent further hostilities and restore peace. Their efforts were often successful, because the Crows, continually at war with their neighbors, fully realized the values of solidarity among bands.

On some occasions, mainly the annual buffalo hunts, the chief and other council warriors had the authority to resort to force rather than persuasion to maintain order. In such instances the senior warriors "severely whipped anyone who prematurely attacked the herd, broke his weapons, and confiscated the game he had illegally killed."[9] The need for a winter's supply of food, and the fact that this need could not be adequately served without the closest coordination of effort, clearly justified, in Crow eyes, the chief's authority over his tribesmen. However, apart from such special occasions as the community buffalo hunt, members of the band were allowed to act pretty much as they pleased, subject only to the discipline of public opinion. The threat of ridicule and the obligations imposed by kinship were normally sufficient deterrents to antisocial behavior.

Band or tribal organizations similar to that of the Crow are widespread among nonliterate peoples. As environment and technology permit higher concentrations of population, bands form into larger tribes. From this stage there emerge even larger political units with recognized power structures.

POWER AND THE AZTEC EMPIRE

The emergence of a state

The most fully developed system of power relationships is the state—the last of our major categories. Power in the state is employed to maintain order among peoples and to carry on large-scale community enterprises, just as in the band or tribe. But power in the state is also closely linked to defense, aggression, and the exploitation of conquered peoples. Frequently states emerge in response to attacks by others. Where there is a fairly high density of population, frequent and continuing contact among bands, and some commonality of language and culture, there is the potential for "national" unity in the form of a state. But a state may not emerge if there is no compelling motivation for large-scale cooperation. This motivation is very often provided initially by the need for defense against outside invasion.

Leadership

States differ from bands or tribes to the extent that there is a *centralized authority* with recognized power, backed by force, to carry out its decrees. This *legitimate use of force* distinguishes the state as a form of power structure from the band or tribe, in which power depends largely on persuasion or the personal achievements of individuals. Power in the state is a more impersonal kind of authority.

Economic patterns

The Aztec empire that was conquered by the Spaniards under Cortez in 1521 is an excellent example of a early state. Anthropologists have been able to trace its beginnings to an earlier tribal order confined to the valley of Mexico. The rich agricultural economy developed by the Aztecs produced far in excess of their immediate needs. With the exchangeable surplus there soon evolved a complex specialization of labor and an extensive trade that brought the Aztecs into frequent and profitable contact with neighboring groups.

Warfare and exploitation

Early in the fifteenth century the Aztecs embarked on a series of military conquests that led ultimately to their economic and political control over most of central and southern Mexico. The Aztecs did not destroy the cities and states that they had conquered. On the contrary, the commercially minded Aztecs permitted these cities and states to retain local autonomy, demanding only political allegiance and a yearly tribute in goods and services to the Aztec emperor. It was this economic empire, politically a loose aggregate of city-states controlled from the Aztec capital city of Tenochtitlán, that Cortez took over in 1521.

At the time of the conquest, the Aztec aristocracy was divided into twenty *calpulli*, small groups composed of nuclear families organized in ranked lineages. Each calpulli owned a tract of arable land, a council house, and a temple. The land was allotted in small farms to each family within the calpulli, to hold as long as the family continued its cultivation. Families could cultivate their own land, retaining the proceeds for their own support, or rent it to others, but it could not be sold or otherwise alienated from the calpulli. Should the family line die out or a family fail to cultivate its land for two successive years, the land reverted to the calpulli for reallotment. Some lands within the territory of a calpulli belonged to the chief, and some were cultivated by subordinates. Others were set aside for the support of religious establishments and for the payment of tributes to the central government. These were cultivated communally.

Calpulli were governed by a council of family heads. The council was under the leadership of a chief, who was in charge of land distribution and who kept a record of landholdings. Together with the council, the chief adjudicated property disputes and other conflicts between calpulli members, administered the public stores, and carried on various other administrative and judicial duties. The chief was selected by the council, but the successor to the position was customarily chosen from among the sons or other near relatives of the chief.

The state council consisted of twenty speakers, who met at frequent intervals to administer affairs of state, declare war, make peace, and judge disputes between calpulli. A speaker or delegate represented the calpulli in the state council. In addition, there was a great council, which included the twenty chiefs (one from each calpulli), the speakers, the warlords, the ranking priests, and a number of other state officials. This council judged exceptional legal cases submitted to it by the state council and, at the death of the king, selected a successor. The king was always chosen from a single royal family and was usually a younger son or nephew of the deceased king. The king was the supreme military commander and collector and distributor of tribute from conquered peoples.

The early Aztec power structure, although more complicated than that of primitive tribes, still retained a measure of democratic procedure. The core of the Aztec empire was ruled by its citizens, the members of the calpulli. While the positions of chief and king were in part hereditary (they were customarily chosen from particular families), the choice of a leader also depended upon reputation and ability. Although the king had great power as a military leader in a state more or less continuously at war, this power was modified by the councils.

However, as the Aztecs grew wealthier from their numerous conquests and ever widening control of trade, the power structure underwent a gradual change. Most importantly, there developed a class division in Aztec society along socioeconomic lines. An upper class appeared, composed of honorary lords known as *tecutin*. These were men, calpulli members, who were given titles for outstanding services to the state as warriors, merchants, public officials, or priests. They were universally esteemed, had many privileges including certain exemptions from taxation, were preferred for high governmental and military positions, and were given large estates and shares of tribute by the king, to be held as private property during their lifetime. These rewards clearly made the tecutin economically independent of their calpulli and, moreover, allied them with the king, who, while he appointed the tecutin their honors, also had the power to withdraw them.

A middle class also emerged, made up of calpulli members who were not tecutin. These formed the bulk of the population of the capital city. They were self-supporting through their membership in the calpulli and had a voice in the government through their representatives in the state and great councils. Often they rented their calpulli lands, and some acquired great wealth.

Finally, a lower class was divided into propertyless freemen and serfs. The latter were attached to the lands of the nobility as slaves. The former were men exiled from the calpulli for various crimes and who were thus without any way of making a living except by hiring themselves out as agricultural laborers or as porters in the caravans of the merchants. Slaves were similarly dependent for a living on their own labor. Neither slaves nor propertyless freemen had a voice in the government. Though initially small, the lower class grew as conquests increased.

As class lines become more sharply drawn, Aztec government moved inevitably in the direction of an *absolute, hereditary monarchy.* Tecutin clearly supported this tendency to their advantage and increasingly, by various devices, managed to pass on their titles and private property to their heirs. Slowly a *hereditary nobility* arose. At the time of the conquest, the Aztec empire was essentially an emerging feudal order, with political power centered more and more in the king and his tecutin, rather than in the elected representatives of the calpulli.

POWER AND SOCIETY—SOME ANTHROPOLOGICAL OBSERVATIONS

Let us summarize the contributions that anthropological studies can make to our understanding of the growth of power relationships in societies. First, it is clear that the *physical environment* plays an important role in the development of power systems. Where the physical environment is harsh and the human population must of necessity be spread thinly, power relationships are restricted to the family and kinship groupings. Larger political groupings are essentially impossible. Elites emerge only after there is some concentration of population, where food resources permit groupings of people larger than one or two families.

Second, power relationships are linked to the *economic patterns* of a culture. In subsistence economies, power relationships are limited to the band or tribal level. Only in surplus-producing economies do we find states or statelike power systems. Developed power systems are associated with *patterns of settled life,* a certain degree of *technological advance,* and *economic surplus.*

Third, *patterns of warfare* are linked to the development of power relationships. Warfare is rare or lacking among people such as the Eskimos who have no real power system outside of the family. Where power relationships emerge at the band or tribal level, as in the culture of the Crows, warfare appears to be continuous, in the form of periodic raiding for small economic gains or the achievement of personal glory and status; victory assumes the form of killing or driving off enemy groups. Only at the state level is warfare well organized and pursued for the purpose of conquest and economic exploitation. This does not mean necessarily that statelike power systems *cause* war, but rather that some common factor underlies both the rise of state power systems and organized warfare. Warfare and conquest are not essential to the maintenance of the state; in fact, in the modern world, warfare between major states may slowly give way to other forms of competition, if only because of the increasing threat of total destruction.

Fourth, anthropological research makes it clear that power relationships exist in simple forms in primitive societies and that *no society is void of a power structure*. Power structures become more complex and hierarchical, and more impersonal and based on physical force, as societies move from the subsistence level with simple technology to a surplus-producing level with advanced technology and large cooperative enterprises. The simpler power systems are frequently headed by chiefs and councils selected for their age, wisdom, or demonstrated capacity as hunters or warriors. These leaders tend to rule more by example and persuasion than by formal decree or force. As more complex state systems emerge, leaders are endowed with the exclusive right to coerce. Characteristically, political and economic power in the state is concentrated in a small hereditary elite. Modern representative government, in the form of European and American democracies, is relatively rare in the history of human societies.

CASE STUDY
Sociobiology: It's All in Your Genes

A recent highly controversial topic in the social sciences is that of *sociobiology*. Sociobiology may be defined as the branch of biology that deals with the biological basis of social behavior in all kinds of organisms, including human beings. In general, sociobiologists argue that at least some aspects of human behavior are based on *genetics*—that is, that these behaviors are the results of millions of years of heredity and evolution. Some sociobiologists, whose ranks include biologists and zoologists as well as social scientists, believe that genetics largely determines culture—from educational and child-rearing practices to sexual behaviors.

In 1975, Harvard zoologist Edward Wilson's book *Sociobiology: The New Synthesis* brought many of the insights of the rapidly advancing field of genetics to the study of human social behavior. The book, and the field of sociobiology itself, is highly controversial. Some people claim that it is reactionary and denies the possibility of improving social conditions because of the pull of the genes. Others fear that genetic explanations of human behavior may be used to justify racism or sexual discrimination.

Sociobiologists, however, claim that their research builds upon our scientific knowledge of genetic evolution and applies this knowledge to animal and human behavior. They maintain that many of the behavioral patterns of humans, as well as of other animals, are not "learned," but are instead the results of genetic coding. Songbirds that have been raised in complete isolation from any other members of their own species can sing the exact melody that their species sings, even though the isolated birds never had any opportunity to "learn" the melody. The melody is built into the DNA sequences in their genes. Many similar animal experiments reveal that behaviors occur in a species even though the animal has never had the opportunity to "learn" the behaviors.

Sociobiology, Natural Selection, and the Selfish Gene Sociobiology is related to Darwin's theory of evolution, which holds that all animals (including humans) evolve by *natural selection*—that those that are better adapted to their environment survive and reproduce; the rest tend to become extinct. Darwin, however, in attempting to explain natural selection, focused on the animal itself, rather than its particular genetic code. Sociobiologists, on the other hand, focus on the genetic coding, for they believe that it is within this coding that natural selection takes place. The genes struggle *within* the animal to protect themselves. Darwin was never really able to explain why some animals (including humans) acted altruistically—giving up their own lives to save others. Such behavior—birds risking their own lives to cry out to warn the flock of danger; dolphins swimming beside an injured companion to keep it from drowning; ants giving up their lives fighting for the colony—seems to contradict the theory of natural selection.

Sociobiologists explain this altruism by claiming that the genetic coding of each animal in these particular species includes directions to save the others in order to protect the same genes. In other words, altruism is really *genetic selfishness*. Moreover, most sociobiologists argue that animals will act more altruistically to save relatives (who share more genes) than nonrelatives. Altruism extended to general charitable acts (even by humans) may simply be a genetic code that urges individuals to exchange favors—"You scratch my back; I'll scratch yours." Many true heroes who feel they acted on impulse in risking their lives to save others may really have been obeying genetically coded directions.

Sociobiological Explanations of Various Behavior   Sociobiologists do *not* necessarily agree that humans are always instinctively aggressive (as suggested by Conrad Lorenz in his popular book *On Aggression*). The optimal genetic coding for survival will include just enough aggression not to be beaten out by others, but not too much to waste energy and risk death by pointless fighting. In other words, genetic coding includes a rough cost-benefit analysis for aggression.

Is it possible that power is acquired by upper social classes because they have acquired superior genes? Responsible sociobiologists reject this notion. It requires millions of years for any significant change to occur in the genetic coding of a group. Culture moves too fast for genes to be able to create any permanent class system. Even the two-thousand-year-old castes of India are not genetically different, despite their prohibitions on intermarriage and rigid separation between castes (restrictions that have been lifted since India's independence). On the other hand, sociobiologists may attribute an individual's success in such areas as sports, business, war, or science to the individual's genetic makeup.

Sociobiologists also offer genetic explanations for sexual

behavior. They contend that the object of sexual behavior in animals and humans is to pass on as many of their own genes to succeeding generations as possible at the lowest possible cost in energy and time. Because a male can start thousands of pregnancies, thus ensuring that some of his offspring will survive, he can ignore the nurturing of his offspring. But a female can only give birth a limited number of times during her lifetime and therefore must invest more time in nurturing her young in order to ensure their survival. Thus, promiscuity among males of many species is common, as is the nesting urge of females. Females of many species stay near to the nest, while males roam far in search of opportunities to breed. Moreover, males often engage in openly aggressive behavior against other males, not only to beat out the competition for available females, but also to impress females with the strength of their genes. Over millions of years of evolution, the result, say the sociobiologists, is a different and stronger male physique. Of course, these views have irritated many women, who fear that sociobiologists are telling them to stay home and mind the babies.

It is difficult to estimate how much human behavior is genetically directed (as the sociobiologists contend), and how much is learned from parents and others (as cultural anthropologists contend). It is impossible to say, for example, that 20 or 30 percent of human behavior is genetically based, and the rest is culturally based. All we know now is that both genetics and culture affect human behavior.

NOTES

1. Clyde Kluckhohn and William Kelly, "The Concept of Culture," in Ralph Linton, ed., *The Science of Man in the World Crisis* (New York: Columbia University Press, 1945), p. 97.

2. Morris E. Opler, *An Apache Life Way* (Chicago: University of Chicago Press, 1941), pp. 409–10.

3. This approach was developed by Bronislaw Malinowski, *A Scientific Theory of Culture and Other Essays* (Chapel Hill: University of North Carolina Press, 1944).

4. Ruth Benedict, *Patterns of Culture* (Boston: Houghton Mifflin, 1934), p. 46.

5. Ibid., p. 172.

6. William W. Stephens, *The Family in Cross-Cultural Perspective* (New York: Holt, Rinehart & Winston, 1963).

7. U.S. Bureau of the Census, *Current Population Reports*, Series P–20, no. 296.

8. Daniel P. Moynihan, *The Negro Family: The Case for National Action* (Washington, D.C.: Government Printing Office, 1965).

9. Robert H. Lowie, *The Crow Indians* (New York: Rinehart, 1935), p. 5.

DISCUSSION QUESTIONS

1. Describe how societies attempt to control the behavior of their members. Discuss the four broad purposes for which societies exercise power.

2. Describe how power relationships begin within the family and how they develop into political organizations. What effect can warfare have on the power structure?

3. Choose a "subculture" that is familiar to you. If you were asked to explain in anthropological terms what sets this subculture apart from the society at large, what cultural categories would you examine? Identify the variations in lifestyle that make this a subculture.

4. Describe how an anthropologist of the functionalist school would approach the study of culture.

5. Discuss Ruth Benedict's contributions to anthropology. In your discussion, describe how an anthropologist of the configurationist school would approach the study of culture.

6. Identify the characteristics of the family that are found in all societies. Explain why these characteristics account for the family being the most important social group. Describe the variations in family arrangements that are found in different societies.

7. "In all societies the child's first experience with authority is within the family. . . . Differences in the type of authority exercised, and whether or not the authority is exercised primarily by the mother or father, can shape the character and personality of the growing individual." Describe the type of adult female you might expect to have grown up within a family in an agricultural society and contrast with an adult female who has grown up within a family in an industrialized society. Describe the influences contributing to the development of both women.

8. Discuss changes in the American family. Comment on the continuing strength of family life; the number of families with a single adult; the declining birth rate; and mothers in the work force.

9. Describe the broad stages of development of power relationships and the power groups associated with them. Compare these groups in terms of leadership, economic systems, patterns of warfare, population density, and patterns of settlement. How have anthropological studies contributed to our understanding of these power relationships?

10. "Culture is learned. . . . culture is transferred from one generation to another, but . . . it is *not* genetically transmitted." What arguments do sociobiologists advance against this contention? Why does sociobiology arouse so much controversy? Identify the areas of human social behavior that sociobiologists believe may be genetically directed. Discuss your opinions about the relative effects of genetics and culture on human behavior.

SUGGESTED READINGS

Ralph L. Beals and Harry Hoijer, *An Introduction to Anthropology* (New York: Macmillan, 1971).

Ruth Benedict, *Patterns of Culture* (Boston: Houghton Mifflin, 1934).

Ruth Bunzel and Margaret Mead, *The Golden Age of American Anthropology* (New York: Braziller, 1960).

Clyde Kluckhohn, *Mirror for Man* (New York: Fawcett, 1960).

Ralph Linton, *The Tree of Culture* (New York: Vintage Books, 1959).

Margaret Mead, *Coming of Age in Samoa* (New York: Mentor Books, 1949).

William H. Stephens, *The Family in Cross-Cultural Perspective* (New York: Holt, Rinehart & Winston, 1963).

Edward O. Wilson, *Sociobiology: The New Synthesis* (Cambridge, Mass.: Harvard University Press, 1975).

Photo from Magnum by Constantine Manos

Photo from Magnum by Alex Webb

Chapter 4
Power and
Social Class

"In worn out, king-ridden Europe, men must stay where they are born. But in America a man is accounted a failure, and certainly ought to be, who has not risen above his father's station in life." These are the words of Charles O'Conor, the self-made son of an Irish immigrant, who himself rose "above his father's station" to acquire the symbols of social status—power and authority as the recognized leader of the New York bar, wealth as the owner of a stately Nantucket mansion, and prestige as the holder of five honorary degrees from universities.[1] Although O'Conor made his statement over a century ago and most Americans would acknowledge that in the meantime the "land of opportunity" has shrunk, his words are still an accurate reflection of the ideology on which the American class system is based.

In this chapter we will look at how Americans "stratify" themselves into social classes; at how sociologists measure this stratification; at the functions that ideology serves; and at the relationship between social class and power. After you have read chapter 4, you should be able to:

- describe the stratification system and the methods that sociologists use to identify and measure stratification.
- discuss the functions of ideology and describe how the American ideology influences social stratification.
- define class consciousness and identify the factors that help to stabilize the existing class system in America.
- discuss the relationships between social class and lifestyle and between social class and political power.

POWER PYRAMIDS AND PECKING ORDERS

Social stratification   All known societies have some system of ranking their members along a superiority-inferiority scale. While some societies claim to grant "equality" to their members, in no society have people in fact been considered equal. The *stratification* of society involves the *class-*

ification of individuals and the *ranking* of classifications on a superiority-inferiority scale. This system of classification and ranking is itself a source of prestige, wealth, income, authority, and power.

Bases of stratification

Individuals can be classified on a wide variety of characteristics—physical strength, fighting prowess, family lineage, ethnic or racial category, age, sex, religion, birth order, and so on. But *the most important bases of stratification in a modern industrial society are the different roles that individuals play in the economic system.* Individuals are ranked according to how they make their living and how much control they exercise over the livelihood of others. Ranking by occupation and control of economic resources occurs not only in the United States but in most other modern nations as well; both communist and noncommunist nations have stratification systems based on these same factors.[2]

Characteristics of stratification

The evaluation of individuals along a superiority-inferiority scale means, of course, a differential distribution of prestige. Thus, the elite strata will receive the *deference* of individuals who are ranked below them. Deference may take many forms: acquiescence in the material advantages or privileges of the elite (the use of titles and symbols of rank, distinctive clothing, housing, and automobiles); accordance of influence and respect; acceptance of leadership in decision making; and so on. The stratification system also involves *different styles of life:* foods eaten, magazines and books read, place of residence, favorite kind of sports, schools attended, pronunciation and accent, recreational activities, and so forth. In addition, of course, the stratification system is associated with the *uneven distribution of wealth and income:* In every society higher-ranking persons enjoy better housing, clothing, food, automobiles, and other material goods and services than persons ranked lower in the scale.

Finally, the stratification system involves the *unequal distribution of power*—the ability to control the acts of others. Sociologists agree that power and stratification are closely related, but they disagree on the specific value of this relationship. Some theorize that power is a *product* of economic well-being or prestige or status. Others believe that power *determines* the distribution of wealth, prestige, and status.[3]

Social class

It is the stratification system that creates social classes. The term *social class* simply refers to all individuals who occupy a broadly similar category and ranking in the stratification system. Members of the same social class may or may not interact, or even realize that they have much in common. Since all societies have stratification systems, all societies have social classes.

STRATIFICATION IN AMERICAN SOCIETY

Social classes are of interest to sociologists, with their concern for the relationships among individuals and groups. Sociologists have devised several methods of identifying and measuring social stratification. These include: (1) the *subjective method*, in which individuals are asked how they see themselves in the class system; (2) the *reputational method*, in which individuals are asked to rank positions in the class system; and (3) the *objective method*, in which social scientists observe characteristics that discriminate between patterns of life associated by them with social class.

Methods of identifying and measuring stratification

The American ideology encompasses the notion that position should be based upon personal qualities and achievements. Individuals in a free society should have the opportunity to achieve the social rankings that they can earn by ability, effort, and moral worth. They are supposed to rise or fall according to their merits. The American ideology does not deny the existence of a superiority-inferiority scale for evaluating people in society; nor does it call for absolute equality or "leveling," with all people given equal income, wealth, position, and prestige regardless of their individual merit. But it does call for *equality of opportunity*; that is, all should have an equal opportunity to achieve high position in accordance with their individual merits and endeavors. In the American ideal "anyone who has it in him can get ahead." The logical sequel to this is that those who are at the top are worthy of being there because of their talents and efforts.

Ideology and subjective identification

In view of this ideology it is not surprising that most Americans think of themselves as middle class. Nearly nine out of ten will describe themselves as middle class when they are forced to choose between this term and either upper or lower class. It is apparent that to characterize oneself as upper class is regarded as "snobbish" and to view oneself as lower class is to admit that one is a loser in the great game of life. Even people who admit to being poor consider it an insult to be called lower class.[4]

However, the fact that most Americans label themselves as middle class does not mean American society is one big middle-class society. In fact, when *working class* is added to the list of choices, and individuals are asked for subjective evaluations of their own class membership, a different picture emerges. Table 4–1 shows the distribution of responses when people are asked to rank themselves on more precise scales. Obviously the inclusion of "working class" reveals that Americans by no means see themselves as members of a single class; more than one-third of a national sample placed themselves in this category.[5]

Table 4-1   Subjective Class Identifications of Americans

Upper class	2.2%
Upper-middle class	16.6
Middle class	44.0
Working class	34.3
Lower class	2.3
Deny idea of class	1.0

Source: Adapted from Robert W. Hodge and Donald J. Treiman, "Class Identification in the United States," *American Journal of Sociology* 73 (March 1968):535–47.

Subjective vs. objective identification

How well does *subjective* evaluation of class conform to the ideas of social scientists about the *objective* meaning of class? As we have already noted, social scientists view occupation and control of economic resources as the principal determinant of social class in America. Sociologist Richard Centers writes, "A man's way of getting his livelihood dominates much of his waking life, and it is out of the forces acting upon him in this economic sphere that class consciousness has been seen to emerge."[6] In an interesting test of this idea, sociologists Hodge and Treiman examined the way that individuals' subjective identification of their own class correlated with their actual income, occupation, education, and ownership of real estate, savings bonds, and corporate stocks and bonds. It turned out that occupation, income, and education were all associated with subjective class identification (occupation was more intimately connected with class identification than anything else), but that ownership of real estate, savings bonds, or corporate stocks and bonds had almost nothing to do with this identification process. Persons who did not own these resources were just as likely to rank themselves as middle or upper-middle class as those who did. Moreover, the authors found that the other objective criteria of class—occupation, income, and education—were not as closely related to subjective evaluations as had been expected. They found it difficult to predict what class people would put themselves in on the basis of occupation, income, or education. In addition, Hodge and Treiman reported that the social class of friends and neighbors affected a person's self-identification. Those whose friends were in the upper occupation and income categories tended to rank themselves as middle class while those whose friends and neighbors were blue-collar workers tended to rank themselves working class. In short, there is some relationship between subjective and objective measures of social class, but subjective evaluation of one's own social class can be affected by factors other than objective circumstances.

Reputational method

Social scientists have spent a great deal of time studying the prestige ranking of occupations as another aspect of the stratification system of modern society. Individuals are asked in national surveys to make a superiority-inferiority ranking of specific occupations—for example, "For each job mentioned, please pick out the statement that best gives *your own personal opinion* of the *general standing* that such a job has." Respondents are then asked to choose *excellent, good, somewhat below average,* or *poor* as their answer. The resulting prestige scores for ninety separate occupations are shown in table 4–2. It is interesting to note that these rankings remained stable

Table 4-2   Prestige Ratings of Occupations

Occupation	Prestige Rank	Occupation	Prestige Rank
U.S. Supreme Court justice	1	Instructor in public schools	27.5
Physician	2	Captain in the regular army	27.5
Nuclear physicist	3.5	Accountant for a large	
Scientist	3.5	business	29.5
Government scientist	5.5	Public school teacher	29.5
State governor	5.5	Owner of a factory that em-	
Cabinet member in the		ploys about 100 people	31.5
federal government	8	Building contractor	31.5
College professor	8	Artist who paints pictures	
U.S. representative in		that are exhibited in	
Congress	8	galleries	34.5
Chemist	11	Musician in a symphony	
Lawyer	11	orchestra	34.5
Diplomat in the U.S.		Author of novels	34.5
foreign service	11	Economist	34.5
Dentist	14	Official of an interna-	
Architect	14	tional labor union	37
County judge	14	Railroad engineer	39
Psychologist	17.5	Electrician	39
Minister	17.5	County agricultural agent	39
Member of the board of		Owner-operator of a	
directors of a large		printing shop	41.5
corporation	17.5	Trained machinist	41.5
Mayor of a large city	17.5	Farm owner and operator	44
Priest	21.5	Undertaker	44
Head of a department in		Welfare worker for a city	
a state government	21.5	government	44
Civil engineer	21.5	Newspaper columnist	46
Airline pilot	21.5	Policeman	47
Banker	24.5	Reporter on a daily	
Biologist	24.5	newspaper	48
Sociologist	26	Radio announcer	49.5

Table 4-2   (Cont.)

Occupation	Prestige Rank	Occupation	Prestige Rank
Bookkeeper	49.5	Clerk in a store	70
Tenant farmer—one who owns livestock and machinery and manages the farm	51.5	Milk route man	70
		Streetcar motorman	70
Insurance agent	51.5	Lumberjack	72.5
Carpenter	53	Restaurant cook	72.5
Manager of a small store in a city	54.5	Singer in a nightclub	74
		Filling station attendant	75
Local official of a labor union	54.5	Dockworker	77.5
		Railroad section hand	77.5
Mail carrier	57	Night watchman	77.5
Railroad conductor	57	Coal miner	77.5
Traveling salesman for a wholesale concern	57	Restaurant waiter	80.5
		Taxi driver	80.5
Plumber	59	Farm hand	83
Automobile repairman	60	Janitor	83
Playground director	62.5	Bartender	83
Barber	62.5	Clothes presser in a laundry	85
Machine operator in a factory	62.5	Soda fountain clerk	86
Owner-operator of a lunch stand	62.5	Sharecropper—one who owns no livestock or equipment and does not manage farm	87
Corporal in the regular army	65.5	Garbage collector	88
Garage mechanic	65.5	Street sweeper	89
Truck driver	67	Shoe shiner	90
Fisherman who owns his own boat	68		

Source: Robert W. Hodge, Paul M. Siegel, and Peter H. Rossi, "Occupational Prestige in the United States," *American Journal of Sociology* 69 (November 1964): 286–302. By permission of the University of Chicago Press.

for several decades. U.S. Supreme Court justice and physician held first and second places respectively from the end of World War II at least through 1964. Sharecropper, garbage collector, street sweeper, and shoe shiner occupied the last four rankings over these years. It should be noted that knowledge about occupational prestige and relatively strong consensus on relative ratings of occupations are widespread throughout the American population. Even more noteworthy is the fact that occupational-prestige rankings are similar from nation to nation among modern societies, both socialist and capitalist, developed and underdeveloped.

Objective method   The *principal objective criteria* of social class are income, occupation, and education. If sociologists are correct in the assumption
that occupation and control of economic resources are the source of
stratification in society, then these indexes are the best available
measures of class. Certainly income, jobs, and education are unequally distributed in American society, as they are in all other
societies. Table 4–3 reveals the distribution of income in the United
States, as well as the distribution of income by education and occupation.

These three measures of social class are related; generally individuals with prestigious occupations and good educations enjoy high
incomes. This is substantiated by table 4–3, which shows that individuals who have acquired higher educations tend to enjoy higher an-

Table 4–3   Distribution of Income, Occupation, and Education in the
United States

Family Income	% of Population
Less than $4,000	7.4
$ 4,000–6,000	8.2
6,000–8,000	9.4
8,000–10,000	9.5
10,000–12,000	10.0
12,000–15,000	14.8
15,000–25,000	34.1
25,000–50,000	15.7
Over $50,000	1.9

Median family income = $14,094

	Median Family Income		
Education	Total	White	Black
Eight years school or less	$10,037	$10,210	$ 8,360
Four years high school	15,077	15,400	10,779
Four years college	21,987	22,124	19,641
Occupation			
White-collar	$19,459	$19,746	$14,240
Blue-collar	14,555	14,791	12,159
Service worker	11,220	12,100	8,425
Farm worker	9,821	10,230	5,069

Source: U.S. Bureau of the Census, *Current Population Reports* Series (Washington,
D.C.: Government Printing Office, March 1978), p. 60.

nual incomes. Moreover, individuals with more prestigious occupations also enjoy higher incomes.

However, table 4–3 also shows that there are two separate scales by which income is distributed—one white and one black. Blacks with equivalent educations tend to earn less than whites. Moreover, blacks at each occupational level also earn less than whites. These disparities between blacks and whites are changing slowly over time. But there is still considerable racial inequality in the distribution of income in America. (See also appendix, table B.)

IDEOLOGY AND STRATIFICATION: DREAMS ABOUT GETTING AHEAD

Functions of ideology

The ideology of a stratification system *explains and justifies the distribution of power and rewards* in society. The ideology *helps to reduce tensions between classes* by explaining and justifying differences in their well-being. At the same time, it *helps to consolidate the power of the elite* by giving legitimacy to their superior standing in society. Thus, ideology itself is a source of power (see chapter 9).

In the American ideal, one who works hard ought to get ahead, does get ahead, and in getting ahead proves that hard work is justified. The American ideology is one of equality of opportunity. Its major points are:

The American ideology

1. The belief in an open opportunity structure in the United States, with equality of chances for upward and downward mobility.
2. Personal responsibility for movement upward or downward in the class system, with movement based largely upon personal effort, ambition, hard work, skill, and education.
3. Relative accessibility of education to everyone who has the ability.
4. The impartial functioning of the political and legal systems.

American attitudes

Do Americans believe in this ideology? A majority of them endorse it when it is presented to them in very general statements. However, when general statements are translated into specific questions, there is much less agreement. Moreover, acceptance of both general and specific statements about opportunity in America varies widely from one social class to another. Wealthy white Americans believe more strongly in the American ideal of equality of opportunity than do black Americans.

To test beliefs about the opportunity structure, sociologists asked a sample of Americans a series of questions relating to the American ideology. First was a general question about the existence of "plenty of opportunity" to get ahead: *Some people say there's not much op-*

portunity in America today—that the average man doesn't have much chance to really get ahead. Others say there's plenty of opportunity and anyone who works hard can go as far as he wants. How do you feel? Then came a more specific question about opportunities to get ahead: Do you think that a boy whose father is poor and a boy whose father is rich have the same opportunity to make the same amount of money if they work equally hard, or do you think that the boy whose father is rich has a better chance of earning a lot more money?

Next there was a general question regarding equal access to education: Do you feel that all young people of high ability have fairly equal opportunity to go to college, or do you feel that a large percentage of young people do not have the opportunity to go to college? This was followed by a more specific question on access to education: Do you think that most young people in college come from families who can give them financial help, or do you think that young people whose parents are poor are just as likely to be in college as anyone else?

There followed a question on power and influence in general terms: Some people think that voting is a vital part of the governmental process in this country while others think it really doesn't make much difference who gets elected because the same people go on running things anyway. What do you think? Finally, there was a more specific question on power and influence: Some people say that, regardless of who gets elected, people who are rich get their way most of the time, while others say that people who are poor have just as much influence in government as people who are rich. What do you think?

The responses to these questions clearly indicate that Americans believe in the ideology of opportunity only when it is stated in the most general and vague terms (see table 4-4). There is far less belief in the existence of equal opportunity when the ideology is presented in concrete, specific situations. White Americans, who feel there is "plenty of opportunity" in general terms, divide over the question of whether or not a boy whose father is poor can achieve as much by working hard as a boy whose father is rich. Likewise the majority of whites think that "all young people of high ability" have a fairly equal opportunity to go to college, but at the same time they do not believe that young people of ability from poor families are as likely to be in college as anyone else. Most Americans will agree with the general proposition that voting influences government, but few are willing to assert that poor people have "just as much influence in government" as rich people. Moreover, support for both specific and general statements about equality of opportunity in America declines with income: lower-income groups have less faith in equality of opportunity than upper-income groups. Finally, it is significant that

Table 4–4   Beliefs about Getting Ahead in America

% in Agreement	Low Income		Middle Income		Upper Income	
	Black	White	Black	White	White	Total
Rich and poor have plenty of opportunity (general)	56	90	58	80	93	78
Rich and poor have equal opportunity (specific)	11	47	21	49	57	42
Rich and poor have equal access to college (general)	22	57	41	75	96	64
Rich and poor have equal access to college (specific)	11	38	28	37	43	38
Rich and poor have equal voting influences (general)	76	88	89	89	94	88
Rich and poor have equal voting influences (specific)	3	30	15	30	55	35

Source: Data from Joan H. Rytina, William H. Form, and John Pease, "Income and Stratification Ideology: Beliefs About the American Opportunity Structure," *American Journal of Sociology* 75 (January 1970): 703–16; from a sample of residents in Muskegon, Michigan.

black Americans are far less likely than white Americans to believe in the existence of equal opportunity.

CLASS AS A DETERMINANT OF STYLE OF LIFE

Life in each social class is different. Differences in ways of life mean differences in culture, or rather (since the style of life in each class is really a variant of one common culture in American society) a division of the culture into *subcultures*. Class subcultures have been described by many sociologists. There are class differences in almost every aspect of life: health, hygiene, vocabulary, table manners, standards of right and wrong, recreation and entertainment, religion, sexual activity, family and child-rearing practices, political beliefs and attitudes, club memberships, dress, birth rates, attitudes toward education, toilet training, reading habits, and so on. It is impossible to provide a complete description of all the class differences that have been reported by sociologists. Moreover, class lifestyles overlap, and there are no rigid boundaries in America between classes. Class subcultures should be thought of as a *continuous scale* with styles of life that blend; hence there are many "in-between" positions. And finally, it should be remembered that any generalizations about broad classes in America do not necessarily describe the style of life of any particular individuals. So the following paragraphs are merely a general summary of these subcultures. (For a general summary of socioeconomic characteristics according to race, see appendix, table C.)

The Upper Class   The typical upper-class individual is future-oriented and cosmopolitan. Persons of this class expect a long life, look forward to this future and the future of their children and grandchildren, and are concerned about what lies ahead for the community, the nation, and mankind. They are self-confident, believing that within limits they can shape their own destiny and that of the community. They are willing to "invest" in the future—that is, to sacrifice some present satisfaction in the expectation of enjoying greater satisfaction in time to come. They are self-respecting; they place great value on independence, creativity, and "developing potentialities to the fullest." In rearing their children, they teach them to be guided by abstract standards of social justice rather than by conformity to a given code ("Do things not because you're told to, but because you take the other person into consideration"). Child rearing is permissive, and the only coercive measures taken against the child are verbal and emotional. Instructions to the child are always rationalized. Upper-class parents are not alarmed if their children remain in school or travel to the age of thirty. Sex life in upper classes is innovative and expressive, with great variety in sexual practices. Women enjoy nearly equal status with men in family relationships. The goals of life include individuality, self-expression, and personal happiness. Wealth permits a wide variety of entertainment and recreation: theater, concerts, and art; yachting, tennis, skiing; travel abroad; and so on.

Upper-class individuals take a tolerant attitude toward unconventional behavior in sex, the arts, fashions, lifestyles, and so forth. They deplore bigotry and abhor violence. They feel they have a responsibility to "serve" the community and to "do good." They are active in "public service" and contribute time, money, and effort to worthy causes. They have an attachment to the community, the nation, and the world, and they believe they can help shape the future. This "public-regardingness" inclines them toward "liberal" politics; the upper classes provide the leadership for the liberal wings of both Republican and Democratic parties.

The Middle Class   Middle-class individuals are also future oriented; they plan ahead for themselves and their children. But they are not likely to be so cosmopolitan as the upper-class person, being more concerned with their immediate families than about "humanity" in the abstract. They are confident about their ability to influence their own futures and that of their children, but they do not really expect to have an effect on community, state, or national events. They show some independence and creativity, but their taste for self-expression is modified by their concern for "getting ahead."

The middle-class individual is perhaps even more self-disciplined and willing to sacrifice present gratification for future advantage than the upper-class individual. In the lower-middle class, investing time, energy, and effort in self-improvement and getting ahead is a principal theme of life. Middle-class people strongly want their children to go to college and acquire the kind of formal training that will help them get ahead. Child rearing in the middle class is only slightly less permissive than in the upper class; it is still based largely upon verbal and emotional punishment. This can be quite severe, however, and the middle-class child may be more closely supervised and disciplined than either upper- or lower-class children. Authority is rationalized for the child, but values and standards of behavior are drawn from surrounding middle-class society rather than from abstract concepts of social justice. In matters of sex, the middle-class individual is outwardly conventional. The middle-class adolescent experiences first intercourse at a later age than the lower-class youth. However, in adult life, vis-à-vis lower-class individuals, the middle-class person enjoys greater variety in sexual activity, women have greater equality in the family, and the family has fewer children (though home activities are frequently child-centered). Recreation and entertainment include golf, swimming, movies, sports events, and travel in the United States. In general, the middle-class person is less able than the upper-class one to afford an interest in theater, art, symphonies, or travel abroad.

As a rule middle-class individuals deal with others according to established codes of conduct and behavior. They are likely to be middle-of-the-road or conservative in politics; they tend to vote Republican. They have regard for the rights of others and generally oppose bigotry and violence. However, they do not hold these attitudes as strongly as do members of the upper class, nor do they feel as much responsibility to the community as the upper-class individual does. Though they join voluntary organizations, many of which are formally committed to community service, they are less willing to give their time, money, and effort to public causes.

The Working Class   Working-class individuals do not "invest" heavily in the future; they are much more oriented toward the present. They expect their children to make their own way in life. They have less confidence than the middle class in their ability to shape the future, and a stronger sense of being at the mercy of fate and other uncontrollable forces. They attach more importance to "luck" in getting ahead than to education, hard work, or self-sacrifice. They are self-respecting and self-confident, but these feelings extend over a narrower range of matters than they do in middle-class individuals. The horizon of the working class is limited by job, family, immediate friends, and neighborhood. Self-improvement or getting ahead is not a major concern of life; there is more interest in having a "good time" with family and companions. The working-class family has more children than do middle-class or upper-class families.

Working-class individuals work to maintain themselves and their families; they do not look upon their jobs as a means of getting ahead and certainly not as a means of self-expression. In rearing their children, they emphasize the virtues of neatness, cleanliness, honesty, obedience, and respect for authority. They seldom rationalize authority over their children ("Because I said so, that is why") and frequently use physical punishment. They are not interested in stimulating their children to self-expression, but rather in controlling them—teaching them traditional family values. They would like their children to go to college, but if they do not do so, it is no great matter. The working-class youth experiences first sexual intercourse at an earlier age than do middle- and upper-class young people, but is much more likely to categorize women as "good" or "bad" depending on their sexual activity. There is very little variety in the adult sexual behavior of the working class, and the female is relegated to a subordinate role in sexual and family affairs. Frequently a double standard allows promiscuity in the male whereas extramarital sex by the female can be the cause of family disruption.

In relationships with others, the working-class individual is often intolerant and sometimes aggressive. Open bigotry is more likely to be encountered in the working class than in the middle or upper classes. Violence is less shocking to the working class than to middle-class persons; indeed, sometimes it is regarded as a normal expression of a masculine style. To the working class, the upper class appears somewhat lacking in masculinity. The working-class individual's deepest attachment is to family. Most visiting is done with relatives rather than friends. Working-class persons do not belong to many organizations other than union and church. Whether Protestant or Catholic, their religious beliefs are fundamentalist in character; they believe in the literal meaning of the scriptures and respect the authority of the church. In their views toward others in the community, they are very "private-regarding"; they believe they work hard for a living and feel others should do the same. They are not interested in public service or "do-goodism"; they look down on people who accept welfare or charity, unless these people are forced to do so by circumstances over which they have no control. When they vote, they generally vote Democratic, but they are often apathetic about politics. Their opinions on public matters are more likely to be clichés or slogans than anything else. They are liberal on economic issues (job security, fair labor standards, government guarantees of full employment, etc.), but conservative on social issues (civil rights, welfare, youth, etc.). The working-class position in politics is motivated not by political ideology, but by ethnic and party loyalties, by the appeal of personalities, or by the hope for occasional favors. For recreation the working-class individual turns to bowling, stock-car racing, circuses, fairs, carnivals, drive-in restaurants, and drive-in movies.

The Lower Class   Lower-class individuals live from day to day, with little interest in the future. They have no confidence in their ability to influence what happens to them. Things happen *to* them; they do not *make* them happen. They do not discipline themselves to sacrifice for the future because they have no sense of future. They look for immediate gratification, and their behavior is governed largely by impulse. When they work at all, it is often from payday to payday, and they frequently drift from one unskilled job to another, taking scant interest in the work. Their self-confidence is low, and occasionally they even suffer from feelings of self-contempt. In relations with others, they are suspicious, hostile, and aggressive. They feel little attachment to community, neighbors, and friends and resent all authority (for example, that of policemen, social workers, teachers, landlords, employers). Lower-class individuals are nonparticipants—they belong to no voluntary organizations, attend church infrequently, have no political interests, and seldom vote.

The lower-class family is frequently headed by a female. Lower-class women not only have more children than middle- or upper-class women, but also have them earlier in life. A woman may have a succession of mates who contribute intermittently to the support of the family but who take almost no part in rearing children. In child rearing, the mother (or the grandmother) is impulsive; children may be alternately loved, disciplined, and neglected, and often do not know what to expect next. The mother may receive welfare aid or work at a low-paying job, but in either case children are generally unsupervised once they have passed babyhood. Physical punishment is frequent. When children enter school, they are already behind other children in verbal abilities and abstract reasoning. For the male offspring of a lower-class matriarchal family, the future is often depressing, with defeat and frustration repeating themselves throughout his life. He may drop out of school in the eighth or ninth grade because of lack of success. Without parental supervision, and having little to do, he may get in trouble with the police. The police record will further hurt his chances of getting a job. With limited job skills, little self-discipline, and low aspiration levels, the lower-class male is not likely to find a steady job that will pay enough to support a family. Yet he yearns for the material standard of living of higher classes—a car, a television set, and other conveniences. He may tie up much of his income in installment debts; because of his low credit rating he will be forced to pay excessive interest rates, and sooner or later his creditors will garnish his salary. If he marries, he and his family will have overcrowded substandard housing. As pressures mount, he may decide to leave his family, either because his inability to support a wife and children is humiliating, or because he is psychologically unprepared for a stable family relationship, or because only in this way will his wife and children be eligible for welfare payments.

Frequently, to compensate for defeat and frustration the lower-class male will resort to risk taking, conquest, and fighting to assert his masculinity. Lower-class life is violent. The incidence of mental illness is greater in the lower class than in any other class. While the lower-class youth may have engaged in sexual activities from a very early age, these are stereotyped in a male-dominant–female-subordinate fashion. Entertainment may be limited to drinking and gambling. Many aspects of lower-class culture are unattractive to women. Sociologist Herbert Gans writes:

> The woman tries to develop a stable routine in the midst of poverty and deprivation; the action-seeking man upsets it. In order to have any male relationships, however, the woman must participate to some extent in his episodic lifestyle. On rare occasions, she may even pursue it herself. Even then, however, she will try to encourage her children to seek a routine way of life. Thus the woman is much closer to working class culture, at least in her aspirations, although she is not often successful in achieving them.[7]

SOCIAL CLASSES: CONFLICT AND CONCILIATION

*Class consciousness vs.
class awareness*

An awareness of class membership is not the same as class consciousness. *Class consciousness is the belief that all members of one's social class have similar economic and political interests that are adverse to the interests of other classes and ought to be promoted through common action.* As we have already seen, Americans are *aware* of class membership, but members of the same class do not always share political interests, or feel that collective class action is necessary, or see themselves as locked in a struggle against opposing classes. Few Americans believe in the militant ideology of class struggle. Americans do not have a strong sense of class consciousness.

Nonetheless, there is some evidence of an awareness of class interest in voting behavior. While Democratic and Republican candidates draw their support from all social classes in America, social class bases of the Democratic and Republican parties are slightly different (see chapter 7). Professional and managerial groups and other white-collar employees give greater support to the Republican party than skilled, semiskilled, and unskilled workers. Likewise, people with some college education tend to vote Republican more often than persons with a high school or grade school education do. Of course not all of the upper-class vote goes to the Republican party, and not all of the lower-class vote goes to the Democratic party. In fact the differences in voter support are not very great. But there is some indication that class has an impact on voting behavior.

The *black consciousness* that has developed in America in recent years is similar in many ways to class consciousness. Prominent themes in militant black politics have been the necessity to foster black pride and dignity, bring about an awareness of oppression, reject the idea of coalition with whites, promote black solidarity, and engage in collective political action to advance black interests. But black consciousness is based on race and *not* upon class membership, Only insofar as black consciousness draws attention to the general problems of lower classes in America will it be contributing to the growth of *class* consciousness.

Why is there no militant class consciousness in America? This is a difficult question to answer precisely, but we can summarize some of the factors that appear to help *stabilize the existing class system* in America and *reduce class conflict:*

Stabilizing factors

1. The high level of real income of Americans of all social classes and the relatively wide distribution of a very comfortable standard of living.
2. A great deal of upward mobility in the American system, which

diverts lower-class attention away from collective class action and focuses it toward individual efforts at "getting ahead."

3. The existence of a large middle-income, middle-prestige class.
4. Widespread belief in the legitimacy of the class structure and the resulting acceptance of it.
5. Many cross-cutting allegiances of individuals to churches, communities, races, unions, professional associations, voluntary organizations, and so forth, which interfere with class solidarity.

In stabilizing the class system, these factors also stabilize the *existing distribution of power* in America.

The American system has produced a high level of material comfort for the great majority of the population. The real possibilities of acquiring greater income and prestige have reinforced efforts to strive within the system rather than to challenge it. Even individuals who realize that their own social mobility is limited can transfer their hope and ambition to their children. A large middle class, diverse in occupation and ambiguous in political orientation, helps to blur potential lines of class identification and conflict. This class stands as a symbol and an embodiment of the reality of opportunity. A widely accepted set of ideologies, beliefs, and attitudes supports the existing system. Finally, cleavages centering around religious affiliations, ethnic backgrounds, and racial categories, as well as other types of diversity (region, skill level, occupational group), have all worked against the development of a unified class movement.

KARL MARX
The Class Struggle

Conflict between social classes is a central feature of communist ideology. In the opening of his famous *Communist Manifesto*, Karl Marx wrote:

The history of all hitherto existing society is the history of class struggles. Freeman and slave, patrician and plebeian, lord and serf, guild-master and journeyman, in a word, oppressor and oppressed, stood in constant opposition to one another, carried on uninterrupted, now hidden, now open fight, a fight that each time ended, either in a revolutionary reconstitution of society at large, or in the common ruin of the contending classes. . . . Our epoch, the epoch of the bourgeoisie, possesses, however, this distinctive feature: it has simplified the class antagonisms. Society as a whole is more and more splitting up into two great hostile camps, into two great classes directly facing each other: Bourgeoisie and Proletariat.

Karl Marx was born in Prussia in 1818. His parents were Jews who converted to Christianity when Marx was a child. He studied history, law, and philosophy at Bonn, Berlin, and Jena and received his doctor of philosophy degree in 1841. Soon after, he entered revolutionary socialist politics as a journalist and pamphleteer; he was expelled from Prussia and engaged in conspiratorial activities in France and Belgium from 1843 to 1849. *The Communist Manifesto,* written with Friedrich Engels, appeared in 1848 as a revolutionary pamphlet. In 1849 Marx fled to London where he spent the remainder of his life writing occasional pamphlets on socialism, advising socialist leaders, and setting forth his views in a lengthy work, *Das Kapital.* He lived largely on the money given him by Friedrich Engels, who was the son of a wealthy textile manufacturer.

Marx's view of economic roles

According to Marx, social classes develop on the basis of the different positions that individuals fulfill in the prevailing "mode of

production"—that is, the economy. In an agricultural economy, the principal classes are landowner and tenant, serf, or slave; in a handicraft economy, guildmaster and apprentice; and in an industrial economy, the capitalist (owner) of the factory and the non-property-owning worker. Marx believed that one's position in the economy determines one's interests, beliefs, and actions. The bourgeoisie who own the factories have an interest in maximizing profit and seek to keep for themselves the surplus of profit that has been created by the worker. Workers are exploited in that they produce more than they receive in wages; this "surplus value" is stolen from the workers by the capitalists. In the long run, bourgeois society is doomed to destruction because gradually the workers will realize they are being exploited, will become aware of their historic role and act collectively to improve their situation, and ultimately will take over the ownership of the instruments of production in violent revolution. In Marx's opinion, it was inevitable that the development of capitalism would lead eventually to the proletarian revolution. He believed that as the capitalist became richer the workers would become poorer:

> Accumulation of wealth at one pole is, therefore, at the same time accumulation of misery, agony of toil, slavery, ignorance, brutality, mental degradation, at the opposite pole.[8]

Class consciousness and the classless society

Class consciousness was viewed by Marx as an important prerequisite to successful proletarian revolution. Class consciousness would increase as the proletariat grew in numbers, as factories concentrated the proletariat in greater masses, as workers communicated among themselves and achieved solidarity in unions and political organizations, and as conflict between workers and owners intensified. The bourgeoisie would not relinquish their control over the means of production without a fight, and therefore violent revolution was necessary and inevitable. Marx said little about the details of revolution; this aspect of communist ideology was developed later by Lenin (see chapter 9). But after the successful proletarian revolution, Marx envisioned a society without social classes. This *classless society* would be a "dictatorship of the proletariat" with all other social class eliminated. The state would control the means of production, and everyone would be in the same relationship to the state as everyone else. Only when all were employees of the state would true equality exist. Class distinctions and class antagonisms would then be abolished. Social relations would be based upon the rule: "From each according to his ability; to each according to his needs." The state, which functions in bourgeois society to help the bourgeoisie oppress the masses, would gradually wither away in a communist society. As soon as there was no longer any social class to be held in subjection, the special repressive force, the state, would no longer be necessary.

Failure of Marx's analysis

The truth of the matter is, of course, that in the end neither capitalist societies nor communist societies conformed to Marx's analysis. There are several reasons why the capitalist society of America failed to meet Marx's expectations. First, Americans do not define their interests strictly on the basis of their class membership. Allegiances to church, ethnic group, racial category, voluntary organizations, union, occupational groups, and so forth, prevent the emergence of a militant class consciousness. Second, and perhaps more importantly, the workers in America did not become poorer over time but improved their standard of living. It turned out that capitalism provided workers with considerable material comfort. Third, American society provided a great deal of social mobility that enabled many individuals in the working class to move into the middle class. Marx did not foresee this growth of the middle class. Moreover, the social mobility of American society encouraged people in the working class to work within the system to improve their life and the lives of their children, rather than to organize to destroy the system.

With regard to the failure of communist societies to conform to Marx's analysis, even though the bourgeois class was eliminated at great cost in human lives, new social groups emerged that were just as oppressive as the former bourgeoisie, if not more so. Communist party officials, government bureaucrats, and military officers monopolized power, prestige, and wealth. The state did not wither away at all, but instead became all-encompassing and all-powerful.

SOCIAL CLASS AND POLITICAL POWER

Social class and legislative power

Government leadership is recruited mainly from the upper social classes. Most government officials, particularly at the national level (cabinet officers, presidential advisers, congressional representatives, Supreme Court judges, and so on), are members of the well-educated, prestigiously employed, successful, and affluent upper and upper-middle classes. Political scientist Donald Matthews studied the occupations of the fathers of representatives and senators in order to obtain a reasonably accurate indicator of their class origins. With few exceptions, they are the children of professional men, business owners and managers, or successful farmers and landowners.[9] Only a small minority are the children of wage earners or salaried workers.

The occupational characteristics of representatives themselves also show that they are generally of higher social standing than their constituents; professional and business occupations dominate the halls of Congress. One reason is, of course, that congressional candidates are more likely to win the election if their occupations are socially "respectable" and provide opportunities for extensive public contacts. The lawyer, insurance agent, farm implement dealer, and real estate dealer establish in their business the wide circle of friends necessary for political success. Another more subtle reason is that candidates and elected legislators must come from occupational groups with flexible work responsibilities. Lawyers, landowners, and business owners can adjust their work to the campaign and legislative schedules, whereas office managers cannot.

The overrepresentation of lawyers as an occupational group in Congress and other public office is particularly marked, since lawyers constitute no more than two-tenths of 1 percent of the labor force.[10] Lawyers have always played a prominent role in the American political system. Twenty-five of the fifty-two signers of the Declaration of Independence and thirty-one of the fifty-five members of the Continental Congress were lawyers. The legal profession has also provided 70 percent of the presidents, vice-presidents, and cabinet officers of the United States and approximately half of all United States senators and members of the House of Representatives. Lawyers are in a reasonably high-prestige occupation, but so are physicians, businessmen, and scientists. Why then do lawyers, rather than members of these other high-prestige groups, dominate the halls of Congress?

It is sometimes argued that lawyers bring a special kind of skill to Congress. Since their occupation is the representation of clients, they make no great change in occupation when they move from representing clients in private practice to representing constituents in Congress. Also, they are trained to deal with public policy as it is reflected in the statute books, so they may be reasonably familiar with public policy before entering Congress. But professional skills alone cannot explain the dominance of lawyers in public office. Another answer is that of all those in high-prestige occupations, only lawyers can really afford to neglect their careers for political activities. For the physician, the corporate businessman, and the scientist, such slighting of their vocations is very costly. However, for the lawyer, political activity can be a positive advantage in terms of occupational advancement; free public advertising and opportunities to make contacts with potential clients are two important benefits. Yet another answer is that lawyers naturally have a monopoly on public offices in the legal and judicial system, and the office of judge or prosecuting attorney often provides a stepping stone to higher public office, including Congress.

Members of Congress are among the most educated occupational groups in the United States. They are much better educated than most members of the populations they represent. Of course, their education reflects their occupational background and their middle- and upper-class origins.

To sum up, information on the occupational background of legislators indicates that more than high social status is necessary for election to Congress. It is also helpful to have experience in interpersonal relations and public contacts, easy access to politics, and a great deal of free time to devote to political activity.[11]

Social class and executive and judicial power

Power in the *executive branch*, which most analysts now see as more important than Congress in policy formulation, is also exercised by individuals from the upper and upper-middle classes. Cabinet secretaries, undersecretaries, and top civil servants tend to come from eastern Ivy League schools; most are lawyers or business people at the time of their appointment; many accept lower salaries out of a sense of obligation to perform "public service."[12] The same class origins are found among judges in federal courts, particularly the Supreme Court.[13]

We know that political power is largely in the hands of individuals from upper social classes, but what does this really mean for the great majority of Americans? We might *infer* that people drawn from upper social classes share values and interests that are different from those of the majority of people. We might also infer that these elites will use their power to implement the values of the upper social classes and that, consequently, public policy will reflect upper-class values more than mass values. These inferences would be consistent

Elitist view of society

with the *elitist view of society*.

On the other hand, several factors may modify the impact of upper social classes in politics. First, there may be considerable conflict among members of upper social classes about the basic directions of public policy—that is, despite similarity in social backgrounds, individuals may *not* share a consensus about public affairs. Competition rather than consensus may characterize their relationships.

Second, elites may be very "public-regarding" in their exercise of power; they may take the welfare of the masses into account as an aspect of their own sense of well-being. Indeed, there is a great deal of evidence that America's upper classes are liberal and reformist and that "do-goodism" is a widespread impulse. Many public leaders from very wealthy families of the highest social status (e.g., Franklin

D. Roosevelt, Adlai Stevenson, John F. Kennedy) have championed the interests of the poor and the downtrodden. Thus, upper-class values may foster public service rather than political exploitation.

Third, upper-class leaders, whatever their values, can be held accountable for their exercise of power by the majority in elections. Our system of parties and elections forces public officials to compete for mass support to acquire public office and the political power that goes with it. This competition requires them to modify their public statements and actions to fit popular preferences. Hence, in a democracy the fact that the upper social classes tend to hold public office does not necessarily mean that the masses are oppressed or exploited or powerless. This interpretation of the relationship between social class and political power reflects the *pluralist view of society* (see chapter 7).

Pluralist view of society

CASE STUDY
The Power Elite

The most popular and controversial analysis of power in America is *The Power Elite*, by sociologist C. Wright Mills.[14] Since its appearance in 1956, most writers have been unable to discuss national power without reference to this important study.

According to Mills, power in America is concentrated at the top of America's corporate, governmental, and military organizations, which closely interlock to form a single structure of power—a *power elite*. Power rests in these three domains: "the corporation chieftains, the political directorate, and the warlords." Occasionally there is tension among them, but they share a broad consensus about the general direction of public policy and the main course of society. Other institutions (the family, churches, schools, and so forth) are subordinate to the three major institutions of power:

Families and churches and schools adapt to modern life;

governments and armies and corporations shape it; and, as they do, they turn these lesser institutions into means for their ends.

The *emergence of the power elite is a product of technology, bureaucratization, and centralization.* The economy—once a scatter of many small competing units—is now dominated by a few hundred giant corporate and financial institutions. The political system—once a decentralized structure of states and communities with a small central government—has become a giant centralized bureaucracy in Washington that has assumed power over nearly every aspect of American life. The military—once a slim establishment depending largely on citizen-soldiers to meet specific crises—has become the largest and most expensive function of government and a sprawling bureaucratic domain.

> The history of modern society may readily be understood as the story of the enlargement and the centralization of the means of power—in economic, in political, and in military institutions.[15]

As each of these sectors of society enlarged and centralized, they increasingly came together to coordinate decision making.

> At the pinnacle of each of the three enlarged and centralized domains, there have arisen those higher circles which make up the economic, the political, and the military elites. At the top of the economy, among the corporate rich, there are the chief executives; at the top of the political order, the members of the political directorate; at the top of the military establishment, the elite of soldier-statesmen clustered in and around the Joint Chiefs of Staff and the upper echelon. As each of these domains has coincided with the others, as decisions tend to become total in their consequences, the leading men in each of the three domains of power—the warlords, the corporation chieftains, the political directorate—tend to come together, to form the power elite of America.[16]

The power elite holds power because of its position at the top of the institutional structures of society. These people are powerful *not* because of any individual qualities—wealth, prestige, skill, or cunning—but because of the *institutional positions* they occupy. As society has concentrated more and more power in a few giant institutions, the people in command of these institutions have acquired enormous power over all of us.

> If we took the one hundred most powerful men in America, the one hundred wealthiest, and the one hundred most celebrated away from the institutional positions they now occupy, away from their resources of men and women and money, away from the media of mass communication that are now focused upon them—then they would be powerless and poor and uncelebrated. For power is not of a man. Wealth does not center in the person of the wealthy. Celebrity is not inherent in any personality. To be celebrated, to be wealthy, to have power requires access to major institutions, for the institutional positions men occupy determine in large part their chances to have and to hold these valued experiences.[17]

Mills is aware that his description of power in America conflicts with the "pluralist" interpretation. But he believes that notions of power holders who balance and compromise interests or who engage in competition between parties and groups apply to middle-level power holders in America and not to the top power elite. Political journalists and scholars write about middle levels because this is all they know about or understand; these levels provide the noisy content of most "political" news and gossip. The major directions of national and international policy are determined by persons beyond the "clang and clash of American politics." Political campaigns actually distract attention from the really important national and international decisions.

The *unity* of the top elite rests on several factors. First of all, these people are recruited from the same upper social classes; they have similar education, wealth, and upbringing. Moreover, they continue to associate with each other, which reinforces their common feelings. They belong to the same clubs, attend the same parties, meet at the same resorts, and serve on the same civic, cultural, and philanthropic committees. Members of the elite incorporate into their own viewpoints the viewpoints, expectations, and values of those "who count." Factions exist and individual ambitions clash, but their community of interest is far greater than any divisions that exist. Perhaps what accounts for their consensus more than anything else is their experience in command positions in giant institutions. "As the requirements of the top places in each of the major hierarchies become similar, the types of men occupying these roles at the top—by selection and by training in the jobs—become similar."

"Tom Willoughby, meet Howard Sylvester—one of us."
Drawing by Bernard Schoenbaum; © 1977 The New Yorker Magazine, Inc.

Mills finds American democracy severely deficient, and his work is frequently cited by radical critics of American society. According to Mills, the power elite is guilty of "a higher immorality," which is not necessarily personal corruption or even mistaken policies and deeds, but rather the moral insensitivity of institutional bureaucracy. More importantly, it is the failure of the power elite to be responsive and responsible to "Knowledgeable publics." Mills implies that true democracy is possible only where persons in power are truly responsible to "men of Knowledge." He is not very specific about who the "men of Knowledge" are, but the reader is left with the impression that he means intellectuals like himself.

NOTES

1. Eric I. Goldman, *Rendezvous with Destiny* (New York: Vintage Books, 1956), pp. 7–8.

2. Alex Inkeles and Peter Rossi, "National Comparisons of Occupational Prestige," *American Journal of Sociology* 61 (January 1956):320–39; R. Murray Thomas, "Reinspecting a Structural Position on Occupational Prestige," *American Journal of Sociology* 67 (March 1962):561–65.

3. Gerhard Lenski, *Power and Privilege* (New York: McGraw-Hill, 1966); Jack Roach, Llewellyn Gross, and Orville R. Gursslin, *Social Stratification in the United States* (Englewood Cliffs, N.J.: Prentice-Hall, 1969).

4. Richard Centers, *The Psychology of Social Classes* (Princeton, N.J.: Princeton University Press, 1949).

5. Robert W. Hodge and Donald J. Treiman, "Class Identification in the United States," *American Journal of Sociology* 73 (March 1968):535–47.

6. Centers, *Psychology of Social Classes*, p. 218.

7. Herbert Gans, *The Urban Villagers* (New York: Free Press, 1962), p. 246. See also Edward C. Banfield, *The Unheavenly City* (Boston: Little, Brown, 1968), ch. 3.

8. Karl Marx, *Capital* (New York: Modern Library, 1936), p. 709.

9. Donald Matthews, *Social Background of Political Decision-Makers* (Garden City, N.Y.: Doubleday, 1954).

10. Heinz Eulau and John D. Sprague, *Lawyers in Politics* (Indianapolis, Ind.: Bobbs-Merrill, 1964).

11. See Joseph A. Schlesinger, *Ambition and Politics* (Chicago: Rand McNally, 1968).

12. David T. Stanley, Dean E. Mann, and Jameson W. Doig, *Men Who Govern* (Washington, D.C.: Brookings, 1966).

13. John Schmidhouser, "The Justices of the Supreme Court: A Collective Portrait," *Midwest Journal of Political Science* 3 (1959):1–10.

14. C. Wright Mills, *The Power Elite* (New York: Oxford University Press, 1956).

15. C. Wright Mills, "The Structure of Power in American Society," in Irving L. Horowitz, ed., *Power, Politics and People: The Collected Writings of C. Wright Mills* (New York: Oxford University Press, 1963), p. 24.

16. Mills, *The Power Elite*, pp. 8–9.

17. Ibid., p. 10.

DISCUSSION QUESTIONS

1. Discuss the social stratification system. Include in your discussion a description of the bases used for stratification, as well as the characteristics associated with the stratification system.

2. If you were studying social class, what methods might you use to identify and measure social stratification? If in the course of your study you were to ask average Americans how they see themselves in the class system, what class would they choose, and why? How might the respondents' subjective evaluations differ from the results you as a social scientist obtain? What are the objective criteria you would use to identify social class?

3. Discuss the functions of the ideology of a stratification system. Describe the American ideology and the attitudes of Americans toward this ideology.

4. Choose two of the American social classes and contrast them according to orientation toward life; individual self-confidence; child-rearing practices; sexual attitudes; women's roles; activities and interests; and political participation and party identification.

5. Contrast class consciousness with class awareness. Discuss the factors that appear to stabilize the existing class system in America and to reduce class conflict.

6. Discuss Karl Marx's views of economic roles and class consciousness in the struggle for power among social classes. What sort of society did Marx envision and what are the reasons for the failure of capitalist and communist societies to conform to his vision?

7. Political power in America is largely in the hands of individuals from upper social classes. Discuss the factors that account for this, what impact it might have on the "masses," and what factors may modify the impact. In your discussion distinguish between the "elitist" view of society and the "pluralist" view of society.

8. Define the *power elite* that was identified by C. Wright Mills and describe the factors that contribute to the emergence of such an elite. What is its actual base of power and on what factors does its unity rest? How does Mills's interpretation of power in America conflict with the "pluralist" interpretation?

SUGGESTED READINGS

Edward C. Banfield, *The Unheavenly City* (Boston: Little, Brown, 1968).

W. J. Goode, Reinhard Bendix, and Seymour Martin Lipset, *Class Status and Power: Social Stratification in Comparative Perspective,* 2nd ed. (New York: Free Press, 1966).

Suzanne Keller, *Beyond the Ruling Class* (New York: Random House, 1963).

Gerhard Lenski, *Power and Privilege* (New York: McGraw-Hill, 1966).

Donald Matthews, *Social Background of Political Decision-Makers* (Garden City, N.Y.: Doubleday, 1954).

C. Wright Mills, *The Power Elite* (New York: Oxford University Press, 1956).

Jack Roach, Llewellyn Gross, and Orville R. Gursslin, *Social Stratification in the United States* (Englewood Cliffs, N.J.: Prentice-Hall, 1969).

Photo by Marshall Henrichs

Photo by Marshall Henrichs

Chapter 5

Power and the Economic Order

"What do I care about the law? Hain't I got the power?" The power to which Cornelius Vanderbilt, buccaneering railroad tycoon of the 1800s, was referring was undoubtedly economic. Indeed, in those days of little or no government interference, men who controlled such vast financial empires could well consider themselves as laws unto themselves. Even today with extensive government regulation of the economy, persons who control the economic resources and make the economic decisions still wield an impressive amount of power. And that power and those decisions have very real and direct implications for our lives.

In this chapter we will examine the content of economic decisions and take a look at how individuals, government, and corporations make them. After you have read it, you should be able to:

- describe the operation of the market in a private enterprise economy.
- define the various cycles that an economy experiences.
- discuss the reasons why government intervenes in the economy, thus creating a "mixed" economic system, and some of the means by which government does this.
- describe how America's wealth is measured and discuss some of the shortcomings of this system of measurement.
- discuss personal wealth in America and the increasing concentration of corporate power.

POWER AND ECONOMIC ORGANIZATION

A great deal of power in America is centered in large economic organizations—corporations, banks, utilities, investment firms, and government agencies charged with the responsibility of overseeing the economy. Not all power, it is true, is anchored in or exercised through these institutions; power is also embodied in class, cultural, political, and ideological institutions and processes, as discussed elsewhere in this volume. But *control of economic resources provides a continuous and important base of power in any society.* Economic organizations decide the basic economic question of *who gets what.* Deciding "who gets what" entails deciding what will be produced, how it will be produced, how much will be produced and how much it will cost, how many people will be employed, who will be employed and what their wages will be, how the goods and services that are produced will be distributed, what technology will be developed, what profits will be made and how they will be distributed, how much money will be available for loans and what interest rates will be charged, how fast the earnings will grow, and so forth.

The decisions of steel companies to raise prices, of defense industries to develop new weapons, of banks to raise or lower interest rates on home mortgages, of electrical companies to market new home products, of the president to freeze wages and prices, of the Federal Reserve Board to tighten credit and to reduce the supply of money—all affect our lives directly. The economic decisions, made by both governments and private corporations, require choices by individuals, corporations, and governments. Control over these choices is obviously a major source of power in society.

THE MARKET SYSTEM, HARD-BOILED AND IMPERSONAL

Economic system

The *economic system* consists of the *institutions and processes by which a society produces and distributes scarce resources.* There is not enough of everything for all of us to have all that we want; if nature provided everything that everyone wanted without work, there would be no need for an economic system. But resources are "scarce," and some scheme must be created to decide who gets what. Scarcity and the problem of choice that it raises are a fundamental problem of economics.

The American economic system is a capitalist, free enterprise system. It is largely "unplanned"; no government bureau tells all 80 million workers in the United States where to work, what to do, or

Private enterprise economy

how to do it. The *private enterprise economy* largely organizes itself, with a minimum of central planning or direction. It would be difficult to consciously plan such a vast and complex cooperative arrangement. The American system relies chiefly on private individuals in search of wages and profits to get the job done. No government agency directs that shirts be produced: If people want shirts, then there is profit to be made in producing them, and business people who recognize this potential profit will begin turning them out. No government agency directs how many shirts shall be produced: as shirt output increases, a point is reached at which there are so many shirts that the price that people are willing to pay falls below the cost of producing them, and business people then begin curtailing their production of shirts. This same production-in-search-of-profits goes on for thousands of other products simultaneously. No government agency directs where workers shall work: Millions of workers go where they wish and search for the best jobs available. A private enterprise economy decides what is to be produced, how it is to be produced, and how it is to be distributed, all in a fashion that is for the most part automatic and impersonal. Everyone, by following self-interest, decides who gets what. The absence of planning and control does not mean chaos. Rather, it means a complex system of production and distribution that no single mind, and probably no government planning agency, could organize or control in all its infinite detail.

The market and its components   A *market* is any place or arrangement that enables people to exchange money for goods, services, or labor. The exchange rate is called the *price*. Under the private enterprise system, the *market determines what is to be produced, how much it will cost, and who will be able to buy it.* Consumers decide what shall be produced by expressing their preferences in terms of the amount of money they spend on various goods and services (*consumer demand*). When consumers are *willing and able to pay* for something, they will bid up the price of that item. The price is an indication of how much of the item consumers want produced. Businesses are out to make *profits*. They gain profits when selling prices are higher than the costs of production. Business people move into industries in which consumers bid prices up and the business people can bring costs down. Where consumer demand bids prices up, business people can afford to pay higher wages; and workers tend to move toward those industries with higher pay and better working conditions. Thus consumer demand shifts both business and labor into industries in which prices are high. Business people play a key role in a private enterprise system because they channel production toward industries having the strongest consumer demand and organize productive activity in the most efficient (lowest cost) way possible. Profits are the mainspring of the market system. In seeking profits, business people perform a vital economic function. And prices play a key role in determining what profits will be, and prices are determined by consumer demand.

Who gets the goods that are produced? The price system allocates them to those who have both the *willingness to pay* and the *ability to pay.* The willingness to pay determines the desirability of producing a certain item. No government agency determines whether we "need" goods and services, the market reveals whether individuals are willing to pay for them. Consumers, however, must also have the ability to pay: They must earn incomes by working to produce goods and services that consumers want. The income received for their labor depends largely on their worth to the businesses that employ them. They are worth more when they contribute more to production and profit. Where production and profits are low, wages will be low and individuals will be frequently unemployed. The *labor market* largely determines where people will work and how much they will be paid.

The market is hard-boiled and impersonal. If a business produces too much of a particular item—more than consumers are willing to buy at a particular price—the price will have to be lowered or production (product supply) will have to be cut back. Competition among businesses also checks prices, for a business that sets a price higher than that set by competitors will lose sales. Thus *consumer demand, product supply, and competition determine prices.* In the absence of interfering factors, the price depends upon a relationship of supply and demand at any given time. If demand increases, prices tend to rise; if demand decreases, prices tend to fall. If supply increases, prices tend to fall; if supply decreases, prices tend to rise.

The market reconciles the interests of buyers and sellers, labor and business, in the process of getting people to agree on prices. The market in a free enterprise system undertakes this reconciliation automatically, without assistance from outside individuals or forces. The ideal conditions for a market operation are:

Ideal conditions for a market operation

1. The existence of a perfect competition exists, in which the market has so many buyers and sellers that no single trader has any control over the price of the good or service being exchanged, and the price is made by the market through the impersonal forces of supply and demand. (If one or a few sellers have control over supply, the market is said to be *monopolistic;* if one or a few buyers have control over demand, the market is said to be *monopsonistic.)*

2. The ability of a buyer of the good to exclude others from the satisfactions that it provides so that no one can enjoy the benefits of someone else's purchase. (When people benefit from the purchases of others, there are said to be *spillover effects,* as, for example, in the case of national defense, which cannot be sold on the open market.)

3. The complete mobility of resources and labor so that they can move in response to changes in prices. (In a completely mobile economy, each individual [or business] is prepared to alter the pattern of spending and working in response to changes in prices of goods and labor.)

In other words, in an ideal market there is a great deal of competition and prices are determined solely by supply and demand. All must pay for the goods and benefits they receive, and resources and labor shift easily in response to changes in prices and wages.

SUPPLY, DEMAND, AND THE MARKET PRICE

Let us try to illustrate what happens in a true market economy, where price is governed by supply and demand.

Along with many other commodities, millions of bushels of wheat are bought and sold every day at the Chicago Board of Trade. Let us suppose that the first buyer of the day offers $2 per bushel for wheat. Let us also suppose that there are buyers for 20 million bushels of wheat at this low price (see table 5–1). However, few owners are willing to sell at this price and therefore there are only 10 million bushels of wheat offered at $2 per bushel. The result is an imbalance in supply and demand—a 10 million bushel shortfall in supply at the low $2 price. Those still wishing to buy must therefore raise their price to attract more wheat to the market. Let us suppose that the price then shot up to $4 per bushel. At this price, there are fewer buyers (let us say only an 8 million bushel demand) and many more sellers (let us say an 18 million bushel supply). The result is an excess supply of 10 million bushels at the high price.

Thus, the price tends to stabilize at a point low enough to attract sufficient demand for wheat, but high enough to attract an equivalent supply of wheat. In our example (table 5–1), this price is $3 per bushel, where 14 million bushels are demanded and 14 million bushels are offered.

Table 5–1 An Example of Supply and Demand

Bushels of Wheat Offered for Sale (Millions)	Price	Bushels of Wheat Demanded (Millions)
18	$4.00	8
16	3.50	11
14	3.00	14
12	2.50	17
10	2.00	20

Figure 5–1 shows our example of supply and demand in graphic form. The supply curve is low at a low price, but increases as the price increases. Demand is high at a low price, but it declines as the price increases. The two curves for supply and demand intersect at a price where the amount demanded just matches the amount supplied. This will tend to be the market price. In our example, it is set at $3 per bushel. Any other price will produce either an excess supply (at a higher price) or an excess demand (at a lower price).

GOVERNMENT AND THE ECONOMY

The free enterprise system that we have just described is subject to major modifications by the activities of government. In fact, government is now so involved in the economy that we might call the American economic system a *mixed* economy rather than a *private enterprise* economy. Government intervenes in the free market for many reasons:

Reasons for government intervention

1. To assure competition among businesses by breaking up monopolies and prohibiting unfair competitive practices.
2. To set minimum standards for wages and working conditions.
3. To regulate industries (like communications, broadcasting, and transportation) in which there is a strong public interest and in which unbridled competition may hurt more than it helps.
4. To protect the consumer from phony goods and services and false or misleading advertising.

Figure 5–1   An Example of Supply and Demand in Graphic Form

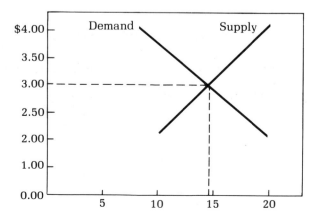

5. To provide a wide range of public services (defense, education, highways, police protection) that cannot be reasonably provided on a private-profit basis.

6. To provide support and care (welfare, social security, unemployment compensation, medicare, health care, etc.) to individuals who cannot supply these things for themselves through the market system.

7. To ensure that the economic system functions properly and avoids depression, inflation, or unemployment.

ADAM SMITH
Laissez-faire Economics

In the same year the Declaration of Independence was signed, Adam Smith, a Scottish professor of philosophy, published his *Wealth of Nations* and thereby secured recognition as the founder of free enterprise economics. Today the economic model set forth by Adam Smith is frequently referred to as *classical economics* or *laissez-faire economics* (from the French phrase meaning "allow to do as one pleases"). Smith wrote *The Wealth of Nations* as an attack on the *mercantilism* of nations in his day—that is, the attempt of governments to intervene in the economy with special tariffs, regulations, subsidies, and exclusive charters to businesses, all designed to maximize the acquisition of gold and silver in government treasuries. Smith argued against mercantilism and in favor of *free competition* in the marketplace. He believed that a worldwide market, *unfettered by government restrictions or subsidies*, would result in lower prices and high standards of living for all. A free market would allow the businesses and nations most capable of producing particular goods cheaply and efficiently to do so. There would be greater specialization as each business and nation concentrated on what it did best. The outcome of the specialization and efficiency created by free competition would be a high standard of living for everyone. Thus, pursuit of private profit was actually in the public interest.

Every individual endeavors to employ his capital so that its produce may be of greater value. He generally neither intends to promote the public interest, nor knows how much he is promoting it. He intends only his . . . own gain. He is in this led by an invisible hand to promote an end which was no part of his intention. By pursuing his own interest he

frequently promotes that of society more effectively than if he really intended to promote it.[1]

Laissez-faire economics is based on the idea that people are
rational, that they will pursue their own economic self-interest, that
they are mobile and able to shift their resources and labor as the
market demands. According to this economic system, there should be
no artificial blocks to the most efficient use of people and materials.
The market has a large number of competitors buying and selling
products, services, and labor; and no one alone has control over supply or demand or price. Buyers buy from producers who make the
best goods at the lowest price. Thus efficiency is rewarded and inefficiency driven out of the economy. Guided by demand and high
prices, producers constantly shift to new lines of production. As competition increases supply and lowers prices, some producers again
shift to more lucrative lines. The market continually corrects unpro-
ductive use of resources. The system is *self-adjusting* and *self-
regulating.*

Smith objected to government interference in the natural operations of the marketplace. Government should do only two things: (1)
create an environment for an orderly marketplace—that is, maintain
law and order, protect private property, enforce contracts, and provide a monetary system; and (2) supply those services that the

*Laissez-faire economics and
traditional democracy*

marketplace cannot provide, such as defense, public works, and care of widows, orphans, and other helpless people.

Laissez-faire economics has much in common with *traditional democracy*. It is important to realize that at the same time that Adam Smith was setting forth a model economic system that stressed individual rationality, freedom of choice, and limited government intervention, democrats in America were developing a model political system emphasizing individual responsibility, freedom of expression, rational voter choice, and limitations on governmental power over individual liberty. The free enterprise economic system *paralleled* the democratic political system. In politics, every man was to be free to speak out, to form a political party, and to vote as he pleased—to pursue his political interests as he thought best. In economic life, every man was to be free to find work, start a business, and spend money as he pleased—to pursue his economic self-interest as he thought best. The ballot box in politics and the market in economics were the impartial arbiters of conflict in society. Government was to be restricted in both its power over individual liberty and its power over economic life.

Today many "classical" economists echo Adam Smith's ideas. Although it is now widely recognized that government must play an important role in stabilizing the economy (avoiding both inflation and depression), protecting consumers, regulating business and labor practices, and assisting individuals who cannot care for themselves, classical economists nonetheless argue that economic planning by government is incompatible with *personal freedom*. They contend that bureaucratic intervention in the economy not only is inefficient and wasteful, but also gradually erodes individual freedom and initiative.

This fear is not unfounded; political scientist Roland Pennock warns of the political consequences of the government-controlled economy:

> The existing freedom to choose one's vocation, one's employer, and the way one would manage his savings or spend his income would give way in greater and lesser degree to regimentation in all these areas by governmental fiat. It might provide greater security or more equality, but it could hardly fail to reduce liberty.[2]

And conservative economist Friedrich Hayek writes:

> We have progressively abandoned the freedom in economic affairs without which personal and political freedom have never existed in the past. . . .
> What our planners demand is central direction of all economic ac-

tivity according to a single plan, saying how the resources of the society should be "consciously directed" to serve particular ends in a definite way.[3]

Thus, the appeal of laissez-faire economics is based not only upon the efficiency of the marketplace in channeling labor and resources into their most productive uses, but also upon the personal freedom in economic affairs that this system guarantees.

JOHN M. KEYNES
The Mixed Economy

The Great Depression of the 1930s significantly altered American thinking about laissez-faire economics. It is difficult to realize today what a tremendous economic disaster befell the nation in those days. Following the stock market crash of October 1929 and in spite of President Herbert Hoover's assurances that prosperity lay "just around the corner," the American economy virtually collapsed. Businesses failed, factories shut down, new construction practically ceased, banks closed, and millions of savings were wiped out. One out of four American workers was unemployed, and one out of six was receiving welfare relief. Persons who had never before known unemployment lost their jobs, used up their savings or lost them when the banks folded, cashed in their life insurance, gave up their homes or farms because they could not continue the mortgage payments. Economic catastrophe struck far into the ranks of the middle classes. Some business executives sold apples and pencils on the street to eke out a living. Homeless men and women stood in breadlines, slept on park benches, or took to the roads searching for work. Tramps abounded and panhandlers plied the streets. Mines were no longer worked; steel mills, foundries, and every variety of industrial plant put out only a fraction of the goods that they could produce; trains ran with no more than a handful of passengers; stores lacked customers, and many closed their doors; hospitals were empty, not because they were unneeded but because people could not afford them. Crops rotted in fields while people suffered hunger and malnutrition. Farmers lost their farms and either stayed on as

sharecroppers or wandered the roads as migrant laborers. Fear was widespread that violent revolution would soon sweep the country. Many lost faith in the free enterprise system and urged the abandonment of the market economy. The "solutions" of fascism in Italy and Germany and communism in the Soviet Union were looked to as alternatives to a "doomed" capitalist system.

Recession

Laissez-faire economics recognized the possibilities of economic cycles. A *recession* occurs when consumer demand declines for any reason, and businesses cut back on production. Cutbacks involve laying off workers and postponing plans for capital investment in new plants or facilities. The resulting increase in unemployment means fewer dollars in the hands of consumers and thus a *further* cutback in consumer demands, leading to *further* cutbacks in production.

Classical economics and
recession

But classical economics believed that the system would eventually adjust itself, reverse this downward cycle, and resume a forward movement. The turnabout would happen largely because of the effect of *interest rates:* While businesses were postponing capital investment, savings would pile up, and the price of money (the interest rate) would decline. The interest rate would fall so low that businesses would be encouraged to borrow money again, to invest in new plants and facilities, and thereby to stimulate employment. As employment rose, consumer demand would increase, and the economy would revive. In short, classical economics relied upon *low interest rates* as incentives to businesses to reinvest in the economy. At the same time, the *lower prices* in a recession would presumably result in an increase in consumer demand. President Hoover, a believer in laissez-faire economics, waited three years for the economy to adjust itself according to the classical model. But the economy continued its downward spiral, and Hoover was overwhelmingly defeated in the 1932 presidential election by Franklin D. Roosevelt.

In 1936 John M. Keynes, a British economist, wrote a landmark book called *The General Theory of Employment, Interest and Money.* Keynes attacked the basic notion of classical economics that the free enterprise system was a self-adapting mechanism that tended to produce full employment and maximum use of resources. He believed that not all savings went into investment. When there was little prospect of profit, savings were likely to be hoarded and un- used. This removal of money from the economy brought depression. Moreover, he argued, low interest rates would not necessarily stir businesses to reinvest; it was the expectation of *profit*, not the availability of money, that motivated investment. Keynes believed that as confidence in the future is diminished, investment will decline, regardless of interest rates.

The Keynesian answer: government countercyclical action

In Keynes's view, only *government* can reverse a downward economic cycle. Private businesses cannot be expected to invest when consumer demand is low and there is no prospect of profit. And consumers cannot be expected to increase their purchases when their incomes are falling. So the responsibility rests on the government to take *countercyclical* action to increase income and consumption.

Fiscal and monetary policy during recession

Governments can act, first of all, by means of *fiscal policy*—that is, by making decisions regarding government expenditures, taxes, and debt. In recessions, government can *increase its own expen- ditures or lower taxes or do both* in order to raise total demand and private income. Government purchases add directly to total demand and stimulate production and employment. Government payments to individuals in the form of social security, unemployment compensa- tion, or welfare make more money available to individuals for con- sumption. Reducing taxes also makes more money available to indi- viduals for purchasing. Of course, increasing expenditures or lower- ing taxes or both means an *increase in government debt*, but only in this fashion can government pump money into the economy.

At the same time, government can act in a countercyclical way by means of *monetary policy*—that is, by making decisions regarding the availability of money and credit and rates of interest. To encourage investment, government can expand the money supply by *lowering interest rates and increasing the amount of money available for circulation.* However, monetary policy may not have a really direct or immediate impact on the economy if businesses do not take advantage of the availability of cheaper money. Thus, *Keynes relied more heavily on fiscal policy than monetary policy to bring about economic recovery during recessions.*

Keynes also argued that governments should pursue counter-cyclical fiscal and monetary policies to offset inflation, as well as

Inflation

depression. *Inflation* means a general rise in the price level of goods and services. Inflation occurs when total demand exceeds or nears the productive capacity of the economy. An excess of demand over supply forces prices up.

Fiscal and monetary policy during inflation

Keynes believed that when inflation threatens, government should gear its *fiscal policy* toward *reducing its own expenditures or increasing taxes or both.* Reducing government purchases would reduce total demand and bring it back into equilibrium with supply. Raising taxes would reduce the money available for consumption and therefore also help bring demand back into equilibrium with supply. These fiscal policies (to be pursued during inflationary times) would enable the government to reduce its debt (which is incurred during depressions).

At the same time, governments would pursue *monetary policies* to fight inflation. Government could *reduce the total amount of money in circulation and increase interest rates.* These policies are fairly certain to reduce total demand. In fact, *monetary policy is more effective in fighting inflation than it is in fighting recession.*

Keynes was no revolutionary. On the contrary, he wished to preserve the private enterprise system by developing effective governmental measures to overcome disastrous economic cycles. In December 1933 he wrote an open letter to Roosevelt emphasizing the importance of saving the capitalist system:

> You have made yourself the trustee for those in every country who seek to mend the evils of our condition by reasoned experiment within the framework of the existing social system. If you fail, rational change will be gravely prejudiced throughout the world, leaving orthodoxy and revolution to fight it out.[4]

THE GOVERNMENT AND ECONOMIC STABILIZATION: CUSHIONING THE UPS AND DOWNS

Today the government of the United States is fully committed to preserving economic prosperity and using fiscal and monetary policies to try to offset the effects of inflation and recession. This much of Keynesian economics is contained in the Employment Act of 1946, which specifically pledges the federal government to assume responsibility for the economy:

> The Congress hereby declares that it is the continuing policy and responsibility of the Federal Government to use all practicable means . . . to coordinate and utilize all its plans, functions, and resources for the purposes of creating and maintaining, in a manner calculated to foster and promote free competitive enterprise and the general welfare, conditions under which there will be afforded useful employment, for those able, willing, and seeking to work, and to promote maximum employment, production, and purchasing power.

To implement this commitment, the act created the Council of Economic Advisers (CEA) to "develop and recommend to the President national economic policies." The CEA is composed of three economists, appointed by the president, and a staff of analysts to collect data on the economy and advise the president on what to do to offset cycles of inflation or recession. The act also requires the president to submit to Congress an annual economic report assessing the state of the economy and recommending economic legislation.

Fiscal Policy During recessions, when consumer demand must be increased, Congress can increase government spending, thereby adding to the total demand, or it can cut taxes and thereby put more money into the pockets of consumers. Conversely, during inflations, when strong consumer demands are pushing prices up, Congress may cut its own spending thereby reducing total demand, or it may raise taxes in order to restrict the spending power of consumers. During recessions, Congress must increase its spending even if it does not have sufficient funds to pay the costs. Governments must run a deficit (debt) in order to pour money into the economy in periods of recession. During inflation, the government must cut its spending or raise taxes and create a surplus in its budget—that is, it must take money out of the economy and reduce its debt in order to lower consumer demand and stabilize prices.

Automatic Stabilizers "Automatic stabilizers" are government programs that automatically act to counter the effects of economic cycles. For example, since income taxes increase in proportion to one's earnings, the income tax automatically restricts spending habits in times of prosperity by taking large bites of income. In times of adversity and low earnings, taxes drop automatically. Welfare programs also act automatically to counter economic cycles: In recessions, more people apply for welfare and unemployment payments, and these payments help to offset declines in income.

Monetary Policy   Since banks are the major source of money and credit for investors, business people, and manufacturers, government can control investment spending by making it easy or difficult to borrow money from banks. The *Federal Reserve Board* (the "Fed") was created in 1913 to regulate the nation's supply of money through its *power to control the amount of money that commercial banks can lend.* The Fed is headed by a seven-person board of governors, appointed by the president, for overlapping terms of fourteen years. In periods of *recession,* the Fed can *loosen controls* on lending and encourage banks to loan more money to business people at lower interest rates. During *inflation* the Fed can pursue *tight money policies*—policies that make it more difficult for banks to lend money and that thus reduce inflationary pressures.

Government Use of Countercyclical Tools   In practice there have been many difficulties in government use of fiscal and monetary policy. (1) *Economic prediction is not an exact science;* honest economists will admit to a lot of uncertainty about just what policy should be adopted and when. Actions taken by the government may not have an impact on the economy until six or nine months later, when conditions have changed from those that existed at the time the policy was adopted. There is a "lag" between government action and its effect. (2) Presidents and congressmen are afraid of being blamed for a depression. Inflation frequently goes unchecked because *public officials fear that "tight money" or reduced spending or higher taxes might set off a recession.* Besides, these counterinflationary actions are politically unpopular. Hence, deficit spending continues even when the nation is not confronting a recession. (3) Monetary policy often results in *overreaction to short-run economic disturbances* and contributes to long-run instability. Very tight money can check an inflation, but it may later cause a recession. Likewise, easy credit may check a temporary downswing but contribute to long-run inflation. Economist Milton Friedman has suggested that the money supply be stabilized through thick and thin. This would allow minor economic fluctuations but avoid big swings. (4) *Inflation and recession can occur at the same time* if prices are pushed up by union demands for higher wages and the expectations of business that inflation is a permanent way of life. Thus, even with high unemployment, prices can continue to climb. In such a situation, the government is forced into the difficult choice of fighting inflation at the cost of continued high unemployment or reducing unemployment at the cost of runaway inflation. (5) Fiscal and monetary policy must be *effectively coordinated* for optimal results. Unless they are, one may offset the other. But the president and Congress largely determine fiscal policy, while the independent Federal Reserve Board determines monetary policy. Occasionally, the Fed has disagreed with politicians about what policy should be applied at what time. The Fed is frequently more concerned with inflation than are the president and Congress (who are usually more concerned with unemployment).

Recent inflation in America is not merely a product of our own government's deficit fiscal policies and expansionist monetary policies. Growing worldwide demand for food and increases in the worldwide price of oil imposed by a new cartel of oil-producing nations (the Organization of Petroleum Exporting Countries—OPEC) have contributed to *worldwide inflation.* Today the United States faces the continuing threat of "double-digit" inflation—inflation rates exceeding 10 percent a year. It is small comfort to know that inflation in many other nations is even higher than in the United States. An annual decline in the value of the dollar (eight to twelve cents) is a serious threat to the stability of the economy. Government *wage and price controls* proved ineffective in halting inflation in the early 1970s, and they were gradually phased out. These controls were supposed to hold the line against inflation while the government continued its fiscal and monetary policies—deficit spending and easy credit—designed to maintain full employment. Some economists think the failure of wage and price controls was due to poor enforcement, while other economists do not believe such controls can ever halt serious inflation.

It is difficult for any democratically elected government to curb inflation by deliberate "belt-tightening"—that is, by cutting down government spending, increasing taxes, and holding down the supply of money and credit. Although these policies are *economically* sound in an inflationary period, they are *politically* unpopular. Members of Congress (and elected officials in other democratic nations) are reluctant to cut favorite spending programs, or confront their constituents with a tax increase, or allow unemployment to rise as a result of cutbacks in the supply of money and credit for business expansion and home buying. In short, good economics is not always good politics.

GOVERNMENT REGULATION OF BUSINESS

American public policy also attempts to maintain competition in the economy. The decline of business competition and the rise of monopolies accompanied America's industrial revolution in the late nineteenth century. As business became increasingly national in scope, only the strongest or the most unscrupulous of the competitors survived. Great producers tended to become the cheapest producers, and little companies tended to disappear. Industrial production rose rapidly while the number of industrial concerns steadily diminished. The result was the emergence of monopolies and near monopolies in each of the major industries of America.

Antitrust legislation

To maintain competition in the economy, Congress has relied on the enactment of legislation designed to control monopolies and restraint of trade. Both the Sherman Anti-Trust Act of 1890 and the Clayton Anti-Trust Act of 1914 are examples of this type of legislation. Although the Clayton Act is more specific than the Sherman Act in its prohibitions, the enforcement of both acts depends upon the action of the Justice Department and the interpretation of the courts. Each case must be handled separately and it is not always clear to businesses or the public what is permitted under these laws.

Direct government regulation

As another way of regulating business policies and practices, Congress has, over the years, established a number of *administrative commissions* with rule-making, administrative, and judicial powers. The first such national regulatory commission was the Interstate Commerce Commission, set up in 1887 for the purpose of regulating railroad practices, including rate setting. This regulatory approach implies that competition alone is not sufficient to guarantee protection of the public interest, that *direct government regulation* is better insurance against abuse of the public by business than reliance upon the indirect effects of competition. However, complaints from regulated industries and consumers alike—of bureaucratic red tape and commissions that represent the interests of the industries they are supposed to regulate—indicate that the commission system, with its reliance on detailed case-by-case regulation, may be ill adapted to modern problems.

Labor laws

Business is also governed by labor laws. The keystone of American labor policy is the *National Labor Relations Act of 1935*, sometimes called the Wagner Act. In this act, government guarantees labor's right *to organize* into unions and its right *to bargain collectively* through union representatives. The act forbids employers to interfere with these rights. Employers' dissatisfaction with the increased strength of organized labor under the Wagner Act led to a dramatic shift in public policy in the *Labor-Management Relations Act of 1947* (the Taft-Hartley Act). While the Taft-Hartley Act reserves for labor all the basic guarantees of the Wagner Act, it places severe restrictions on the activities of unions. Technically, the Taft-Hartley Act is a series of amendments to the Wagner Act. The Taft-Hartley Act has to do with unfair labor practices of *unions* whereas the earlier Wagner Act is concerned with unfair labor practices of *management*.

MEASURING AMERICA'S WEALTH: NATIONAL INCOME ACCOUNTING

Underlying the power of nations is the strength of their economy—their total productive capacity. The United States can produce nearly $2 trillion worth of goods and services in a single year for its 215 million people. This is over $10,000 worth of output per person. To understand America's vast wealth, we must learn how to measure it. We need to know where the wealth comes from and where it goes. The system of *national income accounts* provides these measures.

The GNP

Let us begin with the gross national product. *The gross national product (GNP) is the nation's total production of goods and services for a single year valued in terms of market prices.* It is the sum of all the goods and services that people have been willing to pay for, from wheat production to bake sales, from machine tools to maid service, from aircraft manufacturing to bus service, from automobiles to chewing gum, from wages and salaries to interest on bank deposits. The gross national product is not a moral or an ethical concept; producing and selling cigarettes is part of the GNP, just as physician services and hospital care are. *The gross national product is also the total income received by all sellers of goods and services.* It really does not matter whether we view the GNP as the *value* of all goods and services *produced,* or the sum of all *expenditures* on these goods and services, for they are the same thing.

Computing the GNP

To compute the GNP, economists sum up all the expenditures on goods and services, plus government purchases. Care is taken to count *only the final product* sold to consumers, so that raw materials will not be counted twice—that is, both in original sale to a manufacturer and in the final price of the product. Business investment includes *only new investment goods* (buildings, machinery, and so on) and does not include financial transfers such as the purchase of stocks and bonds. Government purchases for goods and services include the money spent on *goods* (weapons, roads, buildings, parks, etc.), as well as the *wages* paid for the *services* of government employees. "Transfer payments" such as welfare payments, unemployment insurance, or social security payments are *not* part of the gross national product because they are not payments for currently produced goods or services. Thus, the gross national product becomes a measure of the nation's production of goods and services. It can be thought of as the total national pie for a given year, and it is the most widely used measure of total national production. (Table D in the appendix shows the growth of the GNP and its component parts from 1950 to 1975.)

National income accounting helps us to understand the circular flow that makes up both the *income* and *expenditure* sides of the gross national product. Figure 5–2 shows the circular flow of goods and services. Note that the GNP is composed of consumer outlays, plus business investment, plus government purchases of goods and services. Table 5–2 shows national income accounting figures for 1976. The *net national product* is the sum of all goods and services produced (GNP) less "depreciation"—that is, the wearing out of producer goods that must be replaced to maintain the nation's productive capacities. The *national income* is the total of all income

Figure 5–2 Circular Flow of Goods and Services

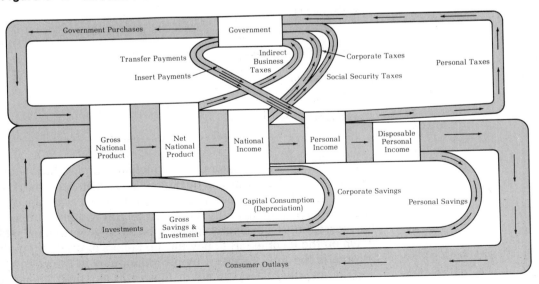

Table 5-2   National Income Accounting and the GNP, 1976

	Billions
Gross National Product	$1,692.6
Less Capital consumption (depreciation of capital goods that must be replaced)	−179.8
Net National Product	1,512.8
Less Indirect business taxes (sales, excise, property taxes that must be paid to government)	−165.7
National Income	1,347.1
Less Corporate profit taxes	−259.8
Social security taxes	−122.8
Plus Government transfer payments (social security, welfare)	184.2
Government interest payments	123.0
Dividends	35.1
Business transfer payments	7.1
Personal Income	1,313.9
Less Personal taxes	−193.6
Disposable Personal Income	1,120.3
Personal Savings	76.5
Consumer Outlays	$1,043.8

earned by the basic factors of production—land, labor, capital, and management—less indirect business taxes. The national income is always less than the net national product because the factors of production do not actually receive the full value of their output; businesses must pay many indirect taxes to government, which cut down on the income left to pay for the factors of production. *Personal income* is the total received by all individuals in the country—what people actually have to spend or to save to pay their taxes. Personal income includes government transfer payments to individuals—mainly social security and welfare payments. Personal income is what remains of national income after corporations have paid their income taxes, made their social security contributions, and decided upon their corporate savings—that is, how much they want to plow back into the business rather than pay out to stockholders. *Disposable personal income* is what people have left after they pay their taxes. Disposable personal income goes either to personal savings or to consumer outlays.

Actual and "dollar" increases

Since prices have increased over time through inflation, to get a meaningful measure of actual growth and output we must view the gross national product in *constant* dollars. Doubling the GNP by merely doubling prices is no real gain in production, so in order to separate actual increases in the GNP from mere "dollar" increases we must adjust for changes in the value of the dollar over the years. Economists account for changes in the value of a dollar by establishing the value of a dollar in a particular time base (for example, 1972) and then using "constant" dollars to measure the value of goods over time. Table 5–3 shows that the GNP has grown rapidly and vigorously both in "real" dollars *and* in "constant" dollars. Thus, America's economic growth is not merely a product of inflation. Between 1950 and 1976 the gross national product in "real" dollars rose from $286 billion to $1.6 trillion. Even with inflation taken into account, the growth is still phenomenal—in "constant" dollars from about $534 billion to $1,265 billion. Real GNP has grown between 3 and 3½ percent per year. An annual growth rate of 3½ percent enables the GNP to double every two decades.

Table 5–3   Growth of the GNP in Real and Constant Dollars

Year Average	GNP in Billions of Current ("Real") $'s	GNP in Billions of 1972 ("Constant") $'s
1950	$ 286	$ 534
1955	399	655
1960	506	737
1965	688	926
1970	982	1,075
1972	1,171	1,171
1976	1,692	1,265

Source: U.S. Bureau of the Census, *Statistical Abstract of the United States, 1977* (Washington, D.C.: Government Printing Office, 1977), p. 429.

THE GROSS NATIONAL PRODUCT
AND THE QUALITY OF LIFE

Weaknesses of the GNP   Although the gross national product is our best measure of economic well-being, it does not necessarily measure the quality of life in American society. First of all, it measures the size of the pie and not how the pie is cut up. Extremes of wealth and poverty can exist in the nation at any level of GNP. We will return to a discussion of the distribution of wealth, but for the moment it is important to realize that the GNP is *not* necessarily a measure of the extent of *poverty*.

The GNP does not identify *what goods and services get produced.* The GNP includes military output—weapons, munitions, and the services of troops and other war activities—as well as expenditures for education, highways, food, and medical care. Not all of these expenditures contribute equally to improving the quality of life.

Some expenditures that are reflected in the GNP represent *costs of life* in a modern industrial society, rather than *benefits.* For example, we must build elaborate subways and mass highway transport systems in our cities to move millions of people to and from work each day. The billions of dollars spent contribute to the annual GNP. But do they mean increased well-being for city dwellers and workers? Or do they simply mean that money is being spent on a painful necessity of life in crowded cities?

Moreover, the GNP does not give any negative weight to the *adverse side effects of economic development.* For example, until recently producers could pollute the air and water freely, and the cost of their products did not reflect the costs of this pollution. Increasingly, efforts to control pollution will add to the cost of goods. But to the extent that the cost of goods does not include the damage done to the environment in the process of production, the GNP is misleading.

Nor does the GNP reflect the *costs of goods and services that are not reflected in money transactions.* The services of women who work in their own home and care for their own children are not included in the GNP; yet if women hire housekeepers and child-care personnel, their wages become part of the GNP.

The GNP places no value on *leisure.* Over the past fifty years, the average workweek has been cut from six long days (over sixty hours) to five short days (less than forty hours) and vacations have greatly lengthened. In consequence, the quality of life has certainly improved. Yet the GNP does not reflect this increase in leisure. The fact that the GNP has continued to rise *despite* the growth in leisure is further evidence of the success of our system in producing goods and services.

Thus, national income accounting focuses largely on the quantity of production rather than on the quality of life. As we noted in chapter 2, social scientists have recently concerned themselves with producing new measures of social well-being, which are known as *social indicators*. A special task force of distinguished social scientists prepared a document, *Toward a Social Report,* for the U.S. Department of Health, Education, and Welfare suggesting the measurement of such social conditions as (1) health and illness, (2) social mobility, (3) physical environment, (4) income and poverty, (5) public order and safety, (6) the learning of science and art, (7) participation and alienation.

The social indicators movement

The social indicators movement has a long way to go. There are, first of all, no *adequate national data,* comparable to the GNP, to measure the quality of life in all these areas. Moreover, *determining what is "quality" in life* is frequently a controversial issue. The selection of which social condition to measure implies the judgment that this social condition has something to do with the quality of life, and even suggests that government ought to do something about it. The political implications of social reporting are obvious—different interests will argue over what should be measured, what is important in life, and what shall be done about it. (Table E in the appendix shows how people differ in their opinions about national priority items.)

WEALTH, TAXES, AND LOOPHOLES

Income concentration

Personal wealth in America is distributed unevenly. The top 20 percent (one-fifth) of income earners earn about 41 percent of all the income. The lowest 20 percent of income earners earn less than 6 percent of all the income. The top 5 percent of income earners earn about 15 percent of all of the nation's income. However, this income concentration has been declining over time (see table 11–2, chapter 11). In 1929 the top 5 percent of income earners received 30 percent of the total income, and the highest one-fifth of income earners received 54 percent of all income. Even since World War II, the decline in income concentration can be observed. The share of the total income received by the top 5 percent of income earners fell from 17.2 percent in 1947 to 14.7 percent in 1970. The income received by the highest one-fifth of the population went from 43 percent in 1947 to 41 percent in 1970. Note, however, that this is only a very modest decline in income concentration over the last twenty-five years.

Tax structure

Although federal income taxes are steeply *progressive* (large incomes are subject to higher tax rates than small ones), they do not succeed in completely leveling incomes in America. In 1977 an average family of four paid no income tax unless its income exceeded about $6,800. On the first $1,000 of income over this figure the family was taxed at 14 percent. The percentage rate increased rapidly as the family acquired more income. Income received over $47,200 was taxed at 50 percent, and the tax rate reached a maximum of 70 percent on income over $200,000. But *effective tax rate* (actual taxes paid as a percentage of total income) is not the same as *marginal tax rate* (the percentage of the last, highest dollar paid into taxes). For example, a family receiving $23,000 in income would be in the 32 percent marginal rate bracket, but its actual income tax bill would total only 20 percent of its income. The first $6,800 or so of income would be free of taxes, the next $1,000 would be taxed only 14 percent, the next $1,000 would be taxed 15 percent, and so on up the rate structure; only that portion of taxable income (after exemptions) over $23,000 would be taxable at the marginal rate of 32 percent.

Tax loopholes

Moreover, various forms of income are either tax exempt or taxed at lower rates, and a great many deductions are permitted for interest payments, depreciation, business and professional expenses, state and local taxes, and so forth. For example, capital gains (that is, profits on assets bought and sold) are taxed at only half the rate of income if the assets are held more than six months. This provision encourages investment in growing industries, but it also allows investors to receive income on which they pay less than the regular tax rates. Traditionally, interest on state and local government bonds has been exempt from federal income tax. Thus, not only are investors encouraged to assist state and local governments in community projects, but wealthy investors can receive tax-exempt income. While each of these tax provisions has special purposes (for example, the capital gains provision is supposed to encourage investment in growing industries, the tax-exempt status of state and local bonds is supposed to encourage investment in state and local governments, etc.), taken as a whole, they can act to reduce the effective tax rate on wealthy taxpayers. Hence, they are frequently referred to as *tax loopholes*.[5]

Effective federal income tax rates are shown in figure 5–3. The top line shows the steady rise of marginal tax rates under the law; the bottom line shows the effective tax rate after exemptions, deductions, and provision for capital gains at different income levels. Plainly, taxation in America does not greatly change the distribution of income.

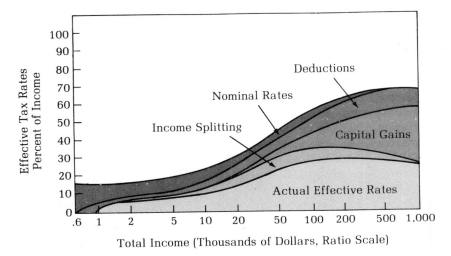

Figure 5–3 Effective Federal Income Tax Rates
Source: Adapted from C. Joseph Pechman, *Federal Tax Policy* (Washington, D.C.: Brookings, 1968), p. 66.

THE CONCENTRATION OF CORPORATE POWER

Control over the economic resources of the nation is becoming increasingly concentrated in the hands of a very few people, largely because of the *consolidation of economic enterprise* into a small number of giant corporations. The following statistics can only suggest the scale and concentration of modern corporate enterprise in America: The 500 largest corporations hold over two-thirds of the industrial assets in the nation. The 100 largest corporations hold over half of the nation's industrial assets (see table 5–4). The 50 largest corporations hold over one-third of all industrial assets; the 5 largest corporations possess over 12 percent of all of the assets of the nation. The combined revenues of 3 industrial corporations—General Motors, Standard Oil of New Jersey, and Ford Motor Company—exceed the total revenues of all of the American states combined. The revenues of General Motors alone are fifty times those of Nevada, eight times those of New York, and slightly less than one-fifth those of the federal government. The rate of corporate mergers in recent years suggests that this concentration is continuing to increase.

A. A. Berle, Jr., a corporation lawyer and corporate director who has written extensively on the modern corporation, commented on the concentration of corporate power:

Table 5–4 Concentration in Industry: The 100 Largest Industrial Corporations by Size of Assets, 1976

Rank	Name	Assets (Billions)
1	Exxon	$36.3
2	General Motors	24.4
3	Mobil	18.8
4	Texaco	18.2
5	IBM	17.7
6	Ford	15.8
7	Standard Oil of Calif.	13.8
8	Gulf Oil	13.4
9	General Electric	12.0
10	Standard Oil (Indiana)	11.2
11	International Tel. & Tel.	11.1
12	U.S. Steel	9.2
13	Atlantic Richfield	8.8
14	Shell Oil	7.8
15	Tenneco	7.2
16	Chrysler	7.1
17	E. I. Du Pont	7.0
18	Dow Chemical	6.8
19	Union Carbide	6.6
20	Standard Oil (Ohio)	6.3
21	Continental Oil	6.0
22	Eastman Kodak	5.5
23	Westinghouse Electric	5.3
24	Western Electric	5.2
25	Phillips Petroleum	5.1
26	Bethlehem Steel	4.9
27	Sun	4.8
28	Xerox	4.6
29	Goodyear Tire & Rubber	4.3
30	R. J. Reynolds Industries	4.3
31	Union Oil of Calif.	4.2
32	Procter & Gamble	4.1
33	Monsanto	3.9
34	Occidental Petroleum	3.9
35	Caterpillar Tractor	3.9
36	RCA	3.8
37	Weyerhaeuser	3.7
38	International Paper	3.6
39	Getty Oil	3.6
40	Cities Service	3.6
41	Philip Morris	3.6
42	International Harvester	3.6

Table 5–4   (Cont.)

Rank	Name	Assets (Billions)
43	Aluminum Co. of America	$ 3.6
44	Gulf & Western Industries	3.5
45	Minnesota Mining & Manufacturing	3.3
46	Firestone Tire & Rubber	3.3
47	Marathon Oil	3.0
48	Deere	2.9
49	Rockwell International	2.9
50	Armco Steel	2.8
51	Amax	2.8
52	National Steel	2.8
53	Amerada Hess	2.8
54	W. R. Grace	2.7
55	United Technologies	2.6
56	Georgia Pacific	2.6
57	Sperry Rand	2.6
58	Burroughs	2.5
59	American Brands	2.4
60	Allied Chemical	2.4
61	IC Industries	2.3
62	Reynolds Metal	2.3
63	Republic Steel	2.3
64	NCR	2.3
65	Kennecott Copper	2.3
66	Honeywell	2.2
67	Owens-Illinois	2.2
68	Continental Group	2.2
69	Kaiser Aluminum	2.2
70	Champion International	2.2
71	Pfizer	2.2
72	McDonnell Douglas	2.2
73	LTV	2.1
74	Ashland Oil	2.1
75	Inland Steel	2.1
76	Litton Industries	2.0
77	PPG Industries	2.0
78	General Foods	2.0
79	American Cyanamid	2.0
80	Anaconda	2.0
81	American Can	1.9
82	Warner-Lambert	1.9
83	FMC	1.9
84	Boeing	1.9
85	Celanese	1.9

Table 5–4   (Cont.)

Rank	Name	Assets (Billions)
86	Coca-Cola	$1.9
87	TRW	1.9
88	Signal Companies	1.9
89	Beatrice Foods	1.8
90	Control Data	1.8
91	Kraft	1.8
92	Penzoil	1.8
93	Borden	1.8
94	Merck	1.8
95	Colgate-Palmolive	1.8
96	Phelps Dodge	1.8
97	Lykes	1.7
98	Esmark	1.7
99	Ingersoll-Rand	1.7
100	Burlington Industries	1.7

Total Assets of 100 Largest Industrial Corporations	= $482.6
Total Industrial Assets	= $883.9
Percentage of Total Industrial Assets Held by 100 Largest Corporations	= 54.9%
Total Number of Corporations	= 204,259

Since the United States carries on not quite half of the manufacturing production of the *entire world* today, these 500 corporations—each with its own little dominating pyramid within it—represent a concentration of power over economics which makes the medieval feudal system look like a Sunday School party. In sheer economic power, this has gone far beyond anything we have yet seen.[6]

According to Berle, corporate power is lodged in the hands of the *directors* of these corporations plus the holders of large *control blocks* of corporate stock:

Directors and control blocks

The control system in today's corporations, when it does not lie solely in the directors as in the American Telephone and Telegraph Company, lies in a combination of the directors of a so-called control block [of stock] plus the directors, themselves. For practical purposes, therefore, the control of power element in most large corporations rests in its group of directors, and it is autonomous—or autonomous if taken together with a control block. . . . This is a self-perpetuating oligarchy.[7]

Corporate power does not rest in the hands of masses of corporate employees or even in the hands of millions of middle- and upper-middle-class Americans who own corporate stock.

Interlocking directorates and corporate ownership

Corporate power is further concentrated by a system of *interlocking directorates*, in which a director of one corporation also sits on the boards of other corporations, and by a *corporate owner-ship* system in which control blocks of stock are owned by financial institutions rather than by private individuals. Interlocking directorates enable key corporate elites to wield influence over a large number of corporations. It is not uncommon for members of the top elite to hold six, eight, or ten directorships.

A. A. Berle, Jr., has also suggested that *managers*, rather than major stockholders, have come to exercise dominant influence in American corporations:

Management control

Management control is a phrase meaning merely that no large concentrated stockholding exists which maintains a close working relationship with the management or is capable of challenging it, so that the board of directors may regularly expect a majority, composed of small and scat-

"Well, to begin, I'm sure this little box needs no introduction."
Drawing by Vietor; © 1976 The New Yorker Magazine, Inc.

tered holdings, to follow their lead. Thus, they need not consult with anyone when making up their slate of directors, and may simply request their stockholders to sign and send in a ceremonial proxy. They select their own successors. . . . Nominal power still resides in the stockholders; actual power in the board of directors.[8]

Economist Gabriel Kolko summarizes the impact of the concentration of corporate power:

> The concentration of economic power in a very small elite is an indisputable fact. . . . A social theory assuming a democratized economic system—or even a trend in this direction— is quite obviously not in accord with social reality. Whether the men who control industry are socially responsive or trustees of the social welfare is quite another matter: it is one thing to speculate about their motivations, another to generalize about economic facts. And even if we assume that these men act benevolently toward their workers and the larger community, their actions still would not be the result of social control through a formal democratic structure and group participation, which are the essentials for democracy; they would be an arbitrary noblesse oblige by the economic elite. When discussing the existing corporate system, it would be more realistic to drop all references to democracy.[9]

THE MANAGEMENT TECHNOSTRUCTURE

Today the requirements of technology and planning have greatly increased industry's need for specialized talent and skill in organization. Capital is something that a corporation can now supply to itself. Thus, there is a shift in power in the American economy from capital to organized intelligence, and we can reasonably expect that this shift will be reflected in the deployment of power in society at large.

Decline of the individual investor

Individual capitalists are no longer essential to the accumulation of capital for investment. Approximately three-fifths of industrial capital now comes from retained earnings of corporations, rather than from the investments of individual capitalists. Another one-fifth of industrial capital is borrowed, chiefly from banks. Even though the remaining one-fifth of the capital funds of industry come from "outside" investments, the bulk of these funds are from large insurance companies, mutual funds, and pension trusts, rather than from individual investors. Thus, *the individual capitalist investor is no longer in a position of dominance in American capital formation.*

American capital is primarily administered and expended by managers of large corporations and financial institutions. Stock-

Nonaction by institutional investors

holders are supposed to have ultimate power over management, but individual stockholders seldom have any control over the activities of the corporations they own. Usually "management slates" for the board of directors are selected by management and automatically approved by stockholders. Banks and financial institutions and pension trust or mutual fund managers occasionally get together to replace a management-selected board of directors. But more often than not, banks and trust funds sell their stock in corporations whose management they distrust, rather than use the voting power of their stock to replace management. Generally, banks and trust funds vote their stock for the management slate. This *policy of nonaction* by institutional investors means that the directors and managements of corporations become increasingly self-appointed and unchallengeable; and this policy freezes absolute power in the corporate managements.

Restraints

Of course, the *profit motive* is still important to the corporate managers, since profits are the basis of capital formation within the corporation. Increased capital at the disposal of corporate managers means increased power; losses mean a decrease in the capital available to the managers, a decrease in their power, and perhaps eventual extinction for the organization. There is also some evidence that management today has more concern for the interests of the public than did the individual industrial capitalists of a few decades ago. The management class is more sympathetic to the philosophy of the liberal establishment, to which it belongs; it is concerned with the public interest and expresses a devotion to the *corporate conscience*. As Adolph Berle explains:

> This is the existence of a set of ideas, widely held by the community and often by the organization itself and the men who direct it, that certain uses of power are "wrong," that is, contrary to the established interest and value system of the community. Indulgence of these ideas as a limitation on economic power, and regard for them by the managers of great corporations, is sometimes called—and ridiculed as—the "corporate conscience." The ridicule is pragmatically unjustified. The first sanction enforcing limitations imposed by the public consensus is a lively appreciation of that consensus by corporate managements. This is the reality of the "corporate conscience."[10]

Management fears loss of prestige and popular esteem. While the public has no direct economic control over management, and government control is more symbolic than real, the deprivation of prestige is one of the oldest methods by which any society enforces its values upon individuals and groups. Moreover, most of the values of the prevailing liberal consensus have been internalized by corporate managers themselves; that is, they have come to believe in a public-regarding philosophy.

CASE STUDY
Inflation: The Silent Thief

Inflation has been stealing buying power from Americans for decades, but the "creeping" inflation of former years is now "galloping" inflation. Today we can expect the value of each dollar earned or saved to decline 6, 8, 10, or even 12 percent in a single year. Americans who live on fixed incomes from pensions or savings watch their buying power plummet and their standard of living decline as inflation robs them of the value of their earnings and savings. Even Americans whose salaries or wages increase to match inflation rates find themselves in higher income-tax brackets paying out more in taxes. Thus, the buying power of millions of working Americans decreases even as salaries and wages increase. (See appendix, table F for a description of consumer price indexes from 1940 to 1976.)

Inflation occurs when there is too much money chasing too few goods. *Demand-pull* inflation results when the supply of money (cash as well as loans) exceeds the ability of the economy to produce the goods desired. *Demand-push* inflation results when workers demand and get pay increases, which, in turn, push up the price of goods. Finally, a new form of inflation might be labeled *anticipated inflation*. This occurs when everyone in the economy—business people, workers, consumers—comes to expect ever higher inflation each year, so that they buy everything possible now, at any price asked, believing that prices will be even higher next year.

Where does the money to fuel inflation come from? The Federal Reserve Board, through the operations described earlier in this chapter, creates money by allowing its member

"So what's it going to be? The same size as last year or the same price as last year?"

Drawing by Modell; © 1978 The New Yorker Magazine, Inc.

banks to make loans and create deposits, literally out of thin air. An influential "monetarist" school of thinking among economists, led by Milton Friedman, believes that if the Federal Reserve Board restrained the growth of the money supply, inflation would gradually disappear. But politicians put heavy pressure on the "Fed" (Federal Reserve Board) to increase the money supply when a recession threatens. Sometimes the quasi-independent Fed can resist these pressures, but more often it cannot. The threat of a recession causes an increase in the money supply, which in turn causes inflation.

Government also contributes directly to inflation by spending billions more than it collects in taxes. (In 1979, President Carter's budget called for $500 billion in spending, but only $440 billion in revenue. This means a $60 billion deficit in one year.) Government makes up its deficits simply by creating more money to cover its borrowing. This adds to the supply of money in the economy and creates more inflation.

Some critics of government believe that the federal

government deliberately creates inflation to raise wages and salaries, which automatically puts more Americans into higher tax brackets. Because inflation creates these tax increases automatically, Congress and the president, by fostering inflation, can actually increase taxes without having to vote for a tax increase. Politicians can thus avoid direct responsibility for politically unpopular tax increases. Another source of demand-push inflation is the proliferation of government rules and regulations, environmental controls, safety rules, and a host of other government restrictions, all of which push business costs up. But perhaps the greatest single inflationary jolt hit America when OPEC (the Organization of Petroleum Exporting Countries) quadrupled the price of oil in a single year (1973).

What does inflation mean to the average American? Let us consider a worker who earned $10,000 per year in 1960. This worker would have paid $1,362 in taxes and kept $8,638 in buying power (see table 5–5). But in 1978 this same worker would have had to earn $22,671 just to keep the same $8,638 in buying power. This is because $10,098 of the salary increase (from $10,000 to $22,671) would go to inflation and $3,935 to taxes. Executives who earned $50,000 in 1960 would have had to earn $118,482 in 1978 in order to have the *same* buying power that they enjoyed in 1960.

What can be done to halt inflation or at least slow it down? There are no easy solutions, as the following list indicates:

Table 5–5   How Inflation Erodes Buying Power

	Worker		Executive	
	1960	*1978*	*1960*	*1978*
Salary	$10,000	$22,671	$50,000	$118,482
Taxes	1,362	3,935	14,187	40,804
Inflation	—	10,098	—	41,865
Buying power	$ 8,638	$ 8,638	$35,813	$ 35,813

1. The Fed could maintain a steady money supply regardless of the temporary ups and downs of the economy. The problem with this solution is that a president or Congress faced with a recession will bring heavy pressure on the Fed to expand the money supply.

2. Government itself could reduce or eliminate its own deficits. However, deficit spending has become a way of life in Washington, and it is politically impossible to decide which programs should be cut to bring expenditures down to revenues.

3. American production could be stimulated by tax credits and the elimination of unnecessary government regulations. An increase in the supply of goods would tend to keep prices down. To reduce our dependence on expensive foreign oil, it is particularly important to stimulate the production of domestic oil, gas, coal, and nuclear energy.

4. Government could impose wage and price controls, ordering businesses and unions to keep their prices and wages at current levels. However, controls have not worked well in the past: A large government bureaucracy is needed to enforce them; wages and prices sneak up despite the controls; shortages occur as suppliers hold back goods at the low controlled prices; a "black market" of illegal selling at higher prices springs up; and so forth.

5. The federal government could "index" all wages and prices and government benefits. This means automatically raising everyone's income to match inflation. Indexing might relieve business and labor of some of the psychological pressure to "get ahead" of inflation. Tax rates could also be indexed so that inflation would not push taxpayers into even higher brackets. However, past savings would still be destroyed.

Government cannot ignore the problem of inflation. Opinion polls show that many Americans believe inflation is the number one problem confronting the nation. Perhaps the worst part about inflation today is the spreading cynicism that nothing will be done about it.

NOTES

1. Adam Smith, *The Wealth of Nations* (New York: Modern Library), p. 423.
2. J. Roland Pennock, *Liberal Democracy: Its Merits and Prospects* (New York: Holt, 1950), p. 333.

3. Friedrich Hayek, *The Road to Serfdom* (Chicago: Phoenix Books, 1957), p. 35.

4. Richard Hofstadter, *American Political Tradition* (New York: Knopf, 1948), p. 332.

5. C. Joseph Pechman, *Federal Tax Policy* (Washington, D.C.: Brookings, 1968); Tax Foundation, *Tax Burdens and Benefit of Government Expenditures by Income Class* (New York: Tax Foundation, 1966).

6. A. A. Berle, Jr., *Economic Power and the Free Society* (New York: Fund for the Republic, 1958), p. 14.

7. Ibid., p. 10.

8. A. A. Berle, Jr., *Power without Property* (New York: Harcourt Brace Jovanovich, 1959), p. 73. See also Ferdinand Lundberg, *The Rich and the Super Rich* (New York: Lyle Stuart, 1968).

9. Gabriel Kolko, *Wealth and Power in America* (New York: Praeger, 1962), pp. 68–69.

10. Berle, *Power Without Property*, pp. 90–91.

DISCUSSION QUESTIONS

1. Identify the components of an economic system. Discuss how the market in a private enterprise economy determines what is to be produced, how much it will cost, and who will be able to buy it. Comment on the roles that the following factors play in a market operation: consumer demands, profits, prices, willingness to pay and ability to pay, labor market, competition, product supply.

2. Describe the ideal conditions for a market operation in a free enterprise system. What are the reasons for government interfering in such a system?

3. Discuss the similarities between laissez-faire (classical) economics and a traditional democratic political system. Describe the conflict between laissez-faire economics and Keynesian economics over the self-adaptability of the free enterprise system.

4. Describe the kinds of fiscal and monetary policies that a Keynesian economist would recommend during a recessionary period and an inflationary period. How do the automatic stabilizers work during each of these periods?

5. Discuss some of the problems that government has in using fiscal and monetary policies.

6. Describe some of the means by which government has attempted to regulate business.

7. Explain how economists compute the gross national product (GNP). Differentiate between actual increases in the GNP and "dollar" increases in the GNP. Describe some of the weaknesses of the GNP

measure and some of the alternative measures that social scientists have suggested. What are the difficulties with *these* measures?

8. Describe the trend of income concentration in America. Discuss some of the "loopholes" of the American taxation system, the reasons for the "loophole" provisions, and the overall effect of taxation on the distribution of income.

9. Discuss the reasons for the increasing concentration of corporate power in America. Describe the factors contributing to the absolute power of corporate management and the factors that work against such absolute power.

10. Describe some of the factors that contribute to inflation. Identify the various counterinflationary measures that might be employed and the problems that would be encountered in employing them. Which measures do you think might be most feasible?

SUGGESTED READINGS

George L. Bach, *Economics: An Introduction to Analysis and Policy,* 7th ed. (Englewood Cliffs, N.J.: Prentice-Hall, 1971).

Adolph A. Berle, Jr., *Power without Property* (New York: Harcourt Brace Jovanovich, 1959).

Congressional Quarterly, *The Power of the Pentagon* (Washington, D.C.: Congressional Quarterly, Inc., 1972).

John Kenneth Galbraith, *The New Industrial State* (New York: Signet Books, 1968).

Gabriel Kolko, *Wealth and Power in America* (New York: Praeger, 1962).

C. Joseph Pechman, *Federal Tax Policy* (Washington, D.C.: Brookings, 1968).

U.S. Department of Health, Education, and Welfare, *Toward a Social Report* (Ann Arbor: University of Michigan Press, 1970).

Photo from Magnum by Burk Uzzle

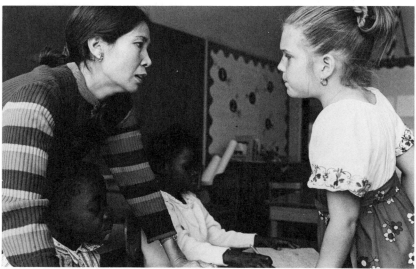

Photo from Magnum by Paul Fusco

Chapter 6
Power and Personality

You are alone in a corridor in an airport in a foreign city. You are tired after an all-night plane trip and in a hurry to catch a connecting flight. You are suddenly stopped by a uniformed policeman and, without explanation, "frisked." How do you react? If you had not been tired and in a hurry, would you have reacted any differently? Is there any similarity between the way you reacted here and the way you reacted when your fourth grade teacher accused you of passing notes? In other words, is this way of responding to this sort of authority characteristic of you? Is it part of your *personality*? If it is, how do you think you came to develop this particular way of responding?

An understanding of personality, of individual behavioral responses and their determinants, is essential to a full understanding of power in society. In this chapter we will explore the meaning of personality and various psychological theories regarding the determinants of personality. We will also see what different schools of psychology have to say about the relationship between personality and power. After you have read chapter 6, you should be able to:

- discuss how psychoanalytic (Freudian) theory views personality and its development and how it interprets individual responses to power and authority.
- discuss behavioral psychology's use of learning theory in its approach to the study of personality, and B. F. Skinner's ideas for the control of human behavior.
- discuss how social psychology views personality and its determinants, and its approach to power relationships.
- describe humanistic psychology's view of the "self," Rollo May's concept of powerlessness, and Abraham Maslow's construction of a "hierarchy of needs."
- discuss how power in the form of authority and legitimacy can command obedience, and the implications of such obedience.

PERSONALITY AND INDIVIDUAL RESPONSES TO POWER

Individuals react toward power and authority in characteristic ways. In many different situations and over a relatively prolonged period of time, their responses to power and authority are fairly predictable. Some individuals regularly seek power and authority while others avoid it. Some individuals are submissive to authority while others are habitually rebellious. Some individuals try to conform to the expectations of other people while others are guided by internalized standards. Some individuals feel powerless, helpless, and isolated; they believe they have little control over their own lives. Other individuals are self-assured and aggressive; they speak out at meetings, organize groups, and take over leadership positions. Some individuals are habitually suspicious of others, unwilling to compromise; they prefer simple, final, and forceful solutions to complex problems. Some individuals are assertive, self-confident, and strong-willed while others are timid, submissive, and self-conscious. There are as many different ways of responding to power as there are types of personalities.

Personality
Personality is all of the characteristic ways of behaving that an individual exhibits; it is the enduring and organized sets of responses that an individual habitually makes when subjected to particular stimuli. By *characteristic* and *habitual* we mean that individuals tend to respond in a similar fashion to many separate situations. For example, their attitudes toward authority in general may affect their response to any number of different leaders, supervisors, directors, or other authority figures, in different situations. By *enduring* we mean that these characteristic ways of behaving may operate over a long time, perhaps through youth, young adulthood, and maturity. Attitudes toward authority in the home may carry over to school, university, job, church, government, and so forth. By *organized* we mean that there are relationships between various elements of an individual's personality. A change in one element (let us say, a growing need for social approval) would bring about a change in another element (let us say, an increased willingness to conform to group norms). Thus, personality is not just a bundle of traits but an *integrated pattern of responses.*

Personality vs. role
It is important to distinguish the concept of "personality" from the concept of "role." A *role* is a pattern of expected behavior associated with a given position in society—such as parent or child, supervisor or supervisee, union member or union official, team coach or team member, and so on. Occasionally it is difficult to distinguish role-determined from personality-determined behavior. Sometimes the

only way to do so is to observe how individuals behave in a number of different roles. If they display a similar characteristic—for instance, if they are authoritarian—in all of their roles, then we can attribute this characteristic to *personality* rather than role.

Psychologists differ over the precise meaning of personality. Psychologist Gordon Allport lists no less than fifty types of definitions.[1] Definitions tend to be linked to major theories or approaches to individual behavior and to the major divisions within psychology itself.

One of those major divisions is *clinical psychology*, which has to do with the treatment of psychological disorder. It is closely related to *psychiatry* in that both clinical psychologists and psychiatrists deal with the diagnosis and treatment of psychological disorders. The psychiatrist, however, is also a medical doctor. Clinicians deal with real persons with real psychological problems. They enter the patient's world and concern themselves with the subjective human experience, including wishes, fears, anxieties, ambitions. Clinical psychology stresses therapy, ranging from chemical therapy and shock treatment to various behavior therapies and insight therapies. *Psychoanalysis* is a type of insight-oriented therapy that encourages patients to think about themselves—their problems, dreams, memories—so that they can gain insight into the causes of their own difficulties. Psychoanalysis enables patients to talk about early childhood experiences and thus to reveal unconscious motivations, emotions, and conflicts. The psychoanalytic approach to personality emphasizes these *childhood experiences* and *unconscious feelings* as determining factors in personality development. Although the practice of psychoanalysis has always been the domain of the Freudian-trained psychiatrist, many clinical psychologists do use *psychoanalytic theory* in their approach to therapy.

Experimental psychology, another major division of psychology, is concerned with the scientific study of the behavioral responses of humans and animals to various stimuli. Experimental psychology focuses on observed behavior—it is frequently termed *behavioral psychology*. Its setting is the academic laboratory, and rats and pigeons are frequent subjects of experimentation. There is an emphasis on careful observation, quantitative data, and statistical methods. Behavioral psychology relies heavily on *learning theory* (stimulus-response theory), which views all behavior as a product of learning or conditioning. Behavioral patterns are learned through a process whereby a stimulus evokes a response that is either rewarded or punished, and habits are formed. The behavioral approach to personality views personality as a *pattern of learned, reinforced responses*.

Social psychology is concerned with the individual's relationship with other individuals and groups. The social psychologist studies the whole person and the impact of the social world on the person—the world of social interaction and group life, which constantly shapes and modifies the individual's goals, perceptions, attitudes, and behavior. The social psychological approach to personality emphasizes the individual's *socialization*—the development of individual identity through *interpersonal experiences*, and the *internalizing of the expectations of significant others*.

Humanistic psychology focuses on human experience and human fulfillment; it emphasizes the individual's innate potential to grow and develop. According to the humanists, human beings are unique among animals because they alone have psychological, as well as biological, needs. The individual is internally motivated to fulfill these needs, to grow and develop and expand the capacity for creativity. Humanistic psychology views personality development as a *continuous process of positive growth* in which the individual, having fulfilled a lower need, pursues the fulfillment of a higher one.

In the following pages, we will see how each of these theories can contribute to our understanding of personality and individual reactions to power and authority. We will begin with an exploration of psychoanalytic (Freudian) theory and a consideration of the Freudian approach to power relationships, as exemplified by *The Authoritarian Personality* study. We will then examine behavioral psychology's reliance on learning (stimulus-response) theory and the ideas of behavioral psychologist B. F. Skinner about the need to control human behavior. Next we will consider how social psychology uses interpersonal-interaction theory to explain personality. To illustrate the general approach of this school of psychology to power relationships, we will explore David Riesman's concept of the "other-directed" person. We will then briefly describe humanistic psychology's theory of personality, Rollo May's views of powerlessness, and Abraham Maslow's construction of a "hierarchy of needs." The chapter concludes with a case study of authority and obedience, which describes the startling results of one of the most interesting social science experiments of recent times.

SIGMUND FREUD AND PSYCHOANALYTIC THEORY

Perhaps no other scholar has had a greater impact on the social sciences than the Viennese psychiatrist Sigmund Freud (1856–1939). Freud completed medical school at the University of Vienna in 1881.

He would have preferred an academic position at a university, but discrimination against Jews forced him to enter private practice. Freud's interest in neurology led him to specialize in the treatment of nervous disorders; he studied hypnosis because a French neurologist, Jean Charcot, had learned that neurotic symptoms could be removed during hypnotic trance. He also collaborated with another Viennese physician, Joseph Breuer, who learned that some worries could be alleviated by having the patient talk about them.

In his initial treatment of neurotic patients, Freud used hypnosis. He soon found that patients did not really need to be in a full hypnotic trance so long as they felt relaxed and uninhibited. He encouraged them to engage in *free association*—that is, to say anything that came into their minds without regard to organization, logic, or embarrassment over socially unacceptable ideas. He wanted to make the patient's *unconscious* motives, drives, feelings, and anxieties *conscious* ones. The goal of psychoanalysis, as it was called, was to help patients attain *insight*, or self-knowledge. Once this was achieved, the neurotic symptoms tended to disappear.

Personality components   According to Freud, the personality is composed of three major systems: the *id*, the *ego*, and the *superego*. The interaction of these components determines an individual's behavior. The *id* is the basic system of life instincts, or drives—hunger, thirst, sex, rest, pain avoidance, and so on. The id is in close touch with the body's needs; these needs produce psychic energy, which is experienced as uncomfortable states of tension. The id endeavors to reduce the tensions—it operates on the *pleasure* principle—but the id has no knowledge of objective reality. A newborn baby's personality is almost pure id. It seeks immediate gratification of bodily urges and has no knowledge of reality or morals.

The *ego* is the part of the personality that is in contact with objective reality. It directs the energies of the id toward real-world objects that are appropriate for the satisfaction of the urge and the reduction of tension. The ego operates on the *reality* principle, formulating plans for the satisfaction of needs, testing these plans, and deciding what needs will be satisfied first and in what manner. The ego exercises important executive functions, coordinating the sometimes conflicting desires of the id with the conditions of the external world.

The *superego*, the last part of the personality to develop, is the internal representative of the values, standards, and morals that the child is taught. The superego is the *moral* arm of the personality and develops through rewards or punishments that the parents impose upon the child and through the child's identification with the parents' standards. The superego decides what is right and wrong, rewarding the individual with feelings of pride or punishing with feelings of guilt. It inhibits the impulses of the id, persuades the ego to direct energies toward moralistic goals rather than realistic ones, and strives for moral perfection.

Anxiety: functions and types

Anxiety is a state of tension that results from an apprehension of impending pain or danger, whether physical or psychological. Anxiety reduction is a drive like hunger or thirst, the difference being that it results from psychological, rather than bodily, discomfort. Anxiety is an important force in structuring early personality development. If it becomes too intense at too early an age when the ego is unprepared to deal with it, it can produce serious personality disorders. However, anxiety should not be construed as being necessarily pathological. It serves the important function of warning us of impending danger, making us more alert, perceptive, and better prepared to deal with the situation. When its intensity and nature are appropriate to the real situation, the anxiety is *normal*. When there does not seem to be adequate cause for it in the real world, when it is caused by unconscious or irrational fears, and when it interferes with the person's functioning, the anxiety is *neurotic*.

Identification and personality development

Identification is important as a process in early personality development and as a way or reducing anxiety. The infant imitates the characteristics of the persons in its environment who satisfy its needs. These characteristics—for example, a parent's way of walking or talking—are incorporated into the child's developing personality. As we have noted, identification is also important in the development of the superego, as the child identifies with and incorporates the parents' moral values.

Identification as a defense against anxiety

Children (or adults) may also identify with persons whom they perceive as aggressive, threatening, or all-powerful, and it is in this sense that identification is used to reduce anxiety. By becoming like the feared person who causes the anxiety, one is able to perceive the aggression as if it were one's own and were under one's own control. This type of identification is known as *identification with the aggressor*, and it constitutes one type of defense against anxiety.

Other defense mechanisms

There are many other *defense mechanisms* that the personality may use, often unconsciously, to reduce anxiety and tension. When it is dangerous to express an instinctual drive, be it in the form of love or hate, the individual may use *displacement* to defend against the anxiety—that is, shift the impulse from the original object to a less dangerous one. For example, a man who is angry at his employer, on whom he is dependent for his livelihood, may become furious with his wife over a petty matter, without realizing why he is acting as he is. A displacement that channels the psychic energy from the blocked instinctual drive into a socially acceptable activity is known as *sublimation*. Freud believed that sublimation of the instinctual drive was a great source of cultural achievement and civilization.

The most important of the defense mechanisms is *repression*. In this defensive maneuver, the ego protects the individual from unbearable impulses by forcing them out of consciousness. This may occur when an impulse would endanger life, risk punishment, or risk feelings of guilt. But there are costs to repression. A severely repressed individual who has denied many strong impulses may suffer fatigue, nervousness, or depression. Repression can even interfere with the functioning of the body; sexual impotence can result from severely repressed sexual impulses. Repression and displacement may operate together. For example, a son who has repressed his hostility toward his father may express displaced hostile feelings against symbols of authority.

Projection occurs when individuals attribute their own impulses to others in the external world because to admit their own impulses would produce too much anxiety or guilt. Instead of saying, "I hate him," the individual says, "He hates me." In this way people can express aggressive impulses toward others under the guise of defending themselves against their enemies. *Reaction formation* is the replacement in the consciousness of an anxiety-producing impulse by its opposite. "I hate you" becomes "I love you," or vice versa. *Regression* is a mechanism whereby one reverses the process of maturity. When growing up entails responsibilities, frustrations and anxieties, a person may regress to an earlier stage of development.

The instinctual drives   Freud never drew up a comprehensive list of instincts or needs. However, he was convinced that of all of our many instincts, those of sex and aggression were the most seriously repressed by society. This repression begins with the newborn infant and extends through adulthood. If we feel hunger, we can immediately go out and buy a hamburger; but if we feel a sexual urge, it usually must be denied until an appropriate outlet is found. Aggressive impulses are also severely restricted. Thus, Freud's seeming emphasis on sex was not a product of his belief that this drive was any more powerful than others, but that it was the most repressed and therefore the source of many personality disorders.

Stages of personality development   Freud believed that an individual passes through a series of *stages of personality development*. The first stages are decisive. The newborn infant at the *oral stage* derives pleasure from sucking and eating. It is a passive and receptive stage that centers on oral gratification. In adulthood, oral characteristics include smoking, overeating, extreme dependence on others. Sarcasm and argumentativeness may be a displaced form of oral aggression or biting.

The *anal stage* centers about control of the sphincter and the tension reduction involved in the release of feces. When toilet training is introduced, the infant experiences its first external regulation of an instinctual pleasure. Overreaction to demands that relief be postponed may lead to *anal-retentive* personality characteristics. The individual becomes possessive, stingy, excessively orderly, interested in collections of various sorts, and frequently constipated. Excessive praise for producing feces on demand may lead to *anal-expulsive* characteristics—an excessive concern with creativity and productivity.

In the *phallic stage* the infant becomes aware of the pleasure to be derived from the genital organs. Autoerotic activity (masturbation) is often quickly repressed by parents. Later the child (three to five years old) feels sexual attraction toward the parent of the opposite sex and hostile feelings toward the parent who appears as a love rival. According to Freud, every small boy goes through a period when he lusts after his mother and wishes his father were out of the way. (The term *Oedipus complex* comes from an ancient Greek play, *Oedipus Rex*, in which Oedipus unknowingly kills his own father and marries a woman who, he later finds out, is his mother.) These feelings produce various anxieties; for example, *castration anxiety* is the boy's fear that his father will retaliate by cutting off the offending organs. But usually the male child resolves his problems by eventually *identifying* with his father and replacing his dangerous sexual attraction to his mother with harmless tender affection. Freud believed that little girls may hold their mothers responsible for the absence of a protruding penis. The girl's love for her father is mixed with a feeling of envy—"penis envy"—because he possesses something that she lacks.

Freud believed that every person is bisexual; each sex is attracted to members of the same sex as well as the opposite sex. However, homosexual impulses are repressed in most people. Bisexuality actually helps reduce the problems of the Oedipus complex because the boy does have some positive feelings for his father and the girl for her mother.

After age five or six the child enters a *latency* period, in which many of the early oral, anal, and phallic problems are repressed. Indeed, the repression of these early feelings is responsible for our loss of memory of early childhood and infancy. It is not until puberty that latent feelings are reawakened by physical maturation, and repression is again attempted.

The *genital stage* represents maturity in personality development. The gratification an individual received from his own body pleasure as a child is redirected toward external love objects. The person approaching adulthood begins to love others not simply for selfish or narcissistic reasons. Earlier, oral, anal, and phallic stages are fused into genital impulses; the personality gradually stabilizes with habitual displacements, sublimations, and identifications. The final organization of personality represents contributions from all four stages.

Perhaps no other social science theory has been subjected to such searching and bitter criticism as Freudian theory. The criticism ranges from charges that Freud was a "sex maniac" (Freud was a dedicated father and husband whose marriage lasted a lifetime; Freud's daughter, Anna, became a distinguished psychoanalyst herself) to more serious scientific reservations. One criticism centers on psychoanalytic therapy: It can be long and costly, and is not always successful. Drugs, shock treatment, and behavioral therapy frequently produce more complete results in less time and at less expense. Another criticism is that Freud's observations were based on abnormal, clinical cases rather than normal adults; most of his patients were middle-class Europeans; and he worked in a cultural period when sexual repression in society was much greater than it is today. All these factors may have produced distortions in his theory.

Another problem with Freudian theory is that it is difficult to test scientifically. Freudian explanations proceed from observed behavior *back* to unconscious feelings and childhood experiences; but they do not permit exact predictions of future behavior from these factors. For example, Freudian theory might hypothesize that a boy who has a severe Oedipus complex and cannot "cut the apron strings" and identify with his father may cope with this problem by becoming a homosexual. But Freudian theory might also hypothesize that the same Oedipus complex could lead the boy to become a "lady-killer," with a string of sexual conquests to prove his masculinity to himself. A scientist may object that Freudian theory provides two completely different behaviors with the same explanation. It does not predict which of the two behaviors may result from an Oedipus complex; hence it is "bad" scientific theory. Nevertheless, psychologist William McDougall concluded, "In my opinion Freud has, quite unquestionably, done more for the advancement of our understanding of human nature than any other man since Aristotle."[2]

THE AUTHORITARIAN PERSONALITY

The Freudian approach to power relationships

The Freudian approach to power relationships focuses upon the channeling and blocking of drives; the conflicts among the id, ego, and superego; unconscious processes; and early childhood determinations of habitual responses to power and authority. Power motives—for example, a need to dominate others or, the opposite, pleasure in leaving decision making to others and accepting direction—are organized into the personality early in life. They are later *displaced* onto general power structures in society—for example, a desire to acquire powerful office or position, or a willingness to accept directions and orders of superiors. The real motives for people's public behavior are largely unconscious, so they *rationalize* their behavior in terms of the public interest.

Perhaps the most influential study of power, authority, and personality, which was conducted mainly within the framework of Freudian theory, is the landmark volume entitled *The Authoritarian Personality.*[3] This study was undertaken after World War II by a group of psychologists who sought to identify potentially anti-democratic individuals—those whose personality structures render them particularly susceptible to authoritarian appeals. The research was supported by the American Jewish Committee because of its interest in finding the causes of anti-Semitism and social prejudice. The study ended with an identification of an entire "syndrome" of authoritarianism—an organized set of related attitudes.

The Authoritarian Personality study employed a variety of methodological tools to identify and explain authoritarianism: questionnaires, in-depth interviews, responses to pictures and ink-blots, and psychiatric clinical observations. One of the tools developed in the course of the study was the F (fascism) Scale, now widely used by social scientists to identify authoritarianism. Part of the original F Scale is reproduced in table 6-1. Persons who agree with all or most of the items in the F Scale are said to be authoritarian.

Characteristics of the authoritarian personality

The central attitudes of authoritarianism are *dominance* and *submission*—dominance over subordinates in any power hierarchy and submissiveness toward superiors. Authoritarians are highly ambivalent in their attitudes toward authority. They are outwardly servile toward those they perceive as their superiors, but in fact they also harbor strong negative feelings toward them. They conceal this hate with the ego defense of *reaction formation*—bending over backward in excessive praise of authority and admiration for the strong. Their repressed rage toward their superiors is redirected into hostility toward the weak and inferior.

Table 6-1 Items from the F (Fascism) Scale

Conventionalism: Rigid adherence to conventional, middle-class values.

Obedience and respect for authority are the most important virtues children should learn.

A person who has bad manners, habits, and breeding can hardly expect to get along with decent people.

Authoritarian Submission: Submissive, uncritical attitude toward idealized moral authorities of the ingroup.

Obedience and respect for authority are the most important virtues children should learn.

Young people sometimes get rebellious ideas, but as they grow up they ought to get over them and settle down.

What this country needs most, more than laws and political programs, is a few courageous, tireless, devoted leaders in whom the people can put their faith.

Authoritarian Aggression: Tendency to be on the lookout for and to condemn, reject, and punish people who violate conventional values.

A person who has bad manners, habits, and breeding can hardly expect to get along with decent people.

What the youth needs most is strict discipline, rugged determination, and the will to work and fight for family and country.

An insult to our honor should always be punished.

If people would talk less and work more, everybody would be better off.

Homosexuals are hardly better than criminals and ought to be severely punished.

Anti-introception: Opposition to the subjective, the imaginative, the tender-minded.

When people have problems or worries, it is best for them not to think about it, but to keep busy with more cheerful things.

Nowadays more and more people are prying into matters that should remain personal and private.

If people would talk less and work more, everybody would be better off.

Superstition and Stereotypy: The belief in mystical determinants of the individual's fate; the disposition to think in rigid categories.

Science has its place, but there are many important things that can never possibly be understood by the human mind.

All persons should have complete faith in some supernatural power whose decisions they obey without question.

People can be divided into two distinct classes: the weak and the strong.

Power and "Toughness": Preoccupation with the dominance-submission, strong-weak, leader-follower dimension; identification with power figures; overemphasis upon the conventionalized attributes of the ego; exaggerated assertion of strength and toughness.

No weakness or difficulty can hold us back if we have enough will power.

What the youth needs most is strict discipline, rugged determination, and the will to work and fight for family and country.

Table 6-1   (Cont.)

People can be divided into two distinct classes: the weak and the strong.

Destructiveness and Cynicism: Generalized hostility, vilification of the human.

Human nature being what it is, there will always be war and conflict.

Familiarity breeds contempt.

Projectivity: The disposition to believe that wild and dangerous things go on in the world; the projection outward of unconscious emotional impulses.

Nowadays more and more people are prying into matters that should remain personal and private.

The wild sex life of the old Greeks and Romans was tame compared to some of the goings-on in this country, even in places where people might least expect it.

Most people don't realize how much our lives are controlled by plots hatched in secret places.

Sex: Exaggerated concern with sexual "goings-on."

Sex crimes, such as rape and attacks on children, deserve more than mere imprisonment; such criminals ought to be publicly whipped, or worse.

The wild sex life of the old Greeks and Romans was tame compared to some of the goings-on in this country, even in places where people might least expect it.

Source: Abridgment of table 7 (pp. 255–57), "The F (Fascism) Scale," in *The Authoritarian Personality* by T. W. Adorno et al. Copyright 1950 by The American Jewish Committee. Reprinted by permission of Harper & Row, Publishers, Inc.

Authoritarians are *oriented toward power*. They tend to think in power terms, to be acutely sensitive in any situation to questions of who dominates whom. They are very uncomfortable when they do not know what the chain of command is. They need to know whom they should obey and who should obey them.

Authoritarians are *rigid*. They are "intolerant of ambiguity." They like order and are uncomfortable in the presence of disorder. When matters are complex, they impose their own rigid categories on them. Their thinking, therefore, is largely in *stereotypes*.

Authoritarians show *exaggerated concern with virility and strength*. Feelings of personal weakness are covered with a facade of toughness. They are unusually preoccupied with masculine virtues, and they also stereotype women as feminine and soft.

Authoritarians are *conventional*. They are particularly sensitive to the prevailing standards of their own social groups. They rigidly conform to these standards themselves and are prepared to severely punish others who deviate from them. They are particularly upset by sexual deviations of any kind.

Authoritarians are *anti-introceptive*. They are impatient with, and opposed to, the subjective and tender-minded. They are unimaginative and reluctant to acknowledge their own feelings and fantasies.

Authoritarians are *cynical and threat-oriented*. They distrust the motives of others and are generally pessimistic about human nature. They are disposed to believe that the world is a jungle and that various conspiracies exist to threaten them and their ways of life.

Authoritarians are *ethnocentric*. They view members of social groups other than their own as outsiders who are different, strange, unwholesome, and threatening. They hold an exalted opinion of their own groups. They reject outsiders and *project* many of their own aggressive impulses on them. They place stereotyped labels on outsiders.

Authoritarians are *superstitious*. They attribute much of what they do not understand in the world to fate or mysticism.

Sources of authoritarianism

The Authoritarian Personality study cites early childhood experiences with authority as one probable cause of authoritarianism:

> When we consider the childhood situation . . . we find reports of a tendency toward rigid discipline on the part of the parents, with affection which is conditional rather than unconditional, i.e., dependent upon approved behavior on the part of the child. Related to this is a tendency apparent in families of prejudiced subjects to base interrelationships on rather clearly defined roles of dominance and submission. . . . Forced into a surface submission to parental authority, the child develops hostility and aggression which are poorly channelized. The displacement of a repressed antagonism toward authority may be one of the sources, and perhaps the principal source, of his antagonism toward outgroups.[4]

Children who have been socialized in warm, close, affectionate interpersonal relationships are less likely to have authoritarian attitudes than children who have been socialized in strict, rigid, punitive situations. (This explanation is also consistent with interpersonal-interaction theory.)

Another psychoanalytic explanation of the authoritarian syndrome is the male child's *sadomasochistic resolution of the Oedipus complex*.[5] According to this theory, love for the mother is severely repressed, and hatred for the father is transformed through reaction formation into a strong identification with authority, masculinity, and toughness. The transformation is a difficult task that never succeeds completely. While part of the original hostility toward the father is transformed into pleasure in obedience and subordination, some of the hostility is left over as sadism, which seeks an outlet in aggressive behavior toward outgroups and subordinates. Authoritarians never perceive the ambivalence of their view: blind submission to authority, yet a readiness to attack those who are deemed weak.

Criticisms of The Authoritarian Personality *study*

A great deal of research followed *The Authoritarian Personality* study, much of it using the F Scale to identify authoritarians and then observing related attitudes, environments, and behaviors. Some of the subsequent research on authoritarianism raised serious criticisms and reservations about the original work. First, it was observed that poorly educated persons tend to agree with F Scale statements more frequently than do well-educated persons. This finding does not necessarily mean that a lack of education *causes* authoritarianism, but it does suggest that differences in F Scale scores may be a product of education and *not* personality development. Well-educated persons, whether they are authoritarian or not, simply know enough not to agree with the obviously biased statements on the F Scale.

Another problem is that the F Scale tests only for *right-wing* (fascist) authoritarianism and fails to identify *left-wing* authoritarianism. Yet there is ample evidence of exaggerated submission to authority in revolutionary and communist movements; aggression and sadism practiced by left-wing authoritarians against the hated outgroup—the "bourgeoisie"; rigidity, toughness, and an orientation toward power among revolutionaries; extreme cynicism toward society among leftists, as well as conspiratorial views about politics; and rigid conformity to stereotyped Marxist ideas. Unfortunately, the F Scale equates authoritarianism with only fascist ideas.

As a result of this problem, some researchers have attempted to develop a measure of dogmatism—the degree to which an individual's belief system is open or closed—that taps both right-wing and left-wing intolerance. Excerpts from one version of the D (dogmatism) Scale are shown in table 6–2.

Another criticism is that authoritarianism is *not* really a *complete* and *separate* syndrome; some of the attitudes of authoritarianism are found in individuals who do not exhibit other attitudes of the supposed syndrome. For example, ethnocentricity is frequently encountered in individuals who are not dominant-submissive. Ethnocentric attitudes may be acquired in a family or subculture that is otherwise warm and affectionate. Thus, stable and loving individuals may have ethnocentric, stereotyped views of outgroups, and even harbor suspicion toward them, simply because their culture or subculture has taught them to do so. In other words, ethnocentricity may be part of a culture or subculture, rather than a component of a personality syndrome. The same may be true of superstition, rigidity, and conventionalism.

Despite these reservations, *The Authoritarian Personality*

Table 6–2   Items from the D (Dogmatism) Scale

In this complicated world of ours the only way we can know what's going on
is to rely on leaders or experts who can be trusted.
Most people just don't know what's good for them.
Of all the different philosophies which exist in this world there is probably
only one which is correct.
The highest form of government is a democracy and the highest form of
democracy is a government run by those who are most intelligent.
The main thing in life is for a person to want to do something important.
I'd like it if I could find someone who would tell me how to solve my per-
sonal problems.
It is only when a person devotes himself to an ideal or cause that life
becomes meaningful.
Most people just don't give a "damn" for others.
To compromise with our political opponents is dangerous because it usually
leads to the betrayal of our own side.
While I don't like to admit this even to myself, my secret ambition is to
become a great man, like Einstein, or Beethoven, or Shakespeare.
Even though freedom of speech for all groups is a worthwhile goal, it is un-
fortunately necessary to restrict the freedom of certain political groups.
It is better to be a dead hero than to be a live coward.

Source: V. C. Troldahl and F. A. Powell, "A Short-Form Dogmatism Scale," *Social Forces* 44 (1965): 211–14.

remains one of the most important studies of the relationship between power and personality. It provides us with invaluable insight
into the psychological mechanisms by which some individuals adjust
themselves to power and authority.

BEHAVIORISM AND LEARNING THEORY

Behavioral psychology is heavily indebted to learning theory or,
more precisely, stimulus-response (SR) theory. It is not an overstate-
ment to say that rats and other animals have had more to do with
shaping this theory than humans; SR theory grew out of experimental
laboratory studies with animals. Academic psychology is based
largely on SR theory; most college courses in psychology are oriented
toward this approach. Behavioral psychology asserts that the goal of
psychologists should be to study *behavior* by employing the same
scientific tests as the natural sciences. Behavioral psychologists dis-
count Freudian notions about the mind or the personality, which can-

Drawing by S. Gross; © 1978 The New Yorker Magazine, Inc.

not be directly observed. For the behaviorists, one is what one does; personality *is* behavior, a pattern of learned, reinforced responses.

The founder of modern stimulus-response theory was the famous Russian physiologist Ivan Petrovich Pavlov (1849–1936), who had already won a Nobel Prize for his studies of digestive glands before he undertook his landmark experiments with salivating dogs. Pavlov's early experiments established the notion of *conditioning*. Saliva flows when meat is placed in a dog's mouth. If a bell is continually sounded just a moment before the meat is placed in its mouth, the dog will soon begin to salivate merely upon hearing a bell even if the meat is not given. Dogs do not normally salivate at the sound of a bell, so such a response is a *conditioned response*. The bell and the meat have become associated in the dog's mind by their occurring together—that is, their "contiguity."

The SR linkage   The learning process is a bit more complex than it first appears. To establish a linkage between a conditioned stimulus and response, there must be a *drive, a cue, a response, and reinforcement*. Learning depends on the establishment of this SR linkage. In simple terms, in order to learn, one must want something as a result of one's action (*reinforcement*). For example, for a rat that is placed in a box and given electric shocks through a wire grid floor, reinforcement is the relief of pain. Pain provides the *drive*, which is the first factor that must be present if learning is to occur. Hunger, thirst or curiosity may also provide the drive to learn. In our example, the electric shocks that the rat receives are accompanied by a buzzer. The buzzer provides the *cue*, the stimulus that is associated with the response. The stimulus may be visual (objects, colors, lights, designs, printed words) or auditory (bells, whistles, spoken words) or related to any of the other senses. Of course, for a response to be linked to a cue, a response must first occur. A critical stage in the learning process is the production of the *appropriate response*. The rat experiencing an electric shock and hearing the buzzer will make a variety of responses; eventually it may pull on the lever that turns off the current. The particular response that satisfies the drive is likely to recur the next time the same situation is encountered. Learning takes place gradually, not so much through "trial and error" as through "trial and success." The rat's first success in pulling the lever will be an accident. After several shocking experiences, however, the rat will learn to pull the lever immediately to stop the current.

The key to the learning process is the *reinforcement* of the appropriate behavior. Reinforcement occurs each time the behavior is accompanied by reduction in the drive. The cue itself will eventually elicit the same response as the original drive. Thus, the rat will pull the lever when it hears the sound of the buzzer whether it is shocked or not. In this way, a previously neutral stimulus (the buzzer) becomes a *secondary drive*, or a *conditioned stimulus*, the organism having learned to respond to it in a particular way.

When a particular conditioned stimulus (the buzzer) gains the capacity to elicit a response because of its being associated with a conditioned stimulus (electric shock), other stimuli that are similar to the conditioned stimuli also tend to produce the same response. Thus, any sound similar to a buzzer may cause the rat to pull the lever. This is called *stimulus generalization*. (A related idea is *response generalization*.)

Stimulus generalization

The strength of the SR linkage depends on (1) the strength of the original drive, (2) the closeness of the drive reduction to the response, and (3) the number of consistently reinforced trials. Thus, the combination of a strong shock, the quick elimination of the shock after the rat pulls the lever, and a large number of trials makes a well-trained rat. Learned behavior can be eliminated by *counterconditioning*— that is, a rat that has learned to pull a lever at the sound of a buzzer can also unlearn this behavior, if a shock is continued even after it pulls the lever.

Higher-order learning

Higher-order learning takes place when an organism establishes elaborate, complex, and abstract linkages between stimulus and response. Higher-order conditioning occurs, for example, when a child learns to associate the written word *bell* spelled on a card with the sound of a bell. Cues become stimuli that provoke a response, which in turn becomes a cue to still another response. Certainly *language* can be viewed as an abstract set of cues. By labeling and naming events, things, and experiences, people can increase their powers of stimulus generalization and discrimination.

Thinking itself may be the tracing out of elaborate and abstract series of linkages between cues and responses. We substitute mental cue-producing responses (thoughts) for overt behavior. It is possible through a series of thoughts to begin at a goal situation and work backward to identify the correct instrumental response. This higher-order learning substitutes for the direct response. Indeed, to think, we must first learn to inhibit or delay direct responses. Without such inhibition or delay, higher-order learning would not have an opportunity to function.

Behavioral therapy   In recent years, behavioral psychologists have come out of the laboratory to engage in some types of treatment for mental disorders. Behaviorists define disorders in terms of the undesirable behaviors that are exhibited. Behavioral psychologists seldom talk about oral or anal personalities or Oedipus complexes; they talk in terms of *functional* (desirable) and *dysfunctional* (undesirable) behaviors. They believe that neurotic behavior has been learned—generally by inconsistent use of rewards and punishment. (Hungry rats that are shocked when they pull a lever that previously produced food develop symptoms similar to "nervous breakdowns"!) Undesirable behaviors can be extinguished by withholding rewards or by punishment. Neurotic behavior can be unlearned by the same combination of principles by which it was taught. Behavioral psychotherapy establishes a set of conditions by which neurotic habits are unlearned and nonneurotic habits learned. The behavioral therapist is regarded as a kind of teacher and the patient as a learner. Thus, the behavioral therapist may reward patients in mental hospitals for good behavior with tokens to be used to buy small luxuries. A therapist of this school believes that smokers can learn avoidance reaction by having thick, obnoxious cigarette smoke blown in their faces; or that bed wetters can unlearn their habit by sleeping on a wired blanket that produces a mild shock when it becomes wet. Even repression (viewed by the behaviorists as "learned nonthinking") can be overcome by forcing individuals to confront situations, events, or experiences they have repressed.

B. F. SKINNER
The Control of Human Behavior

Power is the capacity to control human behavior. What if behavioral science learns to control human behavior and develops a "behavioral technology" to do so? Who will apply this technology and for what purposes? Will the behavioral scientist acquire the ultimate power in society?

Behavioral conditioning and a utopian society

Behavioral psychologist B. F. Skinner believes that society can no longer afford individual freedom and self-determination.[6] He argues that human behavior must be controlled to ensure the survival of humanity and that *behavioral conditioning* must be employed on a massive scale to remold human beings and human culture. In the Skinnerian world, people will be conditioned to be humanitarian rather than selfish, to refrain from polluting, from overpopulating, from rioting, and from making war. Behavioral conditioning will create a utopian society of communal ownership, egalitarian relationships, and devotion to art, music, and literature. Outmoded ideas of individual freedom and self-determination will be discarded in favor of a scientifically designed culture that will condition people to be "good."

Skinner believes that the freedom and dignity of an autonomous human being are "illusions" anyhow. All behavior is determined by prior conditioning. The apparent freedom of human beings is merely inconspicuous control: A permissive government is simply relying on other sources of control—family, church, schools, values, ideologies. If people behave well without government control, it is because they are being controlled by these other agencies. There is, however, ample evidence—war, crime, poverty, racism—that existing control mechanisms are inadequate for survival. Behavioral conditioning replaces imperfect and haphazard control methods with a more effective technology of behavioral control. *Brainwashing* is attacked by scholars who otherwise support changing people's minds by less obvious control mechanisms. Yet, according to Skinner, brainwashing is an effective means of accomplishing behavioral modification.

> A common technique is to build up a strong aversive condition, such as hunger or lack of sleep, and, by alleviating it, to reinforce any behavior which "shows a positive attitude" toward a political or religious system. A favorable "opinion" is built up simply by reinforcing favorable statements.[7]

Skinner believes that all attitudes are developed in this way; the only difference is that formal behavioral conditioning appears obvious and conspicuous.

Skinner developed his ideas through a lifetime of laboratory research on behavioral conditioning. He is the inventor of the famous "Skinner box," a soundproof enclosure with a food dispenser that can be operated by a rat pressing a lever or a pigeon pecking at a bar. Skinner has long been preoccupied with the ideas of conditioning and control:

> I've had only one idea in my life—a true idée fixe. To put it as bluntly as possible—the idea of having my own way. "Control" expresses it. The control of human behavior. In my early experimental days it was a frenzied, selfish desire to dominate. I remember the rage I used to feel when a prediction went awry. I could have shouted at the subjects of my experiments, "Behave, damn you! Behave as you ought!"[8]

Skinner pioneered in the development of teaching machines and programmed instruction, which employ conditioning principles by reinforcing correct answers with a printed statement that the student's response is correct.

Can behavioral conditioning be used on a massive scale? Skinner believes it can. Social science has been slowed, he thinks, because of its concentration on states of mind, feelings, and traits. "Unable to understand how or why the person we see behaves as he does, we attribute his behavior to the person inside." Mistakenly we believe that the individual "initiates, originates, and creates" and that the individual is autonomous. But in fact human behavior is a product of conditioning. "Behavior is shaped and maintained by its consequences. Once this fact is recognized, we can formulate the interaction between the organism and environment in a much more comprehensive way." Behavior that operates on the environment to produce consequences (*operant behavior*) can be modified by arranging environments in which specific consequences are contingent upon it. In short, according to Skinner, the environment can be designed so that "good" behavior is reinforced and "bad" behavior extinguished.

Criticisms of Skinner's utopia

Although arranging effective reinforcements in a laboratory setting is sometimes very complicated, it is far more complex in the real world. Skinner does not provide much specific information on how behavioral technology is to be employed. So the first problem with Skinner's world is that it may be unworkable.

Still more serious dilemmas of power are raised by Skinner's proposals. Who is to determine what is "good" and "bad" behavior? What standards will be used? Who decides what constitutes pleasure and pain and reward and punishment? In Skinner's utopia, immense power would be placed in the hands of the behavioral scientist who designs the culture. Skinner's utopia, although benevolent, is totalitarian. Can the behavioral scientist always be trusted to be "good"? How can the power entrusted in the scientist be checked if the scientist has full capacity to manipulate human behavior? Moreover, what kind of human beings would be produced under a system that manipulates behavior, choices, tastes, and desires? If we believe that individual freedom and dignity are essential components of humanity, then behavioral conditioning on a massive scale is dehumanizing. Giving up freedom and dignity to achieve a secure, comfortable, unpolluted, egalitarian world may be too high a price to pay.

SOCIAL PSYCHOLOGY— THE SELF IN RELATION TO OTHERS

Social psychology is primarily concerned wiith interpersonal interactions—how the individual interacts with others. The social psychologist studies the individual as a whole person, interacting with the environment, rather than studying particular responses, behaviors, or reflexes. Many social psychologists are critical of the "reductionism" of behavioral psychology—the tendency to reduce individual behavior to a series of stimulus-response linkages. Social psychology is strongly influenced by early "Gestalt" psychologists, who argued that the whole person is an entity that cannot be understood by breaking it into sensory elements. (The German word *Gestalt* means "whole," "pattern," or "configuration.")

Interpersonal interaction

Social psychologists view *interpersonal interaction* as the critical determinant of personality development. Indeed, an individual develops an awareness of *self* only by interaction with the environment. The newborn infant cannot distinguish its own body from the outer world. It acquires an identity—a sense of self—only by moving out into the world and relating to other people. As the infant observes and responds to its mother, she becomes a meaningful object, bringing pleasure, frustration, pain, and so on. The infant becomes aware of itself only in relation to others. An infant who is totally ignored withdraws to a corner of its crib, does not talk or develop in any way, and withers away physiologically and psychologically. The emergence of self-identity requires interpersonal interaction; without others there is no self.

Socialization and roles

The process by which an individual internalizes the values, attitudes, and judgments of others is called *socialization*. By *interacting* with others, people come to understand what is expected of them and *internalize* these expectations as part of their personalities. George Herbert Mead conceived the notion of *roles* to explain how the individual internalizes the expectations of others and acquires the values of society. The essential process in the development of self is the individual's taking on the roles of others.

Years ago Charles H. Cooley described the self as a *system of ideas drawn from the social world*. The "looking-glass" self is a product of:

The "looking-glass" self

1. Our image of how we appear to others. We all try to see how we are regarded by others—how our actions are viewed and interpreted.
2. Our image of the judgment of others. We each imagine how others are evaluating us.
3. Our self-feeling. We all react to our perceptions of others' judgments with feelings of pride, shame, guilt, self-esteem, self-hate, and so forth.

In short, our self-conception derives from *interaction* with others from infancy through adulthood.

Through interaction with its parents, the child learns that certain sounds—such as "Mama" and "Daddy"—gain favorable attention. The child begins to repeat these sounds because of the response they evoke in others, and in this way begins to learn language. Children also learn that the things they do are meaningful to those around them, and thus they develop a sense of *self*. Infants who are ignored fail to develop either language or self-identity. Later the small child at play tries on a variety of *roles*—"mother," "father," "fireman," "soldier"—and increases self-realization in the process. Even such basic social roles as male and female may be viewed as a product of socialization rather than biology. Masculine and feminine traits develop through the child's internalization of the expectations of others and through role playing. Schools, games, and group activities provide more and more role-playing opportunities. Of course, not all of the "others" in one's life are equally influential in shaping self-identity; each person has some *significant others* whose judgments carry more weight than the judgments of others. As socialization continues, knowledge of roles and attitudes of others becomes more generalized. We gradually unify and consolidate the many roles we have played into a generalized self-conception. At this point the mature personality emerges.

But the self never stops changing. Every interpersonal interaction has an impact on self-identity. "It is perhaps fair to say that every time a man reacts to his environment he becomes a permanently changed man—be it ever so slight."[9] Throughout life everyone is part of a social "field." The German social psychologist Kurt Lewin extends the idea of self to include the individual's interactions with a field of forces in social situations. Since the field is constantly changing, the individual's behavior is too. Lewin employed the term *life space* to refer to the characteristics of the environment that determine the behavior of an individual. The life space includes *past* as well as *present social experiences*. Even hermits carry with them into the wilderness memories of interpersonal relationships, which continue to influence their personalities.

Life space

Over time, an individual acquires a *distinctive pattern of interpersonal response traits*—relatively consistent and stable dispositions to respond in a distinctive way toward others. These interpersonal response traits constitute the *personality*. They represent the sum of one's socialization, one's role experiences, one's history of successes and failures with various interpersonal responses. Table 6–3 presents twelve interpersonal response traits.

Interpersonal response traits

Many social psychologists believe that interpersonal-interaction theory provides a basis for the treatment of personality disorders.

Table 6–3   Some Interpersonal Response Traits

Role Dispositions

Ascendance *(social timidity)*[1]: defends one's rights; does not mind being conspicuous; is not self-reticent; is self-assured; forcefully puts self forward.

Dominance *(submissiveness):* assertive; self-confident; power-oriented; tough; strong-willed; order-giving or directive leader.

Social initiative *(social passivity):* organizes groups; does not stay in background; makes suggestions at meetings; takes over leadership.

Independence *(dependence):* prefers to do own planning, to work things out in own way; does not seek support or advice; emotionally self-sufficient.

Sociometric Dispositions

Acceptance of others *(rejection of others):* nonjudgmental in attitude toward others; permissive; believing and trustful; overlooks weaknesses and sees best in others.

Sociability *(unsociability):* participates in social affairs; likes to be with people; outgoing.

Friendliness *(unfriendliness):* genial, warm; open and approachable; approaches other persons easily; forms many social relationships.

Sympathy *(lack of sympathy):* concerned with the feelings and wants of others; displays kindly, generous behavior; defends underdog.

Expressive Dispositions

Competitiveness *(noncompetitiveness):* sees every relationship as a contest—other people are rivals to be defeated; self-aggrandizing; noncooperative.

Aggressiveness *(nonaggressiveness):* attacks others directly or indirectly; shows defiant resentment of authority; quarrelsome; negativistic.

Self-consciousness *(social poise):* embarrassed when entering a room after others are seated; suffers excessively from stage fright; hesitates to volunteer in group discussions; bothered at work when people watch; feels uncomfortable if different from others.

Exhibitionism *(self-effacement):* is given to excess and ostentation in behavior and dress; seeks recognition and applause; shows off and behaves in odd ways to attract attention.

---

[a]Opposite trait appears in parentheses.

Causes of personality disorder

They define an *integrated personality* as one in which the individual plays fairly well-defined and stable roles that are not incompatible or conflicting and that are consistent with the values of the groups and culture in which the individual lives. *Personality disorganization* occurs when people find themselves in conflicting roles. Most people can handle mildly conflicting roles, such as being mother and office worker simultaneously; but serious role conflicts, such as an inability to fully assume either a male or a female identification, create deeper problems. Another source of personality disorganization may be an abrupt change in roles—caused, for example, by the loss of a job by a breadwinner, the loss of a wife or husband by a devoted spouse, a change from rural to urban living, even war and natural disaster. Failure to be adequately "socialized" in the first place is another recognized source of personality disorder—for example, the adult who exhibits childlike behavior, or adolescents who cannot "find themselves," that is, find mature responsible roles for themselves in society. *Desocialization* occurs when an individual, encountering consistent defeat and frustration in interpersonal situations, withdraws from contacts with others. Thus, social psychologists tend to view mental disorders in terms of people's relationships to their social environment—whether they are well adjusted and capable of functioning in a socially acceptable fashion.

THE "OTHER-DIRECTED" PERSON

Social psychology and power relationships

Interpersonal-interaction theory approaches power as an attribute of interpersonal relationships. Through the process of socialization, one "internalizes" the expectations of significant others in one's life. Without the ability to interact with others—both to exercise power over others and to respond to their needs and desires—one loses one's sense of significance and self-identity. *Powerlessness*, then, can be viewed as a *threat to individual identity*. Modern mass urban society—with its weakened family, community, religion, and social group ties—may increase the individual's sense of powerlessness. In the absence of meaningful social interaction, people search for synthetic ties to replace the ones lost in the process of modernization. They become *other-directed*—that is, *decreasingly* reliant on their own consciences and *increasingly* dependent upon other people for their ideas and actions. The other-directed person is easily manipulated by the mass media, by demagogic leaders, and by mass political movements.

Riesman's social characters and sources of control

It was David Riesman who, in expressing concern about the relative powerlessness of the modern individual in mass society, identified three broad social characters, in terms of the source of control over personal behavior: *tradition-directed, inner-directed,* and *other-directed*. The *tradition-directed* character is found in traditional societies, where obedience to the family and adherence to traditional ways of life are dominant values. Things that are old and long established are considered good. Traditional norms are the dominant guide for individual behavior. Traditional societies existed in the Western world through the Middle Ages and still exist in many rural areas of the non-Western world.

The *inner-directed* character is associated with the rise of Protestantism and capitalism. Parents implant general values and norms in the child at an early age. Mature, inner-directed adults have internalized these values and norms and use them to guide their behavior throughout life, regardless of changing conditions or the values of others around them. The values of the inner-directed person in the Western world generally include respect for work and self-sufficiency, a desire for personal achievement and production, strong moral restraints on sexual behavior, devotion to family and children, the postponement and sacrifice of pleasure for future well-being, and emphasis on personal savings and the accumulation of wealth. But the important aspect of the inner-directed person is an internalized "gyroscope" for behavioral guidance. Inner-directed people are punished by feelings of guilt when they violate these inner norms.

Riesman believes that modern mass society, particularly twentieth-century urban America, is producing an *other-directed* character type. For the other-directed person, social control lies *outside*, rather than inside, the individual. As parental control weakens and family and church influences wane, the individual seeks guides for behavior in the approval of peers—classmates, friends, groups, society at large. Other-directed persons have few internal restraints upon their behavior, and so are guided primarily by what is fashionable, what is popular, what others are doing. Instead of guilt, they experience anxiety when their behavior does not conform to group expectations. Their parents want them to be popular, and even the school curriculum emphasizes getting along with others—"life adjustment." The mass media, the advertising industry, and the clothing, music, entertainment, and recreation industries reinforce pressures on youth to be fashionable, "hip," "with it." Other-directed adults care more about what their friends and neighbors think than about what they want for themselves and their children. They are "organization men," seeking security in large corporate or governmental bureaucracies. Their values constantly shift as conditions change and social values fluctuate. They are more concerned with leisure and consumption than work and production, less "hung up" about sexual standards, more interested in the immediate "now" than in planning for the future, and oriented toward spending money rather than saving it.

Other-directed people are powerless in the face of group pressures and their own need for group approval. Conformity results from the need to belong and to be accepted by a group. Individual freedom and dignity and self-reliance are submerged in the necessity for conformity and social approval.

HUMANISTIC PSYCHOLOGY—
THE INNATE HUMAN POTENTIAL

Humanistic psychology, like social psychology, focuses upon the *whole* person, rather than upon particular defensive structures or behavioral responses. However, while social psychology focuses upon the process of socialization as the key factor in determining personality, humanistic psychology emphasizes the individual's innate potential for development, the human need to fulfill the "self." According to the humanists, the goal of psychology should be to understand human beings and human experience rather than to predict or control human behavior.

Humanistic psychology, which has been called the "third force" in psychology, came into its own around 1960. It represented a reaction against behaviorism and psychoanalytic theory, the two forces that dominated psychology at that time. Humanistic psychology rejects behaviorism's insistence on using the strictly scientific, objective, value-free methods of the natural sciences. It views behaviorism as lacking in concern for the meaningfulness of human experience; behaviorism, with its narrow focus on behavior itself and its disregard of the subjective human experience, is unable to explain the totality of the person. Humanistic psychology also rejects the Freudian emphasis on the biological needs, or drives, of the body and the defensive structure of the personality. For the humanists, the basic "self" is not a negative force that must be repressed or controlled; the

The "good" self

self is good and has the innate and unique capacity to grow and develop and expand its creativity.

Humanists believe that human beings are unique among animals because they alone have psychological, as well as biological, needs. Psychological needs include the need for safety and security, for friendships and intimacies, for self-esteem and self-expression. The

The need to "self-actualize"

highest psychological need is the need for "self-actualization." Human beings are internally motivated to fulfill these needs, to realize their potential; they have an innate propensity toward self-actualization. Personality development is the continuous process of positive growth in search of fulfilling ever higher needs, the ultimate goal being self-actualization.

"I think that you are potentially a marvellous person. I think I am, too."
Drawing by Handelsman; © 1978 The New Yorker Magazine, Inc.

Factors in personality development

Self-actualization requires first of all that individuals be aware of their own feelings; without such self-awareness, they can never know themselves, let alone realize their innate potential. In addition, self-actualization is affected by social, or environmental, factors. Like the social psychologists, humanistic psychologists believe that an individual's concept of "self" is in large measure socially determined, that others in one's world have an important impact on the way one feels about oneself. Although all people have the innate need to realize their potential, certain types of "socialization" experiences may prevent the individual from achieving self-actualization. If one is fully and unconditionally accepted as a person, then one develops positive feelings about oneself; if, on the other hand, acceptance is contingent on certain types of behavior, then one may experience anxiety and the need to function defensively, to close oneself off from feelings and a subjective experience of the world. This type of functioning interferes with the process of self-actualization.

Humanistic therapies

Because of its orientation toward a "good" human nature and its emphasis on the need for openness and self-awareness, humanistic psychology does not talk in terms of "personality disorder" or "mental illness." Nor does it concern itself with past experiences; the primary focus is on "the here and now." People are not "sick" but simply in need of ridding themselves of anxiety and the defensive functioning that closes them off from subjective experience. The various forms of therapy that fall under the umbrella of humanistic psychology range from individual psychotherapy to consciousness-raising and encounter groups, sensitivity training, biofeedback, and meditation. What these therapies have in common is a focus on promoting self-acceptance and an openness in experiencing the world. Positive personality change is accomplished by bringing people into touch with their feelings, by helping them to become accepting of themselves and others, and by showing them how to assume full responsibility for the direction of their lives. This, in turn, opens the way to self-actualization.

POWERLESSNESS AND SELF-ACTUALIZATION

May's concept of powerlessness

There is a common adage that "power corrupts, and absolute power corrupts absolutely." It reflects our negative view of power, and our association of power with abuse. But the distinguished psychologist Rollo May, whose contributions to the humanistic movement are highly significant, contends that power is a fundamental aspect of the life process. Indeed, he believes that *powerlessness* corrupts the human personality by robbing the individual of a sense of meaning and significance.

Functions of power

Rollo May's argument is that power occurs in an individual's life in five functional forms.[10] The first is the *power to be*. The word *power* comes from the Latin root meaning "to be able." The newborn infant must have the power to make others respond to its needs—it cries and waves its arms violently as signs of its discomfort. An infant who cannot get a response from others fails to develop as a separate personality. *Power as self-affirmation* is the recognition of one's own worth and significance in life. Some power is essential for self-esteem and self-belief. *Power as self-assertion* makes it clear who we are and what we believe. It gives us the potential to react to attack and protect ourselves from becoming victims. Power also occurs in everyone's life as *aggression*—thrusting out against a person or thing seen as an adversary. The constructive aspects of aggression include cutting through barriers to initiate relationships; confronting another person not with the intent to hurt but in order to penetrate that individual's consciousness; and actualizing one's own self in a hostile environment. The destructive side of aggression, of course, includes thrusting out to inflict injury and the taking of power simply to increase one's own range of control. Finally, power occurs as *violence*. May believes that violence is an attempt to exercise power. Violence may result from a failure at self-affirmation or self-assertion, or it may accompany aggression. Nonetheless, it can be regarded as functional to the individual if there is no other way for that person to gain a significance in life.

It is May's belief that modern mass society impairs the individual's self-esteem and self-worth. The feeling of personal powerlessness is widespread.

> To admit our own individual feelings of powerlessness—that we cannot influence many people; that we count for little; that the values to which our parents devoted their lives are to us insubstantial and worthless; that we feel ourselves to be "faceless others," insignificant to other people and therefore not worth much to ourselves—this is indeed, difficult to admit.[11]

He believes that much irrational violence—riots, assassinations, senseless murders—is a product of feelings of powerlessness.

From the point of view of humanistic psychology, the ultimate power of the individual might be regarded as the ability to achieve self-actualization. Abraham Maslow, one of the foremost spokesmen of the humanistic movement, devised a "hierarchy of needs" that distinguishes between the "higher" and "lower" needs that are inherent in each individual. The highest need is, of course, self-actualization. However, before one can fulfill the higher needs, one must first satisfy the lower needs. Individual behavior at any point in time is determined by the individual's strongest need at that time. The higher needs are reflective of later stages of personality development. Figure 6–1 shows Maslow's formulation of the hierarchy of needs. (Note that the peak of an earlier main class of needs must be passed before the next "higher" need can begin to assume a dominant role. Note also that as psychological development takes place, the number and variety of needs increase.)

Maslow's hierarchy of needs

At the base of Maslow's hierarchy are *physiological needs* (food, clothing, shelter). These basic needs must be satisfied first. Once they are, other levels of needs become important and begin to motivate individual behavior. Above physiological needs are the needs for *safety and security*. These needs may not always be apparent to the individual; they may be subconscious and not easily identified. A need for safety or security may become highly motivating depending on early childhood experiences. The insecure child may later prefer occupations that offer insurance, retirement, protection from layoffs, and a predictable life. In contrast, the adult who had a secure childhood may prefer occupations that offer continuing challenges to imagination and ingenuity and that penalize failure.

Once physiological and safety needs are fairly well-satisfied,

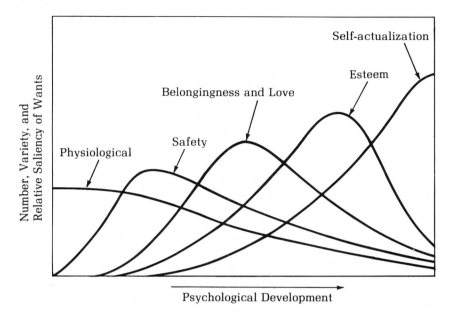

Figure 6–1 Maslow's Hierarchy of Needs, Showing Progressive Changes in Number, Variety, and Relative Importance of Needs

social needs become dominant. The individual, according to Maslow, now seeks group acceptance, friendships, and intimacies. Indeed, studies of group dynamics suggest that group approval may occasionally become so important that it tends to override realistic appraisal of other sources of action. The individual may actually become a victim of group pressures in his or her search to satisfy social needs and find acceptance in life.

Assuming that an individual's social needs are reasonably satisfied, a fourth need comes into prominence—*esteem*. Failure to understand this need may lead parents to complain: "We've given our child everything—a good home, stable family, all the things he ever asked for, even our own time and assistance—yet he is still dissatisfied." However, it may be that it is precisely because children have had the three basic needs sufficiently satisfied that a fourth need emerges—recognition of worth as an individual. Like security or social needs, the need for personal esteem appears in a variety of forms; a search for *recognition* is one manifestation of the need for personal esteem.

Evidence from studies of large corporate and governmental organizations suggests that recognition or symbols of prestige may be more important in motivating management employees than money. Most of the employees make enough money to satisfy their physiological and security needs, and their social needs may be satisfied in relationships with family, work group, neighborhood, church, and so on. But their job performance suffers when they feel they do not receive personal recognition for their work by their supervisors. Their salary carries some prestige value, but often an impressive sounding title (for example, "vice-president for operations," "director of planning," or "deputy secretary") is even more important. In business organizations it is frequently remarked that "a name on the door, and a rug on the floor" is the key to recognition. Many individuals will sacrifice salary to achieve these symbols of esteem.

When these four needs are more or less satisfied, we can expect to witness the emergence of Maslow's fifth and final need—the need for *self-actualization*. It is not always clear what self-actualization really is. According to Maslow, "Self-actualizing people are, without one single exception, involved in a cause outside of their own skin, in something outside of themselves."[12]

Despite problems in defining self-actualization, it does seem true that at some point in life—frequently in the late thirties or early forties—many individuals feel a vague sense of dissatisfaction. This "mid-life crisis" may be related to the need for self-actualization. Individuals who have provided well for themselves and their families, who face no serious threats to their security, who are well accepted by their family, friends, and neighbors, and who have won recognition in their field of work may nonetheless feel that something is "missing." These individuals may have been content while striving to achieve their positions in life, but once they have achieved them, they ask, "Is that all there is?" According to Maslow, these individuals have reached a point where they must turn to their fifth and final need, self-actualization.

CASE STUDY
Authority and Obedience:
The "Shocking" Experiments

A significant theme in the study of human behavior has been the reaction of individuals who were commanded to inflict pain, injury, or death upon others. An estimated 6 million Jews were murdered in Nazi death camps in World War II—men, women, and children—by individuals who frequently claimed they were "only carrying out orders."

"Authority," as we have noted, is a form of power that is perceived as legitimate by society. Doubtlessly, throughout the ages, more pain, injury, and death has been inflicted on humanity by "authorities" than by recognized "criminals." The criminal's claim to power is sanctioned only by a gun, knife, fist, or fraud—not by "legitimacy." But what are the psychological mechanisms that provide legitimacy to the exercise of power, and how far will ordinary Americans go in inflicting pain, injury, or even death if they believe they are acting legitimately?

These are some of the questions explored by psychologist Stanley Milgram in a series of experiments at Yale University in which experimenters told subjects to administer electric shocks to other people.[13] The subjects in these experiments were all adult males of various ages representing a cross section of occupations. Each subject was told that he was participating in a "learning experiment"; the "learner" (actually an associate of the experimenter) was strapped into an "electric chair" and given a list of questions and answers to memorize. The subject was told by the experimenter to administer an ever increasing electric shock every time the "learner" made a mistake. Thirty separate voltage levers were used with signs reading from 15 to 450 volts. Signs also announced that the shocks ranged from "Slight Shock" to "Danger: Severe Shock." Actually the "learner" did not receive any shocks at all, but the subject did not know this. Moreover, the subject could watch the "learner" through a window and hear any sounds the "learner" made. Starting with 75 volts the "learner" begins to twitch, grunt, and groan with each shock. At 150 volts the "learner" demands that he be let out of the experiment. At 180 volts the "learner" screams that he can no longer stand the pain. At 300 volts the "learner" slumps over, refuses to provide any more answers to questions, and appears in dire distress. In response to each of the acts by the "learner," the experimenter tells the subject who is administering the shocks: "You have no choice, you must go on!"

Before the experiments began, Professor Milgram asked forty psychiatrists at a leading medical school to predict the behavior of most subjects; specifically these psychiatrists were asked to predict when the subject would break off the experiment and refuse to administer any more pain to the "learner." These psychiatrists predicted that *most* subjects would refuse to continue beyond the 150-volt level, and that only one-tenth would continue to the full 450-volt level. However, the shocking results of the "shocking" experiments were that 62 percent of the subjects obeyed the experimenter's commands completely and proceeded to administer the highest shock level on the board (450 volts). Only 38 percent of the subjects broke off the experiment when the "learner" groaned, screamed, demanded to be released, and finally pretended to be near death.

Many subjects expressed concern about their "learner" victims but continued the experiment anyway:

150 volts. "You want me to keep going?"

165 volts. "That guy is hollering in there. He's liable to have a heart attack. You want me to go on?"

180 volts. "He can't stand it. I'm not going to kill that man in there! You hear him hollering. He's hollering. He can't stand it. What if something happens to him? . . . I mean who is going to take the responsibility if something happens to that gentleman?" (The experimenter says he will accept responsibility.)

195 volts. "You see he's hollering. Hear that? Gee, I don't know." (The experimenter says, "The experiment requires that you go on.")

210 volts.

225 volts.

240 volts. "Aw, no. You mean I've got to keep going up the scale? No, sir. I'm not going to kill that man! I'm not going to give him 450 volts!" (The experimenter repeats, "The experiment requires that you go on.") The subject proceeds to the highest shock level, 450 volts.

One point made in these experiments is that the subjects were not simply sadistic. They were average men selected from all walks of life. Most objected verbally to what they were doing at some point in the experiment. But in the context of *authority* (an experimenter who told them to continue no matter what happened) and *legitimacy* (the idea that they were participating in a scientific experiment at a prestigious university), these individuals performed acts of brutality that they would not otherwise consider doing.

Psychologist Milgram concluded:

> With numbing regularity good people were seen to knuckle under to the demands of authority and perform actions that were callous and severe. Men who are in everyday life responsible and decent were seduced by trappings of authority, by the control of their perceptions, and by uncritical acceptance of the experimenter's definition of the situation, into performing harsh acts.
>
> What is the limit of obedience? . . .[14]

It is not clear how far we can generalize from these experiments. But it is certainly not farfetched to suspect that under the right conditions otherwise normal people can become unusually cruel. If those who are invested with authority and legitimacy encourage sadistic behavior toward others, we can reasonably expect that a substantial proportion of the population will engage in such behavior. Another holocaust is not impossible.

NOTES

1. Gordon Allport, *Personality* (New York: Holt, 1937), pp. 24–54.
2. William McDougall, quoted in Gardner Lindzey, ed., *Handbook of Social Psychology*, 5 vols. (Reading, Mass.: Addison-Wesley, 1954) vol. I, p. 144.
3. T. W. Adorno et al., *The Authoritarian Personality* (New York: Harper. 1950).
4. Ibid., p. 482.
5. Ibid., pp. 759–72.
6. B. F. Skinner, *Beyond Freedom and Dignity* (New York: Knopf, 1971).
7. Ibid., p. 96.
8. *Time*, 20 September 1971, p. 47.

9. David Krech, Richard S. Crutchfield, and Egerton L. Ballachey, *Individual in Society* (New York: McGraw-Hill, 1962), p. 103.

10. Rollo May, *Power and Innocence* (New York: W. W. Norton, 1972).

11. Ibid., p. 21.

12. A. H. Maslow, *The Farther Reaches of Human Nature* (New York: Viking Press, 1971), p. 43.

13. Stanley Milgram, "Some Conditions of Obedience and Disobedience to Authority," *Human Relations* 18, no. 1 (1965):57–75.

14. Ibid., p. 74.

DISCUSSION QUESTIONS

1. Discuss the psychoanalytic (Freudian) view of the determinants of behavior. Identify the three major systems that Freudians believe compose the personality and describe the roles played by each of these systems. Differentiate between normal and neurotic anxiety and describe the functions of identification. Briefly outline Freud's stages of personality development.

2. Discuss the Freudian approach to power relationships. Describe the authoritarian personality. What are some psychoanalytic explanations of the authoritarian personality? Discuss the criticisms of *The Authoritarian Personality* study.

3. How would a behavioral psychologist define personality and the goal of psychology? Describe how a linkage between a conditioned stimulus and response is established. Define *stimulus generalization* and describe how it is related to higher-order learning.

4. Discuss B. F. Skinner's vision of a utopian society and the methods by which Skinner proposes such a society be created. What are some of the difficulties with Skinner's thesis?

5. Describe how a social psychologist would approach the study of personality. Identify the processes that social psychologists believe are critical determinants of personality development. Discuss the meaning of the *looking-glass self; life space;* and *interpersonal response traits.*

6. Describe how social psychology approaches the subject of power relationships. Discuss David Riesman's identification of social characters and their sources of control.

7. Discuss humanistic psychology's view of the individual, Rollo May's formulation of the functions of power, and Abraham Maslow's "hierarchy of needs."

8. Discuss the results of the experiments that psychologist Stanley Milgram carried out at Yale University. What do these results tell us about the power of authority and legitimacy to command obedience? What are the implications of such obedience?

9. If you were interested in becoming a clinical psychologist, which type of therapy do you think you would want to practice—psychoanalytic therapy, behavioral therapy, a therapy based on the principles of interpersonal-interaction theory, or one that uses the approach of humanistic psychology? Describe how the theory you would choose views "personality disorder."

10. Which of the theories studied do you think provides the most cogent view of personality and the relationship between personality and power? Discuss your reasoning, including any criticisms you may have about any of these theories.

SUGGESTED READINGS

T. W. Adorno et al., *The Authoritarian Personality* (New York: Harper, 1950).

Calvin S. Hall, *A Primer of Freudian Psychology* (Cleveland, Ohio: World Publishing, 1954).

Calvin S. Hall and Gardner Lindzey, *Theories of Personality*, 2nd ed. (New York: Wiley, 1970).

David Krech, Richard S. Crutchfield, and Egerton L. Ballachey, *Individual in Society: A Textbook of Social Psychology* (New York: McGraw-Hill, 1962).

Harold Lasswell, *Psychopathology and Politics* (Chicago: University of Chicago Press, 1930).

Abraham Maslow, *Motivation and Personality* (New York: Harper, 1954).

Rollo May, *Power and Innocence* (New York: W. W. Norton, 1972).

David Riesman, *The Lonely Crowd* (New Haven, Conn.: Yale University Press, 1961).

B. F. Skinner, *Beyond Freedom and Dignity* (New York: Knopf, 1971).

Photo from Pictorial Parade by Jim Wells

Photo from Magnum by Cornell Capa

Chapter 7
Power and Government

Those who remember the Watergate affair may find themselves pausing to reflect upon the title of this chapter. As the chief executive of the national government, Richard Nixon sat at what most of us regard as the pinnacle of power in this country; yet he was ultimately forced to resign that power. What factors were powerful enough in themselves to unseat this nation's chief executive? Was it, as many observers believed, the strength of a parchment document—the Constitution—or was it Richard Nixon's own inability to play by the "rules of the game," the boundaries established by consensus of the elite? Or was it perhaps both?

Those questions are the province of political science, and in this chapter we will see what answers political science can provide. After you have read chapter 7, you should be able to:

- discuss the political philosophy that is embodied in the United States Constitution.
- discuss the separation of powers around which our government is structured and the reasons why the Founding Fathers designed it this way.
- describe changes in the structure of governmental power.
- discuss actual political behaviors and processes in America and describe their effect on the exercise of power.

POLITICS, POLITICAL SCIENCE, AND GOVERNMENTAL POWER

A distinguished American political scientist, Harold Lasswell, defined "*politics as who gets what, when, how.*" "The study of politics," he said, "is the study of influence and the influential. The influential are those who get the most of what there is to get. . . . Those who get the most are the *elite*; the rest are *mass*." He went on to define *political science* as "the shaping and sharing of power."

Admittedly, Lasswell's definition of political science is very broad. Indeed, if we accept Lasswell's definition of political science as *the study of power,* then political science includes cultural, economic, social, and personal power relationships—topics we have already discussed in anthropology, economics, sociology, and psychology.

Although many political scientists have accepted Lasswell's challenge to study power in all of its forms in society, most limit the definition of political science to *the study of government and politics.*

What distinguishes *governmental power* from the power of other institutions, groups, and individuals? The power of government, unlike that of other institutions in society, is distinguished by (1) *the legitimate use of physical force* and (2) *coverage of the whole society* rather than only segments of it. Because government decisions extend to the whole of society, and because only government can legitimately use physical force, government has the primary responsibility for maintaining order and for resolving differences that arise *between* segments of society. Thus, government must regulate conflict by establishing and enforcing general rules by which conflict is to be carried on in society, by arranging compromises and balancing interests, and by imposing settlements that the parties in the dispute must accept. In other words, government lays down the "rules of the game" in conflict and competition between individuals, organizations, and institutions within society.

THE CONCERNS OF POLITICAL SCIENCE

Political philosophy

Political scientists ever since Plato have constructed ideal political systems—notions of what a good "polity" should be like. Today we refer to efforts to devise *good* political systems as *political philosophy.* Political philosophy concerns itself with political norms and values—criteria for judging the "rightness" or "wrongness" of governmental structures and actions. In chapter 9 we will discuss political ideologies—liberalism, conservatism, communism, socialism, and fascism—and examine philosophies more closely.

Structures

Political science also concerns itself with describing *the structure of political systems.* Schemes for classifying political systems are as old as the study of politics itself. Aristotle, for example, produced a classification based on two criteria: (1) the number of citizens who could participate in making rules—one, few, or many; and (2) whether the rulers governed in "the common interest" or in their own selfish interest. Aristotle's classification system (table 7–1) included six types of governments. Note that Aristotle believed that "democracy" was a corrupt form of government in which the masses pursued their selfish interests at the expense of the common good. Not

Table 7-1   Aristotle's Classification of Governments

No. of Persons Who Rule	Interests Served	
	Common	Selfish
One	Monarchy	Tyranny
Few	Aristocracy	Oligarchy
Many	Polity	Democracy

until the nineteenth century did the word *democracy* come to have positive connotation.

The German social and political scientist Max Weber also classified political systems, but he focused on their *sources of legitimacy*. He suggested that the authority of governmental leaders can be based on:

Sources of legitimacy

1. *Tradition:* where legitimacy rests on established beliefs in the sanctity of authority and the moral need to obey leaders.
2. *Charisma:* where legitimacy rests on the personal heroic qualities of a particular leader.
3. *Legality:* where legitimacy is based on a commitment to constitutional rules that bind both leaders and the people.

Weber identified these types of authority in a variety of political systems.

Many modern political scientists have attempted to improve on Aristotle's and Weber's simple typologies. For example, two Yale political scientists applied a statistical technique, known as factor analysis, to sixty-eight measured characteristics of 115 countries and "inductively derived" seven major characteristics of political systems:[1]

Characteristics of political systems

1. Access to political participation
   Authoritarian
   Democratic
2. Differentiation of separate political institutions
   Modern
   Undeveloped
3. Consensus about rules governing political systems
   Governmental stability
   Instability, "personalism"

4. Sectionalism
   Western
   Non-Western
5. Legitimation
   Bureaucratic, rule-oriented, developed ideology
   Traditional, personality-oriented, authoritarianism
6. Patterns of interest groupings
   Two-party systems
   Multiparty systems
7. Executive leadership
   Strong
   Weak

Political processes and behaviors

Political scientists are also concerned with *the political processes and behaviors among individuals and groups.* The study of political processes and behaviors goes beyond the study of political philosophy and ideology and the study of political structures. It asks how voters, interest groups, parties, legislators, executives, bureaucrats, judges, and other political actors behave and why. Social scientists who explore these questions are known as *behavioral* political scientists. Behavioral political scientists study the way individuals acquire political values and attitudes and how these values and attitudes shape their political activity; why people vote as they do or choose not to vote at all; how and why interest groups are formed and what influence they have on governments; how and why city councilmen and state and national legislators vote as they do on pieces of legislation; what motivates the actions of mayors, governors, and presidents, and what influences the decisions of judges; what the attitudes and functions of political parties are before and after elections; and so on.

But political philosophy and ideology, the structure of governments, and the behavior of political figures can seldom be studied separately. Discovering how these important areas of study interact is essential for a better understanding of power in society. In our examination of power and government in this chapter, we will first take up the political philosophies that are influential in shaping American government and politics; then consider how power is structured in American government; and finally describe political processes and behaviors in the presidency, Congress, the courts, voters, and political parties. We will conclude with a case study illustrating the involvement of the president with the nation's "establishment." "A Tale of Two Presidents: Watergate and Its Aftermath" describes what happened when President Nixon failed to abide by the rules established

by elite consensus and the reasons why a supposedly "unknown"
Jimmy Carter was able to win the presidency.

JOHN LOCKE
Constitutionalism

The potential power of governments has worried people for a
long time. Indeed, since the earliest recorded history, people have attempted to limit the powers of government, to set standards of
legitimate authority, and to prevent the arbitrary use of governmental
power. Of course, not all people or societies share the belief that governmental power should be limited. *Totalitarianism* is a belief that
the state should be orderly, harmonious, and unified in purpose and
values, and that the power of government should be unlimited and
all-embracing. In a totalitarian state, government exercises unlimited
authority in all segments of life—the economy, education, the church,
the family, and so on.

Constitutionalism   *Constitutionalism* is the belief that governmental power should
be *limited* and *controlled*. A fundamental ideal of constitutionalism—
"a government of laws and not of men"—suggests that those who exercise governmental authority are restricted in their use of it by a
higher law. A *constitution* governs government. A constitution describes the offices and agencies of government, defines their
prerogatives, prescribes how they should function, sets limits on the
authority of government, and protects the freedoms of individual
citizens. In other words, a constitution defines what governmental
authority can and cannot do. A constitution should not be subject to
change by the ordinary acts of government officials; change should
come only through a process of general public consent. Most importantly, a constitution must truly limit and control the exercise of
authority by government; the so-called constitutions of totalitarian
states, which merely describe government offices and agencies but do
not actually limit their powers, are not genuine constitutions.

Natural law   In the eighteenth century the notion of constitutionalism was
associated with the idea of a higher natural law. *Natural law* is based
on human nature and the nature of society: It is immutable and it pro-

vides the standards and guidelines for governmental institutions and human law. Natural law binds both rulers and the ruled. The natural law includes natural rights possessed by all people; these rights are not derived from, or subject to, government but derive from human nature itself and have an independent and unchanging existence. The natural law *limits governments*; more importantly, it limits the power of majorities over individuals. Thus, natural law deprives even *majorities* of the power to violate the *inalienable rights of individuals to life, liberty, and property.*

A famous exponent of the idea of natural law and constitutional government was the English political philosopher John Locke (1632–1704). Perhaps more than anyone else, Locke inspired the political thought of our nation's Founding Fathers in that critical period of American history in which the new nation won its independence and established its constitution. Locke's ideas are written into both the Declaration of Independence and the Constitution of the United States. His writings, particularly his *Essay Concerning Human Understanding* and his *Two Treatises on Civil Government* were widely read in early America and even plagiarized in part by Thomas Jefferson in the Declaration of Independence.

According to Locke, people are essentially rational beings,

capable of self-government and able to participate in political decision making. Locke believed that human beings formed a contract among themselves to establish a government in order to better protect their natural rights, maintain peace, and protect themselves from foreign invasion. The *social contract* that established government made for safe and peaceful living and for the secure enjoyment of one's life, liberty, and property. Thus the ultimate *legitimacy* of government derived from a contract among the people themselves and not from gods or kings. It was based upon the *consent* of the governed. To safeguard their individual rights, the people agreed to be governed.

The social contract

Since government was instituted as a contract to secure the rights of citizens, government itself could not violate individual rights. If government did so, it would dissolve the contract establishing it. Revolution, then, was justified if government was not serving the purpose for which it had been set up. However, according to Locke, revolution was justified only after a long period of abuses by government, not over any minor mismanagement.

Locke expounded upon six primary features of constitutional government: (1) The authority of government must be limited by the purposes and ends for which government is instituted, that is, preservation and protection of the natural rights of the individual; (2) government must conform to the law of nature and cannot violate the inalienable rights to life, liberty, and property; (3) laws must have the expressed or implied consent of the governed; (4) laws must apply equally to all; (5) laws must not be arbitrary or oppressive; and (6) taxes must not be levied without the consent of the people or their representatives.

Thomas Jefferson eloquently expressed Lockean ideals in the Declaration of Independence:

> We hold these truths to be self-evident, that all men are created equal, that they are endowed by their Creator with certain inalienable rights, that among these are life, liberty, and the pursuit of happiness. That to secure these rights, governments are instituted among men, deriving their just powers from the consent of the governed. That whenever any form of government becomes destructive of these ends, it is the right of the people to alter or to abolish it, and to institute new government, laying its foundation on such principles and organizing its powers in such form, as to them shall seem most likely to effect their safety and happiness.

Notice that Jefferson varied slightly from Locke in his description of inalienable rights. While Locke had affirmed the right of the individual to "life, liberty, and *property*," Jefferson substituted the more general idea in his famous formulation of the right to "life, liberty, and the *pursuit of happiness*."

THE MEANING OF DEMOCRACY

Ideal democracy

Ideally, *democracy* means *individual participation* in the decisions that affect one's life. In traditional democratic theory, popular participation has been valued as an opportunity for *individual self-development*. Responsibility for the governing of one's own conduct develops one's character, self-reliance, intelligence, and moral judgment—in short, one's dignity. Even if a benevolent king could govern in the public interest, the classic democrat would reject him. The argument for citizen participation in public affairs is based not upon the policy outcomes it would produce, but on the belief that such involvement is essential to the full development of human capacities.

Procedural democracy

Procedurally, popular participation was to be achieved through *majority rule* and *respect for the rights of minorities*. Self-development means *self-government*, and self-government can be accomplished only by encouraging each individual to contribute to the creation of public policy and by resolving conflicts over public policy through majority rule. Minorities who had had the opportunity to influence policy but whose views had not succeeded in winning majority support would accept the decisions of majorities. In return, majorities would permit minorities to openly attempt to win majority support for their views. Freedom of speech and press, freedom to dissent, and freedom to form opposition parties and organizations are essential to ensure meaningful individual participation. This *freedom of expression* is also necessary for ascertaining what the majority views really are.

Democratic values

The underlying value of democracy is *individual dignity*. Human beings, by virtue of their existence, are entitled to life, liberty, and the pursuit of happiness. Implicit in the democratic notion of *freedom* is the commitment that governmental activity and social control over the individual be kept to a minimum; hence the removal of as many external restrictions, controls, and regulations on the individual as is consistent with the freedom of other citizens.

Another vital aspect of classic democracy is a belief in the *equality* of all people. The Declaration of Independence expresses the conviction that "all men are created equal." The Founding Fathers believed in equality *before the law*, notwithstanding the circumstances of the accused. A person was not to be judged by social position, economic class, creed, or race. Many early democrats also believed in *political equality*—that is, equal opportunity to influence public policy. Political equality is expressed in the concept of "one man, one vote."

Over time, the notion of equality has also come to include *equality of opportunity* in all aspects of American life—social, educational, and economic, as well as political, and encompassing employment, housing, recreation, and public accommodations. All people are to have equal opportunity to develop their individual capacities to their natural limits.

In summary, democratic thinking involves the following ideas:

1. Popular participation in the decisions that shape the lives of individuals in a society.
2. Government by majority rule, with recognition of the rights of minorities to try to become majorities. These rights include the freedoms of speech, press, assembly, and petition and the freedom to dissent, to form opposition parties, and to run for public office.
3. A commitment to individual dignity and the preservation of the liberal values of liberty and property.
4. A commitment to equal opportunity for all to develop their individual capacities.

THE POLITICAL PHILOSOPHY OF THE FOUNDING FATHERS

The Founding Fathers—those fifty-five men who met in the summer of 1787 in Philadelphia to establish a new national government—shared a political philosophy. They agreed with Locke that the fundamental purpose of government was the *protection of liberty and property*. They believed in government by the *consent of the governed*. They believed that the origin of government is an implied *contract* among citizens: People pledged allegiance and obedience to government in return for the protection of their natural rights, the maintenance of peace, and protection from foreign invasion. They believed that the ultimate legitimacy of government (that is, "sovereignty") rested with the people themselves, and not with kings. But they also feared the *tyranny of the majority*—the tendency of the masses to use their majority position to capture powers of government and use these powers to attack individual rights, particularly rights of *property*. Their greatest fear was not that a *minority* would seize control of government and trample property rights but that a *majority* would do so.

"All power to some of the people."

Drawing by Handelsman; © 1971 The New Yorker Magazine, Inc.

Republican government

The Founding Fathers believed in *republican government*, by which they meant representative, responsible, and nonhereditary government. They did not, however, mean mass democracy with direct participation by people in decision making. Rather, they expected the masses to consent to be governed by men of principle and property out of recognition of their abilities, talents, and education. Many of the Founding Fathers felt that men of wealth and property had a greater "stake in society" than the masses and were therefore more entitled to govern. In their opinion the masses should have only a limited part in the selection of government leaders.

Limited government

The Founding Fathers believed in *limited government*. Government should be designed so it would not become a threat to liberty or property. Not only should the Constitution limit the government in its exercise of power but the structure of government itself should prevent the concentration of power. Power should be divided among separate bodies of the government, capable of checking each other in the event that any one branch should pose a threat to liberty or property.

Strong national government

Finally, the Founding Fathers regarded a *strong national government* as a safer repository of power than state and local governments. State and local governments, they thought, were more vulnerable to takeover by propertyless masses than a national government. Thus, at this period in history, American men of property supported a strong national government while elsewhere most champions of the common people supported strong state and local governments.

The compromises that took place in the Constitutional Convention in 1787 were relatively unimportant in comparison to the consensus among the Founding Fathers on fundamentals. Consensus in this elite group in 1787 was profoundly conservative in that it wished to preserve the status quo in the distribution of power and property in America. At the same time, that consensus was radical in comparison with the beliefs of other elites in the world. Most governments adhered to the principle of hereditary monarchy—and a privileged nobility—while American elites were committed to republicanism. Other elites asserted the divine right of kings, while American elites talked about government by the consent of the governed. American elites believed in the equality of human beings with respect to inalienable human rights, while the elites of Europe rationalized and defended a rigid caste system.

THE STRUCTURE OF GOVERNMENTAL POWER: THE UNITED STATES CONSTITUTION

Foundations of national power

The Constitution delegates authority to the national government. The Founding Fathers tried to implement Locke's idea of limiting government by granting to the national government *only* certain expressed powers (sometimes called *delegated* powers), together with powers that might reasonably be *implied* from the expressed powers. Article I, Section 8, of the Constitution provides a fairly lengthy list of specific powers that are expressly delegated to Congress. They are the foundation stones of the national power.

The national government is given the power to *declare war and make peace.* Congress is authorized to raise and support armies and to provide a navy. It can define and punish piracy and other international offenses. Article II of the Constitution specifies that the president shall be commander in chief of the armed forces and have power to make treaties with the consent of the Senate and to give or withhold diplomatic recognition (that is, to appoint and receive ambassadors). These significant foreign and military powers are expressive of the most urgent of the drives to produce a powerful national government—the drive to provide defense against common enemies.[2]

A second group of powers expressly delegated to Congress prepared the way for the economic and commercial unity and stability of the nation. Congress is authorized to *regulate commerce* among the states, with foreign nations, and with the Indian tribes. It is authorized to coin money, to make uniform rules for bankruptcy, and to borrow money. By way of aiding economic and social development, Congress is authorized to establish post offices and post roads, to provide for patents and copyrights, and to fix standards of weights and measures. (For a listing of the national powers, see table 7–2.)

The national government is also given power to *tax and spend* for the common defense and general welfare. Congress can tax and spend for any purpose—education, welfare, housing, agriculture, business, urban affairs, manpower, and so forth.

Table 7–2   The Constitutional Distribution of Powers

National Powers
Military affairs and defense
  Provide for the common defense (I–8)
  Declare war (I–8)
  Raise and support armies (I–8)
  Provide and maintain a navy (I–8)
  Define and punish piracies (I–8)
  Define and punish offenses against the law of nations (I–8)
  Make rules for the regulation of military and naval forces (I–8)
  Provide for calling forth the militia to execute laws, suppress insurrections, and repel invasions (I–8)
  Provide for organizing, arming, and disciplining militia (I–8)
  Declare the punishment of treason (III–3)

Table 7-2   (Cont.)

Economic matters
  Regulate commerce with foreign nations, among the several states, and with
    Indian tribes (I–8)
  Establish uniform laws on bankruptcy (I–8)
  Coin money and regulate its value (I–8)
  Regulate value of foreign coin (I–8)
  Fix standards of weights and measures (I–8)
  Provide for patents and copyrights (I–8)
  Establish post offices and post roads (I–8)
Taxing Powers
  Levy taxes (I–8)
  Contract and pay debts (I–8)
Governmental organization
  Constitute tribunals inferior to the Supreme Court (I–8, III–1)
  Exercise exclusive legislative power over the seat of government and over
    certain military installations (I–8)
  Admit new states (IV–3)
  Dispose of and regulate territory or property of the United States (IV–3)
  Make rules for appointments (II–2)
Implied powers
  Make necessary and proper laws for carrying expressed powers into execu-
    tion (I–8)

Restrictions on National Power
Economic matters
  No preference to ports of any state (I–9)
  No tax or duty on articles exported from any state (I–9)
Fiscal matters
  No direct tax except by apportionment among states on population bases
    (I–9), now superseded as to income tax (Amendment XVI)
  No money to be drawn from Treasury except by appropriation (I–9)
Social classes
  No title of nobility to be granted (I–9)
Civil and political rights
  Congress not to establish religion or prohibit free exercise of religion
    (Amendment I)
  Congress not to abridge freedom of speech, press, assembly, or right of peti-
    tion (Amendment I)
  Right to bear arms protected (Amendment II)
  Restriction on quartering of soldiers in private homes (Amendment III)
  No unreasonable searches or seizures (Amendment IV)
  Guarantees of fair trials (Amendment V, Amendment VI, Amendment VII)
  No excessive bail or cruel or unusual punishments (Amendment VIII)
  No taking of life, liberty, or property without due process (Amendment V)
  Voting not to be denied because of race, color, previous servitude (Amend-
    ment XV), or sex (Amendment XIX), or age if 18 or over (Amendment
    XXVI)

Table 7–2   (Cont.)

Voting not to be denied because of nonpayment of any tax (Amendment XXIV)

Suspension of habeas corpus limited (I–9)

Limits on the Powers of the States

Foreign affairs

States not to enter into treaties, alliances, or confederation (I–10)

No compact with a foreign state, except by congressional consent (I–10)

Military affairs

No letters of marque and reprisal (I–10)

No standing military forces in peace without congressional consent (I–10)

No engagement in war, without congressional consent, except in imminent danger or when invaded (I–10)

Economic matters

No legal tender other than gold or silver coin (I–10)

No separate state coinage (I–10)

No impairment of the obligation of contracts (I–10)

No emission of bills of credit (I–10)

No levying of import or export duties, except reasonable inspection fees, without consent of Congress (I–10)

Civil and political rights

No slavery (Amendment XIII)

No bills of attainder (I–10)

No ex post facto laws (I–10)

No denial of life, liberty, or property by state without due process of law (Amendment XIV)

No denial by state of the equal protection of the laws (Amendment XIV)

No abridgment by state of privileges and immunities of national citizenship (Amendment XIV)

No abridgment of voting rights because of race, color, or previous condition of servitude (Amendment XV)

No abridgment of voting rights because of sex (Amendment XIX)

No poll or other taxes required for voting in federal elections (Amendment XXIV)

Social restrictions

No titles of nobility (I–10)

General restrictions

Federal law supreme (VI)

No payment of debts for rebellion against United States or for emancipated slaves (Amendment XIV)

The "necessary and proper" clause

At the end of Article I, Section 8, the Constitution makers added, in paragraph 18, the *necessary and proper clause*, which became the basis for much of the ensuing expansion of the powers of the national government. The "necessary and proper clause" states that the Congress shall have power:

> to make all laws which shall be necessary and proper for carrying into execution the foregoing powers [those mentioned in Article I, Section 8], and all other powers vested by this Constitution in the government of the United States, or in any department or officer thereof.

The last part of this clause makes clear that Congress has powers that may be implied from any of the expressly delegated powers in the Constitution.

The federal government is restricted in many ways by the Constitution, largely in the interest of protecting individual rights. In chapter 12, we will examine how the constitutional rights of defendants restrict the powers of the national government.

Restrictions on the states

The powers granted to the national government are accompanied by certain *restrictions* on the powers of the states, which serve to reinforce the grant of authority to the national government. These restrictions are listed in table 7–2, but let us observe generally that the restrictions on the states take them completely out of the field of foreign affairs and partly out of military matters. In addition, the activities of the states in the economic sphere are sharply limited.

States may not enter into relations with foreign states. They cannot make treaties or agreements (unless Congress consents) with other countries. In short, they have no foreign policy. Similarly, although the states have never completely given up their armies (they retain the state militia and the National Guard, with congressional consent), the national government can control these armies; and they have certainly become less significant than they once were. In the economic sphere, the states cannot coin money or create any new legal tender for payment of debts. In addition, the states cannot impair the obligation of contracts and, hence, cannot pass laws that invalidate private agreements. In effect, a limit is placed on changing the rules of the economic game. Finally, states may not levy import and export duties.

THE GROWTH OF POWER IN WASHINGTON

Federalism

The Constitution *divides* power between two separate authorities, the nation and the states, each of which can directly enforce their own laws on individuals through their own courts. This arrangement is known as *federalism*. In a disputed area, only the Constitution can determine whose authority is legitimate. American federalism differs from a "unitary" political system in that the central government has no legal authority to determine, alter, or abolish the power of the states. At the same time, American federalism differs from a "confederation of states," in which the national government is dependent upon its states for power. The American system *shares* authority and power constitutionally and practically.

Debate over state versus national power can never be removed from the *political context* in which it takes place. Interests that are dominant in national politics assert the supremacy of the national government and extol the virtues of national regulation. In contrast, interests that are weak in national politics but dominate politics in one or more states emphasize the preservation of the rights of states. For example, states' rights were vigorously defended in the 1950s and 1960s by southern state leaders seeking to maintain the segregation of the races. In contrast, civil rights groups appealed to the national government for support in their fight against state and local policies, and succeeded—in *Brown v. The Board of Education of Topeka* in 1954, the Civil Rights Act of 1964, the Voting Rights Act of 1965, and the Fair Housing Act of 1968—in moving the national government to overrule the segregationist policies of state and local governments.

The Constitution, in the Tenth Amendment, "reserves" to the states the power to protect and advance the public health, safety, welfare, and morals. Presumably this means that the national government may enact no laws dealing *directly* with housing, streets, zoning, schools, health, police protection, crime, and so on. However, the national government may *tax* or *borrow* or *spend money* to contribute to the general welfare. The national government has vastly expanded its power over states and communities by the provision of *grants-in-aid*. During the Great Depression of the 1930s, it used its taxing and spending powers in a wide variety of areas formerly reserved to states and communities. Grant-in-aid programs were initiated for public assistance, unemployment compensation, employment services, child welfare, public housing, urban renewal, highway construction, and vocational education and rehabilitation. The inadequacy of state and local revenue systems contributed significantly to the increase of national power in states and communities. Federal grants-in-aid to state and local governments have grown rapidly in recent years. Today federal grant money accounts for over one-sixth of all state and local government revenue.

Whenever the national government contributes financially to state or local programs, the state or local officials are left with less discretion than they would have otherwise. Federal grants-in-aid are invariably accompanied by congressional standards, or *guidelines*,

Grants-in-aid

Guidelines

that must be adhered to if states and communities are to receive their federal money. Often Congress delegates to federal agencies the power to establish the conditions attached to grants. Federal standards are designed to ensure compliance with national minimum standards, but they are bound to annoy state and local leaders. Sometimes protests from state and local leaders are loud enough to induce Congress to yield to the view of "sub-elites."

States or communities can reject federal grants-in-aid if they do not wish to meet federal standards, and some have done so. But it is difficult to resist the pressure to accept federal money. State and local officials are "bribed" by the temptation of much-needed funds, and they are "blackmailed" by the thought that the other states and communities will get the money if they do not, although the money was contributed in part by federal taxation of their own citizens.

In short, through the power to tax and spend for the general welfare and through the conditions attached to grants-in-aid, the national government exercises important powers in areas originally "reserved" to the states. Of course, federal grants-in-aid have enabled many states and communities to provide necessary and desirable services that they could not otherwise have afforded, and federal guidelines have often improved standards of administration, personnel policies, and fiscal practices in states and communities. Furthermore, federal guidelines have helped to ensure that states and communities will not engage in racial discrimination in federally aided programs. However, many commentators are genuinely apprehensive that states and communities have surrendered many of their powers to the national government in return for federal money. They argue that the role of states and communities in the American federal system has been weakened by federal grant-in-aid programs and the conditions attached to them. They believe that the centralization of power in Washington and the increased role of the national government in state and community affairs has curtailed the powers of state and local elites.

THE SEPARATION OF POWERS

The system of separated powers in the national government—separate legislative, executive, and judicial branches—was intended by the Founding Fathers as a *bulwark against majoritarianism* and an *additional safeguard for liberty*. The doctrine of separation of legislative, executive, and judicial powers derived from the French writer Montesquieu, whose *Spirit of the Laws* was a political textbook for these eighteenth-century statesmen. *The Federalist* paper No. 51 expresses the logic of the checks and balances system:

> Ambition must be made to counteract ambition. . . . It may be a reflection on human nature, that such devices should be necessary to control the abuses of government. But what is government itself, but the greatest of all reflections on human nature? If men were angels, no government would be necessary. If angels were to govern men, neither external nor internal controls on government would be necessary. In framing a government which is to be administered by men over men, the great difficulty lies in this: you must first enable the government to control the governed; and in the next place oblige it to control itself.[3]

The concept of the separation of powers is expressed in the opening sentences of the first three articles of the Constitution: "All legislative powers herein granted shall be invested in the Congress of the United States. . . . The executive power shall be vested in a president of the United States of America. . . . The judicial power of the United States shall be vested in one Supreme Court and in such inferior courts as the Congress may from time to time ordain and establish." If this system divides responsibility and makes it difficult for the masses to hold government accountable for public policy, then it is achieving one of the purposes intended by the Founding Fathers.

The growth of majoritarianism: direct elections

Originally, each of the four major decision-making bodies of the national government was to be chosen by different constituencies—the House by the voters in the several states, the Senate by the state legislatures, the president by electors chosen by the states, and the judiciary by the president and the Senate. Note that in the Constitution of 1787 only one of these four governing institutions—the House of Representatives—was to be directly elected by the people. There was no direct popular participation in the selection of president, senators, or judges. These arrangements indicate that the Founding Fathers did not fully trust the masses in the selection of governing officials. However, by the early 1800s, presidential electors had begun the practice of running for their posts "pledged" to cast their votes for one party and candidate or another. This permitted popular participation in the selection of the president by enabling voters to choose between electors pledged to particular candidates. The same practice holds today: Voters in presidential elections actually cast their votes for slates of Democratic of Republican electors pledged to either the Democratic or Republican candidate. It was not until the Seventeenth Amendment was added to the Constitution in 1913 that the people won the opportunity to participate directly in the election of U.S. senators. Thus, today three of the four governing bodies of the

Staggered terms

national government are popularly elected. Now only the Supreme Court and federal judiciary remain free from direct popular control.

The Founding Fathers also made a sharp differentiation in the terms of these decision-making bodies, so that a complete renewal of government by popular vote at one stroke is impossible. The House is chosen for two years; the Senate is chosen for six, but not in one election, for one-third of the senators complete their terms every two years. The president is chosen every four years, but judges of the Supreme Court hold office for life. Thus the people are restrained from working immediate change through direct elections; they must wait years to make their will felt in all of the decision-making bodies of the national government.

Checks and balances:
a sharing of power

Moreover, each of these decision-making bodies possesses important *checks and balances* over the decisions of the others. No bill can become law without the approval of both the House and the Senate. The president shares in legislative power through his veto and his responsibility to "give to the Congress information of the State of the Union, and recommend to their consideration such measures as he shall judge necessary and expedient." He can also convene sessions of Congress. But the appointing power of the president is shared by the Senate; so is his treaty-making power. Also, Congress can override executive vetoes. The president must execute the laws, but to do so he must rely upon executive departments, and these must be created by Congress. Moreover, the executive branch cannot spend money that has not been appropriated by Congress. Thus, the concept of separation of powers is really misnamed, for what we are really talking about is a *sharing*, not a separating, of power; each branch participates in the activities of every other branch.

Even the Supreme Court, which was created by the Constitution, must be appointed by the president with the consent of the Senate, and Congress may prescribe the number of judges. More importantly, Congress must create lower and intermediate courts, establish the number of judges, fix the jurisdiction of lower federal courts, and make "exceptions" to the appellate jurisdiction of the Supreme Court.

Judicial review: final check

Perhaps the keystone of the system of checks and balances is the idea of *judicial review*, an original contribution by the Founding Fathers to the science of government. Judicial review is the power of the courts to strike down laws that they believe conflict with the Constitution. Article VI grants federal courts the power of judicial review of *state* decisions, specifying that the Constitution and the laws and treaties of the national government are the supreme law of the land, superseding anything in the constitutions or laws of any of the states. However, nowhere does the Constitution specify that the Supreme

Court has power of judicial review of *executive* action or of laws enacted by *Congress.* This principle was instead established in the case of *Marbury* v. *Madison* in 1803, when Chief Justice John Marshall argued convincingly that the Founding Fathers intended the Supreme Court to have the power of invalidating not only state laws and constitutions, but also any laws of Congress or executive actions that came in conflict with the Constitution of the United States. Marshall reasoned (1) that the "judicial power" was given to the Supreme Court, (2) that historically the judicial power included the power to interpret the meaning of the law, (3) that the supremacy clause made the Constitution the "supreme law of the land," (4) that laws of the United States should be made "in pursuance thereof," (5) that judges are sworn to uphold the Constitution, and (6) that judges must therefore declare void any legislative act that they feel conflicts with the Constitution. Thus, the Supreme Court stands as the final defender of the fundamental principles agreed upon by the Founding Fathers against the encroachments of popularly elected legislatures and executives.

THE POWER OF THE PRESIDENT

Chief legislator

The president does not command American elites, but he stands in a central position in the elite structure. The responsibility for the initiation of public policy falls principally upon him and his staff and executive departments. Through the power of policy initiation alone, the president has considerable impact on American elites. He sets the agenda for public decision making. His programs are presented to Congress in various presidential messages and in his budget, and he thereby largely determines what the business of Congress will be in any session. Few major undertakings get off the ground without presidential initiation; the president frames the issues, determines their context, and decides their timing.

Commander in chief and chief diplomat

On the whole, presidents of the twentieth century have exercised greater power and initiative than those of the nineteenth century, partly because of America's greater involvement in world affairs and the constant increase in the importance of military and foreign policy. The Constitution gives the president unmistakable and far-reaching powers in foreign and military affairs: He is authorized to send and receive ambassadors and to make treaties (with the advice and consent of the Senate) and is made commander in chief of the armed forces. In effect, these powers put him in almost exclusive control of foreign and military policy in the nation.

Chief administrator

A second factor contributing to the power of the president in the twentieth century has been the growth of the executive branch, which he heads. The federal bureaucracy has become a giant power structure, and the president's constitutional powers as chief executive place him at the top of this structure. The Constitution gives the president broad, albeit vague, powers to "take care that the laws be faithfully executed" and to "require the opinion, in writing, of the principal officer of each of the executive departments upon any subject relating to the duties of their respective offices." By this clause the president has general executive authority over the 2.9 million civilian employees of the federal bureaucracy. Moreover, he has the right to appoint (and generally the right to remove) the principal officers of the executive branch of government (the Senate consenting). A major addition to the president's constitutional authority over the executive branch came in the Budget and Accounting Act of 1921, in which Congress vested in the president the control of the initiation and execution of the federal budget. Budgetary control is a major weapon in the hands of the president, for it can mean the life or death of an administrative agency. Although Congress must appropriate all monies spent by executive departments, the president nonetheless has responsibility for formulating the budget. Congress may cut a presidential budget request and even appropriate more than the president asks for a particular agency or program, but by far the greatest portion of the president's budget is accepted by Congress.

Party leader and voice of the nation

The third reason for the importance of the presidency in the twentieth century can be traced to technological improvements in the mass media and the strengthening of the role of the president as party leader and molder of public opinion. Television brings the president directly in contact with the masses, and the masses have an attachment to him that is unlike their attachment to any other public official or symbol of government. Fred I. Greenstein has classified the "psychological functions of the presidency": First, the president "simplifies perception of government and politics" by serving as "the main cognitive 'handle' for providing busy citizens with some sense of what their government is doing." Second, the president provides "an outlet for emotional expression" through public interest in his and his family's private and public life. Third, the president is a "symbol of unity" and of nationhood (as the national shock and grief over the death of a president clearly reveals). Fourth, the president provides the masses with a "vicarious means of taking political action," in the sense that he can act decisively and effectively while they cannot do so. Finally, the president is a "symbol of social stability," in that he provides the masses with a feeling of security and guidance. Thus, for the masses, the president is the most visible elite member.[4]

The president has many sources of power (see table 7–3); he is chief administrator, chief diplomat, commander in chief, chief of state, party leader, and voice of the people. But despite the great powers of the office, no president can monopolize policy making. The president functions within an established elite system, and he can exercise power only within its framework. The choices available to him are limited to those alternatives for which he can mobilize elite support. He cannot act outside existing consensus in the elite, outside of the "rules of the game."

Table 7–3   Presidential Powers

Chief administrator
Implement policy—"take care that laws be faithfully executed"
Supervise executive branch of government
Appoint and remove policy officials
Prepare executive budget

Chief legislator
Initiate policy—"give to the Congress information of the State of the Union
and recommend to their consideration such measures as he shall judge
necessary and expedient"
Veto legislation passed by Congress
Convene special sessions of Congress "on extraordinary occasions"

Party leader
Control national party organization
Control federal patronage
Influence (not control) state and local parties through prestige

Chief diplomat
Make treaties ("with the advice and consent of Senate")
Make executive agreements
Exercise power of diplomatic recognition—"to send and receive am-
bassadors"
Represent the nation as chief of state

Commander in chief
Command U.S. armed forces—"the President shall be Commander in Chief
of the Army and the Navy"
Appoint military officials
Initiate war
Use broad war powers

THE POWER OF CONGRESS

Arbiters of public policy

What are the powers of Congress in the American political system? Policy proposals are initiated *outside* Congress; Congress's role is to respond to proposals from the president, executive agencies, and interest groups. Congress does not merely ratify or "rubber-stamp" decisions; it plays an independent role in the policy-making process. But this role is essentially a deliberative one, in which Congress accepts, modifies, or rejects the policies initiated by others. For example, the national budget, perhaps the single most important policy document, is written by the executive branch and modified by the president before it is submitted to Congress. Congress may make further modifications, but it does not formulate the budget. Of course, Congress is a critical screen through which appropriations and revenue measures must pass. But sophisticated lawmakers are aware that they function as *arbiters* rather than *initiators* of public policy. As Robert Dahl explains:

> The Congress no longer expects to originate measures but to pass, veto, or modify laws proposed by the Chief Executive. It is the President, not the Congress, who determines the content and substance of the legislation with which Congress deals. The President is now the motor of the system; the Congress applies the brakes. The President gives what forward movement there is in the system; his is the force of thrust and innovation. The Congress is the force of inertia—a force, it should be said, that means not only restraint, but stability in politics.[5]

Constitutional prerogatives

From a constitutional point of view, of course, the potential for power in Congress is very great. Article I empowers Congress to levy taxes, to borrow and spend money, to regulate interstate commerce, to establish a national money supply, to establish a post office, to declare war, to raise and support an army and navy, to establish a court system, and to pass all laws "necessary and proper" to implement these powers. Congress may also propose amendments to the Constitution or call a convention to do so. Congress admits new states. In the event that no candidate receives a majority of votes in the electoral college, the House of Representatives may select the president. The Senate "advises and consents" to treaties and approves presidential nominations to executive and judicial posts. The House has the power to impeach, the Senate to try, any officer of the United States government, including the president. Congress may also conduct investigations, discipline its own members, and regulate its internal affairs.

Yet, despite these extensive formal powers, Congress is only one component of America's elite system. Many important decisions, particularly in *foreign* and *military* affairs, are made without the direct participation of Congress. The president may commit Congress and the nation to a foreign policy or military action that Congress cannot prevent or reverse. For example, Congress could do little more than appropriate the necessary funds for the Korean War and the Vietnam War. Often congressional leaders are told of a major foreign policy decision only moments before it is announced on national television.

Congress is more influential in *domestic* than in foreign and military affairs. It is much freer to reject presidential proposals regarding business, labor, agriculture, education, welfare, urban affairs, civil rights, taxation, and appropriations. Congressional committees share with the president control over executive agencies dealing with domestic affairs. For example, the Office of Education, the Social Security Administration, the Housing Assistance Administration, the Department of Agriculture, the Office of Economic Opportunity—all must go to Congress for needed legislation and appropriations. Congressional committees can exercise power in domestic affairs by giving or withholding the appropriations and the legislation wanted by these executive agencies.

THE POWER OF THE COURTS

Sources of judicial power

The Founding Fathers viewed the federal courts as the final bulwark against mass threats to principle and property. Since *Marbury* v. *Madison* empowered the Supreme Court with judicial review of congressional acts, the federal courts have struck down more than eighty laws of Congress and uncounted state laws that they believed conflicted with the Constitution. *Judicial review and the right to interpret the meaning and decide the application of law* are great sources of power for judges. Some of the nation's most important policy decisions have been made by courts rather than by executive or legislative bodies. In recent years, federal courts have taken the lead in eliminating segregation in public life, ensuring the separation of church and state, defining relationships between individuals and law enforcers, and guaranteeing individual voters equal voice in government. Courts are an integral component of America's governmental elite system, for sooner or later most important policy questions are brought before them.

The undemocratic nature of judicial review has long been recognized in American politics. Nine Supreme Court justices—who are not elected to office, whose terms are for life, and who can be removed only for "high crimes and misdemeanors"—possess the power to void the acts of popularly elected presidents, Congresses, governors, and state legislators. The decision of the Founding Fathers to grant federal courts the constitutional power of judicial review of *state* decisions is easy to understand. Federal court power over state decisions is probably essential in maintaining national unity, for fifty different state interpretations of the meaning of the United States Constitution or of the laws and treaties of Congress would create unimaginable confusion. Thus, the power of federal judicial review over state constitutions, laws, and court decisions is seldom questioned.

However, at the national level, why should the views of an appointed court about the meaning of the Constitution prevail over the views of an elected Congress and president? Congressmen and presidents are sworn to uphold the Constitution, and it can reasonably be assumed that they do not pass laws they believe to be unconstitutional. Since laws must be approved by majorities of those voting in both houses and must have the president's formal approval, why should the Founding Fathers have been persuaded by Chief Justice Marshall that the Supreme Courts should have judicial review of the decisions of these bodies?

Insulation of the courts

The answer appears to be that the Founding Fathers distrusted both popular majorities and elected officials who might be influenced by popular majorities. They believed that government should be limited so that it could not attack principle and property, whether to do so was the will of the majority or not. So the courts were deliberately insulated against popular majorities; to ensure their independence, judges were not to be elected, but appointed for life terms. Originally, it was expected that they would be appointed by a president who was not even directly elected himself and confirmed by a Senate that was not directly elected. Only in this way, the writers of the Constitution believed, would they be sufficiently protected from the masses to permit them to judge courageously and responsibly. This insulation is, in itself, another source of judicial power.

The Supreme Court is best understood as an *elite* institution, rather than as a *conservative* or *liberal* institution. During the 1930s, the Supreme Court was a bastion of conservatism; it attacked the economic programs of the New Deal and clung to the earlier elite philosophy of rugged individualism. In recent years, the Court has been criticized as too liberal in its orientation toward racial equality, church-state relations, and individual rights before the law. The apparent paradox can be understood if we view the Court as an exponent of the dominant elite philosophy, rather than as an unchanging liberal or conservative element in national politics. When the dominant elite philosophy was rugged individualism, the Court reflected this fact, just as it reflects a liberal philosophy today. Of course, owing to the insulation of the Court even from other elites, through life terms and independence from the executive and legislative branches, there is a *time lag* between changes in elite philosophy and the Court decisions reflecting these changes. For example, Franklin D. Roosevelt became president in 1933, but the Supreme Court did not generally approve New Deal legislation until after 1937.

A liberal concern for the underprivileged in America by the Supreme Court, under the leadership of Chief Justice Earl Warren, was reflected in the development of civil rights law. The Court firmly insisted that no person in America should be denied equal protection of the law. It defended the right of blacks to vote, to attend integrated schools, and to receive justice in the courts; it upheld the power of Congress to protect blacks from being discriminated against in public accommodations, employment, voting, and housing. It ruled that discrimination against any group of voters by state legislatures in the apportioning of election districts was unconstitutional. It protected religious minorities (and the nonreligious) from laws establishing official prayers and religious ceremonies in public schools. It protected defendants in criminal cases from self-incrimination through ignorance of their rights, through the subtlety of law enforcement officials in extracting confessions, or through lack of legal counsel.

The elevation of Warren Burger to chief justice by Richard Nixon in 1969 did not significantly alter the commitments of the Court to end racial segregation under law, ensure equality in representation, and maintain separation of church and state. Contrary to popular expectations, the Supreme Court, with four Nixon appointees, has continued to uphold these fundamental commitments of the nation's elite. The Burger Court extended the doctrine of *Brown* v. *Board of Education of Topeka* to uphold court-ordered busing of children to end racial imbalance in schools that had a history of racial segregation under law (that is, southern schools). The Burger Court struck down state payments to church schools to pay for nonreligious instruction. Only in the area of rights of criminal defendants has the Burger Court altered the direction of Warren Court holdings. But even here the Burger Court has not reversed earlier declarations of the rights of criminal defendants; it has merely failed to extend them further.

Perhaps the most sweeping declaration of individual liberty in the Supreme Court's history was the assertion, by the Burger Court, of the constitutional right of women to have abortions in the first three months of pregnancy. The ultimate impact of this decision on society—on population growth, the environment, and the role of women in society—may be as far-reaching as that of any decision ever rendered by the Court. Certainly this decision clearly indicates that the Supreme Court continues to be a powerful institution capable of affecting the lives of all Americans.

POLITICAL BEHAVIOR IN AMERICA

Democracy and popular participation

Popular participation in the political system is the very definition of democracy. Individuals in a democracy may run for public office; participate in marches and demonstrations; make financial contributions to political candidates and causes; attend political meetings, speeches, and rallies; write letters to public officials and newspapers; belong to organizations that support or oppose particular candidates and take stands on public issues; wear a political button and place a bumper sticker on their car; attempt to influence friends while discussing candidates and issues; vote in elections; or merely follow an issue or campaign in the mass media. This list of activities constitutes a ranking of the forms of political participation, in inverse order of their frequency. Those activities at the beginning of the list require greater expenditure of time and energy and greater personal commitment; consequently, far fewer people engage in those activities. Less than 1 percent of the American adult population run for public office.

Actual voting behavior

Only about 5 percent are ever active in political parties and campaigns, and only about 10 percent make financial contributions. Less than 60 percent vote in a close presidential election. Fully one-third of the population are politically apathetic: They do not vote, and they are largely unaware of and indifferent to the political life of the nation.[6] Congressional elections bring out less than one-half of the population. Yet in these "off-year" contests the nation chooses all of its U.S. representatives, one-third of its U.S. senators, and about one-half of its governors. Local government elections—for mayor, councilmen, school board, and so forth—frequently attract only one-quarter or one-third of eligible voters.

Voting is the primary form of popular participation in a democracy, and voter participation is highly valued in American political theory. Popular control of government—the control of leaders by followers—is supposed to be accomplished through the electoral process. Voting requires an individual to make not one, but two decisions: The individual must choose whether to vote at all; and if the individual decides to vote, a choice must be made between rival parties or candidates. Both decisions are equally important; decisions about whether or not to vote can clearly influence the outcome of elections.

Before 1970 only three of the fifty states permitted persons eighteen to twenty-one years of age to vote: Georgia, Kentucky, and Alaska. All the rest, in the exercise of their constitutional responsibility to determine the qualifications of "electors," had set the voting age at twenty-one. The movement for eighteen-year-old voting received its original impetus in Georgia in 1944 under the leadership of Governor Ellis Arnall, who argued successfully that eighteen-year olds were then being called upon to fight and die for their country in World War II and therefore deserved to have a voice in the conduct of government. However this argument failed to convince adult voters or leaders in other states; qualifications for military service were not regarded as the same as qualifications for rational decision making in elections. In state after state, voters rejected state constitutional amendments designed to extend the vote to eighteen-year olds. But in 1970 Congress passed and sent to the states the Twenty-sixth Amendment to the Constitution extending voting rights to all persons eighteen years of age or older in all federal, state, and local elections. The legislatures of three-fourths of the states promptly ratified the amendment.

Voting laws in the states are now heavily circumscribed by national authority:

> Fifteenth Amendment—no denial of voting because of race.
>
> Nineteenth Amendment—no denial of voting because of sex.
>
> Twenty-fourth Amendment—no poll taxes in federal elections.
>
> Twenty-sixth Amendment—no denial of voting to persons eighteen years of age or older.
>
> Civil Rights Act of 1964—no discrimination in the application of voter registration laws.
>
> Voting Rights Act of 1965—attorney general may replace local voting officials with federal examiners on evidence of voter discrimination in southern states.
>
> Voting Rights Act of 1970—no denial of voting to persons eighteen years of age or older; no residency requirements in national elections; no literacy tests.

The states, however, continue to administer national, state, and local elections. All but four states (Alaska, Arkansas, North Dakota, and Texas) have established a system of voting registration. Presumably, registration helps to prevent fraud and multiple voting in elections.

DEMOCRATS AND REPUBLICANS
—WHAT'S THE DIFFERENCE?

Functions of political parties

Democracy is ultimately based on majority rule, and one function of political parties is to *put the majority together.* Political parties organize voters for effective political expression at the polls. Voters, in turn, use party labels to help them identify the general political viewpoints of the candidates.

Because American parties are necessarily rather loose coalitions of interests, they do not command the total loyalty of every office-holder elected under a party's banner. The fact that candidates run under a Republican or Democratic label does not clearly indicate where they will stand on every public issue. Even so, these coalitions do have considerable cohesion and historical continuity. The party label *discloses the coalition of interests and the policy views* with which candidates have generally associated themselves. At the least, the party label tells more about a candidate's politics than would a strange name on the ballot with no party affiliation attached.

Especially in two-party systems, such as we have in the United States, parties also *limit the choice of candidates* for public office and thus relieve voters of the task of choosing from among dozens of contending candidates on election day. This preliminary selecting and narrowing of candidates, by conventions and primary elections, is indispensable in a large society.

Political parties help to *define the major problems and issues* confronting society. In attempting to win a majority of the voters, parties inform the public about the issues facing the nation. The comparisons made by parties during political campaigns have an important educational value: Voters come to "know" the opposing candidates for public office, and the problems of national interest are spotlighted.

Finally, the party *out of office* performs an important function for democratic government by *criticizing officeholders.* Moreover, the very existence of a recognized party *outside* government helps to make criticism of government legitimate and effective.

Criticism of the American two-party system

It is sometimes argued that there are few significant differences between the two main American parties. It is not uncommon in European nations to find totalitarian parties competing with democratic parties, fascists with communists, capitalist parties with socialist parties, Catholic parties with secular parties, and so on. In contrast, in America both Republican and Democratic parties accept and strongly support constitutional government, with separation of powers, federalism, and judicial review. The policies of both parties reflect the same general cultural values. In addition, both parties compete for a majority in the electorate and therefore tend to take moderate stands that will encompass the views of the largest number of voters.

Ascertaining the real party differences

If it were true that the American parties offered no real alternatives to the voters, then effective popular control of government through elections would be impossible. This is exactly what Marxists criticize about American democracy—that there are no differences between the American parties and no choices open to the American people. However, within the context of American political experience, the Democratic and Republican parties can be clearly differentiated. There are at least three ways in which to discern the differences: (1) by examining differences in the *coalitions of voters* supporting each party; (2) by examining differences in the *policy views of the leaders* in each party; and (3) by examining differences in the *voting records of the representatives and senators* of each party.

In ascertaining party differences according to support from different groups of voters, we must note first that major groups are seldom *wholly* within one party or the other. For example, in presidential elections all major social groups divide their votes between the parties (see table 7–4). Yet differences between the parties are revealed in the proportions of votes given by each major group to each party. Thus, the Democratic party receives a disproportionate amount of support from Catholics, Jews, blacks, lower-educational and lower-income groups, younger people, blue-collar workers, union members, and big-city residents. The Republican party receives disproportionate support from Protestants, whites, higher-educational and higher-income groups, older people, professionals and managers, white-collar workers, nonunion members, and rural and small-town residents.

The second way of discerning Democratic and Republican party differences involves an examination of the political opinions of the leaders of each party. Political scientist Herbert J. McClosky made a study of party differences by presenting a series of policy questions to over three thousand delegates to the Democratic and Republican national conventions. He found substantial differences of opinion between Democrats and Republicans on important public issues, including public ownership of natural resources, government regulation of the economy, equalitarianism and human welfare, tax policy, and foreign policy. On the basis of this research, McClosky concludes:

> Although it has received wide currency, especially among Europeans, the belief that the two American parties are identical in principle and doctrine has little foundation in fact. Examination of the opinions of

Table 7-4   Voting Behavior of Major American Social Groups in Presidential Elections

	1968			1972		1976		
	Dem.	*Rep.*	*Ind.*	*Dem.*	*Rep.*	*Dem.*	*Rep.*	*Ind.*
Race								
White	38%	47%	15%	32%	68%	46%	52%	1%
Nonwhite	85	12	3	87	13	85	15	—
Education								
College	37	54	9	37	63	42	55	2
High school	42	43	15	34	66	54	46	—
Grade school	52	33	15	49	51	58	41	1
Occupation								
Professional and business	34	56	10	31	69	42	56	1
White collar	41	47	12	36	64	50	48	2
Manual	50	35	15	43	57	58	41	1
Age								
Under 30	47	38	15	48	52	53	45	1
30–49	44	41	15	33	67	48	49	2
50 and older	41	47	12	36	64	52	48	—
Religion								
Protestant	35	49	16	30	70	46	53	—
Catholic	59	33	8	48	52	57	42	1
National total	43.0	43.4	13.6	38.0	62.0	50.0	48.0	1.0

Note: In 1968 the Democratic candidate was Humphrey, the Republican, Nixon and the Independent, Wallace. In 1972 the Democrat was McGovern, the Republican, Nixon. In 1976 the Democrat was Carter, the Republican, Ford and McCarthy ran as an Independent.
Source: Data from the Gallup Opinion Index, December 1976.

Democratic and Republican leaders shows them to be distinct communities of co-believers who diverge sharply on many important issues. Their disagreements, furthermore, conform to an image familiar to many observers and are generally consistent with differences turned up by studies of congressional roll calls. . . . [They] grow out of their group identification and support—out of the managerial, proprietary, and high-status connections of the one, and the labor, minority, low-status, and intellectual connections of the other. . . . Democratic leaders typically display the stronger urge to elevate the lowborn, the uneducated, the deprived minorities, and the poor in general; they are also more disposed to employ the nation's collective power to advance humanitarian and social welfare goals (e.g., social security, immigration, racial integration, a higher minimum wage, and public education). They are more critical of wealth and big business and more eager to bring them under regulation. Theirs is the greater faith in the wisdom of using legislation for redistributing the national product and for furnishing social services on a wide scale. Of the two groups of leaders, the Democrats are more "progressively" oriented toward social reform and experimentation. The Republican leaders, while not uniformly differentiated from their opponents, subscribe in greater measure to the symbols and practices of individualism, *laissez-faire*, and national independence. They prefer to overcome humanity's misfortunes by relying upon personal effort, private incentives, frugality, hard work, responsibility, self-denial (for both men and government), and the strengthening rather than the diminution of the economic and status distinctions that are the "natural" rewards of the differences in human character and fortunes.[7]

The third indication of party differences in America is the roll-call voting behavior of the representatives and senators of each party on controversial issues. Although members of the same party in Congress often have serious and lasting disagreements over important issues, it is possible to show that the *centers* of *gravity* of the two parties are rather widely separated in many issue areas, including government regulation of the economy, labor legislation, education and welfare programs, and foreign affairs.

Party identification

Voters usually think of themselves as Democrats or Republicans, and this *party identification* is the single most important factor in voter decisions. Candidates and issues, two other bases of voter decisions, are influential in elections, but they do not provide the solid core of millions of party supporters who will vote for the party's nominees no matter who they are. This is particularly pertinent because the vast majority of candidates who appear on the ballot are unknown to the voter, especially candidates for the more obscure offices—those of county commissioner, city councilman, registrar of deeds, auditor general, and so on.

People who identify themselves as Democrats outnumber those who identify themselves as Republicans by as much as two to one in national samples. Thus, if the Republican party is to win an election, it must nominate candidates who can attract Democratic voters. However, the Republican party's electoral hopes are aided by the fact that its adherents—higher-education, higher-income, white-color groups —tend to vote more often than the Democrats.

Americans acquire their party identification much as they acquire most of their other values and attitudes: at home. National samples generally show that voters' preferences tend to correspond with those of their parents. This inclination does not necessarily represent blind or shallow thinking. Children get most of their values through their parents, and it would be inconsistent if their political values did not match what they were taught in the home.

CASE STUDY
A Tale of Two Presidents:
Watergate and Its Aftermath

PART 1   THE RESIGNATION OF RICHARD NIXON

The president does not stand above America's elites but among them. Election to the nation's highest office—even by an overwhelming majority—does not entitle the president to govern. It only gives him the opportunity to engage in consultation, accommodation, and compromise with other elites. Richard Nixon's forced resignation from the presidency was not merely a product of specific misdeeds or improprieties associated with Watergate. It also grew out of his general isolation from established elites, his failure to cooperate with Congress and the courts, and his disregard of general "rules of the game."

President Nixon claimed that his critics blew a petty incident—the Watergate break-in—out of all proportion to its importance. And indeed the burglary of a party headquarters is trivial compared to ending the Vietnam War, or reopening relations with China, or securing the SALT agreement to limit nuclear arsenals, or negotiating the Middle East crisis. But Watergate's importance grew as the president escalated his defense, challenged the powers of other elites, attacked the powerful television networks, asserted his own authority, and offended Congress, the courts, and even loyal members of his own party.

The Origins of Watergate   Threats to democracy can originate from elites, as well as masses, even democratically elected elites. Elite repression frequently appears in response to mass unrest—riots, demonstrations, extremism, violence, and threats of violence. These mass activities generate fear and insecurity among men of power, who respond by curtailing liberties and strengthening "national security." Dissenters come under official suspicion and surveillance, the news media are cut off from their sources or censored, free speech is curtailed, political activists are jailed, and police and security forces are strengthened, usually in the name of "law and order."

The origins of Watergate are found in the climate of mass unrest of the late 1960s and early 1970s that seemed to threaten the security of the nation. A decade of disorder began with the assassination of President John F. Kennedy in 1963, which was followed by the assassinations of Martin Luther King, Jr., and Robert F. Kennedy in 1968 and the attempted assassination of George C. Wallace in 1972. Mass demonstrations and civil disobedience were developed and refined as political tactics by various mass movements. Humiliation and defeat in a prolonged and fruitless military effort in Vietnam undermined the legitimacy of the government. The Democratic National Convention in Chicago in 1968 featured violent antiwar protests outside the convention hall, and police responded with counterviolence of their own. College protest activity, which had been relatively restrained for most of the decade, became increasingly prone to violence in the 1970s. In May 1970, National Guardsmen were sent to Kent State University after the ROTC building had been set afire as a protest against United States operations in Cambodia. When students defied an order to disperse, some National Guardsmen fired their weapons; four students were killed and nine were wounded. In that same month, campus protest activity closed down many of the nation's leading universities. More than sixty thousand persons, mostly students, assembled in Washington for antiwar demonstrations. In 1971, the *New York Times* and the *Washington Post* published the so-called Pentagon Papers, which had been taken from the files of the Department of Defense by a former Defense Department adviser, Daniel Ellsberg. The president and his senior advisers were convinced that this important elite—the influential newsmakers—had acted outside the established "rules of the game" in their effort to end the war quickly.

Thus, by the early 1970s all the conditions for elite repression existed: (1) racial unrest and violence; (2) the approval and encouragement of violence in the form of mass protest; (3) defeat and humiliation in war; (4) counterelite violence, including bombing and arson; (5) attacks from the press that went beyond the "rules of the game." The Watergate affair provides an illustration of the response of national elites to these conditions, and their tendency to resort to repressive measures when threatened. It may be psychologically comforting to believe that the "White House horrors" are unique and unprecedented in American history and that the Nixon administration is the only administration that has ever resorted to repression in times of crisis. But this is not the case. Repressive behavior is typical of elites when they perceive threats to the political system—witness the Alien and Sedition Acts in the administration of John Adams; the suspension of due process rights by Abraham Lincoln during the Civil War; the "Red scare" roundup of suspected Bolsheviks in the administration of Woodrow Wilson; the mass internment of thousands of Japanese-Americans by the Roosevelt administration in World War II; and the "loyalty and security" programs of the Truman and Eisenhower administrations, with their persecution of suspected communists and "fellow travelers." Most of the actions revealed in the Watergate hearings—wiretapping, monitoring of the mail, checking of tax returns, surveillance of suspected subversives, infiltration of radical organizations, "surreptitious entry" (burglary), and so forth—have been long-standing practices of federal security agencies. What is different about Watergate is that some of them were used against the national Democratic party headquarters located in the Watergate office complex in Washington, D.C., during the 1972 presidential elections. Repressive tactics applied in "national security" cases were common in Democratic as well as Republican administrations in the past. But for one segment of the nation's established leadership to use such tactics against another segment is to violate the fundamental "rules of the game."

The "Plumbers" at Work   To deal with the increasingly troublesome radical protest activity of the late 1960s and early 1970s, and particularly to halt damaging leaks of secret government information to a hostile press, the president convened an interagency committee composed of the directors of the FBI, the CIA, the Defense Intelligence Agency, and the National Security Council Agency. This group considered a report calling for: (1) intensified electronic surveillance of both domestic security threats and foreign diplomats; (2) monitoring of American citizens using international communications facilities; (3) increased legal and illegal opening and reading of mail; (4) more informants on college campuses; (5) the lifting of restrictions on "surreptitious entry" (burglary); (6) the establishment of an interagency group on domestic intelligence. The president approved a plan, but later FBI Director J. Edgar Hoover objected to it—not because he opposed such measures but because the FBI was not given exclusive control of the program. Hoover's opposition resulted in the formal withdrawal of the plan.

However, the White House still believed that the political system was endangered by disruptive and subversive elements, that disloyal members of the administration were leaking government secrets to the press, and that "extraordinary" measures were required to protect the government. A Special Investigations Unit was created within the White House. The unit was known as the "Plumbers" because it was supposed to stop leaks of secret government information. It was placed under the supervision of John Ehrlichman and his assistant Egil Krogh. The Plumbers unit soon included ex-CIA agent and author of spy novels E. Howard Hunt, Jr., and former FBI agent G. Gordon Liddy. The Plumbers unit worked independently of the FBI and the CIA (although it received occasional assistance from the CIA) and reported directly to John Ehrlichman. It undertook a variety of activities—later referred to as "White House horrors"—including: the investigation of Daniel Ellsberg and the burglary of his psychiatrist's office to learn more about his motives in releasing the Pentagon Papers; the investigation (and later forgery) of the record of the events surrounding the assassination of South Vietnam's President Diem during the administration of John F. Kennedy; the investigation of national security leaks that affected the U.S. negotiating position in the SALT talks; and other undisclosed domestic and foreign intelligence activities. Later John Ehrlichman strongly defended the actions of the Plumbers unit before the Senate Watergate Committee as necessary to protect national security.

The Watergate Break-in The Watergate break-in itself—burglarizing and wiretapping of the Democratic National Headquarters—was an outgrowth of earlier undercover activities by members of the Plumbers unit. The work of the Plumbers had tapered off by the end of 1971, and Hunt and Liddy found new jobs with the president's reelection campaign organization, the Committee to Re-elect the President (CREEP), headed by former Attorney General John M. Mitchell. The "security coordinator" for CREEP was James W. McCord, Jr., who had been an FBI and CIA agent. It was easy for Hunt, McCord, and Liddy to confuse threats to national security with threats to the reelection of the incumbent president and to employ well-known "national security" tactics, including bugging and burglary, against the president's opponents. On the night of 17 June 1972, five men with burglary and wiretapping tools were arrested in the offices of the Democratic National Committee: James W. McCord and Bernard L. Barker and three Cuban exiles. Later a grand jury charged these five men, together with Hunt and Liddy, with burglary and wiretapping; at a trial in January 1973 all seven were convicted. But U.S. District Court Judge John J. Sirica believed that the defendants were covering up for whoever had ordered and paid for the bugging and break-in. The *Washington Post* reported that the defendants were under pressure to plead guilty, that they were still being paid by an unnamed source, and that they had been promised a cash settlement and executive clemency if they went to jail and remained silent. Judge Sirica threatened the defendants with heavy sentences, and soon McCord broke and told of secret payments and a cover-up.

The Cover-up It was probably not the political embarrassment of the Watergate break-in that led the White House to attempt a cover-up (news of the burglary did not seriously affect the president's reelection campaign, and he was re-elected overwhelmingly in November 1972, five months *after* the break-in). Instead the White House seemed concerned over exposure of the whole series of repressive acts undertaken earlier by the Plumbers. The great blunder of the Watergate operation was that certain individuals who were involved in the petty political burglary of the National Democratic Headquarters—Liddy, Hunt, and McCord—had previously served with the Special Investigations Unit of the White House and the CIA. The Watergate burglary mixed partisan politics with national security affairs. The president attempted to limit the Watergate investigation to the partisan political act of the break-in of the Democratic National Headquarters, to protect his close associates, and to prevent exposure of the repressive measures that the White House had been using for several years.

The Senate formed a Special Select Committee on Campaign Activities—the so-called Watergate Committee—headed by Senator Sam J. Ervin to delve into Watergate and related activities. The national press, led by the prestigious *Washington Post*, which had always been hostile to Richard Nixon, began its own "investigative reporting" and, in cooperation with the major television networks, launched a series of damaging stories involving former Attorney General John Mitchell, White House chief of staff H. R. Haldeman, and White House adviser John Ehrlichman. Rumors of a White House cover-up, including secret payments of money to the Watergate burglars and promises of executive clemency, were reported nightly on the national television networks.

In March 1973 the president announced the resignation of his two top aides, Haldeman and Ehrlichman, and at the same time dismissed White House counsel John Dean, who, although deeply involved in the cover-up itself, had been secretly giving information to the FBI and Senate Watergate investigators regarding the cover-up.

Nixon's Use of "Executive Privilege"   President Nixon might have been able to stay in office and weather the Watergate storm if he had publicly repented his own actions, assisted in the Watergate investigation in Congress, and cooperated with

Attorney General Elliot Richardson and (the first) Special Prosecutor Archibald Cox. But it was Nixon's style to confront crisis directly, to avoid surrender, to test his own strength of character against adversity. His gut instinct in a crisis was to "fight like hell" rather than to bargain, accommodate, and compromise. James David Barber believes that such political figures eventually become rigid:

> Such a President will, eventually, freeze around some adamant stand—as did Wilson in the League of Nations fight, Hoover in refusing relief to Americans during the Depression, and Johnson in the Vietnam escalation. Increasingly, as his stance rigidifies, he will see compromise as surrender, justify his cause as sacred, plunge into intense and lonely effort, and concentrate his enmity on specific enemies he thinks are conspiring against him.[8]

As the Watergate affair broadened and intensified, Nixon increasingly viewed it as a test of his strength and character; he perceived a conspiracy among liberal opponents in Congress and the news media to reverse the 1972 election outcome; he became rigid in his stance on "executive privilege"—that is, in withholding tapes, documents, and information. He came to believe he was defending the presidency itself.

When the Senate Watergate Committee learned that the president regularly taped conversations in the Oval Office, it (and later the special prosecutor) issued subpoenas for tapes that would prove or disprove charges by John Dean and others of a cover-up. In response, President Nixon argued that the constitutional separation of powers permits the president to withhold information from both the Congress and the courts. He relied on the doctrine of *executive privilege*—the assertion of the right of the president to keep information, documents, or testimony from either the Congress or the courts if in the opinion of the president it is necessary to do so in the interest of national security or the proper functioning of the executive. He was not acting without precedent in his refusal to cooperate with Congress and the courts in his assertion of executive privilege. Indeed, executive privilege was first invoked against Congress by George Washington in 1796 and employed by many presidents to withhold information from Congress; in 1807 Thomas Jefferson invoked it to

withhold information from the Supreme Court. The claim of
executive privilege has been applied not only to information
affecting national security and international diplomacy, but
to all communications between presidents and their own advisers and cabinet members. Presumably, the doctrine of
executive privilege ensures that advisers can be completely
candid in their conversations with the president. President
Nixon used the doctrine of executive privilege to prevent
Watergate-related tapes of presidential conversations from
becoming available both to Congress and to the courts.

Eventually, however, the dispute over the Watergate
tapes reached the Supreme Court in the important decision
of *The United States* v. *Richard M. Nixon.* The Court denied
the president the power to withhold subpoenaed information
from the courts under the doctrine of executive privilege
when such information was essential to a criminal investigation. The Supreme Court reaffirmed the principle established
in *Marbury* v. *Madison* (1803), which gave the courts the
power to review the actions of other branches of the government. The Court recognized the principle of executive
privilege but denied that it applies to criminal cases or that
the president could refuse judges access to information that
they needed to determine for themselves whether such information applied to criminal cases.

The Impeachment Movement   The movement to impeach
Richard Nixon began in earnest after Attorney General Elliot
Richardson resigned and Special Prosecutor Archibald Cox
was fired. The story of Richardson and Cox illustrates very
clearly the necessity of the president's accommodating established elites. As the Watergate scandal broadened in early
1973, and after the president dismissed Haldeman and
Ehrlichman from the White House, the president seemed to
reach an understanding with congressional leadership about
the handling of the case. He would appoint Elliot Richardson
attorney general, who would appoint Harvard Professor
Archibald Cox special prosecutor, and Cox would have complete independence in conducting his investigations of
Watergate. This pledge was made to the Senate during confir-
mation hearings on Richardson's appointment as attorney
general. But when Cox was installed in office, he quickly

recruited a staff of liberal attorneys and expanded his investigative activities until Nixon began to suspect that Cox was engaged in a conspiracy to destroy him. When Nixon appeared to reach an agreement with Senate Watergate Committee Chairman Sam Ervin to provide transcripts of certain taped conversations and to allow Senator John Stennis to verify the transcripts by listening to the tapes, Cox objected and insisted on obtaining the tapes himself. Cox cited the original promise to give him full independence in pursuing his investigation. Attorney General Richardson supported the position of his old Harvard Law School professor. Nixon acted abruptly in "the Saturday night massacre" to dismiss Cox, which precipitated the resignation of Richardson.

In firing Cox and forcing Richardson out, President Nixon made a serious error. He not only broke a solemn pledge made to the Congress, but more importantly he also cut his last ties with liberals inside and outside his own party, further isolating himself from established leaders.

Nonetheless, the movement to impeach Richard Nixon could not win strong support among Democrats in Congress and the influential news media as long as Spiro Agnew was vice-president. Agnew was even more offensive than Nixon to liberals and newsmen. It was politically essential that Agnew be removed from the vice-presidency before any serious impeachment movement could be launched against Nixon. Removing Agnew turned out to be a relatively easy task. Early in his career Agnew had served as Baltimore County executive and later as governor of Maryland. Baltimore County politics had long been notorious for corruption. Rumors of Agnew's early involvement in corrupt local politics had circulated in Washington cocktail parties for many years. The Justice Department, under pressure from the national news media, obtained indictments against Vice-President Agnew for accepting money from government contractors and failing to report it on his income tax returns. In court Agnew pleaded no contest to the charge of tax fraud, resigned from office, and was given a suspended sentence. The president appointed Gerald R. Ford, Republican minority leader in the House of Representatives and a popular figure in the Congress, to the vice-presidency. Perhaps President Nixon hoped that the popular Ford would prove an asset in congressional relations in the impending impeachment fight. However, the removal of Agnew opened the way for direct frontal attack on Nixon as president.

President Nixon publicly released the transcripts of the subpoenaed White House tapes in a national television broadcast in which he urged the public to read the tapes in their entirety rather than as single excerpts. Nixon contended that the tapes proved his innocence of any prior knowledge of the Watergate break-in or any participation in the cover-up. One of the key tapes recorded a meeting between President Nixon and John Dean on 21 March, 1973. Dean told the president that "a cancer is growing on the presidency," referring to the fact that the Watergate scandal had grown to such large proportions that the cover-up was breaking down. Dean told the president that McCord had already implicated several staff members of the Committee to Re-elect the President. More importantly, Hunt was blackmailing the White House for immediate payment of $120,000 plus pledges of other financial payoffs and executive clemency after conviction. Dean and the president estimated that eventual payoffs to everyone to keep silent would amount to a million dollars or more. The conversations on the tapes are rambling and inconclusive, and subject to varied interpretations. The most common interpretation is that President Nixon approved an immediate payoff to Hunt but declined to promise him clemency. The tape's importance, however, rested not so much on its suggestion of Nixon's complicity in obstructing justice as on the tone and quality of Nixon's leadership. In many taped conversations, Nixon appeared more concerned with narrow and self-serving political interests than with legal or moral questions.

The Judiciary Committee of the House of Representatives, chaired by Representative Peter Rodino of New Jersey, was convened in the spring of 1974 to consider a series of articles of impeachment against President Nixon. The release of the tapes failed to persuade this committee of Nixon's innocence. Indeed, the opposite occurred; the tapes were used by the president's opponents in Congress and the news media to convince the majority of the committee of Nixon's culpability. The committee passed two articles of impeachment. Article One accused the president of obstructing justice in the

Watergate investigation. Article Two accused the president of misusing his executive power and disregarding his constitutional duties to take care that the laws be faithfully executed, specifically in establishing the Plumbers unit and approving its activities.

However, before the House of Representatives could take up these articles of impeachment, Nixon released another tape that damaged his case beyond repair. It was a tape of a meeting between the president and H. R. Haldeman on 23 June 1972, five days after the Watergate break-in. The president withheld this tape until ordered by the Supreme Court to release it to the special prosecutor. The president also acknowledged that he had withheld this evidence even from his own attorney. The tape suggests that the president himself ordered the cover-up of the Watergate affair and tried to restrict the FBI's investigation by implying CIA involvement. With its release, all Republican minority members of the Judiciary Committee who had supported the president publicly announced that they had changed their minds and would vote for impeachment when the articles reached the floor of the House of Representatives. Shortly thereafter, Nixon was informed by congressional leaders of his own party—including Senate Minority Leader Hugh Scott, House Minority Leader John Rhodes, and Senator Barry Goldwater—that impeachment by majority of the House and removal from office by two-thirds of the Senate was assured.

On 9 August 1974, President Nixon resigned his office—the first president of the United States ever to do so. Gerald R. Ford was sworn in as president. On 8 September 1974, President Gerald Ford pardoned former President Richard Nixon "for all offenses against the United States which he, Richard Nixon, has committed or may have committed or taken part in" during his presidency. In accepting the pardon, Nixon expressed remorse over Watergate and acknowledged grave errors of judgment, but he did not admit personal guilt. Despite intensive questioning by the press and Congress, President Ford maintained that his purpose in granting the pardon was to end "bitter controversy and divisive national debate" and "to firmly shut and seal this book" on Watergate.

Nixon and the Elites   The president must govern the nation within the boundaries of elite consensus. Voters may determine who will be president, but *elites* determine what he can do in office. It is ironic that Richard Nixon saw himself as a defender of the people—"the great silent majority"—pitting himself against the liberal establishment that was not popularly elected and that did not reflect grass-roots sentiments. Nixon believed that he understood "middle America," and he probably did. But in the end, elites in Congress and in the news media were able to turn middle America against him. In six months in 1973, Richard Nixon suffered one of the steepest plunges in public opinion approval rating of a president ever recorded. Richard Nixon failed to understand that even landslide victories at the polls are meaningless if the president cannot win the confidence of the Congress, the press, and other segments of the nation's leadership. Popular majorities may elect the president, but they do not permit him to govern in disregard of traditional "rules of the game."

PART 2   THE RISE OF JIMMY CARTER

The Watergate affair, although perhaps the most damaging, was but the latest in a series of setbacks that American national leadership suffered during the 1960s and early 1970s. Defeat and humiliation in Vietnam and rioting, burning, and looting in the ghettos of the nation's large cities had also shaken America's faith in the ability of the establishment to govern. In the wake of Watergate, national opinion polls showed a decline in public trust and confidence in national institutions and leadership. Established leaders realized that many "old" faces had to be replaced to give national leadership a new image. However, this new image was to be cosmetic only and was not to include any fundamental changes in policies or programs.

In December 1974, four months after Nixon's resignation, the relatively "unknown" governor of Georgia, James Earl Carter, Jr., announced his intention to run for the presidency. Carter's background included seven years in the Navy and one lackluster term as Georgia's governor. He had never served in any federal office. The national news media paid little attention to Carter's announcement; political observers everywhere expected that one of the established leaders—Hubert H. Humphrey or Edward M. Kennedy—would win the presidency in 1976. But Carter himself correctly judged that his image as an "outsider" could be turned to his advantage in an era of popular discontent with national leadership over Watergate, inflation and unemployment, and humiliation in Vietnam.

Carter and the Elites   Carter was not, however, the "outsider" that he pretended to be in the 1976 election. He had been introduced to the "political and economic elites" several years before he began his race for the presidency. The Coca-Cola Company is the largest industrial corporation in Atlanta. J. Paul Austin, its chairman of the board and a friend and supporter of Jimmy Carter, nominated the Georgia governor to serve as a U.S. representative on the international Trilateral Commission. The Trilateral Commission, established in 1972 by David Rockefeller (chairman of the board of Chase Manhattan Bank) with the assistance of the Council on Foreign Relations and the Rockefeller Foundation, is a group of officials of multinational corporations and of the governments of several industrial nations, who meet periodically to coordinate economic policy among the United States, the nations of Western Europe, and Japan. Carter's appointment to the commission in 1972 was made by Rockefeller himself and was supported by Coca-Cola and Lockheed, both Atlanta-based multinational corporations.

The commission's membership is a compendium of power and prestige. At the time of Carter's membership, the executive director of the commission was Zbigniew Brzezinski, then a Columbia University professor and now Carter's national security advisor. Other members included Harold Brown, president of Cal Tech (now secretary of defense); Coca-Cola's J. Paul Austin; Hedley Donovan, editor of *Time* magazine; Paul Warnke, senior partner in Averell Harriman's Wall Street investment firm; Alden Clausen, president of the Bank of America, the nation's largest bank; Leonard Woodcock, president of United Auto Workers; Werner M. Blumenthal, president of Bendix Corporation (later secretary of the treasury); Cyrus Vance, senior Wall Street lawyer (now secretary of state); and U.S. Senator Walter Mondale (now vice-president of the United States).

Although Carter brought a new down-home, God-fearing, peanut-farmer image into national politics, he stuck closely to established liberal remedies for society's problems: social programs for the poor and the aged; civil rights commitments for blacks; jobs for the unemployed; a strong national defense; federal aid for cities; support for large labor unions; and even government reorganization, tax "reform," and a balanced budget. Carter defeated weaker candidates in the early primaries—Morris Udall, Henry Jackson, George Wallace, Sargent Shriver, Fred Harris, Milton Schapp, Lloyd Bentsen—although he lost to Edmund G. "Jerry" Brown, Jr., and Frank Church in later primaries. Throughout early 1976, however, the real question was whether either of the heavyweights, Humphrey or Kennedy, would enter the race and take the prize away from Carter. In the end, consultations with other top leaders persuaded both men not to run and to allow Carter to become president.

Polishing the Smile on the Establishment   Thus, Carter as an "outsider" provided the new face, the smile, and the reassuring manner that a worried elite perceived as essential to winning back mass confidence in national leadership. At the same time, Carter reinforced established programs and policies and personified traditional American values—humble beginnings; hard work; success in business and politics; deep roots in the soil, the family, and the community; and pronounced Christian morals and principles. He was welcomed into top elite circles as a man who could restore mass confidence in public institutions and national leadership, and who could do so without changing things much.

Jimmy Carter's rapid rise to national leadership, as well as his welcome into top elite circles, represents a common tactic employed by embattled elites—replacing the old faces associated with past defeats and humiliations with smiling new faces promising honesty, compassion, and good times.

NOTES

1. Philip M. Gregg and Arthur S. Banks, "Dimensions of Political Systems," *American Political Science Review* 59 (September 1965):602–14.

2. William M. Riker, *Federalism: Origin, Operation, Significance* (Boston: Little, Brown, 1964), pp. 17–20.

3. *The Federalist* papers were a series of essays by James Madison, Alexander Hamilton, and John Jay, written in 1787 and 1788 to explain and defend the new Constitution during the struggle over its ratification (*The Federalist*, New York: Modern Library, 1937).

4. Fred I. Greenstein, "The Psychological Functions of the Presidency for Citizens," in Elmer E. Cornwell, ed., *The American Presidency: Vital Center* (Chicago: Scott, Foresman, 1966), pp. 30–36.

5. Robert Dahl, *Pluralist Democracy in the United States* (Chicago: Rand McNally, 1967), p. 136.

6. See Lester Milbrath, *Political Participation: How and Why Do People Get Involved in Politics?* (Chicago: Rand McNally, 1965), pp. 19, 21.

7. Herbert J. McClosky et al., "Issue Conflict and Consensus Among Party Leaders and Followers," *American Political Science Review* 54 (June 1960):425–26.

8. James David Barber, "Tone-Deaf in the Oval Office," *Saturday Review/World*, 12 January 1974, p. 14.

DISCUSSION QUESTIONS

1. Define political science and describe its areas of concern.

2. Describe John Locke's views on constitutionalism and constitutional government, natural law, and the social contract. Discuss the influence of Locke's ideas upon the authors of the United States Constitution. Define what the Founding Fathers meant by *republican government*, *limited government*, and a *strong national government*.

3. Discuss the ideal and procedural meanings of democracy and the democratic values.

4. What are the foundations of national power and how does the Constitution define and limit them? Contrast expressed (delegated) powers with implied powers and identify the clause on which implied powers are based.

5. Define *federalism* and discuss the change that has taken place in the American federalist structure. Include in your discussion definitions of *grants-in-aid* and *guidelines* as well as an identification of the delegated congressional power that has been responsible for the change in the federalist structure.

6. Discuss the Founding Fathers' rationale for structuring the government around a separation of powers. Identify the separate power structures that the Constitution created. Using the original constitutional provisions regarding elections as an illustration, describe how the Founding Fathers' philosophy conflicted with the concepts of democracy. Define what is meant by *sharing of power.*

7. Discuss the sources of presidential power and the factors contributing to the growth of that power in the twentieth century. Briefly describe how Richard Nixon overstepped the boundaries or limitations of presidential power. Comment on how the system of checks and balances and Nixon's own failure to "play by the rules of the game" contributed to Nixon's downfall. Why was Carter, who was relatively "unknown," readily accepted by the political establishment?

8. Identify the sources of judicial power. Define *judicial review* and explain why the Founding Fathers were in favor of this principle. Describe how and why the courts are "insulated."

9. Discuss participation and nonparticipation in democracy. Who participates and how is it possible to participate? Identify the titles and contents of some of the congressional acts and constitutional amendments that have removed obstacles to voting.

10. Describe the functions of political parties. Compare the American two-party system with European political party systems. How is it possible to identify real party differences in America? Identify and describe the most important factor in voting behavior.

SUGGESTED READINGS

Peter Bachrach, *The Theory of Democratic Elitism* (Boston: Little, Brown, 1967).

Stuart G. Brown, *The American Presidency* (New York: Macmillan, 1966).

Thomas R. Dye and Harmon Zeigler, *The Irony of Democracy: An Uncommon Introduction to American Politics* (Belmont, Calif.: Wadsworth, 1969).

Samuel Krislov, *The Supreme Court in the Political Process* (New York: Macmillan, 1965).

Lester W. Milbrath, *Political Participation: How and Why Do People Get Involved in Politics?* (Chicago: Rand McNally, 1965).

New York Times, *The Pentagon Papers* (New York: New York Times, 1971).

Nelson W. Polsby and Aaron B. Wildavsky, *Presidential Elections: Strategies in American Politics* (New York: Scribner, 1968).

Gerald M. Pomper, *Elections in America* (New York: Dodd, Mead, 1968).

Clinton Rossiter, *1787: The Grand Convention* (New York: Macmillan, 1966).

Frank J. Sorauf, *Party Politics in America* (Boston: Little, Brown, 1972).

Chapter 8
Power and History

Over the ages, history seems to have had a variety of meanings for people:

> . . . History with all her volumes vast,
> Hath but one page.
> > Lord Byron (1788–1824)
>
> The history of the world is but the biography of great men.
> > Thomas Carlyle (1795–1881)
>
> History is merely gossip.
> > Oscar Wilde (1856–1900)
>
> So very difficult a matter is it to trace and find out the truth of anything by history.
> > Plutarch (AD 46–120)
>
> History is little else than a picture of human crimes and misfortunes.
> > Voltaire (1694–1778)
>
> Peoples and governments never have learned anything from history, or acted on principles derived from it.
> > Hegel (1770–1831)
>
> The subject of history is the life of peoples and of humanity. To catch and pin down in words. . . to describe directly the life, not only of humanity, but even of a single people, appears to be impossible.
> > Tolstoy (1828–1910)

Despite these somewhat gloomy views, and because of the opposite proof that some of these authors have provided, we believe it is possible to learn something from history, and we hope that after you have read this chapter you will agree. In it, we will take a look at the tasks that historians set themselves, at the various theories they have developed, and at how the perspective of history can increase our understanding of power in society. After you have read this chapter, you should be able to:

- discuss briefly the theories of history developed by Hegel, Marx, Spengler, and Toynbee.
- describe the power elites of various periods of American history, from the American Revolution through the New Deal.
- discuss the historical reinterpretation of the black experience during the Reconstruction era.

HISTORY AND SOCIAL SCIENCE

Can history inform the social sciences about the nature and uses of power in society? The purpose of this chapter is not to teach American history but rather to examine the work of historians to see what contribution they can make to our understanding of power.

History really has two meanings: History may refer to all *past human actions and events*, or it may refer to the *recording, narrating, and interpreting of these events* by historians. History includes the discovery of facts about past events, as well as the interpretation of these events. Many historians contend that their primary responsibility is the disclosure of facts about the past: the accurate presentation of what actually happened, unbiased by interpretive theories or philosophies.

But however carefully historians try to avoid bias, they cannot report *all* the facts of human history. Facts do not select and arrange themselves. The historian must select and organize facts that are worthy of interest, and this process involves personal judgment of what is important about the past. The historian's judgment about the past is affected by present conditions and by personal feelings about the future. So the past is continually reinterpreted by each generation of historians. History is "an unending dialogue" between the present and the past; it is "what one age finds worthy of note in another."

Yet most historians view their task primarily as one of determining and reporting what happened. They leave it to other social scientists to explain why people behave as they do. This division of labor between history and social science does not always work out. In selecting and organizing their facts historians must consider the causes of wars and revolutions, the reasons for the rise and fall of civilizations, the consequences of great events and ideas. They cannot marshal their facts without some notion of *interrelations* among human events. Since they must consider what forces have operated to shape the past, they become involved in economics, sociology, psychology, anthropology, and political science. Historian Henry Steele Commager has observed that "no self-respecting modern historian is content merely with recording what happened; he wants to explain why it happened."[1] Thus, history and social science are intimately related.

THEORIES OF HISTORY:
HEGEL, MARX, SPENGLER, TOYNBEE

Some historians have claimed to perceive *patterns* in the course of human events. From these patterns they have developed theories of history that enable them to interpret great historical movements over time and even to predict the flow of future events. Many other historians condemn theories of history as illusions; they deny that there are any universal patterns in human history. But the temptation to construct theories has attracted many scholars to the task.

Hegelian dialectic

For example, the German philosopher Hegel believed that the history of human beings was explained by the development of human ideals. Every society expressed some ideal in the form of its politics, social life, family life, religion, art, and so on. This historical evolution occurs in *dialectical* fashion: each idea (*thesis*) contains within itself its own contradiction (*antithesis*), and the conflict gives rise to a new and higher ideal (*synthesis*). The dialectical process occurs in civilizations as well as in people's minds. Hegel believed that historical change was the result of the *growth of ideas* and that culture was the expression or embodiment of the ideas.

Marxian dialectic

Marx agreed with Hegel on the dialectic of history but differed profoundly over the moving force in the process. To Hegel the moving force of history was ideological, whereas Marx was convinced it was *material*—the mode of production. According to Marx, history is determined by the *mode of production:*

> The materialist conception of history starts from the proposition that the production of the means to support human life, and, next to production, the exchange of things produced, is the basis of all social structure, that in every society that has appeared in history, the manner in which wealth is distributed, and society divided into classes or orders, is dependent upon what is produced, how it is produced, and how the products are exchanged. From this point of view, the final causes of all social changes and political revolutions are to be sought, not in men's brains, not in man's better insight into external truth and justice, but in changes in the modes of production and exchange.[2]

Both Hegel and Marx believed in the inevitability of progress. Hegel was an idealist and Marx a materialist, but both believed in continuous human progress over time.

The twentieth century has brought war, death, and destruction to human civilization on a scale unprecedented in any previous era of human history. Hence it is difficult to maintain optimism and faith in the historical progress of humankind. Theories of history that stressed continuous human progress have given way to more cyclical theories—encompassing the decay and death of civilizations as well as their birth and growth.

Spengler's cyclical theory

Oswald Spengler's the *Decline of the West* presents a theory of history in which cultures pass through four cycles: springtime, summer, autumn, and winter. Each great civilization lives about a thousand years and follows the same cyclical course. During the springtime of a culture, new myths and values are created that inspire philosophy, science, politics, religion, and art. During its summer, the culture spreads its influence and realizes the full potential of its values and myths; in this period it builds its great architecture and develops its science and mathematics. The autumn brings a questioning of old values and myths. Social cohesion begins to break down, and there is a growth of rationalism and individualism. While this is a creative period for new ideas and philosophies, nonetheless, the initial spirit that inspired the culture fades, old values are lost, and eventually, in its winter, the civilization dies.

Spengler described the rise and fall of eight great cultures: Egypt, Babylonia, India, China, the Maya culture, Greek and Roman civilization, the Arabian culture, and western Europe. Our own Western culture, begun about the year 1000, is declining and approaching death. In this decline, old elites and old values are overthrown in the name of reason, and above all in the name of "the people." Mass rule has replaced the ordered society.

Toynbee's cyclical theory

Another important history of the rise and fall of civilizations is Arnold Toynbee's *Study of History.* Toynbee also perceived a cyclical pattern in the rise and fall of great cultures, but he saw more overall progress than Spengler. Each succeeding civilization can learn from the experiences, values, and myths of earlier civilizations; therefore each succeeding civilization is a little richer in culture than the one preceding it. Toynbee described twenty-one civilizations. Each went through similar stages of growth, maturation, breakdown, and disintegration. Toynbee agreed with Spengler that our own civilization is passing into a period of decline and disintegration.

According to Toynbee, great civilizations emerge as successful, adaptive response to great challenges. The initial challenge is one of overcoming the physical environment, but later challenges may include outside invasion, or industrialization, or revolution. The challenges must be rigorous enough to spur people to surmount them, but not so severe as to overcome a civilization. The best type of challenge is one that evokes an adaptive and creative response. Frequently this response is a dynamic new religion, and new religions often form the foundations of new civilizations.

Toynbee did not accept the idea that civilizations must follow a preordained life cycle and age and die in the fashion of an organism. Instead, civilizations decline when they finally confront a challenge they cannot meet. Disintegration occurs when a civilization loses its adaptive power, its self-determination, its creative leaders. No longer able to cope with the next great challenge, it splits into warring factions and disintegrates in a "time of troubles."

Interesting as those theories may seem, contemporary American historians for the most part avoid overarching theories of history. They search for explanations, but not in terms of grand generalities or laws or theories of history. A quotation from the preface of H. A. L. Fisher's *History of Europe* has become something of a classic in expressing the contemporary disillusionment with theories of history:

> One intellectual excitement has been denied me. Men wiser and more learned than I have discovered in history a plot, a rhythm, a predetermined pattern. These harmonies are concealed from me. I can see only one emergency following upon another as wave follows upon wave; only one great fact with respect to which, since it is unique, there can be no generalizations; only one safe rule for the historian: that he should recognize in the development of human destinies the play of the contingent and the unforeseen.[3]

POWER, CHANGE, AND THE AMERICAN EXPERIENCE

There is a great temptation to romanticize national history. Many national histories are self-congratulating, patriotic exercises. Many historical biographies paint their subjects as larger-than-life figures, free of the faults of common people, who shape the course of events themselves rather than merely responding to the world in which they live. National leaders of the past—Washington, Jefferson, Jackson, Lincoln, Franklin D. Roosevelt—are portrayed as noble men, superior in character and wisdom to today's politicians. Even with the myth of the cherry tree discarded, generations of historians have looked with awe upon the gallery of national heroes as almost superhuman individuals who gallantly saved the nation.

"Great man" approach to history

Some national histories do not rely on "great man" explanations but instead emphasize the origin and growth of governmental institutions. Democracy is traced from its ancient Greek beginnings, through

Institutional approach

"He may be first in war and first in peace, but he's the last to give a hand on the oars."

© 1979 Orlando Busino

English constitutional development, to the colonies and the American constitutional system. Frequently these national histories reinforce reverence for existing political and governmental institutions. Some are written more to support than to explain America.

In the 1890s historian Frederick Jackson Turner argued that the main influence on American history was not the development of political institutions from English or Greek origins, or even the actions of "great men," but the impact of the western frontier upon American society. As historians explained (and occasionally exaggerated) Turner's thesis, they wrote new and even more nationalistic sagas of the American expansion. They hailed western settlement, the Indian wars, the development of transportation and communication, and the rugged individualism of the heroic democratic frontiersman.

Western frontier approach

But historians have also been critical of American institutions. At the beginning of the twentieth century, the reform politicians and the muckraking journalists brought a new iconoclasm to the scene. The Progressive era was critical of the malfunctioning of many governmental institutions that had become sacred over time—and even of the Olympian position of the Founding Fathers. In 1913 Charles A.

Iconoclastic approaches

Beard created an uproar by suggesting that economic motives played a part in leading the Founding Fathers to write the Constitution.

Nevertheless, for the most part the quest for the American past has been carried on in a spirit of sentiment and nostalgia, rather than critical analysis. Historical novels, fictionalized biographies, pictorial collections, books on American regions—all appeal to our fondness for looking back to what we believe was a better era. Americans have a peculiar longing to recapture the past, to try to recover what seems to have been lost.

An incremental approach   Our own bias about the importance of power in society leads us to focus attention on *changing sources of power over time* in American history, and the characteristics of the people and groups who have acquired power. We contend that the Constitution itself, and the national government that it established, reflected the beliefs, values, and interests of the men of power—the elite—of the new republic. If we are to have a true understanding of the Constitution, we must investigate the political interests of the Founding Fathers and the historical circumstances surrounding the Philadelphia Convention in 1787.

Power structures change over time. To understand power in society we have to explore the historical development of power relationships. Any society, to maintain stability and avoid revolution, must provide opportunities for talented and ambitious individuals to acquire power. As an expanding economy created new sources of wealth, power in America shifted to those groups and individuals who acquired the new economic resources. Western expansion and settlement, industrialization, immigration, urbanization, technological innovation, and new sources of wealth—all created new bases of power and new power holders.

But power in America has changed slowly, without any serious break in the ideas and values underlying the American political and economic system. The nation has never experienced a true revolution, in which national leadership is formally replaced by groups or individuals who do not share the values of the system itself. Instead, changes have been *slow* and *incremental*. New national leaders have generally accepted the national consensus about private enterprise, limited government, and individualism.

Historian Richard Hofstadter argues effectively that many accounts of the American past overemphasize the political differences in every era:

> The fierceness of the political struggles has often been misleading; for the range of vision embraced by the primary contestants in the major parties has always been bounded by the horizons of property and enterprise. However much at odds on specific issues, the major political tradi-

tions have shared a belief in the rights of property, the philosophy of economic individualism, the value of competition; they have accepted the economic virtues of capitalist culture as necessary qualities of man. Even when some property right has been challenged—as it was by followers of Jefferson and Jackson—in the name of the rights of man or the rights of the community, the challenge, when translated into practical policy, has actually been urged on behalf of some other kind of property.

The sanctity of private property, the right of the individual to dispose of and invest it, the value of opportunity, and the natural evolution of self-interest and self-assertion, within broad legal limits, into a beneficent social order have been staple tenets of the central faith in American political ideologies; these conceptions have been shared in large part by men as diverse as Jefferson, Jackson, Lincoln, Cleveland, Bryan, Wilson, and Hoover.[4]

Over the years, America's political leadership has been essentially conservative. Whatever the popular label of the American political and economic system—Federalist, Democrat, Whig, Republican, Progressive, Conservative, or Liberal—American leaders have remained committed to the same values and ideas that motivated the Founding Fathers. Although major changes in public policy and in the structure of American government have indeed taken place over two centuries, these changes have been *incremental* rather than revolutionary.

In the following pages, we will examine how sources of power in America have gradually changed over time. We will trace these changes in power elites from the days of the American Revolution, through the boom of the American West and Jacksonian Democracy, to the Civil War and its aftermath—the rise of the industrial capitalist—up to the New Deal and the emergence of a liberal elite.

CHARLES BEARD
The Economic Interpretation
of the Constitution

Charles Beard, historian and political scientist, provided the most controversial historical interpretation of the origin of American national government in his landmark book *An Economic Interpreta-*

tion of the Constitution. Not all historians agree with Beard's interpretation—particularly his emphasis on economic forces—but all concede that it is a milestone in understanding the American Constitution. From an analysis of the economic interests of the Founding Fathers, Beard drew the following conclusions:

> The movement for the Constitution of the United States was originated and carried through principally by four groups of personalty interests which had been adversely affected under the Articles of Confederation: money, public securities, manufactures, and trade and shipping.
>
> The first firm steps toward the formation of the Constitution were taken by a small and active group of men immediately interested through their personal possessions in the outcome of their labors.
>
> No popular vote was taken directly or indirectly on the proposition to call the Convention which drafted the Constitution.
>
> A large propertyless mass was, under the prevailing suffrage qualifications, excluded at the outset from participation (through representatives) in the work of framing the Constitution.
>
> The members of the Philadelphia Convention which drafted the Constitution were, with a few exceptions, immediately, directly, and personally interested in, and derived economic advantages from, the establishment of the new system.
>
> The Constitution was essentially an economic document based upon

the concept that the fundamental private rights of property are anterior to government and morally beyond the reach of popular majorities.

The major portion of the members of the Convention are on record as recognizing the claim of property to a special and defensive position in the Constitution.[5]

Beard argued that to understand the Constitution we must understand the economic interests of the national elite, which included the writers of the document:

> Did the men who formulated the fundamental law of the land possess the kinds of property which were immediately and directly increased in value or made more secure by the results of their labors in Philadelphia? Did they have money at interest [loans outstanding]? Did they own public securities [government bonds]? Did they hold Western lands for appreciation? Were they interested in shipping and manufactures?[6]

Beard was *not* charging that the Founding Fathers wrote the Constitution exclusively for their own benefit. But he argued that they personally benefited immediately from its adoption, and they did not act only "under the guidance of abstract principles of political science." Beard closely studied old unpublished financial records of the U.S. Treasury Department and the personal letters and financial accounts of the fifty-five delegates to the Philadelphia Convention. Table 8–1 summarizes his findings of the financial interests of the Founding Fathers. Beard then turned to an examination of the *Constitution* itself, in the original form in which it emerged from the Convention, to observe the *relationship between economic interests and political power.*

Taxing power and its beneficiaries

There are seventeen grants of power to Congress in Article I, Section 8, followed by a general grant of power to make "all laws which shall be necessary and proper for carrying into execution the foregoing powers." The first and perhaps the most important enumerated power is the power to "lay and collect taxes, duties, imposts, and excises." The *taxing power* is, of course, the basis of all other powers, and it enabled the national government to end its dependence upon the states. The taxing power was of great benefit to the holders of public securities, particularly when it was combined with the provision in Article VI that "all debts contracted and engagements entered into before the adoption of this Constitution shall be as valid against the United States under this Constitution as under the Confederation." This meant that the national government would be obliged to pay off all those investors who held bonds of the United States, and the taxing power would give the national government the ability to do so on its own.

Congress was also given the power to "regulate commerce with foreign nations, and among the several states." The *interstate commerce clause*, which eliminated state control over commerce, and the provision in Article I, Section 9, which prohibited the states from taxing exports, created a free-trade area, or "common market," among the thirteen states. In *The Federalist*, No. 11, Hamilton describes the advantages of this arrangement for American merchants:

Creation of a free-trade area

> The speculative trader will at once perceive the force of these observations and will acknowledge that the aggregate balance of the commerce of the United States would bid fair to be much more favorable than that of the thirteen states without union or with partial unions.

Table 8-1 Founding Fathers Classified by Known Economic Interests

Public Security Interests		Real Estate and
Major	*Minor*	*Land Speculation*
Baldwin	Bassett	Blount
Blair	Blount	Dayton
Clymer	Brearley	Few
Dayton	Broom	FitzSimons
Ellsworth	Butler	Franklin
FitzSimons	Carroll	Gerry
Gerry	Few	Gilman
Gilman	Hamilton	Gorham
Gorham	L. Martin	Hamilton
Jenifer	Mason	Mason
Johnson	Mercer	R. Morris
King	Mifflin	Washington
Langdon	Read	Williamson
Lansing	Spaight	Wilson
Livingston	Wilson	
McClurg	Wythe	
R. Morris		
C. C. Pinckney		
C. Pinckney		
Randolph		
Sherman		
Strong		
Washington		
Williamson		

Table 8-1   (Cont.)

Lending and Investments	Mercantile, Manufacturing and Shipping Interests	Plantations and Slaveholdings
Bassett	Broom	Butler
Broom	Clymer	Davie
Butler	Ellsworth	Jenifer
Carroll	FitzSimons	A. Martin
Clymer	Gerry	L. Martin
Davie	King	Mason
Dickinson	Langdon	Mercer
Ellsworth	McHenry	C. C. Pinckney
Few	Mifflin	C. Pinckney
FitzSimons	G. Morris	Randolph
Franklin	R. Morris	Read
Gilman		Rutledge
Ingersoll		Spaight
Johnson		Washington
King		Wythe
Langdon		
Mason		
McHenry		
C. C. Pinckney		
C. Pinckney		
Randolph		
Read		
Washington		
Williamson		

Protection of money and property

Following the power to tax and spend, to borrow money, and to regulate commerce in Article I, there is a series of *specific powers designed to enable Congress to protect money and property.* Congress is given the power to make bankruptcy laws, to coin money and regulate its value, to fix standards of weights and measures, to punish counterfeiting, to establish post offices and post roads, to pass copyright and patent laws to protect authors and inventors, and to punish piracies and felonies committed on the high seas. Each of these powers is a specific asset to bankers, investors, merchants, authors, inventors, and shippers. Obviously, the Founding Fathers felt that giving Congress control over currency and credit in America would result in better protection for financial interests than if this important responsibility were left to the states. Likewise, control over communication and transportation ("post offices and post roads") was believed to be too essential to trade and commerce to be left to the states.

All the other powers in Article I deal with *military affairs*—raising and supporting armies; organizing, training, and calling upon the state militia; declaring war; suppressing insurrections; and repelling invasions. These powers in Article I, together with the provisions in Article II making the president the commander in chief of the army and navy and of the state militia when called into the federal service, and giving the president the power to make treaties with the advice and consent of the Senate and to send and receive ambassadors—all combined to *centralize diplomatic and military affairs at the national level.* The centralization of diplomatic-military power is confirmed in Article I, Section 10, in which the states are specifically prohibited from entering into treaties with foreign nations, maintaining ships of war, or engaging in war unless actually invaded. It is clear that the Founding Fathers had little confidence in the state militia, particularly when it was under state control. Moreover, if western settlers were to be protected from the Indians, and if the British were to be persuaded to give up their forts in Ohio and open the way to American westward expansion, the national government could not rely upon state militia but must instead have an army of its own. Similarly, a strong navy was essential to the protection of American commerce on the seas (the first significant naval action under the new government was against the piracy of the Barbary States). Thus, a national army and navy were not so much for protection against invasion (for many years the national government would continue to rely primarily upon state militia for this purpose), but rather for the *protection and promotion of its commercial and territorial ambitions.*

Protection against domestic insurrection also appealed to the southern slaveholders' deep-seated fear of a slave revolt. The Constitution permitted Congress to outlaw the *importation of slaves* after the year 1808. But most of the southern planters were more interested in protecting their existing property and slaves than they were in extending the slave trade, and the Constitution provided an explicit advantage to slaveholders in Article IV, Section 2 (later altered by the Thirteenth Amendment abolishing slavery):

> No person held to service or labor in one state, under the laws thereof, escaping into another, shall, in consequence of any law or regulation therein, be discharged from such service or labor, but shall be delivered up on claim of the party to whom such service or labor may be due.

Slaves were one of the most important forms of property in America at the time, and this constitutional provision was an extremely valuable protection for slaveholders. The slave trade lapsed twenty years after the Constitution was written, but slavery as a domestic institution was better safeguarded under the new Constitution than under the Articles of Confederation.

Restrictions on state legislatures

The *restrictions placed upon state legislatures* by the Constitution also provided protection to economic elites in the new nation. States were not allowed to coin money, issue paper money, or pass legal tender laws that would make any money other than gold or silver coin tender in the payments of debts. This restriction would prevent the states from issuing cheap paper money, which could be used by debtors to pay off their creditors with less valuable currency.

The Constitution also forbids states to pass any law "impairing the obligation of contracts." The structure of business relations in a free enterprise economy depends upon government enforcement of private contracts, and it is essential to economic elites that the government be prevented from relieving persons from their obligations to contracts. If state legislatures could relieve debtors of their contractual obligations, or relieve indentured servants from their obligations to their masters, or prevent creditors from foreclosing on mortgages, or declare moratoriums on debt, or otherwise interfere with business obligations, the interests of investors, merchants, and creditors would be seriously damaged.

Criticisms of Beard's interpretation

Some historians disagree with Beard's emphasis on the economic motives of the Founding Fathers. For example:

> The Constitution was adopted in a society which was fundamentally democratic, not undemocratic; and it was adopted by people who were primarily middle-class property owners, especially farmers who owned realty, not just by the owners of personalty. . . . The Constitution was not just an economic document, although economic factors were undoubtedly important. Since most of the people were middle-class and had private property, practically everybody was interested in the protection of property.[7]

Moreover, in the struggle over ratification of the Constitution, it is clear that some people of prestige, reputation, and property opposed accepting the new Constitution. Influential "Anti-Federalists" deplored the undemocratic features of the Constitution, and their criticism about the omission of a bill of rights led directly to the inclusion of the first ten amendments. Supporters of the Constitution were forced to retreat from their demand for unconditional ratification, and they agreed to add the Bill of Rights as amendments as soon as the first Congress was convened under the Constitution.

FREDERICK JACKSON TURNER
AND THE RISE OF THE WEST

As we have noted, power relationships change over time. Industrialization, urbanization, technological change, and new sources
of wealth create new bases of power and new power holders. The
governmental structure of society must provide for changes in the distribution of power or suffer the threat of instability and even revolution. The political system must provide for the "circulation of elites"
as new bases of power and new power holders emerge in society.

The New West: rapid
upward social mobility

According to historian Frederick Jackson Turner, "The rise of the
New West was the most significant fact in American history."[8] Certainly the American West had a profound impact on the political
system of the new nation. People went west because of the vast
wealth of fertile lands that awaited them there; nowhere else in the
world could one acquire wealth so quickly. Because aristocratic
families of the eastern seaboard seldom had reason to migrate
westward, the western settlers were mainly middle- or lower-class
immigrants. With hard work and good fortune, a penniless migrant
could become a rich plantation owner or cattle rancher in a single
generation. Thus, the West meant rapid upward social mobility.

Assimilation

New elites arose in the West and had to be assimilated into
America's governing circles. This assimilation had a profound effect
on the character of America's elites. No one exemplifies the new en-
trants better than Andrew Jackson. Jackson's victory in the presidential election of 1828 was not a victory of the common man over the
propertied classes, but a victory of the new western elites over established Republican leadership in the East. It forced the established
elites to recognize the growing importance of the West and to open
their ranks to the new rich who were settled west of the Alleghenies.

Jacksonian Democracy

Since Jackson was a favorite of the people, it was easy for him to
believe in the wisdom of the masses. But "Jacksonian Democracy"
was by no means a philosophy of leveling equalitarianism. The ideal
of the frontier society was the self-made individual, and wealth and
power won by *competitive skill* were much admired. What offended
the frontiersmen was wealth and power obtained through special
privilege. They believed in a *natural aristocracy*, rather than an
aristocracy by birth, education, or special privilege. It was *not*
absolute equality that Jacksonians demanded but a *more open elite
system*—a greater opportunity for the rising middle class to acquire
wealth and influence through competition.

In their struggle to open America's elite system, the Jacksonians
appealed to mass sentiment. Jackson's humble beginnings, his image
as a self-made man, his military adventures, his frontier experience,

and his rough, brawling style endeared him to the masses. As beneficiaries of popular support, the new elites of the West developed a strong faith in the wisdom and justice of popular decisions. All of the new western states that entered the Union granted universal white male suffrage, and gradually the older states fell into step. Rising elites, themselves often less than a generation away from the masses, saw in a widened electorate a chance for personal advancement that they could never have achieved under the old regime. Therefore, the Jacksonians became noisy and effective advocates of the principle that all men should have the right to *vote* and that no restrictions should be placed upon *officeholding*. They also launched a successful attack upon the congressional caucus system of nominating presidential candidates. Having been defeated in Congress in 1824, Jackson wished to sever Congress from the nominating process. In 1832, when the Democrats held their first national convention, Andrew Jackson was renominated by acclamation.

Jacksonian Democracy also brought changes in the method of selecting presidential electors. The Constitution left to the various state legislatures the right to decide how presidential electors should be chosen, and in most cases the legislatures themselves chose the electors. But after 1832 all states elected their presidential electors by popular vote. In most states the people voted for electors who were listed under the name of their party and their candidate.

THE CIVIL WAR AND ELITE CLEAVAGE

Social scientists can gain insight into societal conflict and the breakdown of elite consensus through the study of history—particularly the history of the American Civil War. America's elites were in substantial agreement about the character and direction of the new nation during its first sixty years. In the 1850s, however, the role of blacks in American society—the most divisive issue in the history of American politics—became an urgent question that drove a wedge between elites and ultimately led to the nation's bloodiest war. The political system was unequal to the task of negotiating a peaceful settlement to the problem of slavery because America's elites were themselves deeply divided over the question.

Southern elites   It was the white elites and not the white masses of the South who had an interest in the slave and cotton culture. On the eve of the Civil War probably not more than four hundred thousand southern families—approximately one in four—held slaves. And many of these families held only one or two slaves each. The number of great planters—men who owned fifty or more slaves and large holdings of land—was probably not more than seven thousand. Yet the views of these men dominated southern politics.

Northern elites

The Northern elites consisted of merchants and manufacturers who depended upon free labor. However, Northern elites had no direct interest in the abolition of slavery in the South. Some Northern manufacturers were making good profits from Southern trade, and with higher tariffs they stood a chance to make even better profits. Abolitionist activities imperiled trade relations between North and South and were often looked upon with irritation in Northern social circles.

Conflict over western land

Both Northern and Southern elites realized that control of the West was the key to future dominance of the nation. Northern elites wanted a West composed of small farmers who produced food and raw materials for the industrial and commercial East and provided a market for eastern goods. But Southern planters feared the voting power of a West composed of small farmers and wanted western lands for the expansion of the cotton and slave culture. Cotton ate up the land and, because it required continuous cultivation and monotonous rounds of simple tasks, was suited to slave labor. Thus, to protect the cotton economy, it was essential to expand westward and to protect slavery in the West. This conflict over western land eventually precipitated the Civil War.

Underlying elite consensus: attempts at compromise

Yet despite such differences, the underlying consensus of American elites was so great that compromise after compromise was devised to maintain unity. Both Northern and Southern elites displayed a continued devotion to the principles of constitutional government and the protection of private property. In the Missouri Compromise of 1820, the land in the Louisiana Purchase exclusive of Missouri was divided between free territory and slave territory at 36°30'; and Maine and Missouri were admitted to the Union as free and slave states, respectively. After the war with Mexico, the elaborate Compromise of 1850 caused one of the greatest debates in American legislative history, with Senators Henry Clay, Daniel Webster, John C. Calhoun, Salmon P. Chase, Steven A. Douglas, Jefferson Davis, Alexander H. Stephens, Robert Toombs, William H. Seward, and Thaddeus Stevens all participating. Cleavage within the elite was apparent, but it was not yet so divisive as to split the nation. A compromise was achieved, providing for the admission of California as a free state; for the creation of two new territories, New Mexico and Utah, out of the Mexican cession; for a drastic fugitive slave law to satisfy Southern planters; and for the prohibition of the slave trade in the District of Columbia. Even the Kansas-Nebraska Act of

1854 was intended to be a compromise; each new territory was supposed to decide for itself whether it should be slave or free, the expectation being that Nebraska would vote free and Kansas slave. Gradually, however, the spirit of compromise gave way to divergence and conflict.

Beginning in 1856, proslavery and antislavery forces fought it out in "bleeding Kansas." Senator Charles Sumner of Massachusetts delivered a condemnation of slavery in the Senate and was beaten almost to death on the Senate floor by Congressman Preston Brooks of South Carolina. Intemperate language in the Senate became commonplace, with frequent threats of secession, violence, and civil war. In 1857 a Southern-dominated Supreme Court decided, in *Dred Scott* v. *Sanford,* that the Missouri Compromise was unconstitutional because Congress had no authority to forbid slavery in any territory.[9] Slave property, said Chief Justice Roger B. Taney, was as much protected by the Constitution as was any other kind of property. In 1859 John Brown and his followers raided the United States arsenal at Harper's Ferry, as a first step to freeing the slaves of Virginia by force. Brown was captured by Virginia militia under the command of Colonel Robert E. Lee, tried for treason, found guilty, and executed. Southerners believed that Northerners had tried to incite the horror of slave insurrection, while Northerners believed that Brown died a martyr.

Lincoln and slavery

Yet historian Richard Hofstadter observes that even in the midst of this disastrous conflict one finds extensive evidence of attempts to maintain consensus among the elite. There were many genuine efforts at compromise and conciliation. Abraham Lincoln never attacked slavery in the South; his exclusive concern was to halt the spread of slavery in the western territories. He wrote in 1845: "I hold it a paramount duty of us in the free states, due to the union of the states, and perhaps to liberty itself (paradox though it may seem), to let the slavery of the other states alone."[10] Throughout his political career, Lincoln consistently held this position. On the other hand, with regard to the western territories, he said: "The whole nation is interested that the best use shall be made of these territories. We want them for homes and free white people. This they cannot be, to any considerable extent, if slavery shall be planted within them."[11] In short, Lincoln wanted the western territories to be tied economically and culturally to the Northern system. As for Lincoln's racial views, as late as 1858, he said:

> I will say, then, that I am not, nor ever have been, in favor of bringing about in any way the social and political equality of the white and black races: that I am not, nor ever have been, in favor of making voters or

jurors of negroes, nor of qualifying them to hold office, not to intermarry with white people. . . .

And inasmuch as they cannot so live, while they do remain together there must be the position of superior and inferior, and I as much as any other man am in favor of having the superior position assigned to the white race.[12]

Hofstadter believes that Lincoln's political posture was essentially *conservative:* He wished to preserve the long-established order and *consensus that had protected American principles and property rights* so successfully in the past. He was *not* an abolitionist, and he did *not* seek the destruction of the Southern elites or the rearrangement of the South's social fabric. His goal was to bring the South back into the Union, to restore orderly government, and to establish the principle that the states cannot resist national authority with force. At the beginning of the Civil War, Lincoln knew that a great part of conservative Northern opinion was willing to fight for the Union, but might refuse to support a war to free slaves. Lincoln's great political skill was his ability to gather all the issues of the Civil War into one single overriding theme—the preservation of the Union. On the other hand, he was bitterly attacked throughout the war by radical Republicans who thought that he had "no antislavery instincts."

As the war continued and casualties mounted, opinion in the North became increasingly bitter toward Southern slave owners. Many Republicans joined the abolitionists in calling for emancipation of the slaves simply to punish the "rebels." They knew that the power of the South was based on the labor of slaves. Lincoln also knew that if he proclaimed to the world that the war was being fought to free the slaves, there would be less danger of foreign intervention. Yet, even in late summer 1862 Lincoln wrote:

My paramount object in this struggle is to save the Union. If I could save the Union without freeing any slaves, I would do it; if I could save it by freeing some and leaving others alone, I would also do that. I shall do less whenever I shall believe what I am doing hurts the cause, and I shall do more whenever I believe doing more will help the cause. I shall adopt new views as fast as they shall appear to be true views.[13]

Finally, on 22 September 1862, Lincoln issued his preliminary Emancipation Proclamation. Claiming his right as commander in chief of the army and navy, he promised that "on the first day of January, . . . 1863, all persons held as slaves within any State, or designated part of a State, the people whereof shall then be in rebellion against the United States, shall be then, thenceforward, and forever free." Thus, one of the great steps forward in human freedom in this nation, the Emancipation Proclamation, did not come about as a result of demands by the people, and certainly not as a result of demands by the slaves themselves. Historian Richard Hofstadter contends that the Emancipation Proclamation was a political action taken by the president for the sake of helping to preserve the Union. It was not a revolutionary action but a conservative one.

POWER AND THE INDUSTRIAL REVOLUTION

The rise of the industrial elite

The importance of the Civil War for America's power structure lay in the commanding position that the new industrial capitalists won during the course of that struggle. Even before 1860, Northern industry had been altering the course of American life; the economic transformation of the United States from an agricultural to an industrial nation reached the crescendo of a revolution in the second half of the nineteenth century. Canals and steam railroads had been opening up new markets for the growing industrial cities of the East. The rise of corporations and of stock markets for the accumulation of capital upset old-fashioned ideas about property. The introduction of machinery in factories revolutionized the conditions of labor and made the masses dependent upon industrial capitalists for their livelihood. Civil War profits compounded the capital of the industrialists and placed them in a position to dominate the economic life of the nation. Moreover, when the Southern planters were removed from the national scene, the government in Washington became the exclusive domain of the new industrial leaders.

Social Darwinism

The new industrial elite found a new philosophy to justify its political and economic dominance. Drawing an analogy from Darwinian biology, Herbert Spencer undertook to demonstrate that, just as an elite was selected in nature through evolution, so also society would near perfection as it allowed natural *social* elites to be selected by *free competition*. Spencer hailed the accumulation of new industrial wealth as a sign of "the survival of the fittest." The *social Darwinists* found in the law of survival of the fittest an admirable defense for the emergence of a ruthless ruling elite, an elite that defined its own self-interest more narrowly, perhaps, than any other in American history. It was a philosophy that permitted the conditions of the masses to decline to the lowest depths in American history.

The industrialists in Congress

After the Civil War, industrialists became more prominent in Congress than they had ever been. They had little trouble in voting high tariffs and hard money, both of which heightened profits. Very little effective regulatory legislation was permitted to reach the floor of Congress. After 1881 the Senate came under the spell of Nelson Aldrich, son-in-law of John D. Rockefeller who controlled Standard Oil. Aldrich served thirty years in the Senate. He believed that geographical representation in that body was old-fashioned and openly advocated a Senate manned officially by representatives from the great business "constituencies"—steel, coal, copper, railroads, banks, textiles, and so on.

The corporate form of business facilitated the amassing of capital by limiting the liability of capitalists to their actual investments and thereby keeping their personal fortunes safe in the event of misfortunes to their companies. The corporate form also encouraged capitalists to take risks in expanding industrial capital through the stock market. "Wall Street," the address of the nation's busiest security market—the New York Stock Exchange—became a synonym for industrial capitalism. The markets for corporation stocks provided a vast and ready money source for new enterprises or for the enlargement and consolidation of old firms.

Typical of the great entrepreneurs of industrial capitalism was John D. Rockefeller. By the end of the Civil War, Rockefeller had accumulated a modest fortune of $50,000 in wholesale grain and meat. In 1865, with extraordinary good judgment, he invested his money in the wholly new petroleum business. He backed one of the first oil refineries in the nation and continually reinvested his profits in his business. In 1867, he and two partners—H. M. Flagler and F. W. Harkness—founded the Standard Oil Company of Ohio, which in that year refined 4 percent of the nation's output. By 1872, with monopoly as his goal, he had acquired twenty of the twenty-five refineries in Cleveland and was laying plans that within a decade would bring him into control of over 90 percent of the oil refineries of the country. Rockefeller bought up pipelines, warehouses, and factories and was able to force the railroad to grant him rebates. In 1882 he formed a giant trust, the Standard Oil Company, with a multitude of affiliates. Thereafter, the Standard Oil Company became a prototype of American monopolies. As Rockefeller himself put it: "The day of combination is here to stay. Individualism has gone, never to return."

THE NEW DEAL AND THE EMERGENCE OF "THE LIBERAL ESTABLISHMENT"

Impact of the Great Depression

Herbert Hoover was the last great advocate of the "rugged individualism" of the old order. The economic collapse of the Great Depression undermined the faith of both the elite and the nonelite in the idea of "social Darwinism." Following the stock market crash of October 1929, and in spite of assurances by the elite that prosperity lay "just around the corner," the American economy virtually stopped. Prices dropped sharply, factories closed, real estate values declined, new construction practically ceased, banks went under, wages were cut drastically, unemployment figures mounted, and welfare rolls swelled.

New era in elite thinking

The election of Franklin Delano Roosevelt to the presidency in 1932 ushered in a new era in American elite philosophy. The Great Depression did *not* bring about a revolution; it did *not* result in the emergence of new elites; but it did have important impact on the *thinking* of America's governing circles. The economic disaster that had befallen the nation caused the elites to consider the need for economic reform. The Great Depression also reinforced the notion that elites must acquire a greater public responsibility. The victories of fascism in Germany and communism in the Soviet Union and the growing restlessness of the masses in America made it plain that *reform and regard for the public welfare* were essential to the continued maintenance of the American political system and the dominant place of the elite in it.

Roosevelt and the New Deal

Roosevelt sought to elaborate a New Deal philosophy that would permit government to devote much more attention to the public welfare than did the philosophy of Hoover's somewhat discredited "rugged individualism." The New Deal was not a revolutionary system but rather a necessary *reform* of the existing capitalist system. In the New Deal, American elites accepted the principle that the entire community, through the agency of the national government, has a *responsibility for mass welfare*. Roosevelt's second inaugural address called attention to "one-third of a nation, ill housed, ill clad, ill nourished." Roosevelt succeeded in preserving the existing system of private capitalism and avoiding the threats posed to the established order by fascism, socialism, communism, and other radical movements.

Historian Richard Hofstadter comments on Roosevelt's liberal, public-regarding philosophy:

> At the beginning of his career he took to the patrician reform thought of the progressive era and accepted a social outlook that can best be summed up in the phrase "noblesse oblige." He had a penchant for public service, personal philanthropy, and harmless manifestos against dishonesty in government; he displayed a broad easy-going tolerance, a genuine liking for all sorts of people; he loved to exercise his charm in political and social situations.[14]

Roosevelt's personal philosophy was soon to become the prevailing ethos of the new liberal establishment.

Thus, liberalism in America today is a product of elite response to economic depression at home and the rising threats of fascism and communism abroad. Its historical origin can be traced to elite efforts to *preserve* the existing political and economic system through reform. This historical perspective on the liberal tradition gives us a better understanding of the origins of change and reform within society. In a broader view, the historical perspective expands our understanding of society in general, and, as we hope this chapter has shown, can indeed contribute to our understanding of the nature and uses of power in society. In the case study that folllows, we will examine the revisions that the historical perspective must sometimes undergo.

CASE STUDY
Reconstruction and Black History

The ideal history, completely objective and dispassionate, is really an illusion. Consciously or unconsciously, all historians are biased. There is bias in their choice of subject, in their selection of material, in their organization and presentation of the material, and, inevitably, in their interpretation of it.

Let us consider the historical interpretation of black experience in America, particularly of black experience in the Reconstruction era following the Civil War. Only a few years ago historians viewed the Reconstruction Congress as vindictive and sinful. The period as a whole was considered destructive, oppressive, and corrupt. Military rule was imposed upon the South. "Carpetbaggers" and "scallywags" confiscated the property of helpless southerners and retarded the economic progress of the South for decades. Maladministration and corruption in the federal government were portrayed as being greater than ever before in American history. The role of blacks in the Reconstruction years was regarded with ridicule: It was implied that blacks were pushed into positions of authority by spiteful military rules in order to humiliate proud southern whites. The accomplishments of blacks during this period were overlooked. Finally, it was suggested that the separation of the races—segregation—was the "normal" pattern of southern life. The belief was fostered that blacks and whites in the South had never known any other pattern of life than slavery and segregation.

A new awareness of black history in recent years has resulted in a thoroughgoing reinterpretation of the Reconstruction era. Historian C. Vann Woodward's work, among others, led the way in bringing new light to this important period. Woodward recorded the progress of blacks during Reconstruction, described the good-faith efforts of the Reconstruction Congress to secure equality for black Americans, and explained the reimposition of segregation in terms of class conflict among whites. (Alex Haley's popular book *Roots*, together with the dramatic television series based on it, is another example of historical interpretation. While many older histories of the pre–Civil War South romanticized plantation life, *Roots* described the cruelties and brutality of slavery.)

A Revised View of Reconstruction: Black Progress   When the radical Republicans (as opposed to the moderate faction within the party) gained control of Congress in 1867, blacks momentarily seemed destined to attain their full rights as United States citizens. Under military rule southern states adopted new constitutions that awarded the vote and other civil liberties to blacks. Black men were elected to state legislatures and to the U.S. Congress. In 1865 nearly 10 percent of all federal troops were black. The literacy rate among blacks rose rapidly as hundreds of schools set up by the federal government's Freedmen's Bureau began providing education for ex-slaves.[15]

The first black actually to serve in Congress was Hiram R. Revels of Mississippi, who in 1870 took over the Senate seat previously held by Confederate President Jefferson Davis. In all, twenty-two southern blacks served in Congress between 1870 and 1901. All were elected as Republicans; thirteen were former slaves. Many of these men made substantial contributions to Reconstruction policy. Robert B. Elliott of South Carolina won national fame when he delivered a two-hour speech on behalf of the Civil Rights Act of 1875. The last black congressman under Reconstruction from the South was George H. White of North Carolina, who finally left the Congress in 1901.

The accomplishments of the Reconstruction Congress were considerable. Even before the radical Republicans gained control, the Thirteenth Amendment, which abolished slavery, had become part of the Constitution. But it was the Fourteenth and Fifteenth Amendments and the important Civil Rights Act of 1875 that attempted to secure a place in America for the black man equal to that of his white neighbor. The wording of the Fourteenth Amendment was explicit:

> No state shall make or enforce any law which shall abridge the privileges or immunities of citizens of the United States; nor shall any state deprive any person of life, liberty, or property, without due process of law; nor deny to any person within its jurisdiction the equal protection of the laws.

The Civil Rights Act of 1875 declared that all persons were entitled to the full and equal enjoyment of all public accommodations—inns, public conveniences, theaters, and other places of public amusement. In this act the Reconstruction Congress committed the nation to a policy of nondiscrimination in all aspects of public life.

Between 1865 and the early 1880s, the success of the civil rights movement was reflected in black voting throughout the South, the ascendance of many blacks to federal and state offices, and the almost equal treatment afforded blacks in theaters, restaurants, hotels, and public transportation facilities. But by 1877 support for Reconstruction policies began to crumble. In what has been described as the "Compromise of 1877," the national government agreed to end military occupation of the South, thereby giving up its efforts to rearrange southern society and lending tacit approval to white supremacy in that region. In return, the southern states pledged their support for the Union, accepted national supremacy, and enabled the Republican candidate, Rutherford B. Hayes, to assume the presidency following the much-disputed election of 1876 in which his opponent, Samuel Tilden, had received a majority of the popular vote.

The Development of the White Supremacy Movement   The withdrawal of federal troops from the South in 1877 did not bring about an instant change in the status of the black man. Southern blacks voted in large numbers well into the 1880s and 1890s. Certainly we do not mean to suggest that discrimination was nonexistent during this period. Perhaps the most debilitating of all segregation—that in the public schools—appeared immediately after the Civil War under the beneficent sanction of Reconstruction authorities. Yet segregation in its full-blown "Jim Crow" form took shape only gradually, and largely as the result of political and economic conflicts that divided southern whites.

Segregation was closely associated with the rise of *populism*—a movement purporting to represent the interests of the common people—in the South. Interestingly, the earliest southern populists adopted a style of equalitarianism and attempted to enlist blacks in a coalition of white and black poor people against their common economic oppressors. However, they soon came to realize that this strategy was bound to fail since racial prejudice was greatest among the poor whites to whom their appeal was directed. These were the classes most subject to deep-rooted fears of the black man. Conservatives, realizing that the populists had erred in their strategy, were able to discredit the early populists by fanning the flames of racial hatred, thus driving a wedge between poor blacks and poor whites. Alarmed by the populists' successes in the 1880s and 1890s (especially after the formation of the Populist party in 1891), the conservatives soon raised the cries of "Negro domination" and "white supremacy," thereby galvanizing the racial fears of southern whites of all classes. The planters of the rich lowland counties needed an issue—even better, a scapegoat—to oppose the growing influence of white farmers from the mountainous counties. Soon the Populists realized that they would have to disassociate themselves from blacks and adopt the white supremacy position.

The first objective of the *white supremacy movement* was to disenfranchise blacks. The standard devices developed for achieving this feat were the literacy test, the poll tax, the white primary, and various forms of intimidation. Following the disenfranchisement of blacks, the white supremacy movement established segregation and discrimination as public policy by the adoption of a large number of Jim Crow laws, designed to prevent the mingling of whites and blacks (Jim Crow was a stereotype Negro in a nineteenth-century song-and-dance show). Between 1900 and 1910, laws were adopted by southern state legislatures requiring segregation of the races in streetcars, in hospitals, in prisons, in orphanages, and in homes for the aged and indigent. A New Orleans ordinance decreed that white and black prostitutes confine their activities to separate districts. In 1913 the federal government itself adopted policies that segregated the races in federal office buildings, cafeterias, and rest-room facilities. Social policy followed (indeed, exceeded) public policy. Little signs reading "White Only" or "Colored" appeared everywhere, with or without the support of law.

Response of Blacks to Segregation   Many early histories of Reconstruction paid little attention to the response of blacks to the imposition of segregation. But there were at least three distinct types of response: (1) accommodation and acceptance of a subordinate position in society, (2) participation in the formation of a black protest movement, and (3) migration out of the South to avoid some of the consequences of white supremacy.

The foremost black advocate of accommodation to segregation was the well-known black educator Booker T. Washington. Washington enjoyed wide popularity among both white and black Americans. He was an adviser to two presidents (Theodore Roosevelt and William Howard Taft) and was highly respected by white philanthropists and government officials. In his famous Cotton States' Exposition speech in Atlanta in 1895, Washington assured whites that blacks were prepared to accept a separate position in society:

> As we have proved our loyalty to you in the past, in nursing your children, watching by the sickbed of your mothers and

fathers, and often following them with tear-dimmed eyes to their graves, so in the future, in our humble way, we shall stand by you. . . . In all things that are purely social we can be as separate as the fingers, yet one as the hand in all things essential to mutual progress.[16]

Booker T. Washington's hopes for black America lay in a program of self-help through education. He himself had attended Hampton Institute in Virginia, where the curriculum centered around practical trades for blacks. Washington obtained some white philanthropic support in establishing his own Tuskegee Institute in Tuskegee, Alabama, in 1881. His first students helped build the school. Training at Tuskegee emphasized immediately useful vocations, such as farming, preaching, and blacksmithing. Washington urged his students to stay in the South, to acquire land, and to build homes, thereby helping to eliminate ignorance and poverty among their fellow blacks. One of Tuskegee's outstanding faculty members was George Washington Carver, who researched and developed uses for southern crops. Other privately and publicly endowed black colleges were founded that later developed into major universities, including Fisk and Howard (both started by the Freedmen's Bureau) and Atlanta, Hampton, and Southern.

While Washington was urging blacks to make the best of segregation, a small band of blacks were organizing themselves behind a declaration of black resistance and protest that would later rewrite American public policy. The leader of this group was W. E. B. Du Bois, a brilliant historian and sociologist at Atlanta University. In 1905 Du Bois and a few other black intellectuals met in Niagara Falls, Canada, to draw up a black platform intended to "assail the ears" and sear the consciences of white Americans. In rejecting moderation and compromise, the Niagara statement proclaimed: "We refuse to allow the impression to remain that the Negro American assents to inferiority, is submissive under oppression and apologetic before insults." The platform listed the major injustices perpetrated against blacks since Reconstruction: the loss of voting rights, the imposition of Jim Crow laws and segregated public schools, the denial of equal job opportunities, the existence of inhumane conditions in southern prisons, the exclusion of blacks from West Point and Annapolis, and the failure on the part of the federal government to enforce the Fourteenth and Fifteenth Amendments. Out of the Niagara meeting came the idea for a nationwide organization dedicated to fighting for blacks, and on 12 February 1909, the one hundredth anniversary of Abraham Lincoln's birth, the National Association for the Advancement of Colored People (NAACP) was founded.[17]

Du Bois himself was on the original board of directors of the NAACP, but a majority of the board consisted of white liberals. In the years to follow, most of the financial support and policy guidance for the association was provided by whites rather than blacks. However, Du Bois was the NAACP's first director of research and the editor of its magazine, *Crisis*. The NAACP began a long and eventually successful campaign to establish black rights through legal action. Over the years, hundreds of court cases were brought at the local, state, and federal court levels on behalf of blacks denied their constitutional rights.

World War I provided an opportunity for restive blacks in the South to escape the worst abuses of white supremacy by migrating en masse to northern cities. In the years 1916–1918, an estimated half-million blacks moved to the North to fill the labor shortage caused by the war effort. Most migrating blacks arrived in big northern cities only to find more poverty and segregation. But at least they could vote and attend better schools, and they were not obliged to step off the sidewalk into the gutter when a white man approached.

The progressive "ghettoization" of black Americans— their migration from the rural South to the urban North and their increasing concentration in central-city ghettos—had profound political, as well as social, implications. The ghetto provided an environment conducive to collective mass action. Even as early as 1928, the black residents of Chicago were able to elect one of their own to the House of Representatives. The election of Oscar de Priest, the first black congressman from the North, signaled a new turn in American urban politics by announcing to white politicians that they would have to reckon with the black vote in northern cities. The black ghettos would soon provide an important element in a new political coalition that was about to take form—

namely, the Democratic party of Franklin Delano Roosevelt.

The increasing concentration of blacks in northern ghettos in large, politically competitive, "swing" states provided black voters with new political power—not only to support the Democratic party coalition in national politics, but also to elect black men to local public office. Today black mayors serve, or have served, in cities as diverse as Los Angeles, Gary, Atlanta, and Newark. Thus, this particular case of "revisionist" history helps social scientists to understand how blacks coped with segregation and emerged from this experience with new power, unity, and purpose.

NOTES

1. Henry Steele Commager, *The Study of History* (Columbus, Ohio: Merrill, 1965), p. 79.
2. Quoted in F. Engels, *Socialism, Utopian and Scientific* (1892), introduction.
3. H. A. L. Fisher, *A History of Europe* (Boston: Houghton Mifflin, 1935), preface.
4. Richard Hofstadter, *The American Political Tradition and the Men Who Made It* (New York: Vintage Books, 1956), p. viii.
5. Charles Beard, *An Economic Interpretation of the Constitution* (New York: Macmillan, 1913), pp. 324–25.
6. Ibid., p. 73.
7. Robert E. Brown, *Charles Beard and the Constitution* (Princeton, N.J.: Princeton University Press, 1956), p. 200.
8. Frederick Jackson Turner, "The West and American Ideals," in *The Frontier in American History* (New York: Holt, 1921).
9. *Dred Scott* v. *Sanford*, 19 Howard 393 (1857).
10. Richard Hofstadter, *The American Political Tradition* (New York: Knopf, 1948), p. 109.
11. Ibid., p. 113.
12. Ibid., p. 116.
13. Ibid., pp. 132–33.
14. Ibid., pp. 323–24.
15. For a general history of Reconstruction politics, see C. Vann Woodward, *Reunion and Reaction* (Boston: Little, Brown, 1951); also see C. Vann Woodward, *The Strange Career of Jim Crow* (New York: Oxford University Press, 1957).

16. Quoted in Henry Steele Commager, ed., *The Struggle for Racial Equality: A Documentary Record* (New York: Harper & Row, 1967), p. 19.

17. Ibid.

DISCUSSION QUESTIONS

1. Choose two of the following historians and discuss their theories of history: Hegel, Marx, Spengler, Toynbee.

2. Describe the various approaches to studying history. Comment on the strengths or weaknesses of each.

3. What were Charles Beard's two main approaches to understanding the Constitution? Describe briefly how the following constitutional provisions were of immediate benefit to the nation's elite: taxing power; interstate commerce clause; congressional powers to protect money and property; power to raise an army and navy; Article IV, Section 2, which required the return of runaway slaves and indentured servants; restrictions on state legislatures; prevention of laws impairing obligation of contracts. Discuss the criticisms of Beard's interpretation of the Constitution.

4. Describe the power elite that was created by expansion into the American West. What factors contributed to the emergence of this elite; what was its power base? Identify the factor that significantly contributed to the assimilation of this elite into American governing circles. Describe the philosophy of this new elite and the impact that it had on both the elite system and the electoral system.

5. Describe the economic interests of Northern and Southern elites on the eve of the Civil War. What were their points of conflict and of agreement? Discuss at least one of the compromises these elites attempted. Describe Lincoln's attitude toward slavery and his attempts at preserving consensus. Why was the Proclamation Emancipation a conservative, rather than a revolutionary, document?

6. Describe the power elite that emerged in the aftermath of the Civil War. What factors contributed to the rise of this elite? Discuss the philosophy that this elite adopted, as well as the influence that this elite had on Congress.

7. Discuss the impact that the Great Depression had on both elite and nonelite philosophy, and the kind of elite thinking that developed in this era. What foreign influences had an impact on this new thinking? Briefly describe Franklin Delano Roosevelt's New Deal philosophy.

8. Show how different historical interpretations of the same historical events can radically differ by contrasting earlier interpretations of the Reconstruction era with the more recent interpretations of historian C. Vann Woodward.

SUGGESTED READINGS

Charles Beard, *An Economic Interpretation of the Constitution* (New York: Macmillan, 1913).

Robert E. Brown, *Charles Beard and the Constitution* (Princeton, N.J.: Princeton University Press, 1956).

John P. Davis, ed., *The American Negro Reference Book* (Englewood Cliffs, N.J.: Prentice-Hall, 1966).

John Hope Franklin, *From Slavery to Freedom, A History of American Negroes* (New York: Knopf, 1956).

Pietor Geyl, Arnold J. Toynbee, and Pitirim A. Sorokin, *The Pattern of the Past: Can We Determine It?* (New York: Greenwood Press, 1968).

Richard Hofstadter, *The American Political Tradition* (New York: Vintage Books, 1956).

Michael E. Murray, *Modern Philosophy of History* (The Hague: Nijhoff, 1970).

Ronald H. Nash, ed., *Ideas of History* (New York: Dutton, 1969).

Clinton Rossiter, *1787: The Grand Convention* (New York: Macmillan, 1966).

Morton Gabriel White, *Foundations of Historical Knowledge* (New York: Harper & Row, 1965).

C. Vann Woodward, *The Strange Career of Jim Crow* (New York: Oxford University Press, 1957).

PART III

THE USES OF POWER

In part III we will explore the major social problems confronting society. As we noted in chapter 1, these problems are interdisciplinary in nature; they do not confine themselves to one or another of the social science disciplines. The problem of crime and violence, for example, is of as much interest and concern to the psychologist as it is to the sociologist. Indeed, because it is a question of human behavior and its consequences, it is also of concern to the political scientist, the historian, the economist, and the anthropologist. Each of these social scientists would, of course, approach the study of crime and violence from a somewhat different perspective. Our perspective will continue to be the unifying one of power in society, but our main focus here will be on how power may be used to confront the crises that afflict human societies. As we shall see, that use of power can be for the betterment or detriment of humanity.

In chapter 9 we will explore the power of ideology and the specific nature of some of the major ideologies that have been the source of conflict in the twentieth century. In chapter 10 we will examine the powerlessness of those discriminated against on the basis of race and sex, and the power of the protest movements through which they have gained some measure of equality. In chapter 11 we will look at the problem of poverty in an affluent America and at governmental efforts to alleviate, prevent, or cure this particular type of powerlessness. In chapter 12 we will explore the ways in which America has struggled to maintain a balance between the exercise of its police powers and the safeguarding of individual freedom, and the continuous role that violence has played in American struggles for power. In chapter 13 we will look at some of the environmental problems that affect the quality of our lives and at some of the conflicting human interests that work against a fully effective use of governmental power to solve these problems. In chapter 14 we will consider the global struggle for power, and the past and present ways in which people have attempted to maintain peace in international relations.

Chapter 9
Power and Ideology

When commanded by authority they perceive as legitimate, ordinary human beings may inflict extreme pain and suffering on their fellow humans. The experiments carried out by Stanley Milgram at Yale University served to confirm that observation; but indeed the pages of history are filled with similar evidence. It is difficult for us to comprehend the atrocities of World War II—6 million Jews murdered; entire villages of Europe eradicated in acts of indiscriminate retaliation; millions of men, women, and children condemned to slave labor; untold numbers suffering the horrors of concentration camps; still others, the hideous "medical experiments" that were surely the very definition of sadism. The list goes on. Incredibly enough, these were the acts of human beings. Not all of them could have been monsters. Many of them pleaded that they were just obeying "orders." Others revealed that despite their Nazi indoctrination, they felt a certain human aversion to their work. One German officer who had been in charge of an "extermination gang" testified at Nuremberg that to relieve the "psychological burden" on his men, he had had them fire as a group, never as individuals, so that they could avoid "personal responsibility."[1]

How is authority invested with such legitimacy that it has the power to command ordinary people to commit acts of such unthinkable brutality and inhumanity? At least part of the answer, but by no means all, may be found in the power of ideology. Ideology, it should be noted, may be used to further humanitarian as well as nonhumanitarian goals, but regardless of the purpose for which it is used, ideology can be an extremely powerful weapon. In this chapter we will examine the nature of that power and describe some of the major ideologies that have been the source of conflict in the contemporary world. After you have read chapter 9, you should be able to:

- define ideology and describe its power to control people's behavior.
- compare and contrast classical liberalism, modern liberalism, and modern conservatism.

- discuss fascism, Marxism, socialism, and the New Left.
- describe the development of Marxism-Leninism in the Soviet Union.

THE POWER OF IDEAS

Ideology

Ideas have power. People are coerced by ideas—beliefs, symbols, doctrines—more than they realize. Indeed, whole societies are shaped by systems of ideas that we frequently refer to as ideologies. *An ideology is an integrated system of ideas that provides society and its members with rationalizations for a way of life, guides for evaluating "rightness" and "wrongness," and emotional impulses to action.* Power and ideology are intimately related. Ideology rationalizes and justifies the exercise of power. By providing a justification of power, ideology itself becomes a source of control over people. Without the added *legitimacy* provided by ideology, power holders would be confronted by an aroused populace who strongly resented what they regarded as the naked power exercised over them. Nothing could be more dangerous to the stability of a power system. Yet the very ideology that legitimizes power also governs the *conduct of power holders.* Once an ideology is deeply rooted in a society, power holders themselves are bound by it if they wish to retain power.

Ideology and behavior

Ideologies control people's behavior in several ways: (1) Ideologies affect perception. Ideas influence what people "see" in the world around them. Ideologies frequently describe the character of human beings in society; they help us become aware of certain aspects of society but often impair our ability to see other aspects. Ideologies may distort and oversimplify in their effort to provide a unified and coherent account of society. (2) Ideologies rationalize and justify a way of life and hence provide legitimacy for the structure of society. An ideology may justify the status quo, or it may provide a rationale for change, or even for revolution. (3) Ideologies provide normative standards to determine "rightness" and "wrongness" in the affairs of society. Ideologies generally have a strong moral component. Occasionally, they even function as "religions"—complete with prophets (Marx), scriptures (the Communist Manifesto), saints (Lenin, Stalin, Mao), and visions of utopia (a communist society). (4) Ideologies provide motivation for social and political action. They give their followers a motive to act to improve world conditions. Ideologies can "convert" individuals to a particular social or political movement and arouse them to action.

THE AGE OF IDEOLOGY

Ideas have always moved people. The crusades of the Middle Ages, the Reformation and Counter Reformation, and the great religious wars of centuries past are sufficient evidence that ideas can produce wide-ranging consequences. But modern ideologies differ somewhat from those of the past. The nineteenth and twentieth centuries are sometimes referred to as *the age of ideology*. Despite their quarrels, modern ideologies—capitalism, liberalism, socialism, communism, fascism—share several important characteristics:

Characteristics of modern ideologies

1. Modern ideologies are typically *utopian*. Their vision is not of a blissful life hereafter or an other-worldly Kingdom of God, but rather of a perfect life on earth. Such a vision stands in marked contrast to earlier periods of history, in which the conditions of human existence were largely taken for granted. The usual expectation was that people would go on living much as their parents and grandparents had done. Utopia was reserved for life in the hereafter. Doubtlessly, the utopianism of modern ideology is a product of revolutionary scientific and technological advances over the last two centuries; the rapid improvements in living conditions inspired people to believe that life on earth could be perfected. Their minds were diverted from heavenly concerns toward the improvement of life here and now.

2. Modern ideologies are typically *optimistic about human progress*. In an age of technological progress, it is easy to conclude that the steady improvement of human welfare is not only possible but inevitable. Frequently ideologies are presented as "the wave of the future." Supporters of various modern ideologies believe that they possess the ultimate "truth" and that they will achieve the ultimate "victory."

3. Modern ideologies are typically *oversimplifications*. Oversimplification is both their strength and their weakness. They inspire habits of thinking in terms of "we" and "they," "friend" and "enemy." The more committed one is to an ideology, the more likely one is to view opponents as sinister and to look upon political disagreement as a struggle between the forces of good and the forces of evil.

It is difficult to summarize a modern ideology in a few brief paragraphs. The risk of oversimplification is great. And since ideologies themselves are oversimplifications, the problem is compounded. Moreover, ideologies are constantly changing. When old utopian hopes are disappointed, they are frequently revised, or replaced by new ones. New ideologies compete with older ones in various stages of revision. To unravel the ideological forces operating in society at any given time is a highly complex affair. With these warnings in mind, however, let us consider some of the major ideologies that influence our contemporary world.

CLASSICAL LIBERALISM: THE LEAST GOVERNMENT IS THE BEST GOVERNMENT

Attitudes toward the individual

Both "classical liberalism" and "modern liberalism" assert the worth and dignity of the *individual*. They both emphasize the rational ability of human beings to determine their own destinies, and they reject ideas, practices, and institutions that submerge individuals into a larger whole and deprive them of their essential dignity. Liberalism grew out of eighteenth-century Enlightenment, the Age of Reason in which great philosophers, such as Voltaire, Locke, Rousseau, Adam Smith, and Thomas Jefferson, affirmed their faith in reason, virtue, and common sense. Liberalism originated as an attack upon hereditary prerogatives and distinctions of a feudal society, the monarchy, the privileged aristocracy, the state-established church, and the restrictions on individual freedom associated with the feudal order. Classical liberalism and modern liberalism differ in important ways on how the freedom and dignity of the individual should be preserved. But both classical and modern liberals agree that the "fundamental assumption is the worth and dignity and creative capacity of the individual."[2]

Classical liberalism helped motivate America's Founding Fathers to declare their independence from England, to write the American Constitution, and to establish the Republic. It rationalized their actions and provided ideological legitimacy for the new nation. John Locke, the English political philosopher whose writings most influenced America's Founding Fathers, argued that even in a "state of nature"—that is, a world in which there were no governments—an *individual* possesses *inalienable rights* to life, liberty, and property. Locke spoke of a "natural law," or moral principle, which guaranteed to every person these rights. They were not given to the individual by government, and no government could legitimately take them away. Locke believed that the very purpose of government was to protect individual liberty. Human beings form a "social contract" with one another in establishing a government to help protect their rights; they agree to accept governmental authority in order to better protect life, liberty, and property. Implicit in the social contract and the liberal notion of freedom is the belief that governmental activity and social control over the individual should be kept to a minimum. This involves a removal of as many external restrictions on the individual as is consistent with the freedom of other citizens.

Approach to government

Thus, classical liberalism included a belief in *limited government*. Since government is formed by the consent of the governed to protect individual liberty, it logically follows that government cannot violate the rights it was established to protect.

Classical liberalism also asserted the value of *popular participation* in government as an opportunity for individual self-development. Procedurally, classical liberalism held that popular participation was to be achieved *through majority rule and respect for the rights of minorities*. Minorities, who have had the opportunity to influence policy but whose views have not succeeded in winning majority support, must accept the decision of the majority. In return, the majority would permit minorities to attempt openly to win majority support for their views. Freedom of speech and press, freedom to dissent, and freedom to form opposition parties and organizations are not only "natural rights," but are also essential to ensure meaningful participation in government. Thus, the procedural requirements for self-government and the underlying ethics of liberal democracy are linked: *Freedom* of speech, press, religion, and political activity can be defended as natural God-given *rights* essential to human dignity, and they can also be defended as necessary for ensuring *individual participation* in government and ascertaining what the *majority views* really are.

Classical liberalism, however, did not place unlimited confidence in the ability of the masses to make public policy. Most classical liberals believed in *republican government*. They were opposed to hereditary monarchies and a privileged aristocracy. But they did *not* support mass democracy, with direct participation by the people in decision making. The classical liberals believed that the role of the masses was to select competent leaders and to turn out of office those who did not govern in a wise and virtuous fashion. But they did not believe that the masses themselves should decide questions of public policy.

Equality of opportunity but not absolute equality

Classical liberalism also affirmed the equality of all human beings. The Declaration of Independence expressed the conviction that "all men are created equal." The Founding Fathers believed in equality for all *before the law* notwithstanding the accused's circumstances. Over time, the notion of equality has also come to include equality of *opportunity* in all aspects of life—social, educational, and economic. Each person should have an equal chance to develop individual capacities to their natural limits; there should be no artificial barriers to personal advancement. It is important to remember, however, that classical liberalism has always stressed *equality of opportunity* and not *absolute equality*. Thomas Jefferson recognized a "natural aristocracy" of talent, ambition, and industry, and classical liberals have always accepted inequalities that are a product of individual merit and hard work. Absolute equality, or "leveling," is *not* a part of classical liberalism.

Classical liberalism and capitalism

Finally, classical liberalism, as a *political* ideology, is closely related to capitalism as an *economic* ideology. The economic version of liberal freedom is the freedom to make contracts, to trade, to bargain for one's services, to move from job to job, to start one's own business, and so forth. Laissez-faire economics and classical liberal democracy are closely related as economic and political systems. Laissez-faire economics stresses individual rationality in economic matters; freedom of choice in working, producing, buying, and selling; and limited government intervention in economic affairs. Liberal democracy emphasizes individual rationality in voter choice; freedom of speech, press, and political activity; and limitations on governmental power over individual liberty. In liberal politics individuals are free to speak out, to form political parties, and to vote as they please—to pursue their political interests as they think best. In liberal economics, individuals are free to find work, to start businesses, and to spend their money as they please—to pursue their economic interests as they think best. The role of government is restricted to protecting private property, enforcing contracts, and performing only those functions and services that cannot be performed by the private market.

MODERN LIBERALISM: POWER TO "DO GOOD"

Governmental power: a positive force

Modern liberalism rationalizes and justifies much of the growth of governmental power in America in the twentieth century. Modern liberalism retains the fundamental commitment to *individualism, civil liberties, and faith in reason and virtue*. But it emphasizes the importance of *social* and *economic security* of a whole population as a prerequisite to individual self-realization and self-development. Classical liberalism looked with suspicion on the state as a potential source of "interference" with personal freedom; but modern liberalism looks upon the *power of government as a positive force* to be used to contribute to the elimination of social and economic conditions that adversely affect people's lives and impede their self-development. The modern liberal approves of the use of governmental power to ensure the general social welfare and to correct the perceived ills of society.

Modern liberals believe they can change people's lives through the exercise of governmental power: end discrimination, abolish poverty, eliminate slums, ensure employment, uplift the poor, eliminate sicknesses, educate the masses, and instill humanitarian values in everyone. The prevailing impulse is to *do good*, to perform public services, and to assist the least fortunate in society, particularly the poor and the black. Modern liberalism is impatient with what it sees as slow progress through individual initiative and private enterprise toward the solution of socioeconomic problems, so it seeks to use the power of the national government to find *immediate* and *comprehensive* "solutions" to society's troubles.

Reform of capitalism   Modern liberalism is frequently critical of certain aspects of capitalism, but it proposes to *reform* capitalism rather than replace it with socialism. Modern liberalism continues to recognize the individual's right to own private property, but it imposes on the property owner social and economic obligations that are designed to reduce capitalism's hardships. It assumes that business will be privately owned, but subject to considerable governmental regulation. Thus, the government intervenes to ensure fair labor standards, minimum wages, healthy working conditions, consumer protection, and so forth. Modern liberalism stresses the utility of government fiscal policies—taxing and spending—for maintaining full employment and economic stability. Modern liberals are committed to a significant *enlargement* of the public (governmental) sector of society—in matters having to do with education, welfare, housing, recreation facilities, transportation, urban renewal, medicine, employment, child care, and so on. Modern liberalism envisions a larger role for government in the future—setting new goals, managing the economy, meeting popular wants, and drastically redirecting national resources away from private wants toward public needs.

Reduction of extreme inequalities   Modern liberalism places much greater emphasis on the value of equality than does classical liberalism. Classical liberalism stresses the value of equality of opportunity: Individuals should be free to make the most of their talents and skills, but differences in wealth or power that are a product of differences in talent, initiative, risk taking, and skill are accepted as natural. In contrast, modern liberalism contends that *individual dignity and equality of opportunity depend in some measure upon reduction of absolute inequality* in society. Modern liberals believe that true equality of opportunity cannot be achieved where there are significant numbers of people suffering from hunger, remediable illness, or extreme hardships in the conditions of life. They believe that the existence of opportunities to "rise" in employment, housing, education, and the like depends upon a certain degree of absolute equality. Thus, modern liberalism supports government efforts to reduce extreme inequalities in society.

CONSERVATISM: THE INSIGHTS
OF EDMUND BURKE

Conservatism and liberalism

In America today, "conservatism" is associated with classical liberalism. Conservatives in this country retain the early liberal commitment to individual freedom from government controls; maximum personal liberty; reliance upon individual initiative and effort for self-development, rather than governmental programs and projects; a free enterprise economy with a minimum of governmental intervention; and rewards for initiative, skill, risk, and hard work, in contrast to government-imposed "leveling" of income. These views are consistent with the early classical liberalism of Locke, Jefferson, and the nation's Founding Fathers. The result, of course, is a confusion of ideological labels: Conservatives today charge modern liberals with abandoning the principles of individualism, limited government, and free enterprise, and today's conservatives claim to be the true "liberals" in society.

Modern conservatism does indeed incorporate much of classical liberalism, but conservatism also has a distinct ideological tradition of its own. Indeed, conservatism had its origins in *reaction* to the excesses of early liberalism, particularly the radical liberalism of the French Revolution. The first important statement of modern conservatism is found in Edmund Burke's assessment of French liberalism, *Reflections on the Revolution in France*, written in 1790.

Conservatism and human nature

Conservatism is not as optimistic as liberalism about human nature. Traditionally, conservatives doubted the supposed wisdom, virtue, and humaneness of the masses; conservatives were unwilling to place supreme confidence in the rational capacities of the masses. Conservatives realized that human nature includes elements of irrationality, intolerance, extremism, ignorance, prejudice, hatred, and violence. Thus they were more likely to place their faith in *law* and *tradition* than in the popular emotions of mass movement. Edmund Burke recognized selfish and irrational human motives. He believed that without law or tradition, people would exist in a jungle of violence, terror, and chaos—a jungle in which only the most powerful would survive by cunning, deceit, and violence. If law and tradition were discredited and exclusive reliance placed upon rationality, the fabric that holds society together would be weakened. Without the protection of law and tradition, people and societies are vulnerable to terror and violence. The absence of law does not mean freedom, but rather exposure to the tyranny of terrorism and violence.

Attitudes toward government

Conservatives doubt the ability of governmental planners to solve all of society's problems. Edmund Burke believed that reason was a valuable and distinctive human gift, but he challenged the views of liberals that the answers to every human problem were already at hand or could easily be discovered. In Burke's eyes, this was unpardonable conceit, and he was convinced that the intellectual arrogance of liberal reformers could lead society into chaos. Conservatives since Burke have doubted the rational powers of governmental bureaucracies. They tend to think that societies are held together not exclusively by government programs and policies but also by *traditional morality* and *force of habit,* and that the progress of civilization depends as much on the *maintenance of social order* as on governmental planning.

Conservatism sets forth an *evolutionary* view of social progress. Burke believed that real progress in society was the outcome of continuous social change over a prolonged period of time. Revolutionary change is far more likely to set back society than to improve it. But over time, people can experiment in small ways with incremental changes; continued from generation to generation, this process of evolutionary change leads to a progressive improvement in the condition of humanity. *No government* possesses the wisdom to resolve all problems, but the cumulative experience of society does produce certain workable arrangements for the amelioration of social ills. Gradual progress is possible, but only if people do not destroy the painfully acquired wisdom of the past in favor of new untried utopian solutions that jeopardize the well-being of society.

Conservatives hold that people are rational beings, but that they are also victims of passion. Irrational drives and impulses—hatred, prejudice, intolerance, violence—are constantly at war with rational judgment and humane feelings. Without the guidance of law, tradition, and morality, people would soon come to grief by the unruliness of their passions, destroying both themselves and others in pursuit of selfish gain. Rationalism is far from a sufficient guide to action; law, tradition, and morality are also needed for the realization of human purposes. Left to their own instincts, without the benefit of the accumulated wisdom of ages, and without institutions to channel and modify their aggressive instincts, people will degenerate to savagery.

Strong institutions—family, church, and even government—are needed to repress selfish and irrational impulses of individuals and to inculcate civilized ways of life.

Conservatives believe in government by the consent of the governed, but they are skeptical of the ability of the masses to decide public policy questions themselves. Edmund Burke believed in *representative* government: The masses should elect wise and virtuous leaders to govern them, and the masses should have the power to replace leaders who misgovern them. But Burke did not believe that the masses themselves should handle public policy matters. Representatives were elected to use their own best judgment in deciding public issues; they should not become slaves of public opinion. To subject leaders to the caprice of public opinion was to invite anarchy. Thus, today the term *Burkean representation* refers to the willingness of elected representatives to ignore public opinion and settle public issues in the light of their own judgment about what is best for society. While Burke did not trust in the wisdom of the masses, he was only slightly more trustful of the wisdom of political leaders. The only real hope for preserving civilization, he felt, lay in the wisdom of *tradition* and *experience*.

Burkean representation

FASCISM: THE SUPREMACY OF RACE AND NATION

Fascism is an ideology that asserts the supremacy of the nation or race over the interests of individuals or classes—in the words of Benito Mussolini: "Everything for the state; nothing against the state; nothing outside of the state." The state is the embodiment of a unifying, ethical "ideal" that stands above the materialistic class interest of a Marxist or the selfish individualism of the liberals. Fascism is presented as a form of lofty idealism—"a religious conception in which man is seen in immanent relation to a higher law, an objective will, that transcends a particular individual and raises him to conscious membership in a spiritual society."

Fascism perceives the state as not merely a governmental bureaucracy but the organic life of a whole people. According to Mussolini, "The Italian nation is an organism having ends, life, and means of action superior to those of the separate individuals or groups of individuals which compose it." In *Mein Kampf*, written prior to his assumption of power, Adolf Hitler added to the concept of an organic state, with his idea of the *Volk* (people) in which race and nation are united.

The highest purpose of the volkish State is the care for the preservation of those racial primal elements which, supplying culture, create the beauty and dignity of a higher humanity. We, as Aryans, are therefore able to imagine a state only to be the living organism of a nationality which not only safeguards the preservation of that nationality, but which, by a further training of its spiritual and ideal abilities, leads it to the highest freedom.[3]

The central ideal of the *Volk*, then, is that of a racial folk or an "organic people" with a life, will, and purpose of its own.

The goal of the fascist state

The *goal* of the fascist state is not the welfare of the mass of people but the *development of a superior type of human being*. The goal is the cultivation of the best qualities of a people—bravery, courage, creativeness, genius, intelligence, and strength. Fascism values the superior individual who rises out of the mire of mass mediocrity—and the superior nation that rises above the vast anthill of humankind. If life is a struggle for existence in which the fittest survive, then strength is the ultimate virtue and weakness is a fault. Good is that which survives and wins; bad is that which fails. Socialism, communism, and democracy mean the worship of mediocrity and the hatred of excellence; not the superior person but the majority person becomes the ideal and the model; everyone comes to resemble everyone else. These ideologies submerge what is best and noble in the people. All of this degrades the race and contradicts the theory of evolution. In contrast, fascism admires heroism in individuals and nations. War frequently brings out the best in a nation: unity, bravery, strength, and courage.

"Will" over "reason"

Fascism asserts the superiority of "will" over "reason." The great deeds of history were performed not by reason but by heroic will. Peoples are preserved *not* by rational thought but by racial intuition. They rise to greatness when their will to power surmounts physical and world handicaps. Happiness is a poor motive in comparison with heroism, self-sacrifice, duty, and discipline. This irrationalism derives from a belief that life is too difficult, too complex, and too changeable to be reduced to a rational formula—that nature is driven by many forces, as yet unknown to science, that can only be understood by intuition and genius. The one universal law is that of the survival of the fittest. The fascist hero is the opposite of the democratic egalitarian. He lives dangerously and is prepared to meet disaster. He does not wish to be mediocre, but instead superior in everything he does. He creates his own rules and tramples down the opposition.

Fascism offers itself as a *merger of nationalism and socialism*. Prior to World War II, fascism in Italy and in Germany put itself

A "cooperative" economy

forward as a socialist regime adopted to national purposes. The party of Adolf Hitler was the National Socialist party or "Nazi" party. Since under fascism, the nation is an organic whole, the economy ought to be *cooperative* rather than competitive. Every class and every interest ought to work together for the *good of the nation*. Thus, national socialism was designed to appeal not only to the working class, but also to the lower-middle class—the small shopkeepers and salaried employees—who suffer from inflation and depression and who are fearful of the prospect of being degraded to the ranks of the proletariat, a fate that Marxism had promised them. A program of national socialism involves *complete control* of the national economy by the national government in the national interest. Against the rights of liberty or equality, national socialism established the duties of *service, devotion, and discipline.* As an extreme form of nationalism, fascism identified internationalism with cowardice and lack of honor. Indeed, fascism depended for its driving force upon sentiments of national patriotism.

A totalitarian power structure

The power structure of a fascist regime is totalitarian. The unity of the fascist state requires "one people, one party, one leader." The fascist believes that a natural, superior, self-made leadership will emerge to provide intelligence and direction to the nation. The Nazi elite emerges from political combat as the fittest and most deserving of political survival; there is no interest in mass vote counting. A Nazi leadership represents *das Volk* simply by embodying more clearly and explicitly its will to power. At the head of the fascist elite is the leader—*Il Duce* in Italy or *Der Fuehrer* in Germany—in whose name everything is done, who is said to be "responsible" for all, but whose acts can nowhere be called into question. The leader is neither a scholar nor a theorist, but a charismatic man of action. Fascism strives for a *totality of power* in which all sectors of society—education, labor, art, science—are incorporated into the state and serve the purposes of the state. No sphere of social activity is free from national scrutiny and control. All of society's resources are viewed as resources of the state.

MARXISM: "WORKERS OF THE WORLD, UNITE"

The roots of socialism and communism

Liberalism began as an eighteenth-century revolt against the aristocracy of a feudal system. Socialism represents a nineteenth-century revolt against the privileged wealth of a capitalist system. Communism is a particularly violent strain of the larger ideological movement of socialism. Both socialism and communism arose out of the *industrial revolution* and the *social evils* it generated. Even though the industrial revolution led to a rapid rise in standards of living in western Europe, what impressed many early observers of this revolution was the economic inequalities it engendered. Throughout much of the nineteenth century, the only beneficiaries of the new industrialism seemed to be the successful manufacturers, bankers, merchants, and speculators, and the lot of the slum-dwelling working classes showed little improvement. This was a bitter disappointment to the humanitarian hopes of many who had earlier embraced liberalism in the expectation that the rewards of economic progress would be shared by everyone. It appeared that liberalism and capitalism had simply substituted an aristocracy of wealth for an aristocracy of birth.

The first stirrings of socialism date back to the days of the French Revolution itself. Although the majority of French revolutionists were liberals whose aim it was to establish *equality of opportunity*, there were already a few who wished to establish *absolute equality* of wealth and income. The rise of Napoleon appeared to check the growth of socialism for a time, but a number of *utopian socialists* continued to develop schemes to replace the free market system with co-operative, egalitarian communities. Much of this effort was directed toward founding small communistic communities that were self-sufficient and organized on a cooperative basis, with profits from labor distributed equally among the members of the community. This socialism was mild and philanthropic; it was neither political nor violent. Utopian socialism and communal living never amounted to a strong political movement or a full-fledged ideology. The man who finally made socialism an effective ideology and a successful political movement was Karl Marx.

Like many socialists, Karl Marx (1818–1883) was an upper-middle-class intellectual. He was educated at the University of Berlin and began his career as a professor of philosophy. When his radicalism barred academic advancement, he turned to journalism and moved to Paris. There he met Friedrich Engels, a wealthy young intellectual who supported Marx financially and collaborated with him on many of his writings. It was Marx's humanitarian sympathy for industrial workers, not his personal experience in a factory, that led him to devote his activities to the cause of the working classes. Marx's first important work, *The Condition of the Working Class in England* (1844), was a protest against the sufferings and inequities of the working classes in the industrial revolution. The *Communist Manifesto* (1848) was a political pamphlet—short, concise, and full of striking phrases. It provided an ideology to what had previously been no more than scattered protest against injustices. The *Manifesto* set forth the key ideas of Marxism, which would be developed twenty years later in great detail in a lengthy work, *Das Kapital.*

Let us summarize the basic ideas of *Marxian communism:* economic determinism, dialectical materialism, the class struggle, the theory of surplus value, the inevitability of resolution, the dictatorship of the proletariat, and the withering away of the state.

Economic Determinism Communism believes that economic arrangements in society, or "modes of production," are basic to all the rest of society. The mode of production determines the class structure, the political system, religion, education, family life, law, and even art and literature. Thus, the mode of production determines the basic social structure of society, and the rest is simply "superstructure," which is also molded by the prevailing economic arrangements. For example, the economic structure of feudalism creates a class structure of a privileged aristocracy and a suffering serfdom. The economic structure of capitalism creates a class structure of a wealthy *bourgeoisie* (a property-owning class of capitalists) who control the government and exercise power over the *proletariat* (the propertyless workers).

Dialectical Materialism Marx borrowed the idea of the "dialectic" from his former teacher, the German philosopher Hegel. Hegel used this word to refer to a process whereby ideas are first advanced (thesis), then challenged by contradictory ideas (antithesis), and then combined into a higher idea (synthesis) that contained elements of each. Hegel argued that the dialectic of ideas determined the historic development of social institutions. While Hegel was an idealist who believed that *ideas* shaped history, Marx was a materialist who believed that economic arrangements or *modes of production* shaped society. The dialectic of Marx, therefore, involved modes of production rather than ideas in any given economy. There is a ruling class that by virtue of its monopoly over the mode of production is able to dominate a whole society. Yet, great as the power of the ruling class may be, it is basically unstable because new modes of production are developed, leading to new forms of economic organizations and the creation of new classes that arise to challenge the monopoly of the older ruling class. History is determined by *dialectical materialism:* The established mode of production with its ruling class is a *thesis,* and new emerging modes of production and new classes are the *antithesis*—the source of social change and revolution. Marx believed that the old aristocracy had been successfully challenged by liberal capitalism because the mode of production had changed from agriculture to industrialism. In the French Revolution, the new class of capitalists had broken the regime of their former rulers, the aristocrats, whose power had been based upon the ownership of land. As strong as the new ruling class appeared, however, the material dialectic of history was moving on, and capitalism was producing its own antithesis—the factory workers, or "proletariat."

The Class Struggle   The first sentence of the *Communist Manifesto* exclaims: "The history of all hitherto existing society is the history of class struggles." These class struggles are created by the mode of production; the class that owns the mode of production is in the dominant position and *exploits* the other classes. Such exploitation creates antagonism, which gradually increases until it bursts into revolution. The means of production in the Middle Ages was land, and the aristocracy that owned the land controlled government and society. The industrial revolution created a new class, the bourgeoisie, which rose to importance because it owned the means of production—money, machines, and factories. But just as the aristocracy was supplanted by the bourgeoisie, so the bourgeoisie will in the course of time be superseded by the proletariat. The capitalist exploits the worker to the point where the worker is forced to revolt against the oppressors and overthrow the capitalist state.

The Theory of Surplus Value   According to Marx, *labor* is the only source of value. Labor is the one thing common to all commodities and gives each commodity its value. As Marx put it, "All wealth is due to labor, and therefore, to the laborer, all wealth is due." Although laborers deserve the full value of the commodity they make, under capitalism they receive only a small part of it, just enough for their subsistence. The rest, which Marx called *surplus*, is taken by the capitalists for their own enrichment. Thus the capitalist system is a gigantic scheme for exploiting the workers by confiscating the surplus value they have created. The practical solution, of course, is to make it impossible for capitalists to exploit workers by establishing "collective ownership of all means of production, distribution, and exchange." In other words, the proletariat must eliminate the capitalist and take over all the tools of production, distribution, and exchange so that the surplus value will not flow to the capitalist.

The Inevitability of Revolution   Not only did Marx predict the coming of the proletariat revolution, he also sought to show that such a revolution was inevitable. According to the *Communist Manifesto*, "What the bourgeoisie produces, above all, is its own grave-diggers. Its fall and the victory of the proletariat are equally inevitable." As capitalists try to maximize their profits, the rich become richer and the poor become poorer. Moreover, competition squeezes out small capitalists, and ownership is gradually concentrated in the hands of fewer and fewer capitalists. As exploitation increases, and as more petty capitalists are forced into the ranks of the proletariat, both the strength and the antagonism of the proletariat increase. The proletariat develops a working-class consciousness and ultimately rises up against the exploiters. As capitalists drive wages down to maximize profits, capitalism becomes plagued by a series of crises or depressions, each one worse than the one before. As wages are forced ever lower, capitalists soon cannot sell their products because of the lower purchasing power of the proletariat, and depression follows. Further, as capitalists introduce more machinery, the demand for labor declines, and unemployment rises. The result of these internal contradictions in capitalism is a great deal of human misery, which eventually explodes in revolution. Thus, in their drive for profit, capitalists really dig their own grave by bringing the revolution ever closer.

The Dictatorship of the Proletariat   Although Marx claimed that the coming of the revolution is inevitable, he nonetheless urged the workers to organize for revolutionary action. The *Communist Manifesto* closes with the words, "The proletarians have nothing to lose but their chains. They have a world to win. Working men of all countries, unite!" The capitalists will never peacefully give up their ruling position. Only a violent revolution will place the proletarians in power. When the proletarians come to power, they, like ruling classes before them, will set up a state of their own—a dictatorship of the proletariat—to protect their class interests. Unlike governments of the past, however, which served oppressive minorities, the proletariat dictatorship will be a government by and for the great majority of workers. It will seize the property of the capitalist majority and place ownership of the modes of production in the hands of the proletariat. The bourgeoisie will be eliminated as a class.

The Withering Away of the State   Since class differences depend upon ownership of the modes of production, the result of *common* *ownership* will be a one-class, or *classless*, society. Since the purpose of government is to assist the ruling class in exploiting and oppressing other classes, once a classless society is established the government will have no purpose and will gradually "wither away." In the early stages of the revolution the rule of distribution will be "from each according to his ability, to each according to his work." But after the victory of communism and the establishment of a full classless society, the rule of distribution will be "from each according to his ability, to each according to his need." After the elimination of classes, society will be peaceful and cooperative, and there will no longer be any need for coercion. Government and its coercive powers will disappear forever.

SOCIALISM: FROM PRIVATE ENTERPRISE TO PUBLIC OWNERSHIP

There is a bewildering variety of definitions of socialism. Communists employ the term as a label for societies that have experienced successful communist revolutions and are in the process of developing a communist society. Occasionally critics of government programs in the United States label as "socialist" any program or policy that restricts free enterprise in any way. Socialism is also frequently confused with egalitarianism—governmental efforts to achieve absolute equality or "leveling" of wealth or income. But fundamentally, socialism means *public ownership of the means of production, distribution, and service.* Socialists agree on one point: Private property in land, buildings, factories, and stores must be transformed into social or collective property. The idea of *collective ownership* is the core of socialism.

Socialism: collective ownership

Socialism shares with communism a *condemnation of the capitalist system* as exploitive of the working classes. Communists and socialists agree on the evils of industrial capitalism—the exploitation of labor, the concentration of wealth, the insensitivity of the profit motive to human needs, the insecurities and sufferings brought on by the business cycle, the conflict of class interests, and the propensity of capitalist nations to involve themselves in war. In short, most socialists agree with the criticisms of the capitalist system set forth by Marx. However, socialists are committed to the *democratic process* as a means of replacing capitalism with collective ownership of economic enterprise. They generally reject the desirability of revolution as a way to replace capitalism and instead advocate peaceful constitutional roads to socialism. Moreover, socialists have

Socialism and communism

rejected the idea of a socialist "dictatorship"; they contend that the goal of socialism is a *free society* embodying the democratic principles of freedom of speech, press, assembly, association, and political activity. They frequently claim that socialism in the economic sector of society is essential to achieving democracy and equality in the political sector of society. In other words, they believe that true democracy cannot be achieved until wealth is widely distributed and the means of production are commonly owned. Wealth must be redistributed in such a way as to make it possible for all persons to share in the benefits created by society. This means a transfer of ownership of all substantial economic holdings to the government. But the transfer must be accomplished in a democratic fashion, rather than by force or violence; and a socialist society must be governed as a true democracy.

Socialists are generally committed to an *evolutionary* approach to the achievement of common ownership of an economic enterprise. They reject the necessity of violent revolution or civil war. They are prepared for a gradual evolutionary restructuring of society—a restructuring that can take place within the framework of liberal democratic traditions. Socialists are ready to *cooperate* with liberal parties to achieve improvements in the conditions of the working classes—to mitigate the conditions of the impoverished, maintain full employment, regulate economic cycles, extend social security, eliminate discrimination, and expand educational and cultural opportunities for the masses. Unlike communists, they envision a gradual change from private to public ownership of property. Thus, socialists may begin by "nationalizing" the railroads, the steel industry, the automobile industry, privately owned public utilities, or other specific segments of the economy. Nationalization involves governmental seizure of these industries from private owners, perhaps accompanied by some form of compensation. Many socialists realize that support for collective ownership must not rest exclusively on a single class. Socialists have learned through hard experience that their programs have to have the approval of a *wide* segment of the public, and not merely the working class.

Socialism is *egalitarian*. Socialists would reduce or eliminate inequalities in the distribution of wealth or income. Socialism attempts to achieve *absolute equality*, rather than mere *equality of opportunity*, which is the goal of liberals.

The development of modern socialism

Modern socialism grew out of revisions of basic Marxian doctrines in western European nations in the twentieth century. One of the most prominent spokespeople for "revisionism" was Edward Bernstein (1850–1932), who revised many Marxian ideas and contributed to the break between communism and socialism. Bernstein rejected the prediction that capitalism would inevitably collapse as a result of its own internal contradictions. He realized that capitalism would not produce the widespread economic misery that would compel workers to rise up in revolution. The only way to achieve socialism, he contended, would be through organized political activity within the democratic constitutional process. Moreover, he argued that capitalist society did indeed provide the working classes with opportunities for effective political action. He realized that socialist parties could be organized to function within the existing political systems of western European nations. Bernstein also rejected Marx's prediction that the rich must get richer and the poor poorer. He believed that through party activity, governmental reforms, and trade union activity, including collective bargaining with employers, the standard of living of workers could be vastly improved without the necessity of revolution. Finally, he urged that socialism reject the communist notion of political dictatorship by the working class and devote its energies to the welfare of all groups in society.

THE NEW LEFT IN AMERICA

The New Left in America covers a wide spectrum that includes reformers, socialists, and violent revolutionaries. It is linked to a subculture or "counterculture" that deliberately and flamboyantly rejects familiar American middle-class ways of life. Much of the New Left movement is devoid of a coherent ideology. However, the writings of philosopher Herbert Marcuse provide contemporary American radicalism with whatever ideological justification it possesses.

Marcuse's radicalism   The radicalism of Marcuse begins with a sweeping condemnation of contemporary society as a highly industrialized, bureaucratized machine, in which human nature is twisted and destroyed in the competitive values and institutions that it encounters. American society with its capitalist ethos is the most materialistic and bureaucratized of all societies, but Marcuse considers his critique to be almost equally applicable to socialist nations such as the Soviet Union. Marcuse is primarily concerned with the quality of human life and spirit, and he sees advanced technological society as destructive of human characteristics. Marcuse believes that the present ruinous use of technology is ironic, because for the first time in history people possess the opportunity to satisfy all their material needs with relatively little work, leaving them free to live a full, free, creative life. The struggle against scarcity is over, and people are free to develop in a true humanistic fashion. When life's sustaining resources were scarce, human beings were violent and competitive, lacking attitudes of human solidarity and cooperativeness, but now they could really become more humane.

Marcuse believes that only a *radical restructuring* of social and economic institutions will succeed in liberating people for humanistic, cooperative lifestyles. The existing institutions have conditioned them to be materialistic, competitive, and violent. The individual has been transformed into a "one-dimensional" person in whom genuine humanistic values are repressed. In other words, *institutions* have thoroughly distorted human nature. The implication is that they have corrupted people, and without these institutions life would be loving, cooperative, and compassionate. The problem of social change is truly monumental because the values and institutions of American society are deeply rooted. Since most people are not aware that they are "one-dimensional," the first step in social change is "consciousness raising"—that is, making people aware of their misery.

Bureaucracy, rationality, efficiency, and productivity are dehumanizing ideas that grow out of technology and materialism. Bureaucracies, both in socialist governments and in capitalist corporations, are insensitive to human needs. But the American capitalist system is the worst of all. Profitability, rather than humanistic values, remains the criterion of decision making in the economy, and this is the reason for poverty and misery, despite material abundance. Bureaucracies being unresponsive, individuals feel powerless to change their condition in life.

Radicalism views American society as a huge, brutal, irrational machine that operates in terms of efficiency and profitability—diverted from human purposes. Contemporary radicals think of modern liberals as being hypocritical in their attempts to reform the system; only a general revolution and radical restructuring of institutions will succeed in ending war, racism, poverty, and alienation. Contemporary radicals are not necessarily committed to work for change within the existing framework of society; many endorse extralegal and sometimes violent alternatives as the only means of dealing with a system they regard as violent itself. The emphasis in contemporary radicalism is on negative goals: destroying institutions—governments, corporations, universities, the military, and so on—that are bureaucratic and inattentive to human needs.

Radicals are vague about the kind of society they want to replace the present one after the revolution. But radical writings imply that

"I think we have a little misunderstanding here. I said 'radials,' not 'radicals'!"

The new society   the new society will be *humanistic* rather than materialistic, and *spontaneous* rather than bureaucratic; popular participation in the spirit of solidarity and brotherhood will replace the bargaining and compromising and competition that are characteristic of contemporary society.

In the new society, based on the principles of cooperation and brotherhood rather than competition, love will overcome materialism. This new society will be organized not to foster technological or material progress, but to develop human qualities. The New Left is not explicitly socialist because socialism implies large unresponsive state bureaucracies. However, the New Left emphasizes the need for *collectivist control* over the economic resources of society and popular participation in decisions about the use of these resources. *Participatory democracy* must replace bureaucratization and centralization in decision making. Participatory democracy does not involve elections, bargains, or compromises, but has to do with group interaction in the spirit of solidarity and brotherhood with a view toward developing consensus. It is not merely a way of registering individual preferences and deciding issues by majority rule, but a group process in which individuals are transformed into a whole community with a shared purpose. Participatory democracy will bring people out of isolation and powerlessness into solidarity and control. Institutions should not be governed from the top down but by the individuals who compose them. Participatory democracy should extend to work, school, neighborhood, prison, welfare recipients, and so forth. Thus, besides political institutions, all major societal institutions must be restructured to meet the criteria for participatory democracy.

Other characteristics of contemporary radicalism include:

Emphasis on the community rather than the individual.

The superiority of sensory experience over rational knowledge.

Stress on cooperation rather than competition.

Emphasis on naturalness (rejection of makeup, bras, suits, ties, etc.).

Concern with self-knowledge, introspection, and self-discovery.

The rejection of rationality and objectivity in finding truth, with emphasis on direct experience and involvement.

Radicalism does not have a clear comprehensive theory of social change. Radicals do not accept the necessity of "working within the system," believing as they do that present institutions are inflexible and incapable of transformation. However, it is not clear how the revolution will come about. Contemporary radicalism has yet to find a mass base on which to found a revolution; most radicals are upper-middle-class intellectuals and students. They know they must form coalitions with broader-based groups in society. Yet the New Left is fragmented over such questions as the role of black people in the movement, the organizational potential of the working class, and the ethics of violence. Radical meetings are frequently endless debates over such questions as: Is violence or nonviolence the better revolutionary tactic? With whom and under what conditions should coalitions be formed? How should popular current issues be exploited? Should radicals cooperate with liberals? Is the youth culture with its interest in drugs, pop music, and communal living a source of social change or a cop-out from the revolutionary struggle?

The growth and decline of radicalism

The Vietnam War was a contributing force to the growth of radicalism in America in the late 1960s and early 1970s. As the war grew in intensity, so did the New Left; but as the war subsided, radicalism declined, particularly on America's campuses. The war was regarded as a "mistake" by most Americans, but it especially inflamed middle-class, idealistic young people who regarded it as immoral and unjust. It cast a shadow over their postcollege plans and produced some guilt over the knowledge that lower-class youth were being drafted to fight while more favored middle-class youth remained on campus. More importantly, the humiliation of national leadership that resulted from the Vietnam War called into question the whole range of societal values and institutions—American resistance to communistic expansion, the military-industrial complex, and mindless governmental bureaucracies. If the nation's leaders (the older generation) could be so disastrously mistaken about Vietnam, they could also be mistaken about many other values in American life. Hence, for many students, opposition to the war in Vietnam grew into a sweeping criticism of American society in general and then into radicalism as an ideology. However, U.S. disengagement from the war, the end of the draft, and perhaps even the Twenty-sixth Amendment to the Constitution giving persons eighteen years of age or older the right to vote and participate directly in the political system seemed to contribute to the decline of radicalism on the campus in the 1970s.

CASE STUDY
Marxism-Leninism in the Soviet Union

The task fell to Lenin to reinterpret Marxism as a revolutionary ideology, to carry out a successful communist revolution, and to construct a communist state in the Soviet Union after the 1917 Revolution. Lenin contributed a great deal to communist ideology—so much so that contemporary communist ideology is frequently referred to as *Marxism-Leninism*.

From the Russian standpoint in 1917, Marxism was a discouraging doctrine because its hopes for the future were based on conditions that were supposed to emerge in the later stages of industrialism. Marx believed that the communist revolution would occur when capitalism itself produced a class of factory workers that would be large enough to overcome its capitalist rulers. But this theory did not apply in pre–World War II Russia, which was still a semifeudal society of peasants and landlords, with only a small number of factory workers and an even smaller number of capitalists. Lenin, however, believed that Russia could skip the capitalist stage of revolution and move directly from a feudal order to a communist society. His belief was based upon the decay of the Russian state after decades of inefficient despotism under the czarist regime. To Lenin the Russian political system appeared so weak that it could be destroyed by a relatively small, disciplined, hard-core group of professional revolutionaries.

The Totalitarian Party   According to Lenin, the *key to a successful revolution* was the creation of a new and revolutionary type of totalitarian political party composed of militant professional revolutionaries. This party would be organized and trained like an army to obey the commands of superior officers. While western European socialist parties were gathering millions of supporters in relatively democratic organizations, Lenin constructed a small, exclusive, well-disciplined, elitist party. First he described such a party in an early pamphlet, entitled *What Is to Be Done;* then he proceeded to organize it. Under his skilled leadership, the Communist party of the Soviet Union became the first modern totalitarian party.

Lenin could justify the creation of a highly disciplined party elite on the basis of Marx's ambiguous attitudes toward democracy. Marx's idea of a *dictatorship of the proletariat,* and his phrase the *vanguard of the proletariat,* seemed to suggest an *elitist* view of the revolutionary process. Lenin seized upon these and amplified them into an elitist and totalitarian notion of a communist party. According to Lenin, the Communist party is the true "vanguard of the proletariat"—the most advanced and class-conscious sector of the proletariat, which has an exclusive right to act as spokesperson for the proletariat as a whole and to exercise the dictatorial powers of the proletariat over the rest of society. There is no need to ask who speaks for the masses, or even who speaks for the proletariat; the Communist party *is* the voice of the proletariat and it can legitimately exercise dictatorial powers in the name of the proletariat.

The Theory of Imperialism Lenin also tried to come to grips with two dilemmas: Why were capitalist societies still flourishing in the twentieth century, contrary to Marx's prediction? And why was the condition of the working classes improving, rather than deteriorating? Lenin's theory of *imperialism* was an attempt to answer these embarrassing questions. According to Lenin, when advanced capitalist countries were unable to find home markets for their products because of depressed worker income, they were obliged to turn outward and to seize colonial markets. This maneuver enabled them, for the time being at least, to expand without forcing the wages of their own workers down to subsistence level. By "exporting poverty abroad" they managed to keep their own workers relatively prosperous, thus delaying the development of true proletariat class consciousness in their own countries. Lenin believed that the whole world was being divided into exploiters and exploited, with backward nations providing the surplus labor for more advanced nations. To shore up the shaky foundations of capitalism, capitalist nations were continually obliged to strive for fresh colonial markets. Of course, they were thus brought into bitter conflict with one another in their attempt to expand their respective empires. The final state of capitalism, therefore, would assume the form of *imperialist warfare* as rival capitalist nations engaged in a struggle to control colonial markets. To Lenin, World War I was proof that this advanced stage of capitalist decay had been reached and the worldwide capitalist system was ready for destruction. The idea of worldwide imperialism and exploitation also helped to explain why revolutionary activities in economically backward regions could be successful despite the absence of industrial capitalism. Since the inhabitants of these regions were the most cruelly exploited of all the world's workers, the revolution need not begin in the industrial heartland, but would arise at the colonial periphery.

Communism in One Country After Lenin came to power in the Soviet Union, he found himself no longer in the position of revolutionary leader; he was the leader of a nation. Should the Soviet Union direct its energies toward immediate worldwide revolution, as envisioned by Marx? Or should it avoid confrontation with the Western world until it became a strong and self-sufficient nation? Gradually abandoning the original hopes for an immediate world revolution, Lenin and his successor, Stalin, turned to the task of creating "communism in one country." With the Communist party more firmly and centrally disciplined than ever, the Soviet leaders turned to the achievement of rapid industrialization through a series of five-year plans designed to convert a backward agrarian country into a modern industrial nation. The sweeping industrialization, brought about by the repression and terror of a totalitarian regime, came at great cost to the people. The Stalinist period saw brutality, oppression, imprisonment, purges, and murders—later officially admitted by the Soviet leaders. The Soviet regime held down the production of consumer goods in order to concentrate on development of heavy industry. As costly and ruthless as it was, the effect of this policy was the modernization of the Russian economy in the course of a single generation. In part, the ideology of communism made it possible to call upon the people for tremendous sacrifices for the good of the communist state.

Neither Marx nor Lenin proved successful as a political prophet. The state never "withered away" in communist Russia. Indeed, to maintain the communist government, a massive structure of coercion—informants, secret police, official terrorism, and a giant prison system—was erected. (The brutality of the system is described by Nobel Prize-winning author and former Soviet political prisoner Aleksandr Solzhenitsyn in *The Gulag Archipelago.*) At the same time, the overall goal of world revolution, while never abandoned by the Soviet leadership, was compromised by the "realities" of world power. Particularly after the death of Stalin, the Soviet Union gradually restored its ties with the Western world. Among the factors that improved relations between ideologically opposed powers were (1) the unspeakable implications of nuclear weapons, which created a balance of terror and provided both sides with a reason to limit conflict; (2) a gradual rise in the standard of living in the Soviet Union and a relaxation of forced industrialization; and (3) the threat of an increasingly powerful Communist China on the eastern border of the U.S.S.R., which compelled the Soviet leadership to seek support against a militant revolutionary rival.

The U.S.S.R. deviated from earlier interpretations of Marxism-Leninism in other ways. More and more, the Soviets have turned to the *principle of material interest*—larger rewards for better labor and management performance—indicating that they are realistic enough to accept a capitalist notion when it is in their interest to do so. Another change involves greater decentralization in industry, along with less reliance on centralized state direction. It is becoming more difficult for the central party apparatus to control the increasingly sophisticated managerial and professional elite required in an advanced technological society. Finally, there has been some decline in terrorism since the Stalinist period, although the Soviet leadership has proved that it can oscillate easily between cruel orthodoxy and relaxed experimentation as it suits its purposes.

Despite these changes, Marxist-Leninist ideology still plays a very important role in the Soviet Union today. There is no lack of interest in the continuing indoctrination of the citizenry in Marxism-Leninism—in schools, factories, collective farms, universities, the military, and social organizations.

Flaws in the Marxist Theory Marxism as a political ideology has reshaped the modern world. More than half of the world's population live under political regimes that call themselves "communist" or "socialist." Yet Marxism as a scientific approach to understanding history and society is clearly inadequate. Let us summarize some of the more serious flaws in Marxism:

1. Capitalism has given the American people the world's highest standard of living—a standard of living that is clearly the envy of people living under socialist and communist regimes. Capitalism does *not* inevitably depress the condition of workers. On the contrary, workers in America own their own homes, automobiles, appliances, and other material luxuries, and the middle class has grown rather than diminished over time. Industrial workers in modern capitalist nations have received larger and larger shares of national income, and standards of living have increased rapidly. Labor under capitalism is *not* becoming progressively miserable and downtrodden.

2. Governments in capitalist nations have responded to

the pressures of organized labor and the masses of voters to provide a wide variety of health, education, and welfare programs. It is difficult to argue that America's national leadership has reflected only the interest of a ruling capitalist class, in view of vast governmental programs and expenditures for social security, welfare, fair labor standards, protection for union organizations, public education, and so forth. Furthermore, these programs have been financed on a progressive income tax structure that takes a larger proportion in taxation from the income of high-income persons than from low-income persons. In short, there are many examples of government programs and policies in capitalist nations that conflict with the interests of capitalists.

3. Capitalist nations have more complex social structures than the simple bourgeois-proletariat distinction of Marxism. There are many crosscutting social, political, economic, religious, and racial interests and allegiances in a modern industrial society. For example, Marx assumed that the interest of farm populations would be the same as those of factory workers, but in most nations farm populations have resisted communism. In America, industrial workers have been neither class conscious nor revolutionary. Ironically, support for Marxism is greater among upper-middle-class intellectuals than among industrial workers.

4. Marxism does not recognize the difference between dictatorship and democracy. The idea of a "dictatorship of the proletariat" justifies suppression, terrorism, violence, purges, imprisonment, and murder when directed against "enemies of the people." After the revolution has occurred, and the proletariat has emerged victorious, there is no reason for political parties, or opposition candidates, or dissent of any kind. In a communist society only the party of the working class—the Communist party—is permitted to exist.

5. Marxism predicts the "withering away" of the state in a communist society, but in fact communist governments have become giant bureaucracies that oversee every aspect of life and society.

NOTES

1. William L. Shirer, *The Rise and Fall of the Third Reich* (New York: Simon and Shuster, 1960), p. 959.
2. Carl Becker, *Modern Democracy* (New Haven, Conn.: Yale University Press, 1941), p. 27.
3. Adolph Hitler, *Mein Kampf* (New York: Reynal and Hitchcock, 1939), p. 595.

DISCUSSION QUESTIONS

1. Define ideology and describe its relationship to power. Discuss the ways in which ideology can control people's behavior. Identify the characteristics of modern ideologies.
2. Compare and contrast classical liberalism and modern liberalism. What is the attitude of each of these ideologies toward the individual? What is their approach to governmental power, the concept of equality, and the capitalist system?
3. Explain the confusion that arises from the ideological labels of *conservative* and *modern liberal*. Define what is meant by *Burkean representation*.
4. Describe the goal of the fascist state. What should the attitudes of a "good" fascist be toward "happiness" and rational thought, and toward the economy and the power structure?
5. Trace the development of socialism and communism. Discuss what Marx meant by economic determinism; dialectical materialism; the class struggle; the theory of surplus value; the inevitability of revolution; the dictatorship of the proletariat; and the withering away of the state.
6. Define *socialism* and discuss how this ideology differs from communism. Describe the development of modern socialism and the contributions of Edward Bernstein to that movement.
7. Discuss the ideological justification that Herbert Marcuse provided for contemporary radicalism. Describe the kind of society envisioned by the New Left. What factors contributed to the growth and decline of radicalism in the United States in the late 1960s and early 1970s?
8. Describe how Lenin adapted the ideology of Marxism to conditions in the Soviet Union. Describe Lenin's totalitarian party and his theory of imperialism. Discuss the "communism in one country" created by Lenin and Stalin. How was the ideology of communism used during Stalin's regime, and what rather recent changes have the goals and methods of Soviet communism undergone?
9. Describe some of the more serious flaws in Marxist theory.

SUGGESTED READINGS

Daniel Bell, *The End of Ideology* (Glencoe, Ill.: Free Press, 1960).

William F. Buckley, *Up from Liberalism* (New York: McDowell and Obstensky, 1959).

John Bunzel, *Anti-Politics in America* (New York: Random House, 1967).

Milton Friedman, *Capitalism and Freedom* (Chicago: University of Chicago Press, 1962).

Barry M. Goldwater, *The Conscience of a Conservative* (New York: Macfadden-Bartell, 1964).

Jeff Greenfield and Jack Newfield, *A Populist Manifesto* (New York: Praeger, 1972).

Lewis Hartz, *The Liberal Tradition in America* (New York: Harcourt Brace Jovanovich, 1955).

Herbert Marcuse, *One-Dimensional Man* (Boston: Beacon, 1964).

C. Wright Mills, *The Marxists* (New York: Delta Books, 1962).

Students for a Democratic Society, *The Port Huron Statement* (Chicago: Students for a Democratic Society, 1966).

Photo from Stock, Boston by Donald Patterson

Chapter 10
Power, Race, and Sex

The United States has a long history of protest. The nation was in fact born as a protest against the injustices of colonialism—against inequality, powerlessness, the lack of a "voice" in controlling its own affairs. Despite that heritage, America's women and racial minorities have had a long and continuing fight against the inequalities imposed on them by their nation's laws and customs. In 1776 Abigail Adams wrote to her husband John, who was then a delegate to the Continental Congress, cautioning him and his fellow delegates that when framing the new nation's laws they should "Remember the Ladies. . . . Do not put such unlimited power into the hands of the Husbands." She added, probably in jest, "If perticuliar care and attention is not paid to the Laidies we are determined to foment a Rebelion, and will not hold ourselves bound by any Laws in which we have no voice, or Representation."[1] The "Ladies" did not find that voice until 1920 when the Nineteenth Amendment finally guaranteed them the right to vote, and although Abigail's prophecy may have been made in jest, it turned out to be accurate: the "Ladies" did indeed foment some rebellions of their own and were fiery participants in others. They were activists in the protest against slavery and had a vital interest in the fight for the Fifteenth Amendment, which extended the franchise to blacks.

In the 1950s black activists launched a new fight for equality, which in turn inspired a rebirth of the feminist movement; the events of the 1960s were of mutual advantage to blacks and women. In this chapter we will explore the struggles and triumphs of both groups, as well as some of the inequalities that these groups suffer. After you have read it, you should be able to:

- discuss the civil rights movement of the 1950s and 1960s and the changes in the laws that it affected.
- describe the inequalities that American blacks and women have protested against.
- identify and describe some of the individual protest movements.
- discuss the conflict between "affirmative action" and equality of opportunity, as well as the Supreme Court's definition of "reverse discrimination."

291

THE CIVIL RIGHTS MOVEMENT: ENDING LAWFUL DISCRIMINATION

Power is exercised when individuals or groups are kept powerless by law or by custom. The long history of slavery and segregation in America is a history of the exercise of power by a white majority over a black minority—first through the institution of slavery, later through laws that segregated the races and imposed an inferior position upon blacks. These exercises of power over specific groups in society may not always involve open, public decisions. The failure to do anything positive about existing discrimination is also an exercise of power—that is, power can involve "non-decision making" as well as "decision making." The civil rights movement of the 1950s and 1960s was successful in forcing America's white majority to make some positive decisions about ending racial discrimination.

Initial goal

The initial goal of the civil rights movement was the elimination of direct *legal* segregation. First, discrimination and segregation practiced by governments had to be prohibited, particularly in voting and public education. Then direct discrimination in all segments of American life, private as well as public—in transportation, theaters, parks, stores, restaurants, businesses, employment, and housing—came under attack. It is important to understand, however, that the elimination of direct lawful discrimination does not in itself ensure *equality*. The civil rights laws of the national government did not affect conditions of equality in America as directly as we might suppose. The problem of racial inequality—inequality between blacks and whites in income, health, housing, employment, education, and so on—is more than a problem of direct legal discrimination. Nevertheless, the first important step toward equality was the elimination of *lawful* segregation.

Led by Roy Wilkins, executive director of the National Association for the Advancement of Colored People (NAACP), and Thurgood Marshall, chief counsel for the NAACP (who was later to become the first black Supreme Court justice), the newly emerging civil rights movement of the 1950s pressed for a court decision that direct lawful segregation violated the guarantee of "equal protection of laws" of the Fourteenth Amendment. Basing their decisions on the case of *Plessy* v. *Ferguson,* the courts for over half a century had upheld laws *separating* the races as long as black and white facilities pretended to be *equal* in tangible respects. The civil rights movement sought a complete reversal of this "separate but equal" interpretation of the Fourteenth Amendment; it wanted a decision that laws separating the races were *unconstitutional.*

The civil rights group chose to bring suit for desegregation in Topeka, Kansas, where segregated black and white schools *were* equal with respect to buildings, curricula, qualifications and salaries of teachers, and other tangible factors. The object was to prevent the Court from ordering the admission of a black person because tangible facilities were not equal, and to force the Court to review the doctrine of segregation itself.

On 17 May 1954, the Court rendered its decision in *Brown* v. *Board of Education of Topeka, Kansas:*

> Segregation of white and colored children in public schools has a detrimental effect upon the colored children. The impact is greater when it has the sanction of law, for the policy of separating the races is usually interpreted as denoting the inferiority of the Negro group. A form of inferiority affects the motivation of a child to learn. Segregation with the sanction of law, therefore, has a tendency to retard the educational and mental development of Negro children and to deprive them of some of the benefits they would receive in a racially integrated school system. Whatever may have been the extent of psychological knowledge of the time of *Plessy* v. *Ferguson*, this finding is amply supported by modern authority. Any language in *Plessy* v. *Ferguson* contrary to this source is rejected.[2]

Brown v. *Board of Education of Topeka, Kansas* marked the beginning of a new era in American politics. The *Brown* decision gave official legitimacy to the aspirations of the black people. It encouraged them to believe that they could achieve power within the constitutional framework. It raised their level of expectations and inspired them to insist upon their full constitutional rights. This turning point in the power of black people in America was the product of a patient, reasoned, and legalistic approach to racial problems.

Of course, the battle over segregation was just beginning in 1954. Although segregation in any state-supported institution after 1954 was unconstitutional, it would remain a part of American life, regardless of its constitutionality, until effective *power* was brought to bear to end it. The Supreme Court, by virtue of the system of *federalism* and the *separation of powers*, has *little formal power* at its disposal. Congress, the president, state governors and legislators, and even occasional mobs of people, have more direct power at their disposal than does the federal judiciary. The Supreme Court must rely largely on other branches of the federal government, on the states, and on private citizens *to implement the law* of the land. In 1954 the practice of segregation was widespread and deeply ingrained in American life.

Implementation

Seventeen states required the segregation of the races in public schools,[3] and four additional states authorized segregation upon the option of the local school boards.[4] Moreover, the Congress of the United States required segregation of the races in the public schools of the District of Columbia.

The Supreme Court did not order immediate nationwide desegregation. Instead, it turned over responsibility for desegregation to state and local authorities under the supervision of federal district courts. The six border states with segregated school systems—Delaware, Kentucky, Maryland, Missouri, Oklahoma, West Virginia—together with the school districts in Kansas, Arizona, and New Mexico that had opted for segregated schools, chose not to resist desegregation formally. The District of Columbia also desegregated public schools the year following the Supreme Court's decision. But

Resistance

resistance to school desegregation was the choice of the eleven states of the old Confederacy. This resistance lasted more than fifteen years. The refusal of a school district to desegregate until it was faced with a federal court injunction was the most common form of delay. Other schemes included state payments of private school tuition in lieu of providing public schools, the amending of compulsory attendance laws so that no child would be required to attend an integrated school, and the use of pupil placement laws to avoid or minimize the extent of desegregation. Pupil placement laws, which guaranteed "freedom of choice," were the most successful of the delaying tactics. Black and white school children were permitted to indicate their choice of schools, and southern school authorities relied on most of them selecting the schools that they had previously attended—that is, segregated schools. Not until the late 1960s did federal courts decline to accept such plans from local school authorities as "good-faith" implementation of desegregation. Finally, state officials themselves—including Governor George C. Wallace of Alabama—attempted to prevent desegregation on the grounds that it would endanger public safety. Violence flared in a number of southern communities; federal troops were used to desegregate Central High School in Little Rock, Arkansas, in 1957 and the University of Mississippi in 1962.

1964: guidelines

Resistance to desegregation was quite successful during the period from 1954 to 1964. Only about 2 percent of the black school children in the eleven southern states that resisted desegregation were attending integrated schools ten years after *Brown* v. *Board of Education of Topeka, Kansas.* But in the *Civil Rights Act of 1964,* the United States Congress finally entered the civil rights field in support of Court efforts to achieve desegregation. Among other things, the act provided that every federal department or agency must take steps to end segregation in all departments or programs receiving *federal financial assistance*. The U.S. Office of Education was authorized to issue *guidelines* to eliminate segregation in schools receiving federal aid; schools that did not meet segregation guidelines faced termination of financial assistance from the federal government. Thus, in addition to Court orders requiring desegregation, school districts also faced federal guidelines and the loss of federal revenues. In 1969 the last legal justification for delay in implementing school desegregation collapsed when the Supreme Court rejected a request by Mississippi school officials for delay. The Court declared that every school district was obliged to end dual school systems "at once" and "now and hereafter" operate only unitary schools. The effect of the decision—fifteen years after the original *Brown* case—was to eliminate any further legal justification for continuation of segregation in public schools.

By 1970, southern school desegregation had proceeded to a point at which more black children were attending integrated schools in the South than in the North. Direct lawful segregation in southern schools had largely been eliminated. But even as the impact of segregation by law in the South was diminishing, more Americans came to realize

De facto segregation

the continuing impact of *de facto* segregation in northern cities. De facto segregation occurs when schools are predominantly white or black as a result of segregated housing patterns and neighborhood schools, rather than as a result of direct lawful discrimination. If the issue is posed as one of "racial isolation," then by 1970 the efforts of federal courts and executive agencies to erase the last vestiges of segregation by law had so reduced racial isolation in the South that it was less than racial isolation in the North. Moreover, efforts to end racial isolation in Boston, Massachusetts, Pontiac, Michigan, and other northern cities produced a type of disorder and violence that was reminiscent of early desegregation efforts in the South.

THE CIVIL RIGHTS ACT OF 1964

As long as the civil rights movement was combating *governmental* discrimination, it could employ the U.S. Constitution as a weapon in its arsenal. Since the Supreme Court and the federal judiciary are charged with the responsibility of interpreting the Constitution, the civil rights movement could concentrate on *judicial* action to accomplish its objective of preventing governmental discrimination. But the

Private discrimination: the need for legislative action

Constitution has considerably less bearing upon the activities of private individuals than do the laws passed by Congress and the various states. Thus, when the civil rights movement turned its attention to combating *private* discrimination, it had to carry its fight into the *legislative* branch of government. The federal courts could help restrict discrimination by state and local governments and school authorities, but *only* Congress could restrict discrimination practiced by private owners of restaurants, hotels, and motels, private employers, and other individuals who were not government officials.

Before 1964 Congress had been content to let other agencies, including the president and the courts, struggle with the problem of civil rights. Yet Congress could not long ignore the nation's most pressing domestic issue. The civil rights movement had stepped up its protests and demonstrations and was attracting worldwide attention with organized sit-ins, freedom rides, picketing campaigns, boycotts, and mass marches. The mass media vividly portrayed the animosity of segregationists and helped to convince millions of Americans of the need for national legislation. After the massive "March on Washington" in August 1963, President Kennedy asked Congress for the most comprehensive civil rights legislation it had ever considered. After Kennedy's assassination, President Johnson brought heavy pressure upon Congress to pass the bill as a tribute to the late president. Everett M. Dirksen of Illinois, Republican leader in the Senate, provided Johnson with the bipartisan support needed to overcome a southern filibuster. The Civil Rights Act of 1964 finally passed both houses of Congress by better than a two-thirds vote and with the overwhelming support of members of both the Republican and Democratic parties. It can be ranked with the Emancipation Proclamation, the Fourteenth Amendment, and *Brown* v. *Board of Education* as one of the most important steps toward full equality for blacks in America.

The act includes the following provisions:

I. It is unlawful to apply unequal standards in voter registration procedures or to deny registration for irrelevant errors or omissions on records or applications. Literacy tests must be in writing and a sixth-grade education is a presumption of literacy.

II. It is unlawful to discriminate or segregate persons on the grounds of race, color, religion, or natural origin in any place of public accommodation, including hotels, motels, restaurants, movies, theaters, sports arenas, entertainment houses, and other places offering to serve the public. This prohibition extends to all establishments whose operations affect interstate commerce or whose discriminatory practices are supported by state action. Private clubs are specifically exempted.

III. The Attorney General shall undertake civil action on behalf of any person denied equal access to a public accommodation. If the proprietor continues to discriminate, he may be held in contempt of court and subjected to preemptory fines or imprisonment without trial by jury. (This mode of enforcement gave proprietors an opportunity to adjust to the new law without being punished, and it also avoided the possibility that southern juries would refuse to convict violators of the act.)

IV. The Attorney General shall undetake civil actions on behalf of persons attempting the orderly desegregation of public schools.

V. The U.S. Commission on Civil Rights, first established by the Civil Rights Act of 1957, shall be empowered (1) to investigate deprivations of the right to vote, (2) to collect and to study information regarding discrimination in America, and (3) to make reports to the President and Congress as necessary.

VI. Each federal department and agency shall take appropriate action to end discrimination in all programs or activities receiving federal financial assistance in any form. These actions may include the termination of assistance.

VII. It shall be unlawful for any firm or labor union employing or representing twenty-five or more persons to discriminate against any individual in any fashion because of his race, color, religion, sex, or natural origins; an Equal Employment Opportunity Commission shall be established to enforce this provision by investigation, conference, conciliation, or civil action in federal court.

MARTIN LUTHER KING, JR.
The Power of Protest

The civil rights movement invented new techniques for minorities to gain power and influence in American society. *Mass protest* is a technique by which groups seek to obtain a bargaining position for themselves that can induce desired concessions from established power holders. It is a means of acquiring a bargaining leverage for those who would otherwise be powerless. The protest may challenge established groups by threatening their reputations (where they might be harmed by unfavorable publicity), their economic position (where they might be hurt by a boycott), their peace and quiet (where noise and disruption might upset their daily activities), or their

security (where violence or the threat of violence is involved).

The protest technique appeals to powerless minorities who have little to bargain with except their promise *not* to protest. Once the protest has begun—or even before it has begun if the *threat* of protest is made credible—the minority can promise not to protest in exchange for the desired concessions. Perhaps more importantly, mass protest frequently motivates members of established elites, who have the political resources the protesters lack, to enter the political arena on behalf of the protesters.

The nation's leading exponent of *nonviolent* protest was Dr. Martin Luther King, Jr. Indeed, King's contributions to the development of a philosophy of nonviolent, direct-action protest on behalf of blacks won him international acclaim and the Nobel Peace Prize in 1964. King first came to national prominence in 1955 when he was only twenty-five years old; he led a year-long bus boycott in Montgomery, Alabama, to protest discrimination in seating on public buses. In 1957 he formed the Southern Christian Leadership Conference (SCLC) to provide encouragement and leadership to the growing nonviolent protest movement in the South.

In 1963 a group of Alabama clergymen petitioned Martin Luther King, Jr., to call off mass demonstrations in Birmingham, Alabama.

King, who had been arrested in the demonstrations, replied in his famous "Letter from Birmingham Jail":

> You may well ask, "Why direct action? Why sit-ins, marches, etc? Isn't negotiation a better path?" You are exactly right in your call for negotiation. Indeed, this is the purpose of direct action. Nonviolent direct action seeks to create such a crisis and establish such creative tension that a community that has constantly refused to negotiate is forced to confront the issue. It seeks to so dramatize the issue that it can no longer be ignored. . . .
>
> You express a great deal of anxiety over our willingness to break laws. . . . One may well ask, "How can you advocate breaking some laws and obeying others?" The answer is found in the fact that there are *unjust* laws. I would be the first to advocate obeying just laws. One has not only a legal but a moral responsibility to obey just laws. Conversely, one has a moral responsibility to disobey unjust laws. . . .
>
> In no sense do I advocate evading or defying the law as the rabid segregationist would do. This would lead to anarchy. One who breaks an unjust law must do it *openly, lovingly* (not hatefully as the white mothers did in New Orleans when they were seen on television screaming "nigger, nigger, nigger") and with a willingness to accept the penalty. I submit that an individual who breaks a law that conscience tells him is unjust, and willingly accepts the penalty by staying in jail to arouse the conscience of the community over its injustice, is in reality expressing the very highest respect for law.[5]

Nonviolent direct action

Nonviolent direct action is a technique requiring direct mass action against laws regarded as unjust, rather than court litigation, political campaigning, voting, or other conventional forms of democratic political activity. Mass demonstrations, sit-ins, and other nonviolent direct-action tactics usually result in violations of state and local laws. For example, persons remaining at a segregated lunch counter after the owner orders them to leave are usually violating trespass laws. Marching in the street frequently entails the obstruction of traffic and results in charges of "disorderly conduct" or "parading without a permit." Mass demonstrations often involve "disturbing the peace" or refusing to obey the lawful orders of a police officer. Even though these tactics are nonviolent, they do entail *disobedience to civil law*.

Civil disobedience is not new to American politics. Its practitioners have played an important role in American history, from the patriots who participated in the Boston Tea Party, to the abolitionists who hid runaway slaves, to the suffragists who paraded and demonstrated for women's rights, to the labor organizers who picketed to form the nation's major industrial unions, to the civil rights marchers of recent years. Civil disobedience is a political tactic of minorities. (Since majorities can more easily change laws through conventional political activity, they seldom have to disobey them.) It is also a tactic attractive to groups wishing to change the social status quo significantly and quickly.

Political purpose

The political purpose of nonviolent direct action and civil disobedience is to call attention or "to bear witness" to the existence of injustices. Only laws regarded as unjust are broken, and they are broken openly without hatred or violence. Punishment is actively sought rather than avoided since punishment will further emphasize the injustices of the law. The object of nonviolent civil disobedience is to stir the conscience of an apathetic majority and to win support for measures that will eliminate the injustices. By accepting punishment for the violation of an unjust law, persons practicing civil disobedience demonstrate their sincerity. They hope to shame the majority and to make it ask itself how far it will go to protect the status quo.

Participation of the news media

Clearly the participation of the mass news media, particularly television, contributes immeasurably to the success of nonviolent direct action. Breaking the law makes news; dissemination of the news calls the attention of the public to the existence of unjust laws or practices; the public sympathy is won when injustices are spotlighted; the willingness of the demonstrators to accept punishment provides evidence of their sincerity; and the whole drama lays the groundwork for changing unjust laws and practices. Cruelty or violence directed against the demonstrators by the police or other defenders of the status quo plays into the hands of the demonstrators by stressing the injustices they are experiencing.

Protest and social change

Perhaps the most dramatic application of nonviolent direct action occurred in Birmingham, Alabama, in the spring of 1963. Under the direction of Martin Luther King, Jr., the SCLC chose Birmingham as a major site for desegregation demonstrations during the centennial year of the Emancipation Proclamation. Birmingham was by its own description the "Heart of Dixie"; it was the most rigidly segregated large city in the United States. King believed that if segregation could be successfully challenged in Birmingham, it might begin to crumble throughout the South. Thousands of black people, including school children, staged protest marches in Birmingham from 2 to 7 May. In response, police and fire fighters under the direction of Police Chief "Bull" Connor attacked the demonstrators with fire hoses, cattle prods, and police dogs—all in clear view of national television cameras. Pictures of police brutality were flashed throughout the nation and the world, doubtless touching the consciences of many white

Americans. The demonstrators conducted themselves in a nonviolent fashion. Thousands were dragged off to jail, including Martin Luther King, Jr. (It was at this time that King wrote his "Letter from Birmingham Jail," explaining and defending nonviolent direct action.)

The most massive application of nonviolent direct action was the great "March on Washington" in August 1963, during which more than two hundred thousand black and white marchers converged on the nation's capital. The march ended in a formal program at the Lincoln Memorial in which Martin Luther King, Jr., delivered his most eloquent appeal, entitled "I Have a Dream."

> I still have a dream. It is a dream deeply rooted in the American dream. I have a dream that one day this nation will rise up and live out the true meaning of its creed: "We hold these truths to be self-evident, that all men are created equal."

Another very significant application of nonviolent direct action occurred in Alabama in the spring of 1965 during the SCLC-organized march from Selma to Montgomery to protest voting inequities. The Selma marchers convinced Congress that its earlier legislation was inadequate to the task of securely guaranteeing the right to vote for all Americans. In response to the march, Congress enacted the *Voting Rights Act of 1965*, which threatened federal intervention in local voting matters to a degree never before attempted. The act authorized the attorney general, upon evidence of voter discrimination in southern states, to replace local registrars with federal examiners, who were authorized to abolish literacy tests, to waive poll taxes, and to register voters under simplified federal procedures. The impact of the Voting Rights Act of 1965 can be observed in increased black voter registration figures in the South and election of blacks to state legislatures in every southern state and to many city and county offices as well.

White racial violence in the early 1960s contributed to the success of the nonviolent direct-action movement in winning the nation's sympathy and support. Murders and bombings shocked and disgusted whites in both the North and the South. In 1963 Medgar Evers, NAACP state chairman from Mississippi, was shot to death by a sniper as he entered his Jackson home. In that same year a bomb killed four black girls attending Sunday school in Birmingham, Alabama. In 1964 three young men (Michael Schwerner and Andrew Goodman, both white, and James Chaney, a black) were murdered in Philadelphia, Mississippi, while working on a civil rights project in education and voter registration. In 1965 a black educator from

Washington, D.C., Lemuel Penn, was murdered as he drove through Athens, Georgia, while returning from military duty as a reserve officer.

On 4 April 1968 Martin Luther King, Jr., was shot and killed by a white man in Memphis, Tennessee. The murder of the nation's leading advocate of nonviolence was a tragedy affecting all Americans. Before his death, King had campaigned in Chicago and other northern cities for an end to de facto segregation of blacks in ghettos and the passage of *fair housing legislation* prohibiting discrimination in the sale or rental of houses and apartments. But King appeared to be having less success in achieving this goal than in his previous efforts to effect change. "Fair housing" legislation had consistently failed in Congress; there was no mention of discrimination in housing even in the comprehensive Civil Rights Act of 1964; and the prospects of a national fair housing law were unpromising at the beginning of 1968. With the assassination of Martin Luther King, Jr., however, the mood of the nation and of Congress changed dramatically. Many people came to feel that Congress should pass a fair housing law as a tribute to the slain civil rights leader. The *Civil Rights Act of 1968* prohibited the following forms of discrimination:

> Refusal to sell or rent a dwelling to any person because of his race, color, religion, or national origin.
>
> Discrimination against a person in the terms, conditions, or privileges of the sale or rental of a dwelling.
>
> Indication of a preference or discrimination on the basis of race, color, religion, or national origin in advertising the sale or rental of a dwelling.

Risks of nonviolent direct action

Despite its successes, nonviolent direct action does pose problems. This tactic is capable of arousing extreme passions on either side of an issue and exciting and provoking masses to act without thinking, perhaps ultimately making disrespect for the law a commonplace attitude. If undertaken too frequently or directed against laws or practices that are not really serious injustices, it may have the effect of alienating the majority, whose sympathies are so essential to the success of the movement. A favorable outcome can be achieved by actions that arouse the conscience of a majority against injustice or that discomfort a majority to the point that it is willing to grant the demands of the minority rather than experience further discomfort. But actions that provoke hostility or a demagogic reaction from the majority merely reduce the opportunities for progress.

Even in a *nonviolent* movement the risk of violence is always great. Though violence on the part of police or counterdemonstrators can assist in achieving the movement's objective, violence by demonstrators usually has the opposite effect. Unfortunately, mass followers do not always fully understand or appreciate the distinction between nonviolent demonstrations directed against injustice, and rioting, looting, and violence directed against society itself.

Finally, while nonviolent direct action may be effective against direct discrimination or an obvious injustice, this strategy is less successful against very subtle discrimination or de facto segregation. Few Americans approve of direct discrimination or cruelty against a nonviolent minority, and direct-action tactics that spotlight such injustice can arouse the conscience of the white majority. But the white majority is less likely to become conscience-stricken over subtle forms of discrimination, segregation, or inequalities that are not the immediate product of direct discrimination.

POWERLESSNESS IN THE GHETTO

Continuing disparities

White Americans can understand the unfairness of legal discrimination, and the majority agree that such discrimination is inconsistent with the norms of a democratic society. Yet, though the *legal* foundations of segregation have collapsed, the *actual* disparity between blacks and whites in terms of income, employment, housing, and other economic conditions has not changed greatly. Though the victories of the civil rights movement were immensely important, they are primarily *symbolic* gains rather than *real* changes in the conditions under which most blacks live in America. Increasingly the problem of inequality is being posed as one of differences in the "life chances" of blacks and whites. (As shown in the appendix, figure E, there is even disparity between blacks and whites in terms of actual life expectancy.) Figures can only suggest the bare outline of a black's life chances in American society (see table 10–1 and appendix figure F). The income of the black family is less than two-thirds that of the

Table 10–1   Life Chances of Blacks and Whites

Income						
Median Income of Families:						
	1947	1960	1968	1970	1972	1975
White	$4,916	$6,857	$8,937	$10,236	$11,549	$13,356
Black	2,514	3,794	5,590	6,516	6,864	7,808

Table 10–1 (Cont.)

Median Family Income of Blacks and Other Minority Races
as a % of White Family Income:

1950	54%	1966	60%
1955	55	1968	63
1959	52	1970	64
1960	55	1972	62
1964	56	1975	58

Persons below Poverty Level:

	Number (Millions)		Percentage of Total Population	
	Black	White	Black	White
1959	11.0	28.5	56	18
1965	10.7	22.5	47	13
1969	7.6	16.7	31	10
1975	7.5	16.3	31	9

Occupation

Blacks and Other Minority Races as a
% of All Workers in Selected Occupations:

	1960	*1970*	*1975*
Professional	4	6	7
Medical Workers	4	8	8
Teachers	7	10	9
Managers	2	3	4
Clerical workers	5	8	9
Sales workers	3	4	4
Craftsmen	5	7	7
Operatives	12	14	13
Nonfarm laborers	27	24	20
Private household workers	46	44	41
Other service workers	20	19	19
Farm workers	16	11	9

Education

% of Persons 25 to 29 Years Old
Completing 4 or More Years of High School:

	Male		Female	
	Black	White	Black	White
1960	37	64	42	66
1968	55	78	58	77
1971	59	81	63	80

average white family. One-third of all black families have annual incomes below the government's "poverty line." Home ownership is greater among whites than blacks. The black unemployment rate is twice as high as that for whites. The average black acquires less education than the average white. Blacks are far less likely than whites to hold prestigious white-collar jobs in professional, managerial, clerical, or sales work. They hold few skilled craft jobs in industry, but are instead concentrated in semiskilled, service, and laboring positions. Black women have more children than white women (see appendix, figure B). They also have them at an earlier age than white women, and bearing too many children too early usually complicates the parents' lives, making it difficult for them to finish school or to save money. Thus, a cycle is at work in the ghettos: Low education levels produce low income levels, which prevent parents from moving out of the ghettos, which deprives children of educational opportunities—and so the cycle repeats.

The ghetto is peopled primarily by lower-class black masses. Individual blacks who have attained middle-class status are generally more acceptable to whites than are blacks living in the ghettos. Whites feel that they can communicate with the black middle class but not with the black masses. They regard blacks at the top of the social pyramid as living examples of what the determined or talented black can accomplish in a democratic capitalist society.

In addition to poverty, family disorganization, and inequality, the ghetto harbors various social pathologies. Crime and delinquency, mental illness, and drug addiction haunt America's ghettos. By and large the victims of these social pathologies are the ghetto residents themselves. Blacks are the *principal* victims of lawlessness in America; they are more likely than whites to be preyed upon by criminals. According to FBI crime statistics, blacks (11 percent of the population) account for 28 percent of all criminal arrests. In all major categories of offenses, the rate of arrests for blacks is higher than that for whites. Assuming that arrests are a rough indicator of the number of crimes committed, the black crime rate is apparently more than *twice* the proportion of blacks in the total population.

Blacks comprise about 40 percent of all persons confined in state prisons, a proportion significantly higher than the black *arrest* rate. They also constitute a disproportionate share of the drug addicts in the United States. Black sociologist Alphonso Pinkney summarized the reasons that social deviance is disproportionately common among blacks:

(1) In the United States black people occupy a separate and subordinate economic and social position which leads to frustration. Their frustrations are usually displaced in acts of aggression against fellow Negroes,

thus leading to a higher proportion of intraracial criminal acts. (2) As
Myrdal has demonstrated, the caste system under which black people
live operates in such a way as to prevent them from identifying with the
society and the law. The very legal system itself is manipulated to discriminate against black people. (3) Black persons, far more than white
persons, are forced to live in deteriorated sections of cities. These areas
are characterized by widespread social disorganization in terms of
criminal values, as well as poverty, poor housing, restrictions on settlement, and limited outlets for recreation and employment. "Out of these
and similar conditions arise elements conducive to greater criminality,
as well as other forms of pathology, among the Negro population." (4)
The high crime rate among black people is partially a function of their
reaction to having their means to success blocked by discriminatory
behavior. "Crime may thus be utilized as a means of escape, ego en-
hancement, expression of aggression, or upward mobility. . . ." (5)
Black people are overrepresented in the lower class, and recorded crime
tends to be concentrated in this class.[6]

"Colonialism"   Powerlessness in black ghettos is reflected in a comparison of
ghettos with the "colonies" of an earlier era. Ghetto residents feel
that they have little control over the institutions in their own communities; businesses, schools, welfare agencies, police departments,
and most other important agencies are controlled from the outside.
Often the agents of these institutions—the store managers, clerks,
teachers, welfare workers, and police officers—are whites who live
outside of the ghetto. Thus, the important institutions of the ghetto are
staffed and controlled almost entirely by outsiders; hence the analogy
with colonialism. Sociologist Kenneth Clark writes:

> The dark ghetto's invisible walls have been erected by the white society,
> by those who have power, both to confine those who have *no* power and
> to perpetuate their powerlessness. The dark ghettos are social, political,
> educational, and—above all—economic colonies. Their inhabitants are
> subject peoples, victims of the greed, cruelty, insensitivity, guilt, and fear
> of their masters.[7]

In analyzing urban riots, the National Advisory Commission on
Civil Disorders also referred to powerlessness, this time as a contributing cause to both urban social disorders and the rise of militant
mass movements:

> Many Negroes have come to believe that they are being exploited
> politically and economically by the white "power structure." Negroes,
> like people in poverty everywhere, in fact lack the channels of communi-
> cation, influence and appeal that traditionally have been available to

ethnic minorities within the city and which enabled them—unburdened by color—to scale the walls of the white ghettos in an earlier era. The frustrations of powerlessness have led some to the conviction that there is no effective alternative to violence as a means of expression and redress, as a way of "moving the system." More generally, the result is alienation and hostility toward the institutions of law and government and the white society which controls them. This is reflected in the reach toward radical consciousness and solidarity reflected in the slogan "Black Power."[8]

Powerlessness and black power

Thus, the ghetto provides an environment that encourages appeals to racial consciousness, black solidarity, and black power. Feelings of powerlessness, alienation, and hostility toward white society can easily be exploited by political movements that reject traditional democratic methods and integrationist goals while asserting the coming of "black power" and black separatism.

THE BLACK POWER MOVEMENT

Black power began not as a program of political action but simply as a slogan.[9] The meaning of this slogan has been widely debated, and there is really no concise definition of what black power means as a political program. However, it is possible to identify several recurrent themes in militant black politics.

Themes in militant black politics

In a book entitled *Black Power: The Politics of Liberation in America*, Stokely Carmichael and Charles V. Hamilton write:

> Black Power . . . is a call for black people in this country to unite, to recognize their heritage, to build a sense of community. It is a call for black people to begin to define their own goals, to lead their own organizations and to support those organizations. It is a call to reject the racist institutions and values of this society. . . .
> . . . Black people must lead and run their own organizations. Only black people can convey the revolutionary idea—and it is a revolutionary idea—that black people are able to do things themselves. . . .
> It does not mean merely putting black faces into office.[10]

One prominent theme in militant black politics is the necessity of *fostering black pride and dignity*. One of the worst effects of segregation and discrimination is that members of the minority group begin to doubt their own worth as human beings. Black leaders therefore endeavor to develop a positive image toward blackness. Carmichael and Hamilton write:

> Throughout this country, vast segments of the black communities are
> beginning to recognize the need to assert their own definitions, to
> reclaim their history, their culture; to create their own sense of com-
> munity and togetherness. There is a growing resentment of the word
> "Negro," for example, because this term is the invention of our op-
> pressor: it is *his* image of us that he describes. Many blacks are now call-
> ing themselves African-Americans, Afro-Americans or black people
> because that is *our* image of ourselves.[11]

The effort to assert pride in blackness is often accompanied by
African dress, African hairstyles, "soul food," "soul music," and the
like.

An important political theme of black militancy is a general
condemnation of white society as "racist." This condemnation of racism in society extends far beyond individual acts of bigotry (for example, the bombing of a black church) to encompass nearly all the
values and institutions of white society. Black militants argue that the
institutions of American society are inherently racist because blacks
are kept segregated in slums, because black unemployment is twice
as great as white unemployment, because black incomes are only half
those of whites, because the infant mortality rate among blacks is
twice that among whites, because the educational level of blacks is
below that of whites, and so on. In other words, the condition of
blacks is itself considered sufficient proof of the racism of established
institutions. Moreover, that condition also inspires black militants to
condemn the value structure of American society, which either has
supported the condition or at least has failed to eradicate it.

The black militant condemnation of existing societal values and
institutions as racist leads to a rejection of traditional democratic and
organizational politics. This disparagement of democratic politics is
usually accompanied by a *rejection of the ideal of coalition with
white liberals.* White liberals want to reform the system, whereas
black radicals want to do away with it. While "limited, short-term
coalitions on relatively minor issues" are possible, "such approaches
seldom come to terms with the roots of institutional racism." In addition to black militants' concern that most white liberals are insuf-
ficiently radical in their politics, there is the fear that black people
will be "absorbed or swallowed up" in white-controlled liberal organizations. There is the fear that white liberals will use black people
to further white liberal objectives, claiming all the while that these
objectives coincide with the aspirations of black people.

This line of reasoning inevitably leads to the conclusion that
black organizations must be led by black people rather than by white

people. The participation of whites in black organizations should be limited to "supportive roles" involving "specific skills and techniques," as, for example, the special knowledge of lawyers. The black militants do not welcome the participation of the

> . . . many young, middle-class, white Americans [who], like some sort of Pepsi generation, have wanted to "come alive" through the black community and black groups. They have wanted to be where the action is—and the action has been in those places. They have sought refuge among blacks from the sterile, meaningless, irrelevant life in middle-class America. They have been unable to deal with the stifling, racist, parochial, split-level mentality of their parents, teachers, preachers and friends. . . . The black organizations do not need this kind of idealism, which borders on paternalism.[12]

The emphasis on black pride and solidarity, as well as the hostility toward existing social values and institutions, frequently leads to a *rejection of integration*. To the militants, integration means assimilation into the white middle-class society that they so vigorously condemn. It means the loss of black identity and the submergence of black culture in the prevailing culture of white society. Thus the black power movement is closely identified with "black separatism." If the prevailing values and institutions of white society were radically altered or abolished, then perhaps genuine racial integration would be possible. The black power movement generally does not envision a separate black nation but merely asserts that black pride and black solidarity are preconditions for bringing about the kinds of social conditions necessary for genuine integration. The kind of integration pictured by advocates of black power is one in which the black masses will become an integral part of a radically different society, rather than one in which individual black people will be absorbed into the existing culture.

Black militancy has won widespread acceptance among black college students. At many major colleges and universities, black students have organized all-black clubs whose activities frequently reflect black power philosophy. These students are critical of established values and institutions of American society; they have demanded greater emphasis on black history and culture, including the establishment of black studies curricula; they have demanded that more black students be accepted for admission; they have demanded that universities hire more black faculty. The black student unions have stressed black consciousness and black pride among their members.

SEXUAL INEQUALITY AND DISCRIMINATION

Sex roles involve power relationships. The recent reconsideration of woman's role in American society, including the publicity given to the women's liberation movement, has brought about a new realization that sexual roles in our culture specify differential treatment, status, and power. The traditional American family was patriarchal, and many cultural practices continue to reflect male dominance. Men still hold most of the major positions in industry, finance, universities, the military, politics, and government. Authority in most families still rests with the male. Over one-third of the work force in America is female, but the average wage of these women is only half the average income of men. Women who work must generally continue to bear

"Founding Fathers! How come no Founding Mothers?"
Drawing by Dana Fradon; © 1972 The New Yorker Magazine, Inc.

the major burden of domestic service and child care in their homes. Women have many special protections in the law, but often these protections limit opportunities for advancement and even encourage women to remain dependent upon men. Sex roles assign domestic service and child care to women, and human achievement, interest, and ambition beyond these to men. (See appendix, figure A and table B, for information on women's enrollment in college and types of occupations held by women.)

Male dominance may stem from a combination of biological factors and cultural practices. Arguments over women's liberation often center around the issue of how much of male dominance can be attributed to *biology* and how much to *culture*.

Cultural conditioning

Many advocates of women's liberation deny that biological differences necessitate any distinctions between male and female in domestic service or child-care responsibilities, or authority in the family, or economic roles in society, or political or legal rights. They contend that existing sex differences are culturally imposed upon women from earliest childhood. The very first item in personality formation is the assignment of sex roles (you are a boy, you are a girl) and the encouragement of "masculine" and "feminine" traits. Aggression, curiosity, intelligence, initiative, and force are encouraged in the boy; passivity, refinement, shyness, and virtue are encouraged in the girl. Girls are supposed to think in terms of domestic and child-care roles, while boys are urged to think of careers in industry and the professions. Deeply ingrained symbols, attitudes, and practices are culturally designated as "masculine" or "feminine" behaviors ("What a big boy!" "Isn't she pretty!"). There are masculine and feminine subjects in school: science, technology, and business are male; teaching, nursing, and secretarial are female. Boys are portrayed in roles in which they master their environment; girls, in roles in which they admire the accomplishments of men. It is this *cultural* conditioning that leads a woman to accept a family- and child-centered life and an inferior economic and political role in society—not her *physiology*.

Many writers have complained about the social-psychological barriers to a woman's full human development. There is a double standard of sexual guilt in which women are subject to greater shame for any sexual liaison, whatever the circumstances. The family and society inculcate greater sexual inhibitions in women, frequently leading to an inability to enjoy sex fully and achieve orgasm. Yet, while denied sexual freedom herself, the female is usually obliged to seek advancement through the approval of males. She may try to overcome her powerlessness by using her own sexuality, perhaps at the cost of her dignity and self-respect. The prevailing male attitude is to value women for their sexual traits rather than their qualities as human beings. Women are frequently portrayed as "sex objects" in advertising, magazines, and literature. They are supposed to entertain, please, gratify, and flatter men with their sexuality; it is seldom the other way around. There is even evidence of self-rejection among women that is similar to that encountered among minority groups: Female children are far more likely to wish they had been born boys than male children are to wish they had been born girls.[13] The "cult of virginity" continues as a traditional sign that the new husband's "property" is received "unused." The power aspects of sex roles are also ingrained in male psychology. Young men are deemed feminine (inferior) if they are not sufficiently aggressive, physical, or violent.

Marriage laws also imply superiority-inferiority relationships for male and female. Marriage has traditionally involved the female's loss of name, her obligation to adopt her husband's place of living, and the exchange of sexual relationships for financial support. Divorce in most states is granted to a male for his wife's failure to grant sexual consortion, but it is not granted to him for his wife's failure to provide financial support. On the other hand, divorce is granted a woman for her husband's failure to support her financially, but it is not granted to her for his failure to engage in sexual relationship. Women are seldom required to pay alimony or child support upon divorce, while men are.

Physiological differences   In contrast to these arguments about *culturally* imposed sex roles, other observers have contended that *physiological* differences between men and women account for differential sex roles. The woman's role in reproduction and care of the young is biologically determined. To the extent that she seeks to protect her young, she also seeks family arrangements that will provide maximum security and support for them. Men acquire dominant positions in industry, finance, government, and so forth, largely because women are preoccupied with family and child-care tasks. Men are physically stronger than women, and their role as economic providers is rooted in this biological difference. Whether there are any biologically determined mental or emotional differences between men and women is a disputed point, but the possibility of such differences exists. Thus, differential sex roles may be partly physical in origin.

Sexual attraction between men and women has certainly been a great force in human affairs since the beginning of time. Attempts to eliminate sex differences—"unisex" in dress, behavior, and manner—may run counter to the biological urges of a great many people, not to mention their preferences. While most Americans today agree that women should have equal opportunities in education and employment, and receive equal pay for equal work, it is quite another matter to try to eliminate all of the distinctions between men and women.

THE POWER OF WOMEN'S PROTEST MOVEMENTS

Women in America have made great progress in acquiring equal rights over the years. The earliest active "feminist" organizations grew out of the pre–Civil War antislavery movement. The first generation of feminists, including Lucretia Mott, Elizabeth Cady Stanton, Lucy Stone, and Susan B. Anthony, learned to organize, to hold public meetings, and to conduct petition campaigns as abolitionists. After the Civil War, the feminist movement concentrated on winning civil rights and the franchise for women. The suffragettes employed mass demonstrations, parades, picketing, and occasional disruptions and civil disobedience—tactics not dissimilar to those of the civil rights movement of the 1960s. The more moderate wing of the American suffrage movement became the League of Women Voters; in addition to women's vote, they sought protection of women in industry, child welfare laws, honest election practices, and the elimination of laws discriminating against the rights of women.

The culmination of the early feminist movement was the passage in 1920 of the Nineteenth Amendment to the Constitution:

Nineteenth Amendment

The right of citizens of the United States to vote shall not be denied or abridged by the United States or by any state on account of sex.

The movement was also successful in changing many state laws that abridged the property rights of the married woman and otherwise treated her as the "chattel" (property) of her husband. But active feminist politics declined after the goal of women's voting rights had been achieved.

1964: equality in employment

Renewed interest and progress in women's rights came with the civil rights movement of the 1960s. The Civil Rights Act of 1964 prevents discrimination on the basis of sex, as well as race, in employment, salary, promotion, and other conditions of work. The Equal Employment Opportunity Commission (EEOC), the federal agency charged with eliminating discrimination in employment, has established guidelines barring stereotyped classifications of "men's jobs" and "women's jobs." State laws and employer practices that differentiate between men and women in terms of hours, pay, retirement age, and so on, have been struck down. Under active lobbying from feminist organizations, federal agencies, including the U.S. Office of Education and the Office of Federal Contract Compliance, have established "affirmative action" guidelines for government agencies, universities, and private businesses doing work for the government. These guidelines set goals and timetables for employers to alter their work force to achieve higher female percentages at all levels.

ERA

Feminist protest activity in recent years has focused on the Equal Rights Amendment (ERA) to the Constitution, which would strike down *all* existing legal inequalities in state and federal laws between men and women. The amendment states simply:

> Equality of rights under the law shall not be denied or abridged by the United States or by any state on account of sex.

ERA passed the Congress easily and was sent to the states for the necessary ratification by three-fourths (thirty-eight) of them. The amendment won quick ratification by half the states, but a developing "Stop-ERA" movement slowed progress and threatened to prevent final ratification. Debate over ratification of ERA in the states has suggested that it may eliminate many legal protections for women—financial support by husbands, an interest in the husband's property, exemption from military service, and so forth. In addition to these specific objections, the opposition to women's liberation has also charged that the movement weakens the family institution and demoralizes women who wish to devote their lives to their family and children.

Changing mores and medical advances

Women are also acquiring greater power over their own lives by means of a series of social and medical developments. First of all, the changing of sexual mores and the lifting of prohibitions against women's pleasure in sexuality have brought about changes in women's attitudes toward sex. Women no longer accept sexual relations as an exclusively male domain. Increased physiological understanding and improved sexual technique have contributed to an assertion of feminine sexuality. Advances in birth control techniques, including "the pill," have freed women's sexuality from the reproductive function. Legal abortions in early months of pregnancy are now a recognized, constitutional right. Women can now determine for themselves whether and when they will undertake childbirth and child rearing.

ABORTION AND THE LAW

Seldom has the United States embarked upon a more important social experiment than in the recent liberalization of the law and practice of abortion. Abortion can dramatically affect a nation's birth rate, its population growth, and ultimately the whole structure and quality of life.

For years, abortions in the United States for any purpose other than saving the life of the mother were criminal offenses under state laws. Then, in the late 1960s, about a dozen states acted to permit abortion in cases of rape or incest, or to protect the physical health of the mother, and in some cases the mental health as well. However, relatively few abortions were performed under these laws because of the red tape involved—review of each case by several concurring physicians, approval of a hospital board, and so forth.

Abortion is a highly sensitive issue. It is not an issue that can be compromised. The arguments touch on fundamental moral and religious principles. Proponents of abortion argue that a woman should be permitted to control her own body and should not be forced by law to have unwanted children. They cite the heavy toll in lives lost in criminal abortions and the psychological and emotional pain of an unwanted pregnancy. Opponents of abortion generally base their belief on the sanctity of life, including the life of the unborn child, which they insist deserves the protection of law—"the right to life." Many believe that the killing of an unborn child for any reason other than the preservation of the life or health of the mother is murder.

Roe v. Wade

Perhaps the most significant decision about the future of the nation's population was the Supreme Court's momentous ruling in *Roe v. Wade* (1973), which recognized abortion as a *constitutional* right of women. In this historic decision the Court determined that the fetus is not a "person" within the meaning of the Constitution, and therefore the fetus's right to life is not guaranteed by law. Moreover, the Court held that the liberties guaranteed by the Fifth and Fourteenth Amendments encompass the woman's decision on whether or not to terminate her pregnancy. The Supreme Court decided that criminal abortion laws that prohibited abortions in any stage of pregnancy except to save the life of the mother were unconstitutional; that during the first three months of pregnancy the abortion decision must be left wholly to the woman and her physician; that during the second three months of pregnancy the state may not prohibit abortion, but only regulate procedures in ways reasonably related to maternal health; and that only in the final three months of pregnancy may the state prohibit abortion except when abortion is necessary for the preservation of life or health of the mother. In this sweeping decision, the Supreme Court established abortion not merely as permissible under law but as a constitutional right immune from the actions of popularly elected legislatures.

CASE STUDY
The Bakke Case: Affirmative Action or Reverse Discrimination?

Aside from busing, perhaps the most sensitive issue affecting relations between blacks and whites in America today is the question of how to achieve real equality in education, jobs, and income. The civil rights movement of the 1960s opened new opportunities for black Americans. But equality of *opportunity* is not the same as *absolute* equality. The problem of inequality today is usually identified as continued disparities in the incomes, educations, and occupations of blacks and whites.

What public policies should be pursued to achieve equality in America? Is it sufficient that government eliminate discrimination, guarantee equality of opportunity for blacks and whites, and apply "color-blind" standards to both blacks and whites? Or should government take "affirmative action" to overcome the results of past unequal treatment of blacks—preferential or compensatory treatment that would favor black applicants for university admissions and scholarships, job hiring and promotion, and other opportunities for advancement in life?

The earlier emphasis of government policy was, of course, nondiscrimination. Although special recruiting techniques, special training, and encouragement of university applicants were stressed, equal employment opportunity "was not a program to offer special privilege to any one group of persons because of their particular race, religion, sex or national origin.''[14] There were no quota systems for black applicants that might result in less qualified blacks being selected over more highly qualified whites for schools, jobs, or promotions.

Increasingly, however, the goal of the civil rights movement shifted from the traditional aim of equality of opportunity through nondiscrimination alone to absolute equality through "goals and timetables" established by affirmative action. Although carefully avoiding the term *quota*, the notion of affirmative action tests the success of equal employment opportunity by observing whether blacks achieve admissions, jobs, and promotions in proportion to their numbers in the population.

Federal policy has been ambiguous—perhaps deliberately so. There has been a question about whether quotas that give preference to blacks because of their race violate the Fourteenth Amendment's guarantee of "equal protection of the laws" to all citizens. Yet federal officials have generally measured progress in affirmative action in terms of the number of blacks admitted, employed, or promoted. The pressure to show progress and retain federal financial support can result in preferential treatment of blacks and "reverse discrimination" against whites with equal or better qualifications.

Affirmative action also puts pressure on traditional measures of qualifications—test scores and educational achievement. Blacks have argued that these are not good predictors of performance on the job or in school and that these measures are biased in favor of white culture. State and local governments, schools, colleges, and universities, and private employers have been under pressure to drop these standards.[15] But how far can any school, agency, or employer go in dropping traditional standards? It is not difficult to drop educational requirements for sanitation workers, but what about physicians, surgeons, attorneys, pilots, and others whose skills directly affect health and safety?

The more perplexing question, however, has been whether affirmative action programs discriminate against whites and thus violate the equal protection clause of the Fourteenth Amendment.

In 1972, after several years of premedical courses and

volunteer work in a hospital, Allan Bakke, a thirty-two-year-old white who was also a Vietnam veteran, applied to the University of California-Davis Medical School. He was rejected two years in a row. He later learned that his college grades and medical aptitude test scores ranked well above those of many who had been accepted. All who had been accepted with these lower scores were black or Mexican-American. Bakke filed a lawsuit arguing that the university had discriminated against him because of race—a violation of the Fourteenth Amendment's guarantee of "equal protection of the laws." The university, which accepted one hundred applicants to medical school per year, admitted that it set aside sixteen places for "disadvantaged students"—a category that never included any whites. Candidates for these sixteen positions were placed in a separate admissions pool and competed only against each other. White applicants with grade point averages below 2.5 (out of a possible 4.0) were always rejected, but many minority students were accepted with averages as low as 2.1 and 2.2. Bakke's average was 3.5.

The university argued that using race as a favorable criterion was in the best interest of the state and the nation. By increasing the number of minority students, the university hoped eventually to improve medical care among the poor and the black. Minority doctors would also provide "role models" for young blacks, giving them something to aspire to in their career development. The university contended that its separation of black and white candidates was "benign" discrimination (meant to help) rather than "invidious" (meant to hurt).

The California Supreme Court, however, believed that the affirmative action program at the University of California-Davis was a quota system based on race and therefore denied white applicants the "equal protection of the laws" guaranteed by the Fourteenth Amendment. The California court said that the purpose of the equal protection clause of the Fourteenth Amendment, "to secure equality of treatment for all, is incompatible with the premise that some races may be afforded a higher degree of protection against unequal treatment than others." The California court upheld Bakke and told the university to find other ways of increasing minority enrollments—such as instituting remedial programs and aggressive recruiting techniques, and increasing the number of students accepted—ways that do not discriminate against whites.

The university appealed the California court's decision to the United States Supreme Court, and the Supreme Court rendered its important judgment on affirmative action programs in *Regents of the University of California* v. *Bakke* (1978).

The Supreme Court divided over the case five to four, with Justices Burger, Powell, Stewart, Rehnquist, and Stevens in the majority and Justices Brennan, White, Marshall, and Blackmun dissenting. The majority held that the affirmative action program at the University of California-Davis Medical School violated Allan Bakke's rights to "equal protection of the law" under the Fourteenth Amendment. They also held that the program violated Title VI of the Civil Rights Act of 1964 because Bakke was "subjected to discrimination under a program receiving federal financial assistance." The Supreme Court ordered the university to admit Bakke to medical school; Bakke was admitted in the fall of 1978 and began his studies six years after his original application.

The Supreme Court was careful to specify the discriminatory aspects of the university's affirmative action program:

> The Davis special admission program involves the use of an explicit racial classification. . . . it tells applicants who are not Negro . . . that they are totally excluded from a specific percentage of seats. . . . No matter how strong their qualifications . . . they [whites] are never afforded the chance to compete with applicants from the preferred groups for the special admission seats.

However, the Supreme Court went on to describe how an affirmative action program *could* be constitutional:

> Race or ethnic background may be deemed a "plus" in a particular applicant's file, . . . [as long as] it does not insulate the individual from comparison with all other candidates for the available seats.

The Supreme Court generally approved of the goal of achieving racial and ethnic diversity in the student body.

In short, the U.S. Supreme Court indicated: (1) that affirmative action programs that set aside specific numbers or percentages of positions for minorities violate the "equal protection" rights of majority candidates; but (2) that affirmative action programs that consider race or ethnic origin as one of many factors in a competition and do not exclude anyone from competing for all available positions do not necessarily violate the constitutional rights of majority candidates.

Thus, the *Bakke* case sets some limits on affirmative action programs, but it still permits schools to consider race as a "plus" factor in competition for admission. Schools throughout the nation are now obliged to review their own affirmative action programs to see if they meet the standards of the *Bakke* case. Government agencies and employers must also review their affirmative action programs. We can expect additional cases to come before the Supreme Court in search of further definitions of the differences between "affirmative action" and "reverse discrimination."

NOTES

1. L. H. Butterfield, Marc Friedlander, and Mary-Jo Kline, eds., *The Book of Abigail and John* (Cambridge, Mass.: Harvard University Press, 1975), p. 121.

2. *Brown v. Board of Education of Topeka, Kansas*, 347 U.S. 483 (1954).

3. Alabama, Arkansas, Delaware, Florida, Georgia, Kentucky, Louisiana, Maryland, Mississippi, Missouri, North Carolina, Oklahoma, South Carolina, Tennessee, Texas, Virginia, and West Virginia.

4. Arizona, Kansas, New Mexico, and Wyoming.

5. A public letter by Martin Luther King, Jr., Birmingham, Alabama, 16 April 1963; the full text is reprinted in Thomas R. Dye and Brett Hawkins, eds., *Politics in the Metropolis* (Columbus, Ohio: Merrill, 1967), pp. 100–09.

6. Alphonso Pinkney, *Black Americans* (Englewood Cliffs, N.J.: Prentice-Hall, 1969), pp. 124–25. For the two quotations, Pinkney cites, respectively, Earl R. Moses, "Differentials in Crime Rates between Negroes and Whites Based on Comparisons of Four Socio-Economically Equated Areas." *American Sociological Review* 12 (August 1947):420:

and Thomas F. Pettigrew, *A Profile of the Negro American* (Princeton, N.J.: Van Nostrand, 1964), p. 156.

7. Kenneth Clark, *Dark Ghetto: Dilemmas of Social Power* (New York: Harper & Row, 1965), p. 11.

8. National Advisory Commission on Civil Disorders, *Report* (Washington, D.C.: Government Printing Office, 1968), p. 205.

9. In June 1966, James Meredith, who in 1962 had been the first black to enroll in the University of Mississippi, was shot on a lone freedom march through Mississippi. Leaders of several civil rights organizations, including Martin Luther King, Jr., of SCLC, and Stokely Carmichael, chairman of SNCC, continued Meredith's march. During this march Carmichael and his associates employed the slogan "Black Power," although King and others disapproved of its use.

10. Stokely Carmichael and Charles V. Hamilton, *Black Power: The Politics of Liberation in America* (New York: Random House, 1967), pp. 44, 46.

11. Ibid., p. 37.

12. Ibid., p. 83.

13. Goodwin Watson, "Psychological Aspects of Sex Roles," in *Social Psychology, Issues and Insights* (Philadelphia: Lippincott, 1966), p. 477. See also Philip Goldberg, "Are Women Prejudiced Against Women?" *Transaction*, April 1968.

14. David H. Rosenbloom, "The Civil Service Commission's Decision to Authorize the Use of Goals and Timetables in Federal Equal Employment Opportunity Programs," *Western Political Quarterly* 26 (June 1973):236–51.

15. Frank J. Thompson, "Bureaucratic Responsiveness in the Cities: The Problem of Minority Hiring," *Urban Affairs Quarterly* 10 (September 1974):40–68.

DISCUSSION QUESTIONS

1. Identify the initial goal of the civil rights movement. Discuss the Supreme Court case that marked the first step in attaining that goal and the constitutional amendment upon which the civil rights movement based its arguments. Why was the Supreme Court unable to implement its decision by itself?

2. Describe the means by which some of the southern states attempted to resist implementation of school desegregation. Define *de facto segregation*.

3. Which provision of the Civil Rights Act of 1964 had an important impact on implementing school desegregation? Describe the intent of the 1964 act and summarize some of its provisions.

4. Discuss the method of protest advocated by Martin Luther King, Jr., its

political purpose, and factors important to its success. What are some of the risks of this method of protest?

5. Describe how King and his followers were instrumental in the passage of the Voting Rights Act of 1965 and the Civil Rights Act of 1968. Briefly describe the content of each act.

6. Discuss the meaning of powerlessness in the ghetto. Include in your discussion an explanation of the analogy between life in the ghetto and "colonialism."

7. Discuss the themes of militant black politics.

8. Discuss the "cultural" and "biological" explanations of male dominance in society. Describe some of the important landmarks for women's protest movements, including the Supreme Court's ruling in *Roe* v. *Wade*. What factors have contributed to women's acquiring greater power over their lives?

9. Discuss the *Bakke* case. How may affirmative action conflict with the concept of equality of opportunity? How may it be in violation of the Fourteenth Amendment?

SUGGESTED READINGS

Harry Bailey, Jr., ed., *Negro Politics in America* (Columbus, Ohio: Merrill, 1968).

Stokely Carmichael and Charles D. Hamilton, *Black Power: The Politics of Liberation in America* (New York: Random House, 1967).

Kenneth Clark, *Dark Ghetto: Dilemmas of Social Power* (New York: Harper & Row, 1965).

Congressional Quarterly, *The Women's Movement* (Washington, D.C.: Congressional Quarterly, Inc., 1973).

Thomas R. Dye, *The Politics of Equality* (Indianapolis, Ind.: Bobbs-Merrill, 1971).

Jo Freeman, *The Politics of Women's Liberation* (New York: David McKay, 1975).

Martin Luther King., Jr., *Why We Can't Wait* (New York: New American Library, 1964).

Donald R. Matthews and James W. Prothro, *Negroes and the New Southern Politics* (New York: Harcourt Brace Jovanovich, 1966).

Alphonso Pinkney, *Black Americans* (Englewood Cliffs, N.J.: Prentice-Hall, 1969).

Hanes Walton, Jr., *Black Politics* (Philadelphia: Lippincott, 1972).

Chapter 11
Poverty and Powerlessness

Captain John Smith's ultimatum to his starving band of settlers in Jamestown in 1609 that "he who would not work must not eat" is probably the first recorded American welfare policy statement. It reflects an attitude that prevailed for many years. The general view that if one were poor in America, one deserved to be poor was fed by a belief in America as the land of unbounded opportunity; by the ideal of rugged individualism and a firmly rooted belief in the individual's right to the permanent possession of property; by the growing nation's need for the labor of every able-bodied person; by a peculiar blending of Calvinism and commercialism that turned poverty into a moral failing; and by the bonanza economics of the nineteenth century and the social Darwinism that justified the social evils of that era. It was not until the frontier had finally and forever closed and the Great Depression of the 1930s had reduced many of the prosperous to the ranks of the paupers that there was any discernible change in the American attitude toward poverty.

When poverty exists in the midst of plenty, as it does today in America, it is more difficult for the poor to bear. The affluence that followed World War II turned poverty into a social, rather than an individual, shame. In this chapter we will explore various definitions of poverty, as well as some of the recent efforts of those in positions of power to lift the poverty-stricken from their positions of powerlessness. After you have read it, you should be able to:

- discuss various definitions of poverty and describe the characteristics of the poor.
- discuss the theory of a subculture of poverty and its implications for social policy.
- describe the strategies of the Social Security Act of 1935 and the current welfare system.
- discuss the "War on Poverty" and some of the current proposals for welfare reform.

POVERTY IN AMERICA

The United States is an affluent society. Indeed, this country is producing more than a trillion dollars' worth of goods and services each year. The median family income exceeds $14,000 per year. Yet many Americans live in poverty. Poverty is nothing new; it was far more widespread a generation ago than it is today. Indeed, what is new today—the reason poverty is now a focus of attention—is a national commitment to *eliminate* poverty. In the Economic Opportunity Act of 1964, Congress and the president declared that it was national policy "to eliminate the paradox of poverty in the midst of plenty in this nation." Nations throughout history have concerned themselves with the lot of the poor. But for the first time the United States has reached a point at which the elimination of poverty has become a serious national aspiration.

But the elimination of poverty—however generally this goal is shared—requires the use of power, and power is a scarce resource. Regardless of widespread agreement that poverty is undesirable, there are conflicts over what should be done about it and important struggles for power over antipoverty activity.

Conflict over poverty begins with conflict over the definition of poverty and differing estimates of its extent in America. Proponents of large-scale government programs for the poor frequently make broad definitions of poverty and high estimates of the number of poor people. They view the problem as a persistent one, even in an affluent society. They contend that millions suffer from hunger, exposure, and remediable illness, and that some people starve to death. Their definition of the problem of poverty practically mandates immediate and massive governmental programs to assist the poor.

On the other hand, opponents of large-scale governmental antipoverty programs frequently minimize the number of poor in America. They see poverty diminishing over time, without major public programs. They view the poor in America as considerably better off than the middle class was fifty years ago—and even wealthy by the standards of most other societies in the world. They deny that Americans need to suffer from hunger, exposure, remedial illness, or starvation if they make use of the services and facilities available to them. Their definition of the problem of poverty minimizes the need for massive public programs to fight poverty.

The poverty line According to the U.S. Social Security Administration, there are about 25 million poor people (those below the poverty line) in the United States, or approximately 12 percent of the population. The poverty line is set by the Social Security Administration. It is derived by careful calculation of the cost of food, housing, clothing, and other items for urban families of different sizes. The dollar amounts are flexible to take into account the effect of inflation. They can be expected to rise each year with the rate of inflation. In 1978 the poverty line for an urban family of four was approximately $6,500.

Subsistence vs. deprivation   This definition of poverty emphasizes *subsistence levels*; it seeks to describe poverty objectively as lack of enough income to acquire the minimum necessities of life. Liberals frequently view the subsistence definition of poverty as insensitive to the variety of needs—including entertainment, recreation, and the relief of monotony. Items that were "luxuries" a generation ago are now considered "necessities." John Kenneth Galbraith writes:

> People are poverty-stricken when their income, even if adequate for survival, falls markedly behind that of the community. Then they cannot have what the larger community regards as the minimum necessary for decency; and they cannot wholly escape, therefore, the judgment of the larger community that they are indecent.[1]

Moreover, the official definition of poverty does not recognize the problems of those who spend their incomes unwisely. If money goes for liquor, dope, or expensive used cars, or is siphoned off by loan sharks, impoverished relatives and friends or by high prices charged by ghetto store owners, then even a reasonably high-income family can live in poverty. Yet despite these shortcomings, the Social Security Administration definition provides the best available estimate of poverty in America.

How poor is "poor"? There is reason to believe that the 25 million Americans living in "official" poverty do not all suffer hardship and privation. About 65 percent own cars, 50 percent own their own homes, and more than half have some savings. Nearly 80 percent of the poor have television sets, and 78 percent have refrigerators or freezers. Over three-quarters have hot water, access to a telephone for receiving calls, a kitchen with cooking equipment, a flush toilet, and a bath. Yet the diets of the poor are nutritionally bad, whether from ignorance or poverty. The poor do not seek medical attention except in emergencies, the result being the great deal of illness.

However, liberals charge that the problem of poverty has been seriously underestimated by government officials. By emphasizing levels of *deprivation* rather than *subsistence* and focusing on an income required for "a healthful, self-respecting mode of life, care of children, and participation in community life," liberals can broaden the definition of poverty to include anywhere from 20 to 40 percent of the population.

WHO ARE THE POOR?

High-risk categories

Poverty occurs in many different kinds of families and in all environmental settings (see table 11–1, as well as appendix, tables C, G, and H). However, its incidence varies sharply among groups living under different circumstances, and several groups experience poverty in greater proportions than the national average.[2] First, *blacks* are three times more likely to experience poverty than whites; the percentage of the black population of the United States falling below the poverty line is 29.4 compared to 9.1 percent of the white population. Second, *female-headed families* experience poverty far more frequently than male-headed families; 34.4 percent of all female-headed families live below the poverty line. Third, the *aged* experience more poverty than persons of working age; 15 percent of the population over sixty-five years of age live below the poverty line. Poverty is a characteristic of persons living in large-city *ghettos;* but *rural* families also experience poverty more frequently than do suburban families.

Are the poor disappearing? Since Franklin D. Roosevelt's depression era estimate that one-third of the nation was "ill housed, ill clad, ill nourished," the American political and economic system has succeeded in reducing the proportion of poor from 33 percent to less than 13 percent (see figure 11–1). If long-run rates in the reduction of poverty in America continue, there will be virtually no poverty in

Table 11–1   Population, by Categories, with Income below Poverty Level (Based on Total Population)

	No. (Millions)	% of Total in Category
White population	16.7	9.1
Black population	8.3	29.4
Those living in central cities	9.5	15.8
Those living in suburbs	5.7	6.9
Those living in rural areas	9.7	14.0
Over age 65	3.3	15.0
Families with male head	12.4	7.1
Families with female head	12.6	34.4
Total	25.0	11.6%

Source: U.S. Bureau of the Census, *Statistical Abstract of the United States, 1977* (Washington, D.C.: Government Printing Office, 1977), pp. 454, 457.

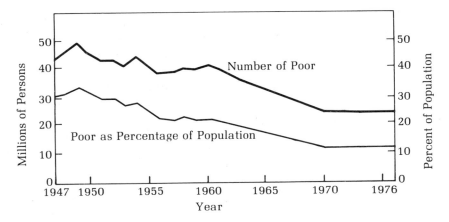

Figure 11—1 Poverty in the United States
Source: Thomas R. Dye, *Understanding Public Policy,* 3d ed. (Englewood Cliffs, N.J.: Prentice-Hall, 1978).

twenty-five to thirty years. However, this optimistic prediction assumes that those remaining in poverty today can rise above the poverty line with the same speed as those who have done so for the last two decades. But there may be a "hard core" of poverty-stricken families and individuals who cannot achieve that status without massive new governmental programs. During the 1970s poverty has not decreased, owing perhaps to the combined effects of recession and inflation.

POVERTY AS INEQUALITY

It is possible to define poverty as *relative deprivation,* which is really to identify it as *inequality.* This definition is not tied to any *absolute* level of subsistence or deprivation. Instead, it characterizes poverty as a sense of deprivation that some people feel because they have less income or fewer material possessions than most other Americans. Even with a fairly substantial income, it is possible to feel relative deprivation in a very affluent society when commercial advertising in the mass media portrays the "average American" as having a high level of consumption and material well-being.

Today the poor in America are wealthy by the standards that have prevailed over most of history, and that still prevail over large areas of the world. Nonetheless, millions of American families are

considered poor, both by themselves and by others, because they
have less income than most other Americans. Actually they are not
any more deprived, even relative to the nonpoor, than in the past. But
they *feel* more deprived, they perceive a wide gap between themselves and an affluent middle class of Americans and they do not accept the gap as legitimate. Blacks are heavily overrepresented among
the poor, and the civil rights movement made blacks acutely aware of
their position in American society relative to whites. The black
revolution contributed to the new awareness of the problem of
poverty in terms of differences in income and conditions of life.
Eliminating poverty when it is defined as relative deprivation really
means achieving *equality* of income and material possessions.

Let us try systematically to examine poverty as relative deprivation. Table 11–2 divides all American families into five groups—from
the lowest one-fifth, in personal income, to the highest one-fifth—and
shows the percentage of total family personal income received by
each group over the years. (If perfect income equality existed, each
fifth would receive 20 percent of all family personal income, and it
would not even be possible to rank fifths from highest to lowest.) The
poorest one-fifth received 3.5 percent of all family personal income in
1929; in 1976, however, this group had increased its percentage of all
family personal income to 5.4. (Most of the increase occurred during
World War II.) The highest one-fifth received 54.4 percent of all
family personal income in 1929; in 1976, however, the percentage had
declined to 41.1. This was the only income group to lose in relation to
other income groups. The middle classes improved their relative in-

Table 11-2   Percent Distribution of Family Personal Income, by Quintiles,
and Top 5 Percent of Consumer Units, Selected Years, 1929–1976

Quintiles	1929	1936	1941	1944	1947	1950	1955	1960	1965	1970	1976
Lowest	3.5%	4.1%	4.1%	4.9%	5.0%	4.5%	4.8%	4.8%	5.2%	5.4%	5.4%
Second	9.0	9.2	9.5	10.9	11.0	12.0	12.3	12.2	12.2	12.2	11.8
Third	13.8	14.1	15.3	16.2	16.0	17.4	17.8	17.8	17.8	17.6	17.6
Fourth	19.3	20.9	22.3	22.2	22.0	23.4	23.7	24.0	23.8	23.9	24.1
Highest	54.4	51.7	48.8	45.8	46.0	42.7	41.3	41.2	40.9	40.9	41.1
Total	100.0	100.0	100.0	100.0	100.0	100.0	100.0	100.0	100.0	100.0	100.0
Top 5 per-cent ratio	30.0	26.5	24.0	20.7	20.9	17.3	16.4	15.9	15.5	15.6	15.6

Source: U.S. Bureau of the Census, *Statistical Abstract of the United States, 1977*
(Washington, D.C.: Government Printing Office, 1977), p. 443.

come position even more than the poor. Another measure of income equalization over time is the decline in the percentage of income received by the top 5 percent. The top 5 percent received 30 percent of all family personal income in 1929 but only 15.6 percent in 1976. There is no doubt that income differences in America are decreasing.

Nevertheless, it is unlikely that income differentials will ever disappear completely—at least not in a society that rewards skill, talent, risk taking, and ingenuity. If the problem of poverty is defined as relative deprivation—that is, *inequality*—then it is not really capable of solution. Regardless of how well off the poor may be in absolute terms, there will always be a lowest one-fifth of the population receiving something less than 20 percent of all income. Income differences may decline, but *some* differences will remain, and even minor differences can acquire great importance and hence pose a "problem."

Relative deprivation: insoluble problem

POVERTY AS POWERLESSNESS

Powerlessness is the inability to control the events that shape one's life. The poor lack economic resources and are hence largely dependent upon others for the things they need. Their lack of power derives from this *dependency*. But powerlessness is also an attitude—a feeling that no matter what one does it will have little effect on one's life. An *attitude* of powerlessness *reinforces* the *condition* of powerlessness among the poor. Their experiences generate feelings of meaninglessness, hopelessness, lack of motivation, distrust, and cynicism. Constant defeat causes many of the poor to retreat into a self-protective attitude characterized by indifference and a pervasive sense of futility.

The poor feel *alienated* because of their lack of success in obtaining important life goals. Persons who are blocked consistently in their efforts to achieve life goals are most likely to express powerlessness and alienation. These attitudes in turn become barriers to effective self-help, independence, and self-respect. Poverty can lead to apathy and aimlessness and lack of motivation.

To be *both* black and poor in a predominantly white and affluent society magnifies feelings of powerlessness and alienation. Social psychologists are not always certain about the processes by which social inequalities are perceived or how these perceptions influence attitudes and behaviors. But black sociologist Kenneth B. Clark has provided some interesting insights into "the psychology of the ghetto."

Professor Clark argues that human beings who live apart from the rest of society, who do not share in society's affluence, and who are not respected or granted the ordinary dignities and courtesy accorded to others will eventually begin to doubt their own worth. All human beings depend upon their experiences with others for clues to how they should view and value themselves. Black children who consistently see whites in a superior position begin to question whether they or their family or blacks in general really deserve any more respect from the larger society than they receive. These doubts, Clark maintains, become the seeds of "a pernicious self- and group-hatred, the Negro's complex and debilitating prejudice against himself."

A sense of inferiority

Clark observed that when black children as young as three years old were shown white and black dolls, or were asked to color drawings of children to look like themselves, many of them rejected the black dolls as "dirty" or "bad" and colored the picture of themselves a light color or even a bizarre shade like purple. The observations suggest that many black children suffer from serious injury to their sense of self-worth at a very young age. The results of this sense of inferiority are revealed when these children begin school—a lack of confidence in themselves as students, a lack of motivation to learn, behavioral problems, and a gradual withdrawal or growing rebellion. Lack of success in school, coupled with poor teaching and poor ghetto schools, tends to reinforce the experience of inferior achievement.

> In Negro adults the sense of inadequate self-worth shows up in a lack of motivation to rise in their jobs or fear of competition with whites; and a sense of impotence in civil affairs, demonstrated in lethargy toward voting, or community participation, or responsibility for others, in family instability and the irresponsibility rooted in hopelessness.[3]

But all human beings search for self-esteem. According to Clark, teenage blacks often pretend to knowledge about illicit activities and to sexual experiences that they have not really had. They use as their models the petty criminals of the ghetto, with their colorful, swaggering style of cool bravado. The inability to succeed by the standards of the wider society leads to a peculiar fascination with individuals who successfully defy society's norms. Some young black men seek their salvation in aggressive and self-destructive behavior. Because the larger society has rejected them, they reject—or at least appear to reject the values of that society.

An antisocial search for self-esteem

Professor Clark believes that the explanation for violence and crime in the ghetto lies in the conscious or unconscious belief of many young blacks that they cannot hope to win meaningful self-esteem through the avenues available to middle-class whites, so they turn to "hustling"—pimping, prostitution, gambling, or drug dealing. They are frequently scornful of what they consider the hypocrisy and dishonesty of the larger society. They point to corruption among respected middle-class whites, including the police force.

Escape from failure

But personal adjustment to ghetto life can take other forms. According to Clark, ghetto dwellers are prone to accept the "evidence" of their personal inferiority and impotence. They express a continuing sense of failure through stagnation and despair; they drop out of school; they turn to narcotics. Or they live in a world of television and motion pictures—a world that supposedly depicts the life of the American middle class. Many poor escape the harshness of poverty in dreams and fantasies of luxury and happiness.

Family instability

Poverty and discrimination have also taken their toll in black family life. Professor Clark observed that under the system of slavery, the only source of family continuity was through the female; children were dependent upon their mothers and seldom knew their fathers. Segregation relegated the black male to menial and subservient jobs. He could not present himself to his wife and children as a consistent wage earner.

> His doubts concerning his personal adequacy were therefore reinforced. He was compelled to base his self-esteem instead on a kind of behavior that tended to support a stereotyped picture of the Negro male—sexual impulsiveness, irresponsibility, verbal bombast, posturing, and compensatory achievement in entertainment and athletics, particularly in sports like boxing in which athletic prowess could be exploited for the gain of others.[4]

It was the black woman who was obliged to hold the family together—to set its goals and to encourage and protect boys and girls. Many young black males had no strong father figure upon which to model their behavior. Many established temporary liaisons with a number of women. The result was a high rate of illegitimacy and family instability.

IS THERE A CULTURE OF POVERTY?

The cycle of poverty

It is sometimes argued that the poor have a characteristic lifestyle or "culture of poverty" that assists them in adjusting to their world. Like other aspects of culture, it is passed on to future generations, setting in motion a self-perpetuating cycle of poverty. The theory of the poverty cycle is as follows: Deprivation in one generation leads, through cultural impoverishment, indifference, apathy, or misunderstanding of their children's educational needs, to deprivation in the next generation. Lacking the self-respect that comes from earning an adequate living, young men cannot sustain responsibilities of marriage and so they hand down to their children the same burden of family instability and female-headed households that they themselves carried. Children born into a culture of alienation, apathy, and lack of motivation learn these attitudes themselves. Thus the poor are prevented from exploiting any opportunities that are available to them.

It is probably more accurate to talk about a *subculture* of poverty. The prefix *sub* is used because most of the poor subscribe to the "middle-class American way of life," at least as a cultural ideal and even as a personal fantasy. Most poor people do not reject American culture but strive to adapt its values to the realities of economic deprivation and social disorganization in their own lives.

Daniel P. Moynihan has argued persuasively that one of the worst effects of slavery and segregation has been their impact on black family life. Segregation, with its implications of inferiority and submissiveness, damaged the male more than the female personality. The black female was not a threat to anyone. But surprisingly, in Moynihan's study the female-headed black family emerged as one of the striking features of life in the ghetto.[5] Almost 25 percent of *all* black families in the nation are headed by women. For the young black male brought up in the matriarchal setting in the ghetto, the future is often depressing, with defeat and frustration repeating themselves throughout his life. He may drop out of school in the ninth grade protesting his lack of success. Perhaps never again will he have an opportunity for further education or job training. Lacking parental supervision and with little to do, he may soon get into trouble with the police. A police record will diminish his chances of getting a job. If he gets a job, his limited job skills will seriously handicap his earning power. His pay is usually not enough to support a family, and he has little hope of advancement. His job is routine and boring. He may tie up much of his income in installment payments for a car, a television set, or the other conveniences that he sees in widespread use. Because of his low credit rating, he will be forced to pay excessive interest rates, and sooner or later his creditors will garnish his salary. If he marries, he is likely to have a large number of children, and he and his family will live in crowded, substandard housing. As pressures and frustrations mount, he may decide to leave his family, either because he has found his inability to support his wife and children humiliating or because only then will his wife and children be eligible for welfare payments. Thus the cycle is at work: Low education levels produce low income levels; low income levels prevent parents from moving out of the ghettos; forced restriction to the ghettos deprives children of educational opportunities; and so the cycle repeats. According to Moynihan:

> At the heart of the deterioration of the fabric of Negro society is the deterioration of the Negro family. . . . Three generations of injustice have brought about deep seated structural distortions in the life of the Negro American. At this point the present tangle of pathology is capable of perpetuating itself without assistance from the white world. The cycle can be broken only if these distortions are set right. In a word, the national effort toward problems of Negro Americans must be directed toward the question of family structure.[6]

Culture of poverty as "present-orientedness"

Another view of the "culture of poverty" emphasizes the "present-orientedness" of the poor. Professor Edward C. Banfield argues that the culture of poverty is primarily an effect produced by extreme present-orientedness rather than a lack of income or wealth. Individuals caught up in the culture of poverty are unable to plan for the future, to sacrifice immediate gratifications in favor of future ones, or to exercise the discipline that is required to get ahead. Banfield admits that some people experience poverty because of involuntary unemployment, prolonged illness, death of the breadwinner, or some other misfortune. But even when severe, this kind of poverty is not squalid, degrading, or self-perpetuating. It ends once the external cause of it no longer exists. According to Banfield, other people will be poor no matter what their "external" circumstances are. They live in a culture of poverty that continues for generations because they are psychologically unable to provide for the future. Improvements in their circumstances may affect their poverty only superficially. Even increased income is unlikely to change their way of life. The additional money will be spent quickly on nonessential or frivolous items. This culture of poverty may involve no more than 10 or 20 percent of all families who live below the poverty line, but it generally continues regardless of what is done in the way of remedial action.[7]

Social conditions or parental transmission?

Opponents of the idea of a culture of poverty argue that this notion diverts attention from the *conditions* of poverty that foster family instability, present-orientedness, and other ways of life of the poor. The question is really whether the conditions of poverty create a culture of poverty or vice versa. Reformers are likely to focus on the conditions of poverty as the fundamental cause of the social pathologies that afflict the poor. They note that the idea of a culture of poverty can be applied only to groups who have lived in poverty for several generations. It is not relevant to those who have become poor during their lifetime because of sickness, accident, or old age. The cultural explanation basically involves *parental transmission of values and beliefs,* which in turn determines behavior of future generations. In contrast, the situational explanation of poverty involves social conditions—differences in financial resources—that operate directly to determine behavior. In this view, the conditions of poverty can be seen as affecting behavior directly, as well as *indirectly* through their impact upon succeeding generations. Perhaps the greatest danger in the idea of a culture of poverty is that poverty in this light can be seen as an unbreakable, puncture-proof cycle, which may lead to a relaxation of efforts to ameliorate the conditions of poverty. In other words, a "culture" of poverty may become an excuse for inaction.[8]

Whether or not there is a culture of poverty is a perplexing question. The argument resembles the classic exchange between F. Scott Fitzgerald and Ernest Hemingway. When Fitzgerald observed, "The rich are different from you and me," Hemingway retorted, "Yes, they have more money." Observers who believe that they see a distinctive lower-class culture will say, "The poor are different from you and me." But opponents may reply, "Yes, they have less money." In other words, are the poor poorly educated, underskilled, poorly motivated, "delinquent," and "shiftless" because they are poor; or are they poor because they are poorly educated, underskilled, unmotivated, "delinquent," and "shiftless"? The question is a serious one because it has important policy implications.

Policy implications

If one assumes that the poor are no different from other Americans, then one is led toward policies that emphasize "opportunity" for individuals rather than drastic changes in the environment. If the poor are like other Americans, it is necessary only to provide them with the ordinary means to achievement of the desires of other Americans—for example, job training programs, good schools, and perhaps some counseling to make them aware of opportunities that are available to them. The intervention that is required to change their lives, therefore, is one of supplying a means of achieving a level of income that most Americans enjoy. It can be argued that this kind of thinking—the denial that a subculture of poverty exists—influenced many of the programs of the Johnson administration's "War on Poverty." The goal of the War on Poverty was not to directly provide resources that would end poverty but to provide opportunities so that people could achieve their own escape from poverty. The assumption behind the programs was that the poor would respond to these opportunities in the same way most middle-class Americans would respond.

On the other hand, if one believes in the notion of a subculture of poverty, it is necessary to devise a strategy to interrupt the transmission of lower-class cultural values from generation to generation. The strategy must try to prevent the socialization of young children into an environment of family instability, lack of motivation, crime and delinquency, and so forth. One rather drastic means to accomplish this would be simply to remove the children from lower-class homes at a very early age and raise them in a controlled environment that transmits the values of the conventional culture rather than of the subculture of poverty. Perhaps a less harsh version of this same idea would involve special day-care centers and preschool programs to remedy cultural deprivation and disadvantage: these programs would be oriented toward bringing about cultural change in young children through "cultural enrichment."

The subculture of poverty has another policy implication: If one believes that such a subculture exists, then one must also conclude that little can be done to help people escape from poverty until after there has been sufficient change in their conditions of life to permit them to take advantage of opportunity programs. According to this line of reasoning, you cannot change people without changing their environment; the poor cannot be changed by schooling, or manpower training, or programs to develop better attitudes while they are still poor. The emphasis on "self-help"—education, information, job training, participation—is incomplete and misleading unless it is accompanied by a program aimed at directly altering the conditions of poverty. Hence, it is argued that a *guaranteed minimum income* is required to bring the poor up to a level where they will be able to take advantage of educational and training information and other opportunity programs.

STRATEGIES IN PUBLIC WELFARE POLICY

Social Security Act: alleviative and preventive

In the Social Security Act of 1935 the federal government undertook to establish a basic framework for welfare policies at the federal, state, and local levels in America. This act embodied both an alleviative strategy (public assistance) and a new preventive strategy (social insurance). The *social insurance* concept was designed to *prevent* poverty resulting from individual misfortune—unemployment, old age, death of the family breadwinner, or physical disability. Social insurance was based on the same notion as private insurance: the sharing of risks and the setting aside of money for a rainy day. Social insurance was not to be charity or public assistance. Instead, it relied upon people's (compulsory) financial contribution to their own protection.

One of the key features of the Social Security Act is the Old-Age, Survivors, Disability, and Health Insurance (OASDHI) program; this is a complusory social insurance program financed by regular deductions from earnings, which gives individuals the legal right to benefit in the event that their income is reduced by old age, death of the head of the household, or permanent disability. OASDHI is not public charity but a way of compelling people to provide insurance against loss of income. (Figure G in the appendix shows numbers of persons receiving OASDHI benefits.) Another feature of the Social Security Act was that it induced states to enact unemployment compensation programs. Unemployment compensation is also an *insurance* program, only in this case the costs are borne solely by the employer. In 1965 Congress amended social security to add comprehensive medical care for persons over sixty-five—"medicare." Medicare provided for prepaid hospital insurance for the aged under social security, and low-cost voluntary medical insurance for the aged under federal administration. Medicare, too, is based upon the insurance principle: Individuals pay for their medical insurance during their working years and enjoy its benefits after age sixty-five. Thus, the program resembles private medical hospital insurance, except that it is compulsory.

Social insurance vs. public assistance

The distinction between the *social insurance* program and a *public assistance* program is an important one, which has on occasion become a major political issue. If the beneficiaries of a government program are required to have made contributions to it before claiming any of its benefits, and if they are entitled to the benefits regardless of their personal wealth, the program is said to be financed on the *social insurance* principle. If the program is financed out of general tax revenues, and if the recipients are required to show that they are poor before claiming its benefits, the program is said to be financed on the *public assistance* principle.

In addition to the insurance programs mentioned above, the federal government undertook in the Social Security Act to help states provide public assistance payments to certain needy persons to alleviate the conditions of poverty. The strategy of public assistance is clearly *alleviative*. There is no effort to prevent poverty or to attack its causes; the idea is simply to provide a minimum level of subsistence to certain categories of needy persons. The federal government gives grants to the states to assist them in providing welfare payments to four categories of recipients: the aged, the blind, the disabled, and dependent children. Welfare aid to persons who do not fall into any of these categories but who, for one reason or another, are poor is referred to as *general assistance* and is paid for entirely from state funds.

In 1965 in its amendments to the Social Security Act, Congress also authorized federal funds to enable states to guarantee medical services to all public assistance recipients. This program is known as "medicaid." Unlike medicare, medicaid is a welfare program designed for needy persons; no prior contributions are required, but recipients of medicaid must be eligible for welfare assistance. In other words, they must be poor.

THE WELFARE MESS

On the whole, the social insurance programs of the government are popular: social security, unemployment compensation, and medicare. But public assistance has turned out to be politically one of the most unpopular programs ever adopted by the Congress. It is disliked by national, state, and local legislatures who must vote the skyrocketing appropriations for it; it is resented by the taxpayers who must bear the ever increasing burdens of it; it is denounced by officials and caseworkers who must administer it; and it is accepted with bitterness by those who were intended to benefit from it.

Criticisms of public assistance

Dependence upon public assistance in America is *increasing* at a very rapid rate (see table 11–3). Whether or not the program itself encourages dependency, one thing is certain: More Americans rely

Table 11–3   Growth of Public Assistance Programs (in Millions of Recipients)

	Total	AFDC	Aged	Disabled	Blind	General Assistance
1950	6.0	2.2	2.8	0.1	0.1	0.9
1955	5.8	2.2	2.5	0.2	0.1	0.7
1960	7.0	3.1	2.3	0.4	0.1	1.2
1965	7.8	4.4	2.1	0.6	0.1	0.7
1970	10.4	6.7	2.0	0.87	0.1	0.8
1971	13.5	9.5	2.0	1.0	0.1	0.9
1972	15.0	10.8	2.1	1.0	0.1	1.0
1976	16.4	11.2	2.1	2.0	0.1	1.0

Source: Past issues of U.S. Bureau of the Census, *Statistical Abstract of the United States.*

upon public assistance today than ever before. Certainly our public assistance programs have not succeeded in reducing dependency. In the last decade the number of welfare recipients has more than doubled, and public assistance costs have quadrupled. Interestingly, it is not programs for the aged, blind, or disabled, or even the general assistance programs, that have incurred the greatest burdens. It is the Aid to Families with Dependent Children (AFDC) program that is the largest, most expensive, and most rapidly growing of all welfare programs—and the most controversial.

The rise in welfare rolls began during a period of high employment. However, the continued rise cannot be attributed to economic depression but is simply due to the fact that more and more people are applying for public assistance. Despite increased dependence upon welfare, and the growing burden of welfare costs, many of the nation's poor do *not* receive public assistance. There were 25 million poor people in America in 1976, yet only 16 million persons on welfare rolls. Many of the nation's poor are *working poor*, who are ineligible for welfare assistance because they hold jobs, even though the jobs pay very little. A low-income family, headed by the father, is not eligible to receive AFDC payments if the father is working, regardless of how poor the family may be.

Not only does welfare fail to assist all of the nation's poor; it does not provide enough to those it does assist to raise them out of poverty. Although welfare benefits differ from state to state, in every state the level of benefits falls *well below* the recognized poverty line.

State administration of welfare has resulted in wide *disparities among the states* in eligibility requirements and benefit levels. For example, in 1976 average AFDC monthly payments ranged from a high of $111 per child in New York to a low of $14 per child in Mississippi.

Operating policies and administration of welfare have produced a whole series of problems. Among other things, they have contributed to the *disintegration of family life.* Until recently, most states denied AFDC benefits if a man was living with his family, even though he had no work. This denial was based on the assumption that an employable man in the household meant that children were no longer "dependent" upon the state. Thus, if a man lived with his family, he could watch them go hungry; if he abandoned them, public assistance would enable them to eat. Moreover, it was easier for an unmarried mother to get on welfare rolls than it was for a married mother (who had to prove she was not receiving support from her husband). These rules have now been relaxed, but it is still more difficult for whole families to get on public assistance than it is for fatherless families.

Welfare policies and administration have also acted as *deterrents to work*. In most states, if a recipient of assistance takes a full job, assistance checks are reduced or stopped. If the recipient is then laid off, it may take some time to get back on the welfare roll. In other words, employment is uncertain, while assistance is not. More importantly, the jobs available to most recipients are low-paying jobs that do not produce much more income than assistance, particularly when transportation, child care, and other costs of working are considered. All these facts may discourage the welfare recipient from seeking work.

While such problems are serious, it is well to note that some of the charges leveled against public assistance are unfounded. For example, there are very few individuals for whom welfare has become "a permanent way of life." The median length of time on AFDC is less than three years; only one-tenth of the persons aided have been receiving assistance for more than ten years. The number of "welfare chiselers"—able-bodied employable adults who prefer public-assisted idleness to work—is probably quite small. Most recipients are either women or children, or aged, blind, or disabled; few employable men are on welfare rolls. The work alternative for the large numbers of AFDC mothers is fraught with problems—child care, lack of skills, no work experience, and so on. It might be more costly to society to prepare these women for work than to support them.

THE WAR ON POVERTY

OEO: a curative strategy

The War on Poverty was an attempt to apply a "curative strategy" to the problem of the poor. The most important governmental effort in the War on Poverty was the Economic Opportunity Act of 1964.[9] This act established the Office of Economic Opportunity (OEO) directly under the president with the authority to support various programs for combating poverty at the community level. The objective was to help the poor and unemployed become self-supporting and capable of earning adequate incomes. The strategy was one of "rehabilitation," not "relief." OEO was given no authority to make direct grants to the poor as relief. Instead, all its programs were aimed, whether accurately or inaccurately, at *curing* the causes of poverty rather than *alleviating* its symptoms.

OEO youth programs

The Economic Opportunity Act established several programs

oriented toward youth. The strategy appeared to be aimed at breaking the cycle of poverty at an early age. The Job Corps was designed to provide education, vocational training, and work experience in rural conservation camps for unemployable youth between the ages of sixteen and twenty-one. The Neighborhood Youth Corps was designed to provide some work, counseling, and on-the-job training for youth who were living at home. A Work-Study program helped students from low-income families remain in school by giving them federally paid part-time employment with cooperating public or private agencies. Volunteers in Service to America (VISTA) was modeled after the popular Peace Corps, but volunteers were to work in poverty-impacted areas within the United States rather than in foreign countries.

Community action programs

But the heart of the Economic Opportunity Act was a grass-roots "community action program" to be carried on at the local level with federal financial assistance. Communities were urged to form a "community action agency" composed of representatives of government, private organizations, and most important, the poor themselves. The idea was that the OEO would *support the antipoverty programs* devised by local community action agencies to combat poverty in their own communities. Projects might include (but were not limited to) literacy training, health services, homemaker services, legal aid for the poor, neighborhood service centers, manpower training, and childhood developmental activities. The act also envisioned that a community action agency would help *organize the poor* so that they could become participating members of the community and avail themselves of the many public programs designed to serve the poor. Finally, the act attempted to *coordinate federal and state programs for the poor* in each community.

Typically a community action agency would begin by hiring a staff, including a full-time director, paid from an OEO administrative grant, and by defining a target area—generally, the low-income area of the county or the ghetto of a city. Neighborhood centers were established in the target area. The centers might offer general counseling services, employment assistance, a recreational hall, a child-care center, and some sort of health clinic. The centers assisted the poor in contacting the school system, the welfare department, the employment agencies, the public housing authority, and so on. Frequently the centers and the antipoverty workers who manned them acted as intermediaries between the poor and public agencies.

Community action agencies also devised specific antipoverty projects for submission to the Washington offices of OEO for funding. The most popular project was "Operation Headstart"—usually a cooperative program between the community action agency and the school district to give preschool children from poor families special preparation before entering kindergarten or first grade. Another type of project was the "Legal Services" program, in which community action agencies set up free legal services to the poor to assist them in rent disputes, contracts, minor police actions, and so on. Other kinds of antipoverty projects funded by OEO included family planning programs, homemaker services, manpower training, and special educational programs. It is important to know that most of the $2 billion per year allocated to the War on Poverty went into salaries and expenses for administrators, teachers, and workers; in other words, the money was spent on efforts to "cure" poverty and not on the poor themselves.

The demise of OEO   The Office of Economic Opportunity was eventually "reorganized" out of existence, and its educational and manpower training programs transferred to other departments. Funds for the War on Poverty faced gradual reallocation. The demise of the economic opportunity programs cannot be attributed to political partisanship. The War on Poverty had become unpopular even before the Johnson administration left office. The reasons for the failure of this effort at a curative strategy are complex.

The Office of Economic Opportunity was always the scene of great confusion. New and untried programs were organized too quickly; there was high turnover in personnel; there were scandal and corruption, particularly at the local level. Community action agencies with young and inexperienced personnel offended experienced governmental administrators, as well as local political figures. Frequently community action agencies became involved in racial politics in local communities. Many people came to believe that the War on Poverty was a "black program." Antipoverty workers competed with local party organizers and even with social workers for the loyalties of the poor. There were duplication of roles, inefficiency, waste, and lack of coordination. Most damaging of all, there was little concrete evidence that the programs that were put into operation were successful in their objective—that is, in eliminating the causes of poverty.

Daniel P. Moynihan has summarized the community action experiences:

> Over and over again the attempts by official and quasi-official agencies (such as the Ford Foundation) to organize poor communities led first to the radicalization of the middle-class persons who began the effort; next to a certain amount of stirring among the poor, but accompanied by

heightened radical antagonism *on the part of the poor* if they happened to be black; next to retaliation from the larger white community; whereupon it would emerge that the community action agency, which had talked so much, been so much in the headlines, promised so much in the way of change in the fundamentals of things, was powerless. A creature of a Washington bureaucracy, subject to discontinuation without notice. Finally, much bitterness all around.[10]

CASE STUDY
Welfare Reform and the
Work Ethic

Growing disillusionment over public welfare programs, combined with failures in the War on Poverty, have stimulated the search for a more effective way of dealing with poverty in America. Today most welfare reform proposals incorporate the idea of *income maintenance*. Income maintenance plans come in many varieties, but essentially they propose to provide the poor with a guaranteed income to allow them to live in decency regardless of the causes of their poverty. The income maintenance strategy does not attempt to deal with the causes of poverty but simply to guarantee a minimum income. An income maintenance program can be designed to help the poor by providing minimum incomes; or it can be designed to eliminate poverty by raising the incomes of the poor high enough to remove them from poverty. In other words, an income maintenance strategy can either ameliorate poverty or eliminate it altogether if the guaranteed minimum income is set high enough.

The problem, of course, is the possibility that a substantial number of recipients would view the guaranteed income as an alternative to work and would choose such an income in preference to work. The destruction of the "work ethic" would diminish total economic output, leaving society less well off than before. It would also tend to reinforce certain individual traits, including dependency, that run contrary to the ideals of individual dignity and self-reliance. Actually it is difficult to predict the effect of a guaranteed income on work incentive. Many people work very hard with little or no monetary incentive and prefer work to the boredom of unemployment. Initial results of experimentation on small groups of individuals who were given guaranteed annual incomes suggested that their work incentive was relatively unaffected. But there is no way of knowing what would happen to the work ethic if the guaranteed income were established for the *whole* society over a *prolonged* period of time. Whatever the results in small-scale experimental situations, how can one foresee the long-run impact of the guaranteed income in America on the qualities of personal independence, self-reliance, and responsibility that appear to be essential to the full development of the individual and to the health of society?

The income maintenance strategy will probably be incorporated into any future welfare reform. It is likely that welfare reform will parallel the proposals for a so-called guaranteed annual income that have been discussed for years in liberal circles. The following features are usually included: (1) All low-income families with children—the *working* as well as the nonworking poor—would be eligible to receive family assistance. (2) For families with no outside income, a minimum federal payment would be provided (perhaps $6,000 for a family of four). (3) Outside earnings would be encouraged, not discouraged. A family could keep the first $750 per year of outside income without reducing federal payment; beyond that amount family assistance would be reduced by only fifty cents for each dollar earned. The break-even point—the level of income at which a family of four would cease to be eligible for family assistance benefits—would be approximately $9,000. (4) This family assistance program would replace the Aid to Families with Dependent Children program. (5) Adult family members would be required to register for work and accept "suitable employment" when it was offered.

This type of welfare reform is clearly designed to remedy many of the dysfunctional consequences of previous welfare policy—deterrents to work, disintegration of family life, inequalities among the states, and discrimination against the working poor. But the long-run impact of such a reform is hard to predict.[11]

The first problem with a guaranteed annual income is the increase in costs that it would involve. It is likely that Congress would want to increase the full minimum guarantee over the years. There is no really reliable information on the number of working poor who would apply or what this additional load would cost. Presumably the costs of AFDC would be eliminated; but the costs of old-age, blind, and disabled assistance would continue, not to mention the continued costs of food stamps, medicaid, and public housing.

Work incentives are probably useless, and perhaps demeaning as well. Previous work-incentive amendments to public assistance programs have not succeeded in reducing dependency. If welfare recipients could find good jobs, they would have done so long ago; the real problem is that most welfare recipients are unskilled, uneducated, and unprepared to function effectively in the work force.

Finally, it is not certain whether such an expansion of welfare assistance to many working families would increase or reduce economic dependency in America. Possibly it would encourage dependency by making the acceptance of welfare assistance a common family practice, extending well up into the middle class. Certainly the percentage of the population receiving some form of public assistance would be greatly increased; it is conceivable that 20 percent of the population would eventually gain access to welfare rolls under a guaranteed annual income.

NOTES

1. John Kenneth Galbraith, *The Affluent Society* (New York: New American Library, 1958), p. 251.

2. U.S. Bureau of the Census, "Poverty in the United States," *Current Population Reports*, P-60, no. 86, 1972.

3. Kenneth B. Clark, *Dark Ghetto: Dilemmas of Social Power* (New York: Harper & Row, 1965), p. 67.

4. Ibid., p. 70.

5. Daniel P. Moynihan, *The Negro Family: The Case for National Action* (Washington, D.C.: Government Printing Office, 1965).

6. Ibid., p. 47.

7. Edward C. Banfield, *The Unheavenly City* (Boston: Little, Brown, 1968), ch. 6.

8. Jack L. Roach and Orville R. Gursslin, "An Evaluation of the Concept Culture of Poverty," *Social Forces* 45 (March 1967):384–92.

9. For a description of all of the different programs in the War on Poverty, see Joseph A. Kershaw, *Government Against Poverty* (Chicago: Markham, 1970).

10. Daniel P. Moynihan, *Maximum Feasible Misunderstanding: Community Action in the War on Poverty* (New York: Free Press, 1969), pp. 134–35.

11. For an excellent example of a rational analysis of welfare reform, see Theodore Marmor, "On Comparing Income Maintenance Alternatives," *American Political Science Review* 65 (March 1971):83–96.

DISCUSSION QUESTIONS

1. Discuss the criteria used by the U.S. Social Security Administration to define the poverty line. Describe the emphasis of this official definition of poverty on subsistence levels. What are the criticisms of this definition of poverty?

2. Identify the groups of people who experience poverty in greater proportions than the national average.

3. Discuss the definition of poverty as relative deprivation or inequality. Explain why it seems unlikely that this type of poverty will ever be eliminated.

4. Discuss the relationship between poverty and feelings of powerlessness. Describe the "psychology of the ghetto." What are the feelings of ghetto residents about themselves? What are their attitudes toward the larger society? Describe some of the forms of personal adjustment in the ghetto and the effect of poverty and discrimination on family life.

5. What is meant by the expression *culture of poverty*? Discuss the theory of the poverty cycle. Comment on Edward C. Banfield's view of the culture of poverty as "present-orientedness." What are the policy implications of a culture of poverty? Discuss the arguments of those who oppose the idea of a culture of poverty.

6. Identify the two basic strategies that are embodied in the Social Security Act of 1935. Differentiate between social insurance programs and public assistance programs in terms of who pays, who benefits, and when they benefit. Give examples of each type of program and specify the type of strategy they express.

7. Discuss the criticisms of current public assistance (welfare) programs.

8. Discuss the curative strategy of the War on Poverty and the objective of the Office of Economic Opportunity. Identify some of the programs established by the Economic Opportunity Act of 1964. Describe some of the antipoverty projects devised by the local community action agencies. What factors contributed to the demise of the economic opportunity programs?

9. Discuss the purposes and strategies of income maintenance plans. What are the criticisms of these plans? Discuss the pros and cons of a guaranteed annual income.

SUGGESTED READINGS

Edward C. Banfield, *The Unheavenly City* (Boston: Little, Brown, 1968).

John C. Donovan, *The Politics of Poverty* (New York: Pegasus, 1967).

John Kenneth Galbraith, *The Affluent Society* (New York: New American Library, 1958).

Michael Harrington, *The Other America: Poverty in the United States* (New York: Macmillan, 1962).

Joseph A. Kershaw, *Government Against Poverty* (Chicago: Markham, 1970).

Daniel P. Moynihan. *The Negro Family: The Case for National Action* (Washington, D.C.: Government Printing Office, 1965).

———, *Maximum Feasible Misunderstanding: Community Action in the War on Poverty* (New York: Free Press, 1969).

Gilbert Y. Steiner, *Social Insecurity* (Chicago: Rand McNally, 1966).

Charles A. Valentine, *Culture and Poverty* (Chicago: University of Chicago Press, 1970).

Chapter 12
Power, Crime, and Violence

Over two thousand years ago, Aristotle wrote of the problem of crime that "the generality of men are naturally apt to be swayed by fear rather than by reverence, and to refrain from evil rather because of the punishment that it brings, than because of its own foulness." Since people will not police themselves, society must do it for them. Power must be exercised for the very basic purposes of maintaining order and protecting the citizenry. The way that a society exercises that power obviously has enormous implications for the lives of all who live in it. Nazi Germany and Stalinist Russia are but two examples of how the unconstrained use of police power can turn the lives of citizens into nightmares. A free democratic society must struggle with maintaining a balance between its exercise of police power and its safeguarding of individual freedom. In this chapter we will examine America's struggles with this problem. We will also examine the violence that has been a part of most of the important social movements in American history.

After you have read chapter 12, you should be able to:

- describe the current status of crime and punishment in America as evidenced by crime rates, the constitutional rights of defendants, and judicial decisions regarding defendants' rights and capital punishment.
- discuss some of the law enforcement problems that police encounter, as well as the law enforcement problems created by the judicial system itself.
- discuss the history of violence in America and some of the social-psychological explanations of violence.
- discuss violence as political protest and the conclusions reached by the National Advisory Commission on Civil Disorders regarding the nature and causes of the ghetto riots of 1965–1968.

POWER AND INDIVIDUAL FREEDOM

For thousands of years people have wrestled with the question of balancing social power against individual freedom. How far can indi-

351

vidual freedom be extended without undermining the stability of a
society, threatening the safety of others, and risking anarchy? The
early English political philosopher Thomas Hobbes (1588–1679)
believed that society must establish a powerful "Leviathan"—the
state—in order to curb the savage instincts of human beings. A
powerful authority in society was needed to prevent people from at-
tacking each other for personal gain—"war of every man against
every man" in which "notions of right and wrong, justice and injustice, have no place." According to Hobbes, without law and order
there is no real freedom. The fear of death and destruction permeates
every act of life: "Every man is enemy to every man"; and "Force and
fraud are the two cardinal virtues."

> In such condition, there is no place for industry; because the fruit
> thereof is uncertain: and consequently no culture of the earth; no naviga-
> tion, nor use of the commodities that may be imported by sea; no com-
> modious building, no instruments of moving, and removing, such things
> as that require much force; no knowledge of the face of the earth; no ac-
> count of time; no arts; no letters; no society; and which is worst of all,
> continual fear, and danger of violent death; and the life of man solitary,
> poor, nasty, brutish, and short.

Freedom, then, is *not* the absence of law and order. On the contrary,
law and order are required if there is to be any freedom in society at
all.

   To avoid the brutal life of a lawless society—where the weak are
at the mercy of the strong—people form governments and endow
them with powers to secure peace and self-preservation. Hobbes
believed that "the social contract"—the agreement of human beings
to establish governments and grant them the powers to maintain
peace and security—is a collective act of self-preservation. People
voluntarily relinquish some of their individual freedom to establish a
powerful government that is capable of protecting them from their
neighbors as well as from foreign aggressors. This government must
be strong enough to maintain its own existence or it cannot defend
the rights of its citizens. But what happens when a government
becomes too strong and infringes the liberties of its citizens? People
agree to abide by law and accept restrictions on their personal freedom for the sake of peace and self-preservation; but how much liberty must be surrendered to secure an orderly society? This is the
The classic dilemma   *classic dilemma of free government*: People must create laws and
governments to protect freedom, but the laws and governments them-
selves restrict freedom.

THE PROBLEM OF CRIME

Crime rates   Crime rates are the subject of a great deal of popular discussion. Very often they are employed to express the degree of social disorganization or even the effectiveness of law enforcement agencies. Crime rates are based upon the Federal Bureau of Investigation's *Uniform Crime Reports*, but the FBI reports themselves are based on figures supplied by state and local police agencies (see table 12–1). The FBI has succeeded in establishing a uniform classification of the number of serious crimes per 100,000 people that are known to the police—murder and nonnegligent manslaughter, forcible rape, robbery, aggravated assault, burglary, larceny, and theft, including auto theft. But record keeping is still a problem, and one should be cautious in interpreting official crime rates. They are really a function of several factors: the diligence of police in detecting crime, the adequacy of the system for reporting and tabulating crime, and the amount of crime itself. Yet the evidence seems inescapable that crime in the United States is increasing at a rapid pace. The greatest increase in crime rates occurs in nonviolent crimes—burglary, larceny, theft—and lesser increases are found in crimes involving violence against the person—murder, nonnegligent manslaughter, and robbery. (For a graphic view of the increases in property crime and violent crime, see appendix figures H and I. Table I in the appendix shows loss of life from violent crimes, 1940–1973.)

Inaccuracy of crime statistics   Police statistics vastly understate the real amount of crime. Citizens *do not report* many crimes to police. The National Opinion Research Center of the University of Chicago asked a national sample of individuals whether they or any member of their household

Table 12–1   Crime Rate—Number of Offenses Known to Police per 100,000 Persons

Year	Total	Criminal Homicide	Forcible Rape	Robbery	Assault	Burglary	Larceny	Auto Theft
1960	1,126	5.0	10	60	85	502	283	182
1965	1,516	5.0	12	71	110	653	410	255
1970	3,985	7.9	19	172	165	1,025	2,079	457
1972	3,961	9.0	22	180	187	1,141	1,994	426
1976	5,266	8.8	26	196	229	1,439	2,921	446

Source: U.S. Bureau of the Census, *Statistical Abstract of the United States, 1977* (Washington, D.C.: Government Printing Office, 1977), p. 168.

had been a victim of crime during the past year. This survey revealed that the actual amount of crime is several times greater than that reported by the FBI. There are more than twice as many crimes committed as are reported to the police. The number of forcible rapes was more than three and one-half times the number reported; burglaries were three times, aggravated assaults and larcenies were more than double, and robbery was 50 percent greater than the reported rate. Only auto theft statistics were reasonably accurate, indicating that most people call the police when their cars are stolen.

Interviewees gave a variety of reasons for their failure to report crimes to the police. The most common reason was the belief that police could not be effective in dealing with the crime. This is a serious commentary on police protection in America today. Other reasons included the feeling that the crime was "a private matter" or that the victim did not want to harm the offender. Fear of reprisal was mentioned much less frequently, usually in cases of assaults and family crimes.

The current system of criminal justice is certainly no serious deterrent to crime. Most behavioral research suggests that it is not the *severity of punishment* that affects behavior but the establishment of a *sure linkage* between the criminal behavior and punishment. In other words, crime is more likely to be deterred by making punishment sure, rather than severe. However, the best available estimates of the ratio between crime and punishment suggest that the likelihood of an individual's being jailed for a serious crime is less than one in a hundred (see figure 12–1). Most crimes are not even reported by the victim. Police are successful in clearing only about one in five reported crimes by arresting the offender. The judicial system convicts only about one in four of the persons arrested and charged; others are not prosecuted, handled as juveniles, found not guilty, or permitted to plead guilty to a lesser charge and released. Only about half of the convicted felons are given prison sentences.

THE CONSTITUTIONAL RIGHTS OF DEFENDANTS

Guarantee of the Writ of Habeas Corpus   An ancient right in common law is the right to obtain a writ of *habeas corpus*, a court order directing a public official who is holding a person in custody to bring the prisoner into court to explain the reasons for the confinement. If a judge finds that the prisoner is being unlawfully detained, or that there is not sufficient evidence that a crime has been committed or

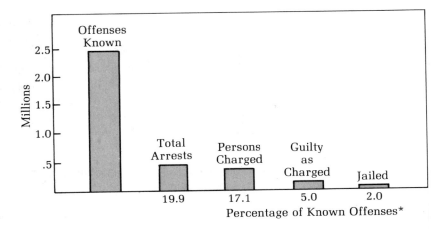

Figure 12–1 Law Enforcement in Relation to Crime
*Actual crime is estimated to be two and a half times the known offenses. If the base were actual crime, the percentages would be less than half of those appearing in the figure. Thus, persons jailed as a percentage of actual crime is less than 1 percent.
Source: *Statistical Abstract of the United States, 1970*, p. 146.

that the prisoner could have committed it, the judge orders the prisoner's immediate release.

Prohibition of Bills of Attainder and of Ex Post Facto Laws Protection against bills of attainder and against ex post facto laws was, like the guarantee of habeas corpus, considered so fundamental to individual liberty that it was included in the original text of the Constitution. A *bill of attainder* is a legislative act that inflicts punishment without judicial trial. An *ex post facto law* is a retroactive criminal law that works to the detriment of the accused—for example, a law that makes an act a criminal one *after* the act is committed, or a law that increases the punishment for a crime and applies it *retroactively*.

Prohibition of "Unreasonable" Searches and Seizures The Fourth Amendment provides: "The right of the people to be secure in their persons, houses, papers, and effects, against unreasonable searches and seizures, shall not be violated, and no warrants shall issue but upon probable cause, supported by oath or affirmation, and particularly describing the place to be searched, and the persons or things to be seized." The requirement that the things to be seized must be described in the warrant is meant to prevent "fishing expeditions" into an individual's home and personal effects on the possibility that some evidence of unknown illegal activity might crop up. An exception to the requirement for a warrant is made if the search is "incident to a lawful arrest." A "lawful arrest" can be made by the police if they have reasonable grounds to believe a person has committed a felony or if a misdemeanor is committed in their presence; a search of the person and the person's property is permitted without a warrant at the time of such an arrest.

Freedom from Self-Incrimination   Although the Fifth Amendment establishes a number of procedural guarantees, perhaps the most widely quoted clause of that amendment guarantees that no person "shall be compelled in any criminal case to be a witness against himself." The sentence "I refuse to answer that question on the ground that it might tend to incriminate me" is, today, a household standard. Freedom from self-incrimination has its origins in English resistance to torture and confession. It now embodies the ideas that individuals should not be forced to contribute to their own prosecution and that the burden of proof of guilt is on the state. The constitutional protection against self-incrimination applies not only to accused persons in their own trials, but also to witnesses testifying in any public proceedings, including criminal trials of other persons, civil suits, congressional hearings, or other investigations. The silence of an accused person cannot be interpreted as guilt; the burden of proving guilt rests with the prosecution.

The Right to Counsel   The right to avoid self-incrimination is closely connected with the right to counsel, as provided in the Sixth Amendment, because counsel may advise the accused to remain silent and claim protection against self-incrimination. The Sixth Amendment states: "In all criminal prosecutions, the accused shall enjoy . . . the assistance of counsel for his defense." An accused individual has the right to ask for counsel before answering any police questions. If the person in custody is indigent and requests counsel, the police must see that counsel is provided.

Guarantee of a Fair Jury Trial   Trial by jury is guaranteed in both the original text of the Constitution and the Sixth Amendment: "In all criminal prosecutions, the accused shall enjoy the right to a speedy and public trial, by an impartial jury . . . and to be informed of the nature and cause of the accusation; to be confronted with the witnesses against him; to have compulsory process for obtaining witnesses in his favor. . . ." The requirement of a "speedy" trial protects the accused from long pretrial waits; but the accused may ask for postponements in order to prepare a defense. A "public" trial prevents secret proceedings, and "impartial" means that each juror must be able to judge the case objectively. Discrimination in the selection of the jury is forbidden. The guarantee of a fair trial can be violated if sensational pretrial publicity or an unruly courtroom hinders the jury from making an unbiased verdict. By old canon law, a jury consisted of twelve persons, and the vote of the jurors had to be unanimous. This is still the requirement in most cases, but recently the Supreme Court indicated that unanimity might not be required in some cases.

The burden of proof rests with the prosecution. It is up to the prosecution to convince a jury "beyond reasonable doubt" that the accused is guilty. Witnesses must appear in person against the accused. The accused or the counsel for the accused has the right to cross-examine those witnesses and may present witnesses on behalf of their own case. The accused may even obtain a "summons" to compel people to testify at the trial. If a guilty verdict is rendered, the defendant may appeal any errors in the trial to a higher court.

Protection Against Double Jeopardy The Fifth Amendment states: "Nor shall any person be subject for the same offense to be twice put in jeopardy of life or limb. . . ." Once a person has been tried for a particular crime and the trial has ended in a decision, that person cannot be tried again for the same crime. However, this right does not prevent a new trial if the jury cannot agree on a verdict (a "hung jury"), or if the verdict is reversed by an appeal to a higher court because of a procedural error. Moreover, an individual may be tried by different jurisdictions on slightly different charges stemming from the same act.

Protection Against Excessive Bail Arrested persons are considered innocent until tried and found guilty. They are entitled to go free prior to trial unless their freedom would unreasonably endanger society, or unless there is reason to believe that they would not appear for trial. Bail is supposed to ensure that the accused will appear. Bail may be denied for major crimes, but most accused persons are entitled to be released on bail pending their trial. Bail must not be "excessive," although there are no fixed standards for determining what "excessive" is.

Landmark Decisions   The Warren Court—the Supreme Court of the 1950s and 1960s, under the guidance of Chief Justice Earl Warren—greatly strengthened the rights of accused persons in criminal cases. Several key decisions, which were the result of split votes, drew heavy criticism from law enforcement officers and others as hamstringing police in their struggle with lawlessness. These decisions include:

> *Mapp* v. *Ohio* (1961), barring the use of illegally seized evidence in criminal cases by applying the Fourth Amendment guarantee against unreasonable searches and seizures. Even if the evidence seized proves the guilt of the accused, it cannot be presented in a trial.
>
> *Gideon* v. *Wainwright* (1963), ruling that equal protection under the Fourteenth Amendment requires that free legal counsel be appointed for all indigent defendants in all criminal cases.
>
> *Escobedo* v. *Illinois* (1964), ruling that suspects are entitled to confer with counsel as soon as police investigation focuses on them, or once "the process shifts from investigatory to accusatory."
>
> *Miranda* v. *Arizona* (1966), requiring that police, before questioning suspects, must inform them of all their constitutional rights including the right to counsel (appointed free, if necessary) and the right to remain silent. Although suspects may knowingly waive these rights. the police cannot question suspects who at any point ask for a lawyer or indicate "in any manner" that they do not wish to be questioned.

To what extent these decisions have really hampered efforts to halt the rise in crime in America is very difficult to ascertain. The Supreme Court under Chief Justice Burger has not reversed any of these landmark decisions. Whatever progress is made in law enforcement, therefore, will have to be made within the current definition of the rights of defendants. It is important to note that Chief Justice Burger's recommendations for judicial reform center on the speedy administration of justice and not on changes in the rights of defendants.

CRIME AND THE COURTS

Chief Justice Warren E. Burger has argued persuasively that rising crime in America is partly due to inadequacies in our system of criminal justice. "The present system of criminal justice does not deter criminal conduct," he said in a special State of the Federal Judiciary message. "Whatever deterrent effect may have existed in the past has now virtually vanished."[1] He urged major reform in law enforcement, courts, prisons, probation, and parole.

A major stumbling block to effective law enforcement is the current plight of America's judicial machinery:

Inadequacies of the criminal justice system

Major congestion on court dockets that delays the hearing of cases for months or even years. Moreover, actual trials are now on the average twice as long as they were ten years ago.

Failure of courts to adopt modern management and administrative practices to speed and improve justice.

Increased litigation in the courts. Not only are more Americans aware of their rights, but more of them are also using every avenue of appeal. Seldom do appeals concern the suit or the innocence of the defendant; usually they focus on procedural matters.

Excessive delays in trials. "Defendants, whether guilty or innocent, are human; they love freedom and hate punishment. With a lawyer provided to secure release without the need for a conventional bail bond, most defendants, except in capital cases, are released pending trial. We should not be surprised that a defendant on bail exerts a heavy pressure on his court-appointed lawyer to postpone the trial as long as possible so as to remain free. These postponements—and sometimes there are a dozen or more—consume the time of judges and court staffs as well as of lawyers. Cases are calendared and reset time after time while witnesses and jurors spend endless hours just waiting."[2]

Excessive delays in appeals. "We should not be surprised at delay when more and more defendants demand their undoubted constitutional right to trial by jury because we have provided them with lawyers and other needs at public expense; nor should we be surprised that most convicted persons seek a new trial when the appeal costs them nothing and when failure to take the appeal will cost them freedom. Being human a defendant plays out the line which society has cast him. Lawyers are competitive creatures and the adversary system encourages contention and often rewards delay; no lawyer wants to be called upon to defend the client's charges of incompetence for having failed to exploit all the procedural techniques which we have deliberately made available."[3]

Excessive variation in sentencing. Some judges let defendants off on probation for crimes that would draw five- or ten-year sentences by other judges. While flexibility in sentencing is essential in dealing justly with individuals, perceived inconsistencies damage the image of the courts in the public mind.

Excessive "plea bargaining" between the prosecution and the defendant's attorney, in which the defendant agrees to plead guilty to a lesser offense if the prosecutor will drop more serious charges.

CAPITAL PUNISHMENT

The pros and cons

One of the more heated debates in correctional policy today concerns capital punishment. Opponents of the death penalty argue that

"If the larceny charge can be dropped, my client is prepared to plead guilty to the lesser charge of creating a climate of larceny."

Drawing by Handelsman; © 1978 The New Yorker Magazine, Inc.

it is "cruel and unusual punishment," and is thus in violation of the Eighth Amendment of the Constitution. They also contend that nations and states that have abolished the death penalty have not experienced higher homicide rates, and hence there is no concrete evidence that the death penalty discourages crime. They also argue that the death penalty is applied unequally. A large proportion of those executed have been poor, uneducated, and nonwhite. In contrast, there is a strong sense of justice among many Americans that demands retribution for heinous crimes—a life for a life. A mere jail sentence for a multiple murderer or a rapist-murderer seems unjust compared with the damage inflicted upon society and the victims. In most cases, a life sentence means less than ten years in prison, under the current parole and probation policies of many states. Convicted murderers have been set free, and some have killed again. Moreover, prison guards and other inmates are exposed to convicted murderers who have "a license to kill" because they are already serving life sentences and have nothing to lose by killing again. Public opinion polls continue to support the death penalty, although opponents have been gaining supporters over time.

Before 1972, the death penalty was officially approved by thirty states; only fifteen states had abolished capital punishment.[4] Federal laws also retained the death penalty. However, no one had actually suffered the death penalty since 1967, because of numerous legal tangles and direct challenges to the constitutionality of capital punishment.

1972: the question of constitutionality

In *Furman v. Georgia* (1972), the Supreme Court ruled that capital punishment *as then imposed* violated the Eighth and Fourteenth Amendments in that it constituted cruel and unusual punishment and denied due process of law. The decision was made by a five to four vote of the justices, and the reasoning in the case is very complex. Only two justices—Brennan and Marshall—declared that capital punishment itself is cruel and unusual. The other three justices in the majority—Douglas, White, and Stewart—felt that death sentences had been applied unfairly; a few individuals were receiving the death penalty for crimes for which many others were receiving lighter sentences. These justices left open the possibility that capital punishment would be constitutional if it were specified for certain kinds of crime and applied uniformly.

New state laws

After this decision, a majority of states rewrote their death penalty laws to try to insure fairness and uniformity of application. Generally, these laws mandate the death penalty for murders committed during rape, robbery, hijacking, or kidnapping; murders of prison guards; murder with torture; and multiple murders. Two trials must be held—one to determine guilt or innocence and another to determine the penalty. At the second trial, evidence of "aggravating" and "mitigating" factors is presented; if there are aggravating factors but no mitigating factors, the death penalty is mandatory.

1976: Court upholds death penalty

In a series of cases in 1976 (*Gregg v. Georgia, Profitt v. Florida, Jurek v. Texas*), the Supreme Court finally held that "the punishment of death does not invariably violate the Constitution." The Court upheld the death penalty with the following rationale: The men who drafted the Bill of Rights accepted death as a common sanction for crime. It is true that the Eighth Amendment prohibition against cruel and unusual punishments must be interpreted in a dynamic fashion, reflecting changing moral values. But the decisions of more than half of the nation's state legislatures to reenact the death penalty since 1972, as well as the decisions of juries to impose the death penalty on more than four hundred and fifty persons under these new laws, are evidence that "a large proportion of American society continues to regard it as an appropriate and necessary criminal sanction." More-

over, said the Court, the social purposes of retribution and deterrence justify the use of the death penalty. This ultimate sanction is
"an expression of society's moral outrage at particularly offensive
conduct."

The Court reaffirmed that *Furman* v. *Georgia* (1972) only struck
down the death penalty where it was inflicted in "an arbitrary and
capricious manner." The Court upheld the death penalty in states
where the trial was a two-part proceeding, the second part of which
provided the judge or jury with relevant information and standards
for deciding whether to impose the death penalty. The Court approved the consideration of "aggravating and mitigating circumstances." The Court also approved of automatic review of all death
sentences by state supreme courts to insure that the sentence was not
imposed under the influence of passion or prejudice, that aggravating
factors were supported by the evidence, and that the sentence was
not disproportionate to the crime.

POLICE AND LAW ENFORCEMENT

Police perform at least three important functions in urban
society—enforcing the law, keeping the peace, and furnishing services. Actually, law enforcement may take up only a small portion of
a police officer's daily activity—perhaps as little as 10 percent.[5] The
service function occupies far more time: attending accidents, directing traffic, escorting crowds, assisting stranded motorists, handling
drunks, and so on. The function of peacekeeping is also a prominent
part of police duties: breaking up fights, quieting noisy parties, handling domestic or neighborhood quarrels, and the like. It is in this function that police exercise the greatest discretion in the application of
the law. In most such incidents, blame is difficult to determine, participants are reluctant to file charges, and police must use *personal
discretion* in handling each case.

Police are generally recruited from working-class families; only a
handful come from middle-class backgrounds, and few have more
than a high school education. Yet the tasks they are assigned in
society would confound highly trained social scientists. Formal police
training emphasizes self-control and caution in dealing with the
public, but on-the-job *experiences* probably reinforce distrust of
others. The element of danger in their work makes the police naturally suspicious of others. They see much of the "worst kind" of people, and even the "best kind" at their worst.

Police are members of a semimilitary organization. They are concerned with *authority* themselves, and as they engage in law enforcement, they expect others to respect authority. It is often difficult for even the most well-meaning police officer to develop respect or sympathy for ghetto residents. One police officer described the problem as follows:

> The police have to associate with lower class people, slobs, drunks, criminals, riffraff of the worst sort. Most of these . . . are Negroes. The police officers see these people through middle class or lower middle class eye-balls. But even if he saw them through highly sophisticated eye-balls he can't go in the street and take this night after night. When some Negro criminal says to you a few times, "you white mother-fucker, take that badge off and I'll shove it up your ass," well it's bound to affect you after a while. Pretty soon you decide they're all just niggers and they'll never be anything but niggers. It would take not just an average man to resist this feeling, it would take an extraordinary man to resist it, and there are very few ways by which the police department can attract extraordinary men to join them.[6]

VIOLENCE IN AMERICAN HISTORY

Violence is not uncommon in American society. The nation itself was founded in armed revolution, and violence has been a *source of power* and a *stimulus to social change* ever since. Violence has been associated with most of the important movements in American history: the birth of the nation (revolutionary violence), the freeing of the slaves and the preservation of the union (Civil War violence), the westward expansion of the nation (Indian wars), the establishment of law and order in frontier society (vigilante violence), the organization of the labor movement (labor-management violence), the civil rights movement (racial violence), and attempts to deal with the problems of cities (urban violence). History reveals that the patriot, the humanitarian, the pioneer, the lawman, the laborer, the black man, and the urban dweller have all used violence as a source of power. Despite pious pronouncements against it, Americans have frequently employed violence even in their most idealistic endeavors.

Guerrilla warfare in the Revolution

Perhaps the most famous act of organized mob violence occurred in 1773 when a group of "agitators" in Boston, Massachusetts, illegally destroyed 342 chests of tea. The early Revolutionary War fighting in 1774 and 1775, including the battles of Lexington and Concord, was really a series of small guerrilla skirmishes designed more to intimidate Tories than to achieve national independence. The old American custom of tarring and feathering was a product of the early patriotic campaign to root out Tories. Aside from the regular clash of Continental and British armies, a great deal of violence and guerrilla strife occurred during the Revolution. Savage guerrilla forays along the eastern coast resulted in the killing of thousands of Tory families and the destruction of their property. The success of this violence enshrined it in our traditions.

Shays' Rebellion

After the Revolutionary War, many armed farmers and debtors resorted to violence to assert their economic interests. If taxes owed to the British government and debts owed to the British merchants could be denied, why not also the taxes owed to state governments and the debts owed to American merchants? In several states, debtors had already engaged in open rebellion against tax collectors and sheriffs. The most serious rebellion broke out in the summer of 1786 in Massachusetts, when a band of insurgents, composed of farmers and laborers, captured courthouses in several western districts of that state and momentarily held the city of Springfield. Led by Daniel Shays, a veteran of Bunker Hill, the insurgent army posed a direct threat to the governing elite of the new nation. Shays' Rebellion, as it was called, was put down by a small mercenary army paid for by well-to-do citizens who feared that a wholesale attack on property rights was imminent. The growing domestic violence in the states contributed to the momentum leading to the Constitutional Convention of 1787, where propertied men established a new central government with the power to "ensure domestic tranquility," guarantee "the republican form of government," and protect "against domestic violence." Thus, the Constitution itself reflects a concern of the Founding Fathers about domestic violence.

Violence of the Civil War era

The Civil War was the bloodiest war America ever fought. Total casualties of the Northern and Southern armies equaled American casualties in World War II—but when the Civil War occurred, the nation was only half as large as it was during the latter conflict. There were few families that did not suffer the loss of a loved one during the Civil War. In addition to military casualties, the toll in lives and property among civilians was enormous. A great deal of domestic violence also occurred both before and after the war. In 1856 the brutal events surrounding the "bleeding Kansas" issue took place. In 1859 came John Brown's raid at Harper's Ferry, meant to start the freeing of the slaves in Virginia. Brown's capture, trial for treason, and execution made him a hero to many abolitionists, though Southerners believed that he had tried to incite slave uprisings. The guerrilla war that took place in the West during the Civil War has seldom been equaled for savagery; the fearsome Kansas Jayhawkers traded brutalities with Confederate guerrillas headed by William Quantrell.

Later, western bandits, including Frank and Jesse James and the Younger brothers, who had fought as Confederate guerrillas, continued their forays against banks and railroads and enjoyed considerable popular prestige and support. Moreover, after the war, racial strife and Ku Klux Klan activity became routine in the old Confederate states. The Ku Klux Klan was first employed to intimidate the Republicans of the Reconstruction era by violence and threats, and later to force blacks to accept the renewed rule of whites.

The Indian wars
Unquestionably the longest and most brutal violence in American history was that between whites and Indians. It began in 1607 and continued with only temporary truces for nearly three hundred years, until the final battle at Wounded Knee, South Dakota, in 1890. The norms of Indian warfare were generally more barbaric than those in other types of warfare, if such a thing is possible. Women and children on both sides were deliberately and purposefully killed. Torture was accepted as a customary part of making war. Scalping was a frequent practice among both Indians and Indian-fighters.

Vigilante violence
Vigilante violence (taking the law into one's own hands) arose as a response to a typical American problem: the absence of effective law and order in the frontier region. Practically every state and territory west of the Appalachians had at one time or another a well-organized vigilante movement. The first vigilante movement appeared in 1767–1769 in South Carolina, where the vigilantes were known as *regulators*—a term later used by San Francisco vigilantes in the 1850s. Vigilantes were frequently backed by prominent men; many later became senators, representatives, governors, judges, businessmen, and even clergymen. Like Indian-fighters, vigilantes became great popular heroes. Antithief and antirustling associations flourished in the West until World War I. Vigilantes often undertook not only to establish law and order but also to regulate the morals of the citizens—punishing drunks, vagrants, ne'er-do-wells, and occasional strangers.

Labor-management violence
Violence was also a constant companion of the early labor movement in America. Both management and strikers resorted to violence in the struggles accompanying the industrial revolution. In 1887 in the bitter railroad strike in Pittsburgh, Pennsylvania, an estimated sixteen soldiers and fifty strikers were killed, and locomotives, freight cars, and other property were destroyed. The famous Homestead strike of 1892 turned Homestead, Pennsylvania, into an open battlefield. The Pullman strike of 1893 in Chicago resulted in twelve deaths and the destruction of a great deal of railroad property. In 1914, Ludlow, Colorado, was the scene of the famous Ludlow Massacre, in which company guards burned a miner tent city and killed nearly a hundred

persons including women and children. The Molly McGuires were a secret organization of Irish miners who fought their employers with assassination and mayhem. The last great spasm of violence in the history of American labor came in the 1930s with the strikes and plant takeovers ("sit-down strikes") that accompanied the successful drive to unionize the automobile, steel, and other mass-production industries.

Racial violence

The long history of racial violence in America continues to plague the nation. Slavery itself was accompanied by untold violence. It is estimated that one-third to one-half of the blacks captured in African slave raids never survived the ordeal of forced marches to the sea, with thirst, brutalities, and near starvation the rule; the terrible two-month voyage in filthy holds packed with squirming and suffocating humanity; and the brutal "seasoning" whereby African blacks were turned into slaves. Nat Turner's slave insurrection in 1831 resulted in the deaths of fifty-seven white persons and the later execution of Turner and his followers. Following the end of slavery, the white supremacy movement employed violence to reestablish the position of whites in the southern social system. Racial violence directed against blacks—whippings, torture, and lynching—was fairly common from the 1870s to the 1930s. During World War II, serious racial violence erupted in Detroit. Black and white mobs battled each other in June 1943, causing thirty-five deaths and hundreds of injuries, over a thousand arrests, and finally the dispatch of federal troops to restore order.

Political violence

Political assassinations have not been uncommon. Four presidents (Lincoln, Garfield, McKinley, and Kennedy) have fallen to assassins' bullets, and others were the intended objects of assassination. Only Lincoln was the target of a proven assassination conspiracy; the other presidential victims were the prey of presumably free-lance assassins in varying states of mental instability. In the 1930s Senator Huey P. Long of Louisiana was murdered, and a bullet narrowly missed President Franklin Delano Roosevelt and killed Mayor Anton Cermak of Chicago, who was standing near the president. The wave of political assassinations in more recent years, which cut down John F. Kennedy, Robert F. Kennedy, and Martin Luther King, Jr., and crippled George C. Wallace, may represent a "contagion phenomenon," unstable individuals being motivated to violence by highly publicized and dramatic acts of violence. But an even more grim possibility is that political assassination may become a persistent feature of American society.

SOCIAL-PSYCHOLOGICAL
PERSPECTIVES ON VIOLENCE

Social psychologists have different explanations of violence. One explanation relies heavily upon learning theory (stimulus-response theory); we shall refer to this as the *frustration-aggression* explanation. Another relies upon Freudian notions of instinctual behavior in the "unlocking" of inhibitions; we shall call this the *aggressive instinct* explanation. Yet another explanation focuses on the violence that is triggered when rising hopes and expectations outstrip the ability of the system to fulfill them. We shall refer to this as the *relative deprivation* explanation.

*Frustration-aggression
explanation*

The frustration-aggression explanation is perhaps the most popular explanation of social violence—of political turmoil, racial conflict, urban disorders, even crime and juvenile delinquency. Over thirty years ago psychologist John Dollard and several colleagues at Yale University set forth the proposition that "aggression is always the result of frustration."[7] They argued, "The occurrence of aggressive behavior always presupposes the existence of frustration and, contrariwise, the existence of frustration always leads to some form of aggression." Frustration occurs when there is a blocking of ongoing, goal-directed activity, and it evokes a characteristic reaction—aggression—whereby the individual seeks to reduce the emotional anxiety produced by this blocking. Aggression helps to lessen frustration brought on by the blocking of the original need, but it fails to satisfy the original need. The aggressive behavior merely copes with the emotional reaction to the blocking. The degree of frustration is affected by the intensity of the original need, and by the degree of expectation that the goal-directed activity would be successful. Aggressive behavior is a function of this degree of frustration, which in turn is determined by the strength of the original need, the degree of interference with its satisfaction, and the number of times its satisfaction has been blocked. Minor frustrations added together can produce a stronger aggressive response than would normally be expected from a frustrating situation that appears immediately before aggression. Thus, frustration can build up over time. Of course, society attempts to inhibit aggressive behavior by threats of punishment. Dollard and his colleagues added, "The strength of inhibition of any act of aggression varies positively with the amount of punishment anticipated to be the consequence of that act."

Acts of physical violence are the most obvious forms of aggression. But other forms include fantasies of "getting even," forays against the frustrating persons (stealing from them or cheating them, spreading malicious rumors about them, or verbal assaults), and generalized destructive outbursts. Dollard contended that frustration and aggression can characterize group action as well as individual action: "Remonstrative outbursts like lynchings, strikes, and certain reformist campaigns are clearly forms of aggression as well." Aggression is generally directed at the person or object that is perceived as causing the frustration, but it may also be *displaced* to some altogether innocent source, or even toward the self, as in masochism, martyrdom, and suicide. The act of aggression is presumed to reduce the emotional reaction to frustration. Dollard and his colleagues referred to the reduction as *catharsis*. "The expression of any act of aggression is a catharsis that reduces the instigation to all other acts of aggression." Dollard also contended that (1) the strongest aggression is usually directed against the agent perceived to be the source of frustration, (2) the inhibition of acts of direct aggression is an additional frustration that instigates additional aggression, (3) inhibited aggression may be displaced to different objects and expressed in modified forms, (4) aggression turned against the self may occur when other forms of expression are strongly inhibited.

The frustration-aggression explanation of violence is frequently espoused by political liberals because it implies that violence is best avoided by eliminating barriers to the satisfaction of human needs and wants. In other words, liberals believe that violence can be reduced if human needs and wants are satisfied and aggression-producing frustration is reduced. In contrast, if it should turn out that aggressive behavior is innate, then no amount of need or want satisfaction would eliminate it. Only strong inhibiting forces would be able to cope effectively with innate aggressive instincts. This is frequently the view of political conservatives.

Aggressive instinct explanation

The research on the innate aggressive tendencies of organisms—humans as well as animals, fish, and birds—suggests that aggressive behavior may be deeply rooted in human genetic history. In his interesting book *On Aggression*, eminent zoologist Konrad Lorenz argues that aggressive behavior is rooted in the long human struggle for survival.[8] The human being is by nature an aggressive animal. The external stimulus that seems to produce aggressive behavior only "unlocks" inhibitory processes, thereby "releasing" instinctual aggressive drives. Aggressive behavior is not just a reaction to some external condition but an inner force or instinct that is let loose by the stimulus. "It is the spontaneity of the [aggressive] instinct that makes it so dangerous." Aggressive behavior "can explode without demonstrable external stimulation" merely because inner drives for aggression have not discharged through some previous behavior. Lorenz believes that "present day civilized man suffers from insufficient discharge of his aggressive drive." Civilization has inhibited people from expressing themselves aggressively; for the greatest part of human history, people released their aggressive drives in hunting, killing, and the struggle for survival. Now, however, these drives must be checked. The instincts that helped people to survive millions of years in a primitive environment today threaten their very existence. Lorenz believes that frustrations are, at best, an unimportant source of aggression. According to this formulation, an excellent way to prevent people from engaging in aggression is to provide them with "safe" ways of venting their aggressive urges. For example, competitive, body-contact sports provide "safe" outlets; even observing their activities, as in the case of televised professional football, affords some release of aggressive drives.

A number of experimental psychologists disagree with Lorenz's proposed remedy for aggression. Laboratory experiments have indicated that attacks upon supposedly safe targets do not lessen, and can even increase, the likelihood of later aggression. Angry people may perhaps feel better when they can attack a safe target, but their aggressive tendencies are not thereby necessarily reduced. For example, recent laboratory studies have demonstrated that giving children an opportunity to play aggressive games does not decrease the attacks they will later make upon another child, but in fact actually increases the strength of subsequent attacks.[9] These studies do not rule out the notion of innate determinants of aggression; indeed, there is today among social psychologists much greater recognition of the role of inherent determinants of human behavior. However, it is clear that other factors—such as fear of punishment or learning to respond in nonaggressive ways to frustrations—can prevent the human potential for violence from being realized.

Relative deprivation explanation
Another explanation of violence centers about the "relative deprivation" of individuals and groups. Relative deprivation is the discrepancy between people's expectations about the goods and conditions of life to which they feel justifiably entitled and what they perceive to be their chances of getting and keeping them. Relative deprivation is not merely a complicated way of saying that people are deprived and therefore angry because they have less than they want. Rather, it focuses on (1) what people think they deserve, not just what they want in an ideal sense, and (2) what they think they have a chance of getting, not just what they have. According to this theory, it is relative deprivation that creates aggression.

Contrary to the earlier frustration-aggression hypotheses, many psychologists now insist that deprivations alone are inadequate to account for most aggressive behavior. According to the newer theorizing, much greater weight must be given to the anticipations of satisfaction than to the duration or magnitude of deprivation itself. The *stimulation arising from anticipation* is held to be the major determinant of the vigor and persistence of the goal-seeking activity. Thus, deprivation alone does not bring about striving toward a goal; such striving is also a product of some *hope* that goals can be achieved. There is more frustration when one's hopes and expectations of success are thwarted than when one is simply deprived and without hope.

Relative deprivation is an expression of the distance between current status and levels of expectation. According to this explanation, neither the wholly downtrodden (who have no aspirations) nor the very well off (who can satisfy their aspirations) represent a threat to civil order; that threat arises from those whose expectations about what they deserve outdistance the capacity of society to satisfy them. Often rapid increases in expectations are the product of symbolic or token improvements in conditions. This situation leads to the apparent paradox of the eruption of violence and disorder precisely when conditions are getting better. Hope, not despair, generates civil violence and disorder. As Bowen and Masotti observe, "The reason why black Americans riot is because there has been just enough improvement in their condition to generate hopes, expectations, or aspirations beyond the capacity of the system to meet them."[10]

The politicial counterpart of this explanation of violence is frequently referred to as *the revolution of rising expectations.* Poverty-stricken people who have never dreamed of owning automobiles, television sets, or new homes are not frustrated merely because they have been deprived of these things; they are frustrated only after they have begun to hope that they can obtain them. Once they have come to believe that they can get them and have anticipated having them, the inability to fulfill their anticipations is a frustrating experience. The dashing of hopes is more likely to breed violence than privation itself. Political scientist James C. Davies has employed this type of reasoning in developing a theory of revolutions.[11] Revolutions do not arise because people are subjected to long severe hardships. Revolutions occur when there is a sudden, abrupt thwarting of hopes and expectations that had begun to develop during the course of gradually improving conditions. Thus, modernization in traditionally backward societies is associated with a great increase in political instability. Hope outstrips reality, and, even though conditions are improving in society as a whole, many people become frustrated.

VIOLENCE AS POLITICAL PROTEST

Violence can also be interpreted as a form of political protest. For example, the ghetto riots of the 1960s expressed the hostility many blacks felt toward white people in general and toward established authority. To be sure, this form of political protest is a criminal one. And it may be irrational and self-defeating. The majority of casualties in ghetto riots—the dead, the injured, and the arrested—were rioters themselves. Much of the property destroyed belonged to ghetto residents. Many businesses and other conveniences will never again venture into the ghetto. Moreover, the riots may have hardened the attitudes of whites toward blacks. Certainly violence itself cannot solve the complicated social problems facing the ghetto. Nonetheless, not all riots were "senseless" or without political purpose.

The view that ghetto riots were a form of political protest is supported by evidence indicating that a large percentage of the black population in the ghetto supported the riots. For example, a survey in Watts, California, after the 1964 riot determined that roughly one-fifth of blacks in that ghetto actually participated in the riot and more than one-half of the residents supported the activities of the rioters.[12] Interviewers found that 58 percent of the Watts residents felt that the long-run effect of the riot would be favorable; 84 percent said that whites were now more aware of black problems; 62 percent regarded the riot as a black protest. In the eyes of a large proportion of blacks, riots were a legitimate protest against white society, and this protest was expected to produce improvement in the condition of the blacks. Of those blacks who claimed that riots had a political purpose, each cited one or more of the following "purposes": (1) to call attention to black problems; (2) to express black hostility to whites; and (3) to serve as an instrument for improving conditions, ending discrimination, and communicating with the "power structure."[13]

Stokely Carmichael once remarked, "Violence is as American as apple pie." And the uncomfortable fact is that the most important social movements in American history *have* been accompanied by violence. Frequently, the American political system is moved by crises when it is not moved by anything else. The civil rights protest movement sought to create *nonviolent* crises that would impel the system to end discrimination. But many black militants argue that white America will not respond to black demands for full equality until whites feel their own physical well-being directly threatened. In commenting on the role of violence in the struggle for power, Masotti and others note:

Perhaps the black power advocates understand better than most whites that Americans have traditionally paid lip service to their notion of consensus when critical issues arose; that in fact when critical issues arise, they can no longer be solved in the normal political channels based on common understandings; that, indeed, the only common interest a challenging minority and an unresponsive majority have is violence, with the minority offering peace only when the majority makes the requisite concessions.[14]

Thus, in the struggle for power in America, blacks face an agonizing choice: whether to work within the established democratic processes to effect change or to resort to violence or threats of violence.

The vast majority of black Americans clearly reject violence. But violence in our society, and increasing rhetoric of violence, has brought about a gradual increase in the number of blacks who believe that "the blacks will probably have to resort to violence to win rights." Louis Harris reported that during a ten-year period the percentage of blacks who believed that was the case rose from 21 percent in the early 1960s to 31 percent in the early 1970s. The percentage of blacks asserting that violence is probably necessary was even higher among younger and urban blacks.[15]

"RIOTING MAINLY FOR FUN AND PROFIT"

Another explanation of violence centers about the social and cultural characteristics of lower-class city life. Political scientist Edward C. Banfield argues *against* the notion that urban riots are always a form of black political protest or a result of rage and frustration over racial discrimination. He contends that the causes of rioting are complex and deeply rooted in the culture of lower-class life. (In fact, the title of the present section is the title of chapter 9 in his *Unheavenly City*.) In his view there are four principal motives in riot behavior, each of which implies a corresponding type of riot:

> *The rampage.* This is an outbreak of animal—usually young, male animal—spirits. Young men are naturally restless, in search of excitement, thrills, "action." . . . The rampage begins not because the incident made the rampagers angry (although they may pretend that) but because they were looking for an excuse (signal?) to rampage. . . .
> *The foray for pillage.* Here the motive is theft, and here also boys and young adults of the lower class are the principal offenders. Stealing is ordinarily most conveniently done in private, of course, but when disasters—earthquakes, fires, floods, power failures, blizzards, enemy invasions, police strikes—interrupt law enforcement it may be done as well or better in public. . . .

The outburst of righteous indignation. Here the rioters are moved by indignation at what they regard, rightly or wrongly, as injustice or violation of the mores that is likely to go unpunished. . . .

The demonstration. Here the motive is to advance a political principle or ideology or to contribute to the maintenance of an organization. The riot is not a spontaneous, angry response to an incident. Rather, it is the result of the prearrangement by persons who are organized, have leaders, and who see it as a means to some end. The word "demonstration" is descriptive, for the event is a kind of show staged to influence opinion. Those who put it on are usually middle or upper class, these being the classes from which the people who run organizations and espouse political causes are mostly drawn.[16]

Professor Banfield contends that all of these motives may be operating in any particular disorder. Some individuals participate "for the fun of it," others to steal liquor and cigarettes and television sets, still others out of some momentary rage and a felt injustice, and a few (probably a tiny minority) for political purposes.

Banfield believes that television is an "accelerating cause" in riots and disorders. He contends that sensational television coverage of riots helps to recruit rampagers and pillagers. Moreover, television informs urban dwellers that they can throw a great city into turmoil by hurling rocks, smashing windows, and setting fires. Once the possibility of such action has been established, the probability of someone's taking it is very much increased. Thanks to television, the knowledge that riots are a possibility is widely disseminated. Finally, the probability of rioting is increased when spokespeople give legitimacy on television to rioting. The knowledge that "everybody is doing it" is transformed into the idea that "it can't be wrong." By explaining riots, commentators tend to justify them and hence to encourage them. Many civil rights leaders predicted that violence would occur if reforms were not implemented at a faster pace. The riots, of course, made these predictions much more credible. But as Martin Luther King, Jr., acknowledged, "A prediction of violence can sometimes be an invitation to it." Thus, explanations and predictions of disorder made rioting appear to be more natural, normal, and hence justifiable.

Professor Banfield believes that society must brace itself for a certain amount of violence:

It is naïve to think that efforts to end racial injustice and to eliminate poverty, slums, and unemployment will have an appreciable effect upon the amount of rioting that will be done in the next decade or two. . . . Boys and young men of the lower classes will not cease to "raise hell" once they have adequate job opportunities, housing, schools, and so on. Indeed, by the standards of any former time, they have these things now. . . . As for the upwardly mobile and politically minded Negro who has a potential for outbursts of righteous indignation and for demonstrations, even serious and successful efforts at reform are likely to leave him more rather than less angry. The faster and farther the Negro rises the more impatient he is likely to be with whatever he thinks prevents his rising still faster and still farther.[17]

CASE STUDY
The Ghetto Riots

Even though domestic violence has played a prominent role in America's history, the ghetto riots of the 1960s shocked the nation beyond measure. More than one hundred and fifty major riots were reported in American cities from 1965 to 1968. All these riots involved black attacks on established authority—on policemen, firemen, National Guardsmen, whites in general, and property owned by the whites. Three riots—Watts in 1965 and Newark, New Jersey, and Detroit in 1967—amounted to major civil disorder.

The Watts riot from 11 to 17 August 1965 was set off when a white motorcycle officer arrested a black youth for drunken driving in a black district of Los Angeles known as Watts. In the words of the McCone Commission's report on the Watts violence:

> In the ugliest interval . . . perhaps as many as 10,000 Negroes took to the streets in marauding bands. They looted stores, set fires, beat up white passers-by whom they had hauled from stopped cars, many of which were turned upside-down and burned, exchanged shots with law enforcement officers, and stoned and shot at firemen. The rioters seemed to have been caught up in an insensate rage of destruction. . . .
>
> Of the 34 killed, one was a fireman, one was a deputy sheriff, and one a Long Beach policeman. . . . [The remainder were blacks.][18]

The Newark riot was set off when police arrested a black cabdriver for reckless driving, driving without a license, and resisting arrest. Fellow black cabdrivers led a crowd to the police station in the overwhelmingly black central ward of Newark. Soon rocks and bottles were clattering against the station house walls. Tension mounted throughout the ghetto, some fires were set, some windows were broken, looting began, and when police and firemen arrived at the scenes of disturbances they were met with hostility and violence. Frequently police, untrained in riot control, responded in a heavy-handed and undisciplined fashion. Within twenty-four hours Newark was in the throes of a major civil disorder. For four consecutive days and nights, snipers fired at police and firemen, looters made off with the inventories of scores of stores, and arsonists set fire to large portions of commercial property in the black section of Newark. New Jersey's governor proclaimed Newark a city "in open rebellion," declared a state of emergency, and called out the National Guard. More than four thousand city policemen, state troopers, and National Guardsmen were required to restore order. Before the riot was over, twenty-three persons had been killed, and property damage was widespread. Of the dead, only two were white—a policeman and a fireman. Of the black dead, two were children and six were women.

In the violent summer of 1967, Detroit became the scene of the bloodiest racial violence of the twentieth century. A week of rioting in Detroit, from 23 to 28 July, left forty-three dead and more than one thousand injured. Of the forty-three persons killed during the riot, thirty-three were black and ten were white. Among the dead were one National Guardsmen, one fireman, one policeman, and one black private guard. Both the violence and the pathos of the ghetto riots were reflected in the following report from Detroit:

> A spirit of carefree nihilism was taking hold. To riot and destroy appeared more and more to become ends in themselves. Late Sunday afternoon it appeared to one observer that the young people were "dancing amidst the flames."
>
> A Negro plainclothes officer was standing in an intersection when a man threw a Molotov cocktail into a business establishment at the corner. In the heat of the afternoon, fanned by the 20 to 25 m.p.h. winds of both Sunday and Monday, the fire

reached the home next door within minutes. As its residents uselessly sprayed the flames with garden hoses, the fire jumped from roof to roof of adjacent two- and three-story buildings. Within the hour the entire block was in flames. The ninth house in the burning row belonged to the arsonist who had thrown the Molotov cocktail. . . .

. . . Employed as a private guard, 55-year-old Julius L. Dorsey, a Negro, was standing in front of a market when accosted by two Negro men and a woman. They demanded he permit them to loot the market. He ignored their demands. They began to berate him. He asked a neighbor to call the police. As the argument grew more heated, Dorsey fired three shots from his pistol in the air.

The police radio reported: "Looters, they have rifles." A patrol car driven by a police officer and carrying three National Guardsmen arrived. As the looters fled, the law enforcement personnel opened fire. When the firing ceased, one person lay dead.

He was Julius L. Dorsey. . . .[19]

In its official report, the National Advisory Commission on Civil Disorders cited "white racism" as one of the factors responsible for ghetto rioting. The commission enumerated "three of the most bitter fruits of white racial attitudes":

Pervasive discrimination and segregation. The first is surely the continuing exclusion of great numbers of Negroes from the benefits of economic progress through discrimination in employment and education, and their enforced confinement in segregated housing and schools. The corrosive and degrading effects of this condition and the attitudes that underlie it are the source of the deepest bitterness and at the center of the problem of racial disorder.

Black migration and white exodus. The second is the massive and growing concentration of impoverished Negroes in our major cities resulting from Negro migration from the rural South, rapid population growth and the continuing movement of the white middle-class to the suburbs. The consequence is a greatly increased burden on the already depleted resources of cities, creating a growing crisis of deteriorating facilities and services and unmet human needs.

Black ghettos. Third, in the teeming racial ghettos, segregation and poverty have intersected to destroy opportunity and hope and to enforce failure. The ghettos too often mean men and women without jobs, families without men, and schools where children are processed instead of educated, until they return to the street—to crime, to narcotics, to dependency on welfare—and to bitterness and resentment against society in general and white society in particular.[20]

However, the commission acknowledged that "these facts alone—fundamental as they are—cannot be said to have caused the disorders." The commission identified three "powerful ingredients" that had "begun to catalyze the mixture":

Frustrated hopes. The expectations aroused by the great judicial and legislative victories of the civil rights movement have led to frustration, hostility and cynicism in the face of the persistent gap between promise and fulfillment. The dramatic struggle for equal rights in the South has sensitized Northern Negroes to the economic inequalities reflected in the deprivations of ghetto life.

Legitimation of violence. A climate that tends toward the approval and encouragement of violence as a form of protest has been created by white terrorism directed against nonviolent protest, including instances of abuse and even murder of some civil rights workers in the South; by the open defiance of law and federal authority by state and local officials resisting desegregation; and by some protest groups engaging in civil disobedience who turn their backs on nonviolence, go beyond the constitutionally protected rights of petition and free assembly, and resort to violence to attempt to compel alteration of laws and policies with which they disagree. This condition has been reinforced by a general erosion of respect for authority in American society and reduced effectiveness of social standards and community restraints on violence and crime. This in turn has largely resulted from rapid urbanization and the dramatic reduction in the average age of the total population.

Powerlessness. Finally, many Negroes have come to believe that they are being exploited politically and economically by the white "power structure." Negroes, like people in poverty everywhere, in fact lack the channels of communication, influence and appeal that traditionally have been available to ethnic minorities within the city and which enabled them—unburdened by color—to scale the walls of the white ghettos in an earlier era. The frustrations of powerlessness have led some to the conviction that there is no effective alternative to violence as a means of expression and redress, as a way of "moving the system." More generally, the result is alienation and hostility toward the institutions of law and government and the white society which controls them. This is reflected in the reach toward racial consciousness and solidarity reflected in the slogan "Black Power."[21]

The commission warned that "our nation is moving toward two societies, one black, one white—separate and unequal." The principal "blame" for the riots was placed upon whites rather than blacks: "What White Americans have never fully understood—but what the Negro can never forget—is that white society is deeply implicated in the ghetto. White institutions created it, white institutions maintain it, and white society condones it."[22] The commission recommended massive federal aid programs in employment, education, welfare, and housing, but it suggested no new departures from traditional programs in these areas.

NOTES

1. Chief Justice Warren E. Burger, address on the State of the Federal Judiciary to the American Bar Association, 10 August 1970.
2. Ibid.
3. Ibid.
4. Alaska, Hawaii, Iowa, Maine, Michigan, Minnesota, New Hampshire, New Mexico, New York, North Dakota, Oregon, Rhode Island, Vermont, West Virginia, and Wisconsin (although in Michigan, New York, North Dakota, Rhode Island, and Vermont there were provisions for certain exceptions—for example, killing a prison guard).
5. James Q. Wilson, *Varieties of Police Behavior* (Cambridge, Mass.: Harvard University Press, 1968), p. 18; Arthur Niederhoffer, *Behind the Shield* (New York: Doubleday, 1967), p. 71.
6. Niederhoffer, *Behind the Shield,* p. 43.
7. John Dollard et al., *Frustration and Aggression* (New Haven, Conn.: Yale University Press, 1939), p. 1.
8. Konrad Lorenz, *On Aggression* (New York: Harcourt Brace Jovanovich, 1966).
9. For an excellent review of the implications of laboratory studies on frustration and aggression, see Leonard Buckewitz, "The Study of

Urban Violence," in Louis H. Masotti and Don R. Bowen, eds., *Riots and Rebellion* (Beverly Hills, Calif.: Sage, 1968).

10. Don R. Bowen and Louis H. Masotti, "Civil Violence: A Theoretical Overview," in Masotti and Bowen, eds., *Riots and Rebellion*, pp. 24–25.

11. James C. Davies, "Toward a Theory of Revolution," *American Sociological Review* 27 (1962):5–19.

12. President's Commission on Law Enforcement and Administration of Justice, *Crime and Its Impact—An Assessment* (Washington, D.C.: Government Printing Office, 1967), p. 116.

13. William McCord and John Howard, "Negro Opinions in Three Riot Cities," in Masotti and Bowen, eds., *Riots and Rebellion.*

14. Louis H. Masotti et al., *A Time to Burn?* (Chicago: Rand McNally, 1969), p. 162.

15. *Time*, 6 April 1970, p. 29.

16. Edward C. Banfield, *The Unheavenly City* (Boston: Little, Brown, 1970), pp. 187–91.

17. Ibid., pp. 205–06.

18. Governor's Commission on the Los Angeles Riots, *Violence in the City—An End or a Beginning?* (Sacramento: Office of the Governor, State of California, 1965), pp. 3–5. The commission was headed by John A. McCone, former director of the Central Intelligence Agency.

19. National Advisory Commission on Civil Disorders, *Report* (Washington, D.C.: Government Printing Office, 1968), p. 4.

20. Ibid., pp. 203–04.

21. Ibid., pp. 204–05.

22. Ibid., p. 2.

DISCUSSION QUESTIONS

1. Discuss the "classic dilemma" of a free government and Thomas Hobbes's ideas regarding the need for a powerful state.

2. Discuss crime rates. How are they used, how are they determined, and what factors contribute to their inaccuracy? What is their current trend?

3. Suppose you have just been arrested by the police. Describe how the following constitutional rights of defendants would be of use to you: guarantee of the writ of habeas corpus; prohibition of bills of attainder and of ex post facto laws; prohibition of "unreasonable" searches and seizures; freedom from self-incrimination; the right to counsel; guarantee of a fair jury trial; protection against double jeopardy; protection against excessive bail.

4. Choose two of the following cases that were decided by the Warren Court

and discuss how each of them strengthened the rights of accused persons in criminal cases: *Mapp* v. *Ohio* (1961); *Gideon* v. *Wainwright* (1963); *Escobedo* v. *Illinois* (1964); *Miranda* v. *Arizona* (1966).

5. Discuss the judicial stumbling blocks to law enforcement that Chief Justice Warren E. Burger outlined in his State of the Federal Judiciary message. What are some of the difficulties that the *police* may encounter in their law enforcement function?

6. Discuss the arguments for and against capital punishment. Describe the 1972 Court decision regarding the constitutionality of capital punishment and the changes in state laws that followed it. Discuss the reasoning of the justices in the 1976 Court decision on capital punishment.

7. Discuss the history of violence in America. Using at least three specific eras or social movements as examples, describe the type of violence that was used and the kind of social change that was its goal.

8. Discuss two of the following social-psychological explanations of violence: the frustration-aggression explanation; the aggressive instinct explanation; the relative deprivation explanation.

9. Contrast the interpretation of violence as a form of political protest with Edward Banfield's "fun" or "profit" explanation of violence.

10. Discuss the conclusions and findings of the National Advisory Commission on Civil Disorders regarding the ghetto riots of 1965–1968. Was "white racism" responsible for ghetto rioting? What other factors may have acted as catalysts in the rioting?

SUGGESTED READINGS

Don R. Bowen and Louis H. Masotti, eds., *Riots and Rebellion* (Beverly Hills, Calif.: Sage, 1968).

James C. Davies, ed., *When Men Revolt and Why* (New York: Free Press, 1971).

John Dollard et al., *Frustration and Aggression* (New Haven, Conn.: Yale University Press, 1939).

Hugh Davis Graham and Ted Robert Gurr, *Violence in America*, A Report Submitted to the National Commission on the Causes and Prevention of Violence (New York: Bantam Books, 1969).

Konrad Lorenz, *On Aggression* (New York: Harcourt Brace Jovanovich, 1966).

National Advisory Commission on Civil Disorders, *Report* (Washington, D.C.: Government Printing Office, 1968).

Arthur H. Niederhoffer, *Behind the Shield* (New York: Doubleday, 1967).

President's Commission on Law Enforcement and Administration of Justice,

Crime and Its Impact—An Assessment (Washington, D.C.: Government Printing Office, 1967).

James Q. Wilson, *Varieties of Police Behavior* (Cambridge, Mass.: Harvard University Press, 1968).

Photo from Stock, Boston by W. B. Finch

Division Of
Accounts & Control

Photo by Marshall Henrichs

Chapter 13
Power and the Quality of Life

Ever since we emerged from the caves, we have looked to the power of government to keep ourselves from clubbing each other to death. It was not, however, until the twentieth century that we had to look to the power of government to keep us from depleting the world of its resources and from polluting or overcrowding ourselves out of existence. But the United States government is a democracy, which Plato once described as "a charming form of government, full of variety and disorder." It is a human institution run by different human beings who promote the different policies they think best and, in a peculiarly democratic way, contribute to a great deal of "variety and disorder." The results are both good and bad. We have made some progress in dealing with environmental pollution, but we lack a coordinated policy for dealing with the problem of dwindling sources of energy. The centers of many of our cities are monuments to how poor the quality of life in an affluent democratic society can be; and the quality of inner-city life is made poorer still by the "white flight" to the suburbs.

In this chapter we will examine some of the problems that affect the quality of our lives and the efforts of government to do something about them. After you have read it, you should be able to:

- discuss the sources and major types of environmental pollution, their impact on health and the environment, and the preventive measures that government has instituted.
- discuss the causes of the energy crisis, the solutions proposed by industry, environmentalists, and government, and the conflict that exists between the government agencies that deal with energy and those that deal with pollution.
- discuss the growth of the metropolis and its effect on pollution, and describe the patterns of urban life.
- discuss the differences between life in the inner city and life in the suburbs and the effect on the inner city of the exodus to the suburbs.

POLLUTION AND THE ENVIRONMENT

Ecology is the study of humanity's relationship with its environment. The ability of humanity to insure its own survival has become a central theme of life as we approach the twenty-first century. It is not only the threat of nuclear war or worldwide famine that confronts the world's population. Humanity could suffocate in its own waste material long before war or famine strikes. Or it could deplete the world's nonrenewable resources. Subsistence is not enough; the question is *how* we want to live—the quality of our life. The immediate environmental problems in America center about the pollution of the environment and the use of natural resources.

Sources

Air Pollution   The air we breathe is about one-fifth oxygen and a little less than four-fifths nitrogen, with traces of other gases, water vapor, and the waste products we spew into it. Most air pollution is caused by gasoline-powered internal combustion engines—cars, trucks, and buses. Motor vehicles send about 90 million tons of contaminants into the atmosphere every year—about 60 percent of the total polluting material (see table 13-1). Industries and government facilities contribute another 60 million tons. The largest industrial polluters are petroleum refineries, smelters (aluminum, copper, lead, and zinc), and iron foundries. Electrical power plants are another major source of air pollution; 95 percent of the nation's electrical power is produced by burning coal or oil. The demand for electrical power has doubled every decade since 1940, and it is expected that Americans will triple their use of electricity in the next two decades.

Table 13-1   Pollution and Its Sources: Annual Emissions of Five Major Air Pollutants and Percentage of Total Emissions by Type

Type of Emission	Automobile	Major Industries	Electrical Power	Space Heating	Refuse Disposal
Carbon monoxide	92%	3%	1%	3%	1%
Hydrocarbons	64	21	5	5	5
Nitrogen oxides	46	15	23	8	8
Sulfur oxides	4	35	46	11	4
Particulates	9	50	25	8	8
Total	60%	16%	14%	6%	4%

Source: Congressional Quarterly, *Man's Control of the Environment* (Washington, D.C.: Congressional Quarterly, 1970).

Heating is also a major source of pollution; homes, apartments, and offices use coal, gas, and oil for heat. Another source of pollution is the incineration of garbage, trash, metal, glass, and other refuse, by both governments and industries.

Air pollutants fall into two major types, particles and gases. The particles include ashes, soot, and lead, which is the unburnable additive in gasoline. Often the brilliant red sunsets we admire are caused by large particles in the air. Less obvious but more damaging are the gases: (1) sulfur dioxide, which in combination with moisture can form sulfuric acid; (2) hydrocarbons—any combination of hydrogen and carbon; (3) nitrogen oxide, which can combine with hydrocarbons in the sun's ultraviolet rays to form smog; and (4) carbon monoxide, which is produced when gasoline is burned.

Impact on health   It is difficult to assess the full impact of air pollution on health. We know that when the smog or pollution count rises in a particular city, there are more deaths than would normally have been expected. Carbon monoxide is toxic and has been measured at toxic levels in the streets of certain cities at certain hours of heavy traffic. Carbon monoxide is tasteless, colorless, and odorless, but it can deprive the body of oxygen; persons exposed to relatively low levels of this gas exhibit drowsiness, headache, poor vision, impaired coordination, and reduced capacity to reason. One polluting hydrocarbon, benzo-a-pyrene, has been implicated as a possible cause of cancer; it is present in cigarette smoke, but even nonsmokers in a highly polluted area inhale as much benzo-a-pyrene daily as they would from smoking. Nitrogen oxide irritates the eyes, nose, throat, and respiratory system; it damages plants, buildings, and statues. Smog is particularly dangerous to victims of emphysema. Emphysema is a pollution-related disease in which the lungs lose their capacity to function normally; it is currently the fastest growing cause of death in the United States. Finally, urban residents have been found to be twice as likely to contract lung cancer as rural residents.

Prevention   What is being done? In a series of Clean Air acts passed over the last decade, the federal government has gradually raised the standards for clean air, tightened enforcement procedures, and increased penalties for violators. The Environmental Protection Agency (EPA) sets standards for emission control for industries and governments. More importantly, the Environmental Protection Agency enforces provisions of the Clean Air acts controlling automobile emissions. The 1975 federal standards for automobile emissions required major technological innovations that the automobile industry had to install on cars. The laws are also forcing other industries to search for non-polluting methods of burning fuel.

Sources and treatments

Water Pollution   Debris and sludge, organic wastes, and chemical effluents are the three major sources of water pollutants. *Primary* sewage treatment—screens and settling chambers where filth falls out of the water as sludge—is fairly common. *Secondary* sewage treatment is designed to remove organic wastes, usually by trickling water through a bed of rocks three to ten feet deep, where bacteria consume the organic matter. Remaining germs are killed by chlorination. *Tertiary* sewage treatment uses mechanical and chemical filtration processes to remove almost all contaminants from water. The present federal goals of the program for abatement of water pollution call for the establishment of secondary treatment in 90 percent of American communities. In most industrial plants, tertiary treatment ultimately will be required to deal with the flow of chemical pollutants. But tertiary treatment is expensive; it costs two or three times as much to build and operate a tertiary sewage treatment plant as it does a secondary plant. Even today, however, one-third of all Americans live in communities where their sewage gets nothing but primary treatment. Municipalities are frequently unwilling to pay the high costs of secondary and tertiary sewage treatment.

Prevention

The Environmental Protection Agency is responsible for enforcing a series of federal Water Quality acts. In 1972 the federal government banned production of detergents containing phosphates in an attempt to reduce the mountains of soap bubbles in the nation's waterways. Phosphates are major water pollutants that overstimulate plant life in water, which in turn kills fish. Paper manufacturing is another major industrial polluter.

Environmental impact

Waterfronts and seashores are natural resources that Americans can no longer take for granted. The growing numbers of waterfront homes, amusement centers, marinas, and pleasure boats, together with the frequent occurrence of offshore oil spills, are threatening to alter the environment of the nation's coastal areas. Marshes and estuaries at the water's edge are essential to the production of seafood and shellfish, yet they are steadily shrinking with the growth of residential-commercial-industrial development. Oil spills are unsightly and they kill fish and birds whose bodies and gills become coated. Coastal pollution is much greater in Europe than in America, but America's coastal areas still require protection. The Water Quality acts make petroleum companies liable for the cleanup cost of oil spills, outlaw flushing of raw sewage from boat toilets, restrict thermal pollution, and set general water quality standards for all the states. In addition, the federal government has purchased certain coastal areas to preserve the coastal wilderness.

Sources and environmental impact

Solid Waste Disposal Only a very wealthy country could afford to be as wasteful as the United States. Every American discards between six and eight pounds of solid waste per day! This per capita waste production is expected to double in weight in the next twenty years. The annual load of waste dumped on the environment includes 48 billion cans, 26 billion bottles and jars, 4 million tons of plastic, 8 million television sets, 7 million automobiles and trucks, and 30 million tons of paper. Already the nation spends billions of dollars annually on hauling all of this away from homes and businesses. The problem is where to put it. Burning creates air pollution. Open dumps are eyesores and create health hazards. The Environmental Protection Agency urges cities to rely on sanitary landfills where the waste is spread in thin layers over specific land areas and covered at least once a day with a layer of earth. But many cities are running out of landfill sites.

Methods of disposal

Solving the problem of solid waste disposal requires that we find better methods of disposal, ways to reduce the amount discarded, or ways to recycle wastes. Recycling could decrease the volume of solid wastes that must be disposed and at the same time reduce the amount of virgin materials taken from the earth. Yet recycling is hampered by the difficulties of separating reusable materials from other refuse. It is frequently cheaper to use virgin materials than it is to separate refuse and recycle it.

THE ENERGY CRISIS

The energy crisis is real; it is not mere speculation about possible future disasters. Gasoline shortages and power blackouts are now facts of life. Americans guzzle a third of the world's energy production, and our appetite is growing; energy demand will more than double by the year 2000. But dwindling domestic supplies of oil and gas, unstable and costly reliance on foreign oil, and lagging development of new electric power plants threaten to curtail growth in energy production in America.

The energy crisis has several causes:

Causes

1. Skyrocketing demand for energy, and styles of life (electric appliances, air conditioning, etc.) that use increasing amounts of energy (see figure 13–1).
2. Leveling off of output of domestic fuels—particularly oil and gas—and a decline in coal production.

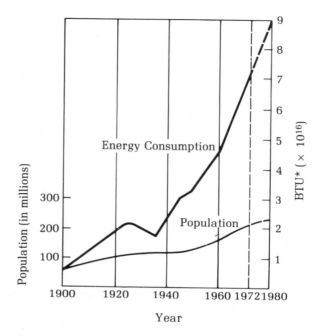

Figure 13–1 U.S. Population Growth and Energy Consumption (1900–1980)

*BTU (British thermal unit): the quantity of heat required to raise the temperature of one pound of water one degree Fahrenheit.

Source: Congressional Quarterly, *Man's Control of the Environment*, (Washington, D.C.: Congressional Quarterly, 1970).

3. Government regulation of the price of electricity and natural gas making it more difficult for power companies to acquire the capital to construct new plants.

4. Attacks by environmentalists forcing cutbacks in the use of polluting fuels and holding up development of new power plants, particularly nuclear power plants.

5. The formation of a cartel of petroleum-exporting countries (OPEC), which forced steep increases in the price of oil and threatened oil embargoes against nations that opposed the political aims of OPEC countries.

Petroleum products supply 44 percent of the nation's energy needs; natural gas, 32 percent; coal, 18 percent; and nuclear power and hydropower together, only about 5 percent (see figure 13–2). Most of America's oil that was relatively easy to find has already been discovered and used. Oil producers must now drill deeper and costlier

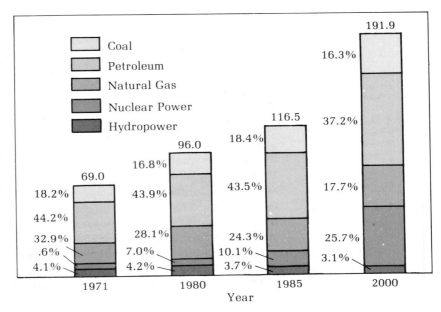

Figure 13–2 Estimated U.S. Power Consumption by Source (Quadrillion BTUs)

Source: U.S. Department of Interior, "United States Energy through the Year 2000."

wells in their search for oil. Currently the United States imports 40 percent of its oil, but dependency on foreign sources is rising. We may soon be importing 50 to 65 percent. This reliance on foreign sources—particularly Middle Eastern Arab nations—raises fears of "political blackmail." Moreover, the cost of gasoline must certainly rise as the United States increases its dependency on imported, rather than domestic, oil.

Government regulation of the rates charged for gas and electricity has hampered investment in new drilling and new plant construction. Natural gas is clean burning and popular for heating houses and buildings; factories also consume gas. For decades gas was very cheap in relation to other fuels because the Federal Power Commission held down prices. This encouraged waste, and drilling declined as investors sought more profitable ventures. *State* governments, rather than the federal government, regulate rates charged for electrical power. Power companies claim that continued delays and cutbacks in rate increases by states make it difficult to attract investment capital to expand capacity, particularly when demand is growing so rapidly.

Electrical power plants that burn coal or oil are major sources of pollution (see table 13–1). Environmentalists actively oppose the construction of new power plants, and their legal efforts have brought new plant construction to a standstill in many parts of the country. According to a leader of the influential environmentalist lobby, the Sierra Club, "Our strategy is to sue and sue and sue."

Environmental concerns

Nuclear power plants offer a new means of generating electricity. Nuclear power does not diminish the world's supply of oil, coal, and gas, which will someday run out. A "fast breeder" reactor can create as much fissionable material as it uses to generate heat, thus solving the problem of the uranium supply. However, nuclear plants use water for cooling and send the water back into streams at a higher temperature. The result is "thermal pollution," which increases algae and chokes off fish life. Environmentalists also object to radioactive waste materials from nuclear reactors being buried in the ground. In addition, they are concerned that overheating accidents could have dire, perhaps lethal, effects. Nevertheless, the result of objections by environmentalists has been to slow the nation's conversion to this future source of energy.

Coal is the nation's most abundant fuel. But the mining of coal scars the land and the burning of coal pollutes the air. Despite the demand for energy, coal production has declined, owing in part to pressures from environmentalists. The Clean Air acts have forced many electrical plants to switch from coal to oil in order to meet air pollution standards. So far, the "gasification" of coal—its conversion to clean-burning gas before use—is too costly to be feasible.

Lack of a coordinated energy policy

Perhaps the overriding problem is that the United States has no coordinated national energy policy. Industry, labor, environmentalists, and Congress and other governmental agencies have failed to agree on such questions as: whether to rely primarily on energy conservation or stimulate the search for new energy sources; whether to speed up the development of nuclear energy or continue to use fossil fuels; whether or not to "trade off" clean air standards in order to ensure adequate energy supplies; whether to proceed slowly or quickly in developing new oil, gas, and coal reserves in the interests of independence from foreign powers; whether to reduce energy consumption by relying on voluntary conservation, allowing fuel prices to rise, and adding new taxes to fuel, or by imposing governmental allocations and rationing.

THE REGULATORY QUAGMIRE

Competing interests

Within the federal bureaucracy, various agencies appear to

"We've taken care of the checks and balances."

represent competing interest groups. The Environmental Protection Agency and the Council on Environmental Quality (CEQ) both owe their existence to increased concern with the environment, and both therefore reflect the views of environmental groups. On the other hand, the new Department of Energy has several component parts with other goals in mind: the Federal Power Commission is concerned with maintaining the nation's supply of gas and electric power, and the Federal Energy Administration is charged with the responsibility of developing new sources of energy as well as a coordinated energy policy. The EPA and CEQ frequently come in conflict with these other executive agencies. Who wins often depends upon the strength of various interests, the stand of the news media and their impact on public opinion, and the access of various agencies and interest groups to the White House.

The EPA   The Environmental Protection Agency was created by executive order in 1970 to bring together a number of separate agencies in different departments charged with enforcing environmental regulations. The EPA director reports to the president. The EPA administers and enforces federal programs and laws regarding water quality control, clean air control, solid waste disposal, pesticide control, toxic substance control, noise abatement, and even radiation control. Many of the laws that it enforces grant much discretion to the EPA itself. The EPA has been obliged to make some difficult decisions—for example, granting the auto industry more time to meet emission standards; banning DDT; banning mirex, which had been used to fight fire ants; and publishing automobile gasoline mileage reports. The EPA also distributes grants to state and local governments and conducts research on the possible harmful effects of various products.

The CEQ   The Council on Environmental Quality also plays a key role in environmental policy making. The CEQ was established by Congress in the National Environmental Policy Act of 1969. The CEQ has no direct enforcement powers; instead it "advises" the president on environmental questions. For example, the CEQ advised the president against the Cross-Florida Barge Channel (a project that was already under construction to minimize shipping time between the East coast and the Gulf coast), and the president ordered the Corps of Engineers to cease its construction. However, the CEQ's real power derives from a provision in the National Environmental Policy Act of 1969 that all federal agencies must submit statements to the CEQ on the impact of any action that affects the environment. These "environmental impact statements" require federal agencies, as well as state, local, and private organizations receiving federal monies, to file lengthy reports on "environmental impacts." If the CEQ wants to delay or obstruct a project, it can ask for endless revisions, changes, additions, and so forth, in the environmental impact statement. The CEQ cannot by itself halt a project, but it can conduct public hearings for the press, pressure other governmental agencies, and make recommendations to the president. The courts have ruled that the requirement for an environmental impact statement is judicially enforceable.

The Department of Energy   On the other hand, the new Department of Energy was created by the Carter administration to help resolve the energy crisis not only by encouraging conservation of energy (which environmentalists support), but also by encouraging new oil and gas exploration, switching many plants from oil to coal, increasing coal supplies, and moving faster to develop safe nuclear energy (all of which environmentalists generally oppose).

THE GROWTH OF THE METROPOLIS

In worldwide perspective, the environment is still relatively free of pollution. Most pollutants of the air and water are removed by natural processes, as long as there is time and room for dispersal and settling. But no one really knows what the limits of environmental pollution are. Actually, most of the nation's pollution problems do *not*

Pollution and population density   arise from the *total* numbers of people in America or even the *total* amount of pollution produced, but rather from excessive concentration of people and pollution in the metropolitan areas of the United

States. The quality of life is determined primarily by how our population has chosen to distribute itself (density) rather than by its size.

Two out of three Americans live in population clusters called metropolitan areas. Most of the nation's population increase is occurring in these metropolitan areas—the increase in metropolitan area population from 1960 to 1970 was 24.4 million, in contrast to a 1.1 million *decline* in the rest of the United States (see table 13–2). Moreover, most of this increase is taking place *outside* of the core cities—in the nation's booming suburbs. The suburban population grew by an amazing 36 percent in a single decade, while the core cities grew by only 8.4 percent. Today more Americans are suburbanites than either city or rural residents. (See table J in the appendix for an overview of how urbanites, suburbanites, and rural residents evaluate life in the United States.)

Metropolitan area   What is a metropolitan area? Briefly, it consists of a central city of 50,000 or more persons together with the surrounding suburbs, which are socially and economically tied to the central city. The Census Bureau calls a metropolitan area a "Standard Metropolitan Statistical Area" (SMSA) and defines it as a city of 50,000 or more persons together with adjacent counties that have predominantly urban in-

Table 13–2 Population Growth in Cities and Suburbs of Metropolitan Areas in the United States

	Total U.S. Population	Metropolitan Areas			Outside Metropolitan Areas
		Total	Central Cities	Suburbs	
1970					
Population (thousands)	203,185	136,330	62,193	74,137	66,855
% of U.S. total	100.0	67.1	30.6	36.5	32.9
1960					
Population (thousands)	179,993	111,886	57,360	54,526	68,107
% of U.S. total	100.0	62.3	31.9	30.3	37.7
% increase	12.9	21.8	8.4	36.0	−1.9

Source: U.S. Bureau of the Census, *1970 Census of Population*, PC (P3)–3 (Washington, D.C.: Government Printing Office, 1971).

dustrial populations with close ties to the central city (see figure 13–3) on page 396.

The growth of the suburbs   In the last decade nearly 20 million Americans moved to the suburbs. No other sector of American life has grown so rapidly. Very few large *central cities* are growing in size; metropolitan areas are growing because their *suburbs* are growing. Suburbanization is due to technological advances in transportation—the automobile and the expressway. In the nineteenth century industrial workers had to live within walking distance of their places of employment. Hence, the nineteenth-century American city crowded large masses of people into relatively small central areas, often in tenement houses and other high-density neighborhoods. But new modes of transportation— first the streetcar, then the private automobile, and finally the expressway—eliminated the necessity for workers to live close to their jobs. Now one can spend one's working hours in a central business district office or industrial plant and pass one's evenings in a residential suburb miles away. The same technology that led to the suburbanization of residences has also influenced commercial and industrial location. Originally industry was tied to waterways or railroads for access to supplies and markets. This dependence has been reduced by the development of motor truck transportation, the highway system, and the greater mobility of the labor force. Now many industries can locate in the suburbs, particularly light industries, which do not require extremely heavy bulk shipment that can be handled only by rail or water. When industry and people move to the suburbs, commerce follows. Giant suburban shopping centers have sprung up to compete with downtown stores. Thus, metropolitan areas are becoming decentralized as people, business, and industry spread over the suburban landscape.

SOCIAL PATTERNS OF URBAN LIFE

Sociological theory of urbanism   What is the impact of urbanism on the way people interact? To deal with this question, sociologists first had to formulate a sociological definition of urbanism—one that would identify those characteristics most affecting social life. Sociologist Louis Wirth provided a classic definition of urbanism more than three decades ago: "For sociological purposes a city may be defined as a relatively large, dense, and permanent settlement of socially heterogeneous individuals." Thus, according to Wirth, the distinguishing characteristics of urban life were *number*, *density*, and *heterogeneity*—large numbers of people living closely together who are different from one another.

Large numbers of people involve a great range of individual

variation. The modern economic system of the metropolis is based upon a highly specialized and complex division of labor. We are told that in the simple farm community a dozen occupations exhausted the job opportunities available to people. In an agricultural economy nearly everyone was a farmer or was closely connected to or dependent upon farming. But in the modern metropolis there are tens of thousands of different kinds of jobs. An industrial economy means highly specialized jobs; hence the heterogeneity of urban populations. Different jobs result in different levels of income, dress, and styles of living. People's jobs shape the way they look at the world and their evaluations of social and political events. In acquiring a job, one attains a certain level and type of education that also distinguishes one from those in other jobs with other educational requirements. Differences in educational level in turn produce a wide variety of differences in opinions, attitudes, and styles of living. Urban life concentrates people with all these different ecconomic and occupational characteristics in a very few square miles.

Ethnic and racial diversities are also present. A few decades ago opportunities for human betterment in the cities attracted immigrants from Ireland, Germany, Italy, Poland, and Russia; today the city attracts blacks, Puerto Ricans, and rural families. These newcomers bring with them different needs, attitudes, and ways of life. The "melting pot" tends to reduce some of the diversity over time, but the pot does not melt people immediately, and there always seem to be new arrivals.

Urban dwellers also differ in where they live and in how they live. There is a certain uniformity to rural life; day-to-day family life on the farm is remarkably similar from one rural place to the next. But urban dwellers may live in apartments in the central city or in single-family homes in the suburbs. Some urban dwellers choose a *familistic* style of life—raising two or more children in their own single-family house, with the wife functioning as a homemaker. Others are less familistic—raising no children or a single child in a rented apartment with the wife holding down a job outside the home.

Increasing the numbers of people in a community limits the possibility that each member of the community will know everyone else personally. Multiplying the number of persons with whom an individual comes into contact makes it impossible for that individual to know everyone very well. The result is a "segmentalization of human relationships," in which an individual comes to know *many* people but only in highly *segmental, partial* roles. According to Wirth, "The contacts of the city may indeed be face to face, but they are nevertheless impersonal, superficial, transitory, and segmental. The reserve, the indifference, and the blasé outlook which urbanites manifest in their

Figure 13-3 Standard Metropolitan Statistical Areas
Source: U.S. Bureau of the Census.

Duluth-Superior

Minneapolis-St. Paul

Rochester

La Crosse

Appleton-Oshkosh

Green Bay

Bay City

Madison

Milwaukee

Muskegon-Muskegon Heights

Lansing-East Lansing

Saginaw

Sioux City

Waterloo

Dubuque

Kenosha

Grand Rapids

Battle Creek

Kalamazoo

Flint

Buffalo

Rochester

Elmira

Binghamton

Lewiston-Auburn

Portland

Utica-Rome

Albany Schenectady-Troy

Manchester

Nashua

Lawrence-Haverhill

Boston

Brockton

New Bedford

Pittsfield

Syracuse

Poughkeepsie 4

Omaha

Des Moines

Cedar Rapids

Rockford

Gary Hammond-East Chicago

Jackson

Ann Arbor

South Bend

Lorain-Elyria

Cleveland

Erie

Youngstown-Warren

Wilkes-Barre-Hazleton

Scranton

Williamsport

Fall River

Providence-Warwick-Pawtucket

Norwich-Groton-New London

Meriden

New Haven

Bridgeport

Davenport Rock Island Moline

St. Joseph

Chicago

Peoria

Bloomington-Normal

Decatur

Lafayette West Lafayette

Fort Wayne

Anderson

Muncie

Mansfield

Lima

Dayton

Akron Canton

Steubenville-Weirton

Pittsburg

Altoona

Harrisburg

Johnstown

Norwalk

Stamford

New York

Jersey City

Long Branch-Asbury Park

Philadelphia

Atlantic City

Vineland-Millville-Bridgeton

Wilmington

Topeka

Kansas City

Columbia

St. Louis

Springfield

Terre Haute

Champaign-Urbana

Indianapolis Hamilton Middletown

Springfield

Cincinnati

Columbus

Wheeling

York

Baltimore

Washington

Richmond

Springfield

Evansville

Louisville

Lexington

Owensboro

Huntington-Ashland

Charleston

Parkersburg-Marietta

Lynchburg

Roanoke

Petersburg

Colonial Heights-Hopewell

Durham

Newport News-Hampton

Norfolk-Virginia Beach-Portsmouth

Nashville-Davidson

Knoxville

Winston-Salem-High Point

Greensboro-High Point

Raleigh

Fort Smith

Chatanooga

Asheville

Gastonia

Charlotte

Fayetteville

Little Rock-North Little Rock

Memphis

Huntsville

Greenville

Spartanburg

Columbia

Wilmington

Pine Bluff

Florence

Gadsden

Atlanta

Charleston

Birmingham

Augusta

Texarkana

Tyler

Shreveport

Jackson

Tuscaloosa

Macon

Savannah

Monroe

Montgomery

Columbus

Alexandria

Bryan-College Station

Lake Charles

Baton Rouge

Lafayette

Biloxi-Gulfport

Mobile

Pensacola

Jacksonville

Albany

Tallahassee

aston

Beaumont-Port Arthur-Orange

Galveston-Texas City

New Orleans

Gainesville

Daytona Beach

Orlando

Melbourne-Titusville-Cocoa

Tampa-St. Petersburg

Lakeland-Winter Haven

West Palm Beach

Sarasota

Fort Lauderdale-Hollywood

Fort Myers

Miami

0   100   200   300   400   500 Miles

Albers Equal-Area Projection

1 Lowell, Mass.
2 Fitchburg-Leominster, Mass.
3 Worcester, Mass.
4 Springfield-Chicopee-Holyoke, Mass.-Conn.
5 Hartford, Conn.
6 New Britain, Conn.
7 Bristol, Conn.
8 Waterbury, Conn.
9 Danbury, Conn.
10 Paterson-Clifton-Passaic, N.J.
11 Newark, N.J.
12 Allentown-Bethlehem-Easton, Pa.-N.J.
13 Trenton, N.J.
14 New Brunswick-Perth Amboy-Sayreville, N.J.
15 Reading, Pa.
16 Lancaster, Pa.

San Juan

Mayaguez

Ponce

Caguas

0   50   100   150

Scale in Miles

relationship may thus be regarded as devices for immunizing themselves against the personal claims and expectations of others."[1] Moreover, urban dwellers frequently interact with others by utilizing them as means to an end, thus giving a *utilitarian* quality to interpersonal relations.

Large numbers mean a certain degree of freedom for the individual from the control of family groups, neighbors, churches, and other community groups. But urbanism also contributes to a sense of *anomie*—a sense of social isolation and a loss of the personal recognition, self-worth, and feeling of participation that comes with living in a small integrated society. The social contacts of urban dwellers are more anonymous than those of rural dwellers; they interact with persons who have little if any knowledge of their life histories.

Rural life emphasized *primary group* ties—interactions within the extended family. Early sociological theory believed that urban life emphasized *secondary group* ties—interactions between members of age and interest groups rather than between families and neighbors. Family life was set to center around voluntary associations and secondary group memberships—crowds, recreation groups, civic clubs, business groups, and professional and work groups. Sociologists believe that urban dwellers have a greater number of interpersonal contacts than rural dwellers and that the people with whom urban dwellers are more likely to interact are the occupants of specific social roles. In contrast, rural dwellers are more likely to interact with individuals as full personalities.

Urban society also presents problems of social control. The anomie of urban life is believed to weaken social mores and social group controls. External controls through a series of formal institutions, such as laws, and organizations, such as the courts and the police, become more essential. Thus, *social control* in the cities depends in large degree upon *formal mechanisms*. But laws generally express the minimum behavioral standard, and urban life involves a much wider range of behavior than rural life. Moreover, laws do not always succeed in establishing minimum standards of behavior; crime rates increase with increases in urbanism.

Another characteristic of urban life is *mobility*, or ease of movement. Urban mobility is both *physical* (from one geographic area to another) and *social* (from one position of social status to another). Rural communities are more stable than urban communities in both respects. Traditionally rural dwellers were more likely to stay near the place of their birth. In contrast, urbanites frequently move from city to city, or from one section of a city to another. Social mobility is also greater in the city, because of the wider range of economic opportunities there. Moreover, urban dwellers are judged far less by their family backgrounds (which are unknown) than by their own appearances, occupational accomplishments, incomes, and lifestyles. While mobility creates opportunities for individuals, it weakens the sense of community. City dwellers do not think of their city as a community to which they belong but rather as a place they happen to live—a geographical entity commanding little personal allegiance.

Yet another fundamental characteristic is *interdependence*. Rural living involves little interdependence. Although the traditional farm family was not wholly self-sufficient, its members were much less dependent on the larger community for employment, goods, and services than is the modern urban dweller. Urban dwellers are highly dependent upon one another in their daily *economic* and *social* activities. Suburbanites, for example, rely upon the central city for food, clothing, newspapers, entertainment, hospitalization, and a host of other modern needs. More importantly, they rely upon the central city for employment opportunities. Conversely, the central city relies upon the suburbs to supply its labor and management forces. Downtown merchants look to the entire metropolitan area for consumers. This interdependence involves an intricate web of economic and social relationships, a high degree of communication, and a great deal of physical interchange among residents, groups, and firms in a metropolitan area. Just as specialization produces diversity, it also produces interdependence, and the need for coordinated activity.

Urban life presents a serious problem in *conflict* management. Since a metropolitan area consists of a large number of different kinds of people living closely together, the problem of regulating conflict and maintaining order assumes tremendous proportions. Persons with different occupations, income, and educational levels are known to have different views on public issues. The way that persons well equipped to compete for jobs and income in a free market view government housing and welfare programs may differ from the way that others not so well equipped view them. People at the bottom of the social ladder look at police—indeed, governmental authority in general—differently from the way those on higher rungs do. Persons who own their homes and those who do not own their homes regard taxation in a different light. Families with children and those without children have different ideas about school systems. And so it goes. Differences in the way people make their living, in their income and educational levels, in the color of their skin, in the way they worship, in their style of living—all are at the roots of political life in the metropolis.

Thus, sociological theory provides us with a series of characteristics to look for in urban life:

Large numbers of people
Population density
Social and economic heterogeneity
Ethnic and racial diversity
Differences in family lifestyle
Numerous but superficial, segmental, utilitarian relationships
Impersonality and anonymity
Greater interaction in secondary groups
Reliance upon formal mechanisms of social control
Physical and social mobility
Economic and social interdependence
Greater potential for conflict

Weaknesses of early theory

Not all of these characteristics of urban life have been documented. Indeed, in a highly industrialized and urbanized society, such as the United States, it is difficult to discern any differences between rural and urban dwellers. Moreover, urban dwellers display a great range and variation in styles of life; some reflect the "typical" style described by sociological theory while others do not. Many retain their commitment to the extended family, and many city neighborhoods are stable and socially cohesive communities. Despite the plausibility of the hypothesis that urban life leads to anonymity, impersonality, and segmentalization in social relationships, it is hard to prove systematically that urban dwellers are getting more impersonal or anonymous than are rural dwellers. Finally, sociologists can no longer focus upon central-city lifestyles in describing urban living. We must now take account of suburban lifestyles, since more people live in suburbs than in central cities. And the suburban way of life is in many ways quite different from the way of life described in early sociological theory.

THE SUBURBAN TREND

Why people move to the suburbs

One explanation of the suburbanization of America is that people strive to avoid many of the unpleasant characteristics of urban life. The move to the suburbs is in part generated by a desire to get away from the numbers, density, and heterogeneity of big-city life, the problems created by large numbers of people—the crowds, dirt, noise, smog, congestion, gas fumes, crime, and delinquency. People move to the suburbs seeking more land (less density) on which to build their own homes, enjoy backyard recreation, and give their children more room in which to play; they want sunshine, fresh air, quiet, privacy, and space.

Moreover, people often move to the suburbs to place physical distance between themselves and those whose cultures and lifestyles are different from theirs—the poor, the black, the lower class. They seek to replace the *heterogeneity* of big-city life by the *homogeneity* of the small suburban community—congenial neighbors, people like themselves, who share their interest in good schools, respectable neighborhoods, and middle-class lifestyles. The suburban community, with a local government small in scale and close to home, represents a partial escape from the anonymity of mass urban life. Suburbanites identify their communities by reference to their suburban homes—Scarsdale, or Mineola; they do not feel much identification with the "New York-Northeastern New Jersey Standard Metropolitan Area." A separate suburban government and a separate school district provide suburbanites with a sense of personal effectiveness in the management of public affairs.

Suburbs offer escape from the worst problems of urban life—racial conflict, crime, violence, poverty, slums, drugs, congestion, pollution, and so forth. A move to the suburbs permits a family, for the time being at least, to avoid the problems of poor schools, deteriorating housing, expanding welfare rolls, muggings and robberies, and violence and rioting in the central cities. Yet at the same time suburbanites retain the positive benefits of urban life. The city offers economic opportunity—high-paying jobs, openings for highly skilled professionals and technicians, and upward social and economic mobility. This is the reason most people come to the city in the first place. The big city also offers theater and entertainment, professional sports, civic and cultural events, specialized shops and stores, and a host of other attractions. Suburban living allows people to enjoy the advantages of urban life while avoiding some of its hardships.

Of course, it is not really possible to argue that the major social problems of urban society—racial conflict, poverty, drugs, crime, undereducation, slum housing, and so on—are problems of central cities and not of suburbs. John C. Bollens and Henry J. Schmandt in *The Metropolis* addressed themselves to this point very effectively:

> Some myopic defenders of suburbia go so far as to say that the major socioeconomic problems of urban society are problems of the central city, not those of the total metropolitan community. Where but within the

402 Chapter 13

boundaries of the core city, they ask, does one find an abundance of racial strife, crime, blight of housing, and welfare recipients? Superficially, their logic may seem sound, since they are in general correct about the prevalent spatial location of these maladies. Although crime and other social problems exist in suburbia, their magnitude and extent are substantially less than in the central city. But why in an interdependent metropolitan community should the responsibility for suburbanites be any less than that of the central city dwellers? Certainly no one would think of contending that residents of higher income neighborhoods within the corporate limits of the city should be exempt from responsibility for its less fortunate districts. What logic then is there in believing that neighborhoods on the other side of a legal line can wash their hands of social disorders in these sections?

. . . No large community can hope to reap the benefits of industrialization and urbanization and yet escape their less desirable byproducts. The suburbanite and the central city resident share the responsibility for total community and its problems. Neither can run fast enough to escape involvement sooner or later.[2]

Generalizing about cities and suburbs is dangerous. Although we will compare some characteristics of cities and suburbs, students are cautioned that individual suburbs and cities may be quite different from one another, just as there are wide differences among social and economic groups living in central cities.

Occupation, income, and education

Cities and suburbs can be differentiated, first of all, on the basis of occupation, income, and educational levels of their populations. The suburbs house greater proportions of white-collar employees, of college graduates, and of affluent families than any other sector in American life. And social differences between city and suburb are increasing rather than decreasing, as middle-class Americans continue to flee from the central city to the suburbs, and lower income, occupational, and educational groups are concentrated in central cities.

Family lifestyles

Perhaps the most frequently mentioned reason for a move to the suburbs is the "kids." Family after family lists consideration of its young as the primary cause for the move to suburbia. The city is hardly the place for most child-centered amenities. A familistic or child-centered lifestyle can be identified in certain social statistics. There are proportionately more children in the suburbs than in the central cities; a larger proportion of suburban mothers stay at home to take care of these children; and a larger proportion of suburban families are housed in single-family homes. A nonfamilistic lifestyle is characteristic of the central city, where there are proportionately fewer children, greater numbers of employed mothers, and more apartment dwellers.

Racial composition

But the most important difference between cities and suburbs is their contrasting *racial composition*. Although blacks constitute only 11 percent of the total population of the United States, they are rapidly approaching a numerical majority in many of the nation's largest cities. Blacks are already in the majority in Washington, Atlanta, and Newark, and they make up more than 40 percent of the population of Detroit, Baltimore, St. Louis, New Orleans, Oakland, Birmingham, and Gary. They are nearing a third of the population of Chicago, Philadelphia, Cleveland, Memphis, Columbus, and Cincinnati.

The concentration of blacks in large central cities is a product of the availability of low-priced rental units in older, run-down sections of central cities and of discriminatory housing practices of private owners and developers. Of course, underlying the concentration of blacks in run-down sectors of central cities is a lack of sufficient income to purchase housing in suburbs or in better city neighborhoods. The poverty and unemployment that contribute to the concentration of blacks in "ghettos" are in turn a product of inadequate training and education, low aspiration levels, and often a lack of motivation. And problems in education and motivation are themselves related to a breakdown in family life, delinquency, and crime. Thus, urban blacks face a whole series of interrelated problems in addition to discrimination: poverty, slum housing, undereducation, lack of job skills, family troubles, lack of motivation, delinquency, and crime. It is difficult to talk about any one of these problems without reference to them all.

The migration of blacks into cities, particularly in the North, has been accompanied by a heavy out-migration of whites fleeing to the suburbs for a variety of reasons. The total populations of many large central cities have remained stagnant in recent years or even declined slightly; black population percentages have increased because black in-migration has compensated for white out-migration.

Many whites have fled to the suburbs to get away from concentrations of black people in central cities. One reason suburbanites may want to remain politically separate from the central cities is so they can more easily resist "invasion" by blacks. However, as blacks gain majorities in central cities, they too, may resist metropolitan governmental consolidation in order to avoid dilution of their political power through merger with white suburbs. The restriction of suburban home sales to whites only and the generally higher costs of suburban homes and property have made it difficult or impossible for blacks to follow whites to the suburbs in any significant number. The nonwhite percentage of all central cities is 21 percent.

Thus, American life is becoming more, not less, segregated. These population statistics clearly show that America is building racial ghettos in its large central cities and surrounding them with white middle-class suburbs. As the exodus to the suburbs continues, cities are becoming bereft of their middle-class, white, high-income, high-taxpaying populations. Increasingly, nonwhite, low-income, low-education, unskilled, nonfamilistic populations are being concentrated in the central cities. Hence, the problems of these people (racial imbalance, crime, violence, inadequate education, poverty, slum housing) have also been concentrated in the central cities. By moving to the suburbs, white middle-class families not only separate themselves from blacks and poor people, but also place physical distance between themselves and the major social problems that confront metropolitan areas.

CASE STUDY
Power, Energy, and the Environment:
The Competing Interests

Environmentalists actively oppose the methods of development of all current domestic energy sources—coal mining, offshore oil drilling, nuclear power plants—and instead stress conservation. The federal government has imposed a national speed limit of fifty-five miles per hour on highways and has urged Americans to turn down their thermostats in winter to sixty-eight degrees. Instead of the annual 4 or 5 percent growth in energy consumption that was previously projected, recent figures indicate that energy consumption is now growing at only 2 or 3 percent per year. But there are limits to what can be achieved by conservation; can we really expect Americans to slow down to forty miles per hour, or heat their homes to only fifty-five degrees, or give up their cars for public transportation?

Industry has urged that existing controls on domestic oil and gas be removed and that prices be allowed to increase. They argue that increased prices would not only encourage conservation, but would also stimulate new exploration and drilling. Consumers would buy smaller, gas-saving cars and limit their travel if American gasoline were priced at world market prices—two dollars per gallon or more. However, many liberals in Congress oppose the unregulated market solution as placing too great a burden on consumers.

Nuclear power holds out the hope of clean, plentiful energy. Environmentalists have opposed nuclear plants as unsafe, despite an enviable record of safety in the 162 reactors operating in the world today (only 60 of them in the United States). There have been malfunctions, but never a serious injury or death due to radiation. Indeed, the electric power industry contends that the pollution caused by alternative fuels—coal and oil—is infinitely more dangerous to health. Nonetheless, environmentalists have filed lawsuits that have slowed, and in some cases halted, the construction and operation of nuclear plants. These suits have increased the costs of nuclear power plants and caused the cancellation of many orders for nuclear facilities. More serious, perhaps, is that at best it takes years to get a nuclear plant working properly, and technical problems have plagued most major nuclear plants, reducing their output. Environmentalists were also successful in creating a new Nuclear Regulatory Commission to license nuclear plants, removing that power from the Atomic Energy Commission, which the environmentalists had attacked as too sympathetic toward nuclear power. The Atomic Energy Commission was replaced by a new Energy Research and Development Administration.

Perhaps no other issue provokes more fear and misinformation than nuclear energy. Prior to the 1979 "Three Mile Island incident," a majority of Americans supported the development of nuclear power. For example, in 1976 California voters supported the continued development of nuclear energy in a statewide referendum. However, in 1979 a nuclear power plant on Three Mile Island near Harrisburg, Pennsylvania, accidentally released a small amount of radioactive steam. The cooling apparatus of the plant threatened to fail and release additional radioactivity. Engineers brought the plant to "cold shutdown" but not before news media and opponents of nuclear power had publicized the possibility of danger. No deaths or injuries occurred at Three Mile Island and nuclear power retained its perfect safety record, but the public image of nuclear energy was badly tarnished.

The early emphasis of federal policy was on speeding up the development of nuclear energy. But the combined weight of legal attacks by environmentalists, difficulty in obtaining licenses, and the time and technical difficulties in making nuclear plants operational has resulted in a shift of emphasis to *coal.* However, an emphasis on coal requires that Congress relax strip mining laws and air quality standards for coal-burning power plants; and environmentalists are in a good position to block the legislation required for stepped-up coal production. So the nation is back where it started—with no coordinated energy policy.

Finally, to develop new energy sources of any kind—to build new electrical power plants or nuclear energy plants, to expand oil and gas exploration, or even to fund new experiments in solar energy—requires heavy capital investment. The power companies and oil companies are unable and unwilling to make large investments unless price controls are lifted and some guarantees are made that their efforts will not be hindered by court action. Moreover, the estimates of the capital required to develop new sources of energy run into the hundreds of billions of dollars—more than industry can generate from profits. Hence, the late Nelson Rockefeller, former vice-president, suggested the creation of a new government agency with large amounts of money to invest in energy development. However, even if such an agency were established, it might quickly bog down in conflicting notions about how to spend its money.

The Carter administration promised a new coordinated national energy policy and created a new cabinet-level Department of Energy that now includes the Federal Power Commission, the Federal Energy Administration, the Nuclear Regulatory Commission, the Energy Research and Development Administration, and other agencies with energy-related responsibilities. President Carter proposes a balanced energy package, which would require all major interests to make some sacrifices. Carter's plan emphasizes conservation of energy. Price controls will be gradually removed from oil and gas, but most environmental controls remain in place, and "fast breeder" plants remain censored. The president proposes a national effort to develop synthetic fuels—an effort which will be financed by a "windfall profits" tax on oil companies whose income will be increased by rising gasoline prices. The president hopes to increase coal production and to provide tax incentives for Americans who insulate their homes or use solar power devices. Nuclear energy will not be abandoned, but it will play a minor role as a national energy source. Long-range experimentation with solar power, wind power, and other sources of energy will be encouraged by the government. Finally, the price of all fuels—gasoline, home heating oil, natural gas, coal—will be allowed to rise gradually.

NOTES

1. Louis Wirth, "Urbanism as a Way of Life," *American Journal of Sociology* 44 (July 1938).
2. John C. Bollens and Henry J. Schmandt, *The Metropolis* (New York: Harper & Row, 1965), pp. 249–50.

DISCUSSION QUESTIONS

1. Compare and contrast the three major types of environmental pollution in terms of sources, impact on health and the environment, and methods of prevention or treatment.
2. Discuss the causes of the energy crisis and the relationship of the energy crisis to the problems of environmental pollution.
3. Compare and contrast the purposes and authority of the Environmental Protection Agency, the Council on Environmental Quality, and the Department of Energy. Why do the EPA and CEQ often come into conflict with agencies of the Department of Energy?
4. Define a *metropolitan area* and discuss the growth patterns of these areas, the reasons for growth, and the effect of population concentration upon the environment.
5. Discuss some of the characteristics of urban life as defined by early sociological theory and some of the weaknesses of that theory.
6. Discuss the reasons for the "suburbanization" of America, the general differences between urban and suburban populations, and the effect of the exodus to suburbia on the central city and on American society in general.
7. Discuss the solutions to the energy crisis proposed by environmentalists, industry, and the Carter administration. What solution do you think would be most likely to solve the energy problem without having a detrimental effect on our quality of life?

SUGGESTED READINGS

John C. Bollens and Henry J. Schmandt, *The Metropolis* (New York: Harper & Row, 1965).

Congressional Quarterly, *Man's Control of the Environment* (Washington, D.C.: Congressional Quarterly, Inc., 1970).

——, *Earth, Energy and the Environment* (Washington, D.C.: Congressional Quarterly, Inc., 1977).

J. Clarence Davies, *The Politics of Pollution* (New York: Pegasus, 1970).

William M. Dobriner, *Class in Suburbia* (Englewood Cliffs, N.J.: Prentice-Hall, 1963).

Jeffery K. Hadden and Lewis H. Masotti, eds., *Metropolis in Crisis* (Itasca, Ill.: Peacock, 1971).

Sue Titus Reid and David L. Lyon, eds., *Population Crisis: An Interdisciplinary Perspective* (Glenview, Ill.: Scott, Foresman, 1972).

Roger Revelle and Hans H. Landsberg, eds., *America's Changing Environment* (Boston: Houghton Mifflin, 1970).

Photo from United Press International

Photo from Wide World Photos

Chapter 14
Power and the International System

Since the earliest recorded times, and no doubt before, people have been fighting wars. They have fought them for every conceivable reason—and even for some reasons that may seem *inconceivable* by today's standards. They have fought to defend themselves or to subjugate others; they have fought for territorial, economic, or political gain; they have fought for ideological reasons and for leaders whose sole reason was to secure a place for themselves in history; they have fought class wars and race wars; they have undoubtedly even fought just for fun. But in our age, the threat of a nuclear holocaust makes it imperative that the world's superpowers avoid war. War on the grand scale can have no meaning today, no reason worth the annihilation of civilization as we know it.

In this chapter we will explore some of the means, past and present, by which people have sought to avoid war. After you have read it, you should be able to:

- discuss the meaning of sovereignty and describe the nature of international law.
- discuss the concepts of a balance of power, collective security, and regional security.
- discuss the concepts of deterrence and "MAD" and the means by which these policies are implemented.
- discuss the "minibalances of power" and the reasons why it is necessary for the superpowers to maintain conventional armed forces.

RELATIONS AMONG NATIONS

The distinguished political scientist Hans Morgenthau wrote:

International politics, like all politics, is a struggle for power. Whatever the ultimate aims of international politics, power is always the immediate aim. Statesmen and peoples may ultimately seek freedom, security, prosperity, or power itself. They may define their goals in terms of a religious, philosophic, economic, or social ideal. . . . But whenever they strive to realize their goal by means of international politics, they are striving for power.[1]

In brief, we are reminded that the struggle for power is global—it involves all the nations and peoples of the world, whatever their goals or ideals.

There are nearly two hundred nations in the world today. One hundred and sixty-five of these nations are members of the United Nations. Others are too small or too poor to claim membership in that body. Yet all the nations of the world—inside and outside of the U.N., whatever their size, location, culture, politics, economic system, or level of technological development—claim *sovereignty*. Sovereignty means formal, legal power over internal affairs, freedom from external intervention, and political and legal recognition by other nations.

Sovereignty

Sovereignty is a legal fiction, or course: Many nations have difficulty controlling their internal affairs; they are constantly meddling in each other's internal affairs and even trampling on each other's political and legal authority. Nonetheless, the *struggle* to achieve sovereignty is an important force in world politics, particularly among nations that were once colonies of other nations. The demand for national control over internal affairs and freedom from outside interference is frequently heard among the newer nations of Asia and Africa. But muffled cries for sovereignty are also heard from inside communist "satellite" nations of the Soviet Union and China.

While sovereignty is highly valued by all nations, it creates an international system in which no authority—not even the United Nations—is given the power to make or enforce rules binding on all nations. There is *no world government*. Nations cooperate with each other only when it is in their own interest to do so. Nations can make treaties with each other, but there is no court to enforce these treaties, and they can be (and are) disregarded when it becomes advantageous for a nation to do so.

The fiction of international law

There are a series of customs and principles among nations—known as *international law*—that help to guide relations among nations. But international "law" is also a fiction: There is no international "police force" to enforce the law, and it is frequently broken or ignored. An International Court (at The Hague, the Netherlands) exists to decide conflicts according to international law, but nations do not have to submit to the authority of this court and can, if they wish to, ignore its decisions. The United Nations, as we shall see, is largely a debating society. The U.N. has no real power to enforce its resolutions, unless one or more nations (acting in their own self-interest) decide to try to enforce a U.N. resolution with their own troops, or contribute troops to a joint "U.N. force." But "U.N. forces" are really the forces of sovereign nations that have voluntarily decided to contribute troops to enforce a particular resolution.

The international system can be viewed as a global game of power that is played continuously. All the players pursue different goals against all the other players. Some players are more powerful than others, and occasionally players team up against each other. (Some team up willingly, while others are coerced into doing it.) Periodically, fights break out, but there is no referee with enough power to stop the fighting (unless one or more stronger players step in to restrain the fighting nations). The players belong to a club called the United Nations where they sit around and quarrel about the game. But the players never agree to a referee or to rules of the game for fear that a referee or rules might interfere with their own style of play. The game has been played for centuries. No one really knows all the goals that each player seeks (although we all know that power is the key instrument in achieving any goal). Yet all of the players are deadly serious and play to win.

BRINGING ORDER TO INTERNATIONAL RELATIONS

The instability and insecurity of "the global game of power" have led to many attempts over the centuries to bring order to the international system. Indeed, wars among nations have averaged one every two years,[2] and if "civil wars" and "indirect aggressions" are counted, the rate of armed conflict is even greater.[3]

The Balance of Power System   One method of trying to bring order to international relations is the *balance of power* system. The nineteenth century saw a deliberate attempt to stabilize international relations by creating a system of alliances among nations that was designed to balance the power of one group of nations against the power of another and thus to discourage war. If the balance worked, war would be avoided and peace would be assured. For almost an entire century, from the end of the Napoleonic Wars (1815) to World War I (1914), the balance of power system appeared to be at least partially effective in Europe. But an important defect in the balance of power system is that a small conflict between two nations that are members of separate alliances can draw all the member nations of each alliance into the conflict.

This defect in the balance of power system can result in the rapid expansion of a small conflict into a major war between separate alliances of nations. Essentially this is what happened in World War I, when a minor conflict in the Balkan nations resulted in a very destructive war between the Allies (England, France, Russia, and eventually the United States) and the Central Powers (Germany, Austria-Hungary, and Turkey).

The Allies and the Central Powers

Indeed, World War I proved so destructive (10 million men were killed on the battlefield between 1914 and 1918) that there was a worldwide demand to replace the balance of power system with a new arrangement—"collective security."

Collective Security *Collective security* originally meant that *all* nations would join together to guarantee each other's "territorial integrity and existing political independence" against "external aggression" by any nation.[4] This concept resulted in the formation of the League of Nations in 1919. However, opposition to international involvement was so great in the United States after World War I that after a lengthy debate in the Senate, the United States refused to join the League of Nations. More importantly, the League of Nations failed completely to deal with rising militarism in Germany, Japan, and Italy in the 1930s. During that decade, Japan invaded Manchuria; Italy invaded Ethiopia; Germany invaded Czechoslovakia; and the League of Nations failed to prevent any of these aggressions. Fascism in Germany and Italy, and militarism in Japan, went unchecked. The result was a war even more devastating than World War I: World War II cost over 40 million lives, both civilian and military.

The League of Nations

Yet, even after World War II, the notion of collective security remained an ideal of the victorious Allied powers—especially the United States, Great Britain, the Soviet Union, France, and China. The Charter of the United Nations was signed in 1945. The new organization included fifty-one members. The U.N. provided for (1) a Security Council with eleven members, five of them being permanent members (the U.S., the U.S.S.R., Britain, France, and China) and having the power to veto any action by the Security Council; (2) a General Assembly composed of all the member nations, each with a single vote (except the U.S.S.R., which obtained three votes by claiming that Byelorussia and the Ukraine were independent); (3) a secretariat headed by a secretary-general with a staff at U.N. headquarters in New York; and (4) several special bodies to handle specialized affairs—for example, the Economic and Social Council, the Trusteeship Council, and the International Court at The Hague.

The United Nations

The Security Council has the "primary responsibility" for maintaining "international peace and security." For this reason, the world's most powerful nations have permanent seats on the council and veto powers over all but procedural matters. The General Assembly has authority over "any matter affecting the peace of the world" although it is supposed to defer to the Security Council if the council has already taken up a particular matter. No nation has a veto in the General Assembly; every nation has one vote, regardless of its size or power. Most resolutions can be passed by a majority vote.

Since 1945, the United Nations has disappointed all but its most ardent admirers. It has grown to a membership of 165 nations, but the vast majority of these nations are headed by authoritarian regimes of one kind or another. The Western democracies are badly outnumbered. Nonetheless, the United States, because of its wealth, pays the largest share of U.N. expenses. In the General Assembly, the prevailing voice is that of small, authoritarian regimes, usually backed by communist powers. The votes of tiny populations headed by absolute dictators count for just as much as the votes of large democracies, including the United States. "One man, one vote" does not operate in the U.N.; the rule is "one country, one vote." Moreover, the U.N. has been ineffective in dealing with many major international disputes. This is true largely because parties to these disputes have no confidence in the U.N. and decline to bring their problems to it. Except on rare occasions (in Korea and, at times, in the Middle East), member nations of the U.N. have failed to commit their troops to enforce U.N. decisions. Finally, in recent years, anti-Western and anti-democratic speeches in the General Assembly have become common. Former U.N. Ambassador Daniel Patrick Moynihan (now U.S. senator from New York) countered these attacks on democracy with strong language of his own. But many of our Western allies, not to mention the bulk of authoritarian regimes in the U.N., thought his speeches were impolite. So the United States has quietly returned to a position of listening to U.N. debate, but not giving much weight to U.N. resolutions.

NATO and the Warsaw Pact

Regional Security   The general disappointment with the United Nations as a form of collective security gave rise as early as 1950 to a different approach: *regional security*. In response to aggressive Soviet moves in Europe,[5] President Harry S. Truman created the North Atlantic Treaty Organization (NATO). In the NATO treaty, the United States made a specific commitment to defend Western Europe in the event of a Soviet attack. Indeed, fifteen Western nations agreed to collective *regional security*: they agreed that "an armed attack against one or more . . . shall be considered an attack against them all." Moreover, a joint NATO military command was established with a

U.S. commanding officer (the first was General of the Army Dwight D. Eisenhower) to command and coordinate the defense of Western Europe. After the formation of NATO, the Soviets made no further advances into Western Europe, and NATO remains today as a deterrent to Soviet expansion in the area. The Soviets themselves, in response to NATO, drew up a comparable treaty among their own Eastern European satellite nations—"the Warsaw Pact."

These regional security agreements—NATO and the Warsaw Pact—remind us more of the nineteenth century *balance of power* alliances than of the true concept of *collective security*. The original notion of collective security envisioned agreement among *all* nations, while NATO and the Warsaw Pact are similar to the older systems of separate alliances.

The Emergence of the Superpowers   Collective security and balance of power concepts have been overshadowed in recent years by the confrontation of the world's two "superpowers"—the United States and the Soviet Union. Indeed, international conflicts throughout the world—in the Middle East, Africa, Southeast Asia, and elsewhere— are usually affected by some aspect of the superpower struggle. The superpowers are distinguished from the rest of the world by their capacity to destroy each other with nuclear weapons. Other nations— Great Britain, France, China, India, South Africa, and Israel—may possess nuclear weapons, but none can deliver the kind of devastating blow that could destroy a large industrial society.

PEACE AND DETERRENCE

To maintain peace and protect the national interests, the United States today relies primarily upon the notion of *deterrence*. In a general sense, deterrence means that war and overt aggression can best be prevented by making the consequences of such acts clearly unacceptable to rational leaders of other nations.

Assured Destruction Deterrence   The policy of *assured destruction* is based on the notion that one can dissaude a potential enemy from war or aggression only by maintaining the capacity to destroy the enemy's society *even after* one has suffered a well-executed surprise attack by the enemy. Assured destruction deterrence assumes the worst may happen—a surprise first strike against our own offensive forces. It emphasizes our *second-strike capability*—the ability of our forces to survive a surprise attack by the enemy and then to inflict an unacceptable level of destruction on the enemy's homeland. Assured destruction deterrence, then, requires: (1) that the U.S. maintain the *capability* to destroy an enemy even after absorbing a full-scale surprise attack (second-strike capability); (2) that the U.S. *communicate* its second-strike capability to the enemy (deterrence is achieved only if the enemy *knows* that you have the capacity to deliver unacceptable damage even after absorbing a first strike); (3) that the U.S. make its threat *credible* (the enemy must believe that you would in fact retaliate if attacked); and (4) that the enemy is a *rational* decision maker (only an irrational enemy would go to war knowing that it would result in the destruction of his society).

A psychological concept

Deterrence, then, is a *psychological* concept: It is not enough for a nation to be confident of its own capability; the potential aggressor must be clearly aware of that nation's capabilities and intentions. Capacities and intentions must be fully communicated to the enemy. Hence, U.S. policy makers regularly publicize the strength and size of U.S. strategic offensive forces.

The key concept

But advertising numbers of missiles or megatonnage or "overkill capacity" is not enough either. The key component of assured destruction deterrence is the *survivability* of an effective strike force *after* a successful surprise attack by the enemy—that is, second-strike capability.

The Triad   American defense policy currently relies on a "triad" of land-based missiles, submarine-launched missiles, and manned bombers to provide its assured destruction deterrence. This combination of forces is believed to be a more effective deterrent than reliance on any single weapons system, because the diversity and multiplicity of forces makes it difficult for an enemy to develop a "first-strike capability"—the capability of destroying all three retaliatory systems simultaneously and thereby avoiding our "second-strike retaliation."

ICBMs

In striving for assured destruction deterrence, both the U.S. and the U.S.S.R. have developed long-range intercontinental ballistic missiles (ICBMs) that can travel between the U.S. and the U.S.S.R. in less than forty minutes. These are dispersed in underground "hardened" silos—concrete structures designed and constructed so that they can be destroyed only by a large explosion very nearby. They are far enough apart so that a single explosion, regardless of its size, can destroy no more than one missile silo. Thus, for an attacker to eliminate with confidence the defender's entire force on a first strike, he would have to evade early detection of his own missile firings (otherwise the defender's missiles would be fired before the attacker's missiles arrived) and either accurately target each of the defender's missile silos or else fire several warheads at each silo to insure a hit.

ULMs

Another approach to assured destruction deterrence is to place missiles in submarines. Submarines with underwater-launched missiles (ULMs) are difficult to detect, follow, and destroy. The coordinated destruction of this deterrent on a first strike is very unlikely with the technology presently available.

Manned bombers

The third approach to assured destruction deterrence is through the development of advanced manned bomber forces. In general, manned bomber forces are considered vulnerable to a first strike; one nuclear explosion can destroy all the aircraft at a single base. Bombers are only safe when they are in the air, and keeping a large bomber force in the air at all times is expensive. However, given sufficient warning, bombers can be effective. An advanced bomber (the B-1) flies at supersonic speeds (over two thousand miles per hour); it is small yet carries a heavy payload of nuclear weapons; its guidance system allows it to fly very low to escape radar detection; and it can launch nuclear warheads in air-to-surface missiles without having to fly over the target area. Moreover, advanced manned bombers are flexible: They can change targets in flight; they can be recalled if the alert is an error; and they can be used in conventional non-nuclear wars if needed. However, in 1977 Carter stopped the further development of the B-1 bomber. The president chose to concentrate on the development of a new low-flying, inexpensive, unmanned, *Cruise* missile. Hundreds of the Cruise missiles can be launched from old B-52 bombers or ships or submarines to saturate enemy air defenses.

Damage Limitation   Damage limitation is the capacity to reduce the damage inflicted by an enemy. A damage limitation strategy assumes that assured destruction deterrence has been provided, but it adds that if deterrence should fail, whether by accident or miscalculation, it is still essential that forces be provided to limit the damage of an enemy attack. Although most defense analysts accept the assured destruction deterrence notion, there is disagreement over the utility, costs, and effectiveness of damage limitation efforts.

ABMs

One major dispute over damage limitation centers on the development of defensive, antiballistic missile systems (ABMs). ABMs are surface-to-air missiles designed to intercept and destroy incoming missiles. The U.S. built one ABM complex with 100 missiles to defend its ICBM sites. The U.S.S.R. built two complexes, each with 100 missiles, protecting Moscow and some of its ICBM sites. The SALT I agreement between the U.S. and U.S.S.R. prohibited both nations from having more than two ABM sites each with 100 missiles. The U.S. never built its second allowable site and has deactivated its first site.

Civil defense

In an all-out enemy first strike against cities, an effective nationwide civil defense program could reduce U.S. fatalities to 80 million out of a population of 215 million. (Without *any* civil defense, U.S. fatalities in such an attack might run to 150 million.) The additional civil defense required to reduce fatalities below 80 million would be very costly and easily offset by less costly increases in the enemy's offensive striking force. Thus, it is difficult to justify a *heavy* civil defense effort. Nonetheless, the U.S. has failed to provide even a modest civil defense program. In contrast, the U.S.S.R. has built an impressive system of civil defense shelters. In addition, its dispersed population gives it a natural advantage in damage limitation.

Credible First-Strike Capability   *First-strike capability* is the capacity to threaten the enemy with a first strike and to make the threat a credible one. Although the notion that "we will never strike first" is common, the United States for many years provided a protective nuclear shield for Western Europe by pledging to come to the aid of NATO nations in the event of an attack. This commitment included an implied pledge to use our strategic nuclear forces against the Soviet heartland if Soviet troops invaded Western Europe. It is generally assumed that this threat played a major role in halting Soviet expansion in Europe in the years following World War II. The history of Soviet expansion into Eastern Europe includes postwar Communist takeovers in Poland, Hungary, Czechoslovakia, Bulgaria, and Rumania; the use of Soviet troops in East Germany, Poland, and, particularly, Hungary to maintain Communist governments in these nations, and military blockades of Berlin. This history suggests that the Soviets can and will use force in Europe to further their political goals. They clearly have superiority in conventional military strength—troops, tanks, artillery, support aircraft, and the like. Hence, most defense analysts believe that the threat of nuclear retaliation was an essential component of the defense of Western Europe.

Outdoing the enemy's second-strike capability

Credible first-strike capability does not simply mean the capability of hurting the other side on a first strike. *Credible* first-strike capability really depends on how much harm the enemy can do in retaliation. A first-strike threat is not really credible if the enemy knows that you know he can inflict unacceptable damages on you in response. Developing a credible first-strike capability would entail: (1) a massive buildup of offensive weapons—enough to take over all or nearly all of the enemy's offensive weapons on a first strike; (2) a massive buildup of damage limitation systems to reduce his second-strike damage to acceptable levels; or (3) both of these moves in combination.

Current U.S. defense policy does *not* include the force levels required for a credible first-strike capability. Indeed, in the last few years makers of defense policy have avoided references to "superiority" of force levels and have talked instead about "sufficiency." This means that U.S. defense policy has emphasized assured destruction deterrence; we now recognize the loss of our credible first-strike capability.

A BALANCE OF TERROR: "MAD"

If *both* sides have assured destruction deterrence—that is, second-strike capability—then *neither* side is likely to begin a nuclear war. Mutual assured destruction, or "MAD," refers to this kind of balance of power. However, if either side should lose its second-strike capability, this would upset the balance by providing an incentive for the other side to proceed with a first-strike of its own, knowing that it would not suffer any serious consequences.

MAD: a type of stability

Mutual assured destruction, or MAD, represents *stability* in the international balance of power. American defense planning strives to maintain MAD as insurance against nuclear war. But many observers consider MAD a balance of terror—each side is restrained from war because of the knowledge of the terrible consequences that the other side can inflict upon it even after an attack. In other words, peace is maintained because of the terrible consequences to both sides in the event of war.

Threats to stability

Research and *technological advancement* are constant threats to stability. For example, to counter the perceived threat from a large-scale Soviet ABM system, the U.S. developed a multiple independently targeted reentry vehicle (MIRV) for its land-based and submarine-launched missiles. MIRV enables *each* missile to launch three, six, or even fourteen separate warheads at separate targets while still high in space over the enemy's homeland. MIRV makes *any* ABM system obsolete; it has the potential of multiplying U.S. striking power by six times. A thousand ICBMs with MIRV could deliver six thousand separately targeted nuclear warheads. Such an attack would easily overwhelm an ABM system and saturate the target areas with multiple hits. Initially the Soviets were behind the U.S. in the development of MIRVs, but they have now begun to catch up.

Stabilizing elements

To maintain second-strike assured destruction deterrence against a fully developed MIRVed ICBM attack, it is essential that a nation develop a *submarine deterrent force* equipped with underwater-launched missiles. MIRVed missiles have a potential first-strike capability against land-based missiles and aircraft, but they have no ability to attack missile-carrying submarines lurking in the depths of the oceans. If the U.S. and U.S.S.R. both have effective MIRV systems, deterrence depends upon each nation's capacity to launch a second-strike retaliatory attack with ULMs from submarines that are on station at the time of attack (and not destroyed in port). These submarine forces may become major stabilizing elements in the nuclear war game in the 1980s. They give each nation a second-strike capability—offensive power that cannot be destroyed in a MIRVed ICBM, saturation type of first strike. Thus, although MIRV appears to threaten stability, submarine forces promise to maintain stability.

The new *Cruise* missile developed by the U.S. is an effort to counter the larger and heavier ICBMs of the U.S.S.R. Cruise missiles are low flying, difficult to spot on radar, inexpensive, and unmanned. They can be launched from airplanes, submarines, or surface ships, but they have a short range (1,500 miles at most) and must be carried a part of the way to their targets. Nonetheless, the U.S.S.R. perceives the Cruise missile as a serious threat to its security.

Satellite reconnaissance is another major stabilizing force in the nuclear war game. Good intelligence reduces uncertainty about offensive and defensive capabilities and hence reduces the likelihood of war through miscalculation. One result of the U.S. space program was the development of "spy-in-the-sky" satellites capable of constant photo reconnaissance of enemy territory. These satellites can take amazingly detailed pictures from outer space. (High-altitude airplane overflights of enemy territory—"U2" flights—are no longer essential.) It is now virtually impossible for the enemy to develop offensive or defensive weapons without the president knowing about it as soon as construction begins. The development of "spy-in-the-sky" satellites has also made arms limitations agreements easier, because each nation can identify cheating with their space photography.

STRATEGIC ARMS LIMITATION AGREEMENTS: SALT I AND SALT II

SALT I

In 1972, the U.S. and U.S.S.R. concluded two and one-half years of talks about limiting the strategic arms race. The agreement that resulted from the first Strategic Arms Limitation Talk (SALT I) marks a milestone in the long journey toward arms control. The SALT I agreement consists of a treaty limiting ABMs and an agreement placing a numerical ceiling on offensive missiles.

The ABM treaty

The ABM treaty limits each side to one ABM site for defense of its national capital and one ABM site for defense of an offensive ICBM field. The total number of ABMs permitted is 200 for each side, 100 at each location. (The U.S.S.R. has one ABM site defending Moscow; the U.S. deactivated its only site in 1975.)

The offensive arms agreement

Under the offensive arms agreement, each side was frozen at the total number of offensive missiles completed or under construction. The Soviet Union was permitted 1,618 land-based missiles. The U.S. was permitted to maintain 1,054 land-based missiles. Both sides could construct new missiles if they dismantled an equal number of older missiles. Both sides were limited to the number of missile-carrying submarines operational or under construction at the time of the agreement; this meant forty-three for the Soviets and forty-one for the U.S. Both sides could replace older submarines and missiles, as long as their number remains unchanged. Each nation agreed not to interfere in the satellite intelligence-gathering activities of the other nation. There were no limitations on MIRV. There are no limitations on bombers. There are no limitations on advanced research on totally new weapons systems like the Cruise missile. The SALT I agreements were to last until October 1977, at which time both nations were to continue efforts at further arms control—the SALT II talks.

Gains

Why would the U.S. and U.S.S.R. enter into such an agreement? First of all, the U.S.S.R. achieved what it had been struggling toward for decades: official recognition by the U.S. of Soviet superiority in the number and size of offensive weapons. The U.S., on the other hand, achieved a slowing of the Soviet momentum in the building of ICBMs and missile-carrying submarines—a momentum that would have given the Soviet Union even greater superiority in the years to come.

Effects

At the time of the SALT I agreement (1972), the U.S. with its advanced MIRV program could actually deliver greater numbers of warheads on the Soviet Union than the Soviets could deliver on the U.S. However, this advantage dissipated as the Soviet MIRV program progressed. Both sides agreed not to build large-scale ABM systems to defend their own cities. This means that each agreed to curtail its damage limitation efforts. Satellite reconnaissance makes the SALT agreement self-enforcing; without satellite photography the question of inspection would have doomed negotiations. Each nation holds the population of the other as hostage (a "stabilizing" condition) as long as neither develops a credible first-strike capability. However, further technological advances in MIRV, advanced manned bombers, Cruise missiles, and antisubmarine warfare could threaten the

Drawing by Ed Fisher; © 1979 The New Yorker Magazine, Inc.

current stability if it gives either or both nations the capacity to take out the other's ICBMs, submarines, and bombers in a coordinated first strike. Hence, to insure stability, the U.S. and U.S.S.R. must find some ways of further curbing the technological race.

SALT II The U.S. and the Soviet Union signed the lengthy and complicated SALT II treaty in 1979. The United States hopes that this treaty will provide for "equivalence" of forces (meaning that any advantages enjoyed by the Soviets are offset by other advantages enjoyed by the U.S.) and will help maintain "stability" in the strategic balance of power. SALT II includes:

A total limit of 2,400 strategic nuclear launchers—ICBMs, SLBMs, bombers, and long-range Cruise missiles—for each side. This ceiling will be lowered to 2,250 in 1981.

A limit of 1,320 on the total number of missiles that can be MIRVed.

A ban on new types of ICBMs, with an exception of one new type of light ICBM for each side.

A limit of 10 MIRVed warheads on any ICBM, 14 MIRVed warheads on any SLBM.

Ceilings on the size and weight of missiles.

Advance notification of test launches.

Agreement not to interfere with electronic or satellite reconnaissance or use deliberate concealment of weapons testing or deployment.

This treaty will allow the Soviets to keep 314 very heavy SS-18 missiles for which the U.S. has no equivalent. However, it will allow the U.S. to develop a mobile missile (MX) that can be moved about to prevent the enemy from accurately targeting it for destruction. The U.S. could place Cruise missiles in some of its old bombers, but land-based and sea-based Cruise missiles will be banned until 1982 and maybe beyond that date if SALT III negotiations begin. The advanced supersonic Soviet "Backfire" bomber (equivalent to the U.S. B-1 that President Carter canceled) is not covered by the treaty.

MINIBALANCES OF POWER

Although the balance of power between the world's two superpowers—the United States and the Soviet Union—overshadows world events, smaller areas of the world are also confronted with the problem of achieving stability by balancing the power of conflicting local forces. We have labeled this process of achieving local stability by balancing the forces of smaller nations as *minibalances of power.*

It is difficult to achieve stability in all parts of the world, not only because of the large number of nations involved, each with its own goals, but also because of frequent intervention by the superpowers on one side or the other. This type of intervention, coupled with local hostilities, makes local war a common occurrence in areas of Africa, Asia, and the Middle East. The danger of superpower intervention is, of course, *escalation*—the growth of a local conflict into a larger war, perhaps even a nuclear war between the superpowers themselves.

The danger of escalation

Vietnam Indochina, which had been a French colony, was occupied by Japanese troops during World War II. Before Allied troops reached Indochina, an independent native Democratic Republic of Vietnam was proclaimed in September 1945, with the revolutionary Communist leader Ho Chi Minh as premier. By December 1946, the French Army had organized itself for an invasion of Vietnam and the recovery of the lost colony. Ho Chi Minh requested United States, British, and even Nationalist Chinese support against the French, but the Allies instead supported the French. Eight years of bloody war ensued, ending in the defeat of a sizable French force at Dien Bien Phu.

Representatives of the Democratic Republic of Vietnam and the French met at Geneva in 1954 and agreed to a cease-fire along a temporary military demarcation line at the 17th parallel, separating Communist North Vietnam from Western-supported South Vietnam. Both sides agreed that the line did not constitute a political or territorial boundary, but they promised not to introduce foreign troops or military bases anywhere in Vietnam, Laos, or Cambodia. The Geneva Agreement also called for free elections in all of Vietnam, to be held in July 1956. An International Council Commission composed of India, Canada, and Poland was to supervise the cease-fire and the elections. The Communist North Vietnamese established their capital in Hanoi in the North, while the anticommunist South Vietnamese rallied in Saigon in the South.

The United States declined to sign the Geneva Agreement, largely because the Republican administration did not wish to be a party to a victory of communism in the area. Although the South Vietnamese government had relatively little popular support in the villages and countryside, it was able, with American backing, to call off the elections of 1956. When the North Vietnamese moved south in large numbers to support Communist "Viet Cong" units fighting the South Vietnamese government, the United States gave heavy military and economic assistance to save South Vietnam from communism. This action was fully consistent with America's containment policy and with its membership in SEATO, because without American intervention, South Vietnam would certainly have come under the control of Ho Chi Minh's Communist regime in Hanoi.

In February 1965, President Lyndon Johnson sent American ground combat units into action in South Vietnam and sharply escalated bombing north of the 17th parallel. The president explained that the U.S. military effort was necessary because of our commitment to the South Vietnamese, who were victims of North Vietnam's aggression. But years of fighting, the commitment of a half million men to Vietnam and the loss of over fifty thousand American lives failed to achieve victory. On 31 March 1968, President Johnson announced an end to U.S. bombing in North Vietnam, issued a new call for negotiations, and withdrew from the presidential race. The North Vietnamese agreed to hold discussions with the United States in Paris, but even while discussions were under way, the war continued unabated with heavy civilian and military casualties on both sides.

The Nixon administration began a slow withdrawal from a situation that looked more and more like a disaster for American policy. However, to cover our withdrawal, Nixon mounted a brief but large-scale attack into Cambodia in 1970. Finally, after renewed heavy bombing of the North Vietnamese capital of Hanoi, the North Vietnamese signed the Paris Peace Agreement in early 1973. The agreement called for an end to fighting, with all forces holding areas they controlled, a withdrawal of all U.S. troops, and the return of U.S. prisoners held by the North Vietnamese. The Paris Peace Agreement lasted only two years; after American troops were withdrawn, the

North Vietnamese launched a massive and successful attack on the South, leading to a complete collapse of the South Vietnamese government in 1975. Communist forces took over all of Vietnam, Laos, and Cambodia. The presidency, weakened by Watergate and lacking the support of Congress, was helpless. The American public was disgusted with the long and costly jungle war. The United States did nothing. A few refugee survivors were helped to find homes in America, but the war in Vietnam ended in American defeat.

China   President Nixon's decision to seek a reconciliation with Red China, suddenly and dramatically revealed in mid-1971, signaled a new American effort to balance Soviet power in the world. In 1979 the Carter administration opened full diplomatic relations with the Peoples Republic of China and cut off U.S. relations with the non-communist government of the Republic of China in Taiwan. The new policy has caused anxiety in the Soviet Union and forecast a considerable shift in the balance of power in the world community. It was Henry Kissinger's view that the United States should, by taking advantage of the growing split between China and the Soviet Union, play a power-balancing role between these communist giants. In contrast, President Carter has tried to reassure the Soviets that the U.S. is not playing its "China card" against the U.S.S.R.

The Middle East   In 1948 immediately after Britain withdrew from its old League of Nations "mandate" to govern Palestine and the United Nations recognized the new nation of Israel, the Arab-Israeli conflict broke out into open warfare. Although vastly outnumbered, the Israelis were successful in their war of independence. Despite the fact that neither Israelis nor Arabs received much outside military assistance, tensions continued. Palestinian Arabs who were displaced from Israel were not integrated into surrounding Arab nations, but were instead kept in squalid camps in Egypt, Jordan, and Syria. These camps became the source of the "Palestinian" question.

In 1956, after Egyptian President Nasser seized the British-built and -owned Suez Canal, a combined force of British, French, and Israeli forces captured the canal, with Israelis doing most of the fighting in the Sinai desert. The United States, seeking to maintain its influence in the oil-rich Arab world, forced a return of the canal and of all captured lands to Egypt. Nonetheless, Egypt and Syria turned increasingly to the Soviet Union for military aid (although Lebanon and Jordan did not). In 1967 Egypt and Syria, heavily armed by the Russians, raced their armies to the Israeli frontier. But in the Six Day

War in a lightning military strike, the Israelis, though heavily outnumbered, defeated the forces of Egypt, Syria, and Jordan. The Israeli border expanded to the Suez Canal in the west, the Jordan River in the east, and the Golan Heights in the northeast. The Israelis asked for a permanent peace agreement that would recognize the right of Israel to exist, but the defeated Arabs, having received a rapid influx of new Russian arms, refused to negotiate under any conditions.

In 1973 the Arabs were prepared for another major military attack on Israel—the fourth in twenty-five years. The Yom Kippur War resulted in yet another defeat for the Arab nations, but this time the Israelis suffered a greater loss of men and material than they had in previous wars. The Yom Kippur War also resulted in the United States becoming directly involved in negotiations. The Arab nations placed a temporary embargo on oil shipped to America as a way of forcing the United States to pressure Israel into concessions. When Egyptian armies were threatened with annihilation in the desert and the Syrian capital of Damascus was under Israeli attack, the Soviets prepared to send in their own troops. A direct confrontation with the Soviets was avoided only when Henry Kissinger succeeded in getting the Israelis to pull back. Kissinger was later able to obtain additional limited Israeli withdrawals and demilitarized zones in the Sinai and Golan areas. Indeed, Kissinger began to win the Egyptians away from the Soviets and to move Israel and the Arab states closer to a permanent peace.

However, hostilities in the area run deep. "Palestinian" terrorists continued to inflame old hatreds, and the Soviets continued to stir unrest. In 1977 President Anwar Sadat of Egypt surprised the world by announcing that he was prepared to go to Jerusalem and talk with Israel's Prime Minister Menachem Begin in an effort to achieve a permanent peace. This announcement changed the long-standing Arab policy of refusing even to recognize the existence of Israel. The subsequent talks between Egypt and Israel did not bring immediate peace. "Hard-line" Arab states, such as Iraq, Libya, Algeria, and Syria, and the militant Palestinian Liberation Organization denounced the Egyptian-Israeli talks. However, with the forces of the Arab nations and Israel reasonably balanced, the atmosphere for peace in the Middle East improved. President Carter succeeded in moving Egypt and Israel closer to peace in talks between himself, President Sadat of Egypt, and Prime Minister Begin of Israel, at the presidential conference site at Camp David, Maryland.

The signing of a peace treaty by Anwar Sadat and Menachem Begin at the White House in 1979 brought a new promise of hope to the embattled Middle East. The Israelis agreed to a gradual withdrawal of all occupied Egyptian lands (the Sinai) and to open negotiations regarding the future of Arabs living in the Israeli controlled areas of the West Bank of the Jordan River and the Gaza strip. In exchange, Egypt agreed to recognize the right of Israel to exist and to exchange ambassadors. But even this limited agreement was denounced by other Arab states, and peace in the Middle East is by no means assured.

CASE STUDY
The Balance of Forces: U.S. and U.S.S.R.

Because of the high risks and costs of all-out nuclear war and the *recognition* of their risks and costs by the United States and the Soviet Union, limited conventional war is a more likely occurrence than a thermonuclear exchange. The notion of deterrence in nuclear war strategy involves the *psychological* use of *very* destructive weapons. Conventional war strategy is much more likely to involve the *actual* use of *less* destructive weapons—artillery, tanks, troops, and tactical aircraft.

America's active involvement in limited conventional wars in Korea and Vietnam has made most Americans realize that "war" is not a single, simple, or uniform action. Wars come in different varieties and sizes. Sometimes it is difficult for Americans to understand why this is so—why the United States does not seek "total victory" in every war and use any and every weapon in its arsenal to achieve that victory.

If the object of war becomes total victory over the enemy, there will be no limit on the enemy's use of force. Total victory for one nation implies total defeat for its opponent—a threat to national survival that justifies unlimited levels of violence. Political objectives are set aside for possible resolution after the war, and every effort is directed toward the complete destruction of the enemy's war-making power. As the dimensions of violence and destruction increase, the war arouses passionate fears and hatreds, which themselves come to replace rational objectives in the conflict. As the level of suffering and sacrifice increases, the goal becomes the blind unreasoning destruction of the enemy.

In a "stable" nuclear balance of terror, where each side possesses assured destruction second-strike capability, conventional war becomes a more likely possibility than nuclear war. America's strategic nuclear forces have been designed to deter a direct attack on the continental United States and a major attack on Western Europe. In *all* other conflicts, the United States will probably rely on conventional weapons, or perhaps in extremely rare circumstances, it will rely on "tactical" nuclear weapons. *Exclusive* reliance on nuclear weapons would place the United States in a terrible dilemma when confronted with limited aggression—a dilemma involving a single choice between surrender or nuclear war. In contrast, if the United States maintains a balance of forces—strategic nuclear, tactical nuclear, and conventional—it will be able to confront aggression anywhere in the world with weapons and forces appropriate to the situation.

Apart from their strictly military purposes, conventional forces also have an important psychological role to play. The deployment of U.S. troops in Berlin and Western Europe serves notice to the U.S.S.R. that it cannot send Soviet divisions across those borders without engaging U.S. troops. Even though these U.S. troops are no match for the massive Soviet armies, the very fact that American troops would have to be killed in a Soviet attack on Western Europe *insures* U.S. involvement in such a conflict. U.S. troops in Europe form a "plate-glass window": the Soviets know that to take Western Europe they would have to kill American troops, and this knowledge is a deterrent to such an attack. Deploying U.S. troops in Europe notifies friend and foe alike of the seriousness of our commitment to defend the area.

U.S. troops in Europe are equipped with tactical nuclear weapons. Obviously, this fact has additional deterrent value. Not only do the Soviets know that U.S. troops would be immediately involved in any defense against aggression, but they also know that such a defense would involve the use of nuclear weapons, at least at the tactical level.

It is very difficult to make an overall estimate of the relative military strength of the United States and the Soviet Union. Military forces differ in *quality* as well as *quantity*, and they also differ in their *mission* or purpose.

Consider the balance of conventional forces. The U.S.S.R. has a vast superiority over the U.S. in numbers of ground combat troops, tanks, and artillery. However, the U.S.S.R. must defend its eastern boundaries against possible Chinese incursion, and this diverts nearly one-third of Soviet ground combat forces. The Soviets must also use military forces to keep the populations of Eastern European nations in subjection. Nearly 20 percent of Soviet ground combat forces appear to be used to control the populations of Poland, Hungary, East Germany, Rumania, Bulgaria, and Czechoslovakia. Thus, it can be argued that the U.S.S.R. needs a larger ground combat capability than the U.S.

However, the overwhelming numerical superiority of the U.S.S.R. in ground combat troops, tanks, and artillery clearly exceeds that nation's need to protect itself from the Chinese and to maintain control of its Eastern European satellite nations. It is this excess capability that worries U.S. and NATO military commanders. The only element in the European equation that offsets the Soviet excess capability is superiority in U.S. tactical nuclear weapons. (The U.S. is estimated to have seven thousand tactical nuclear weapons in Europe, compared to a maximum of three thousand for the Soviets.) But clearly the Soviets have a preponderance of conventional ground combat forces.

American conventional arms—tactical, aircraft, conventional bombs, tanks, antitank missiles, artillery, and battlefield missiles—are technologically equal or superior to Soviet conventional arms. But the U.S.S.R. produces so many more conventional arms than the U.S. that the Soviets can send advanced arms to various nations in the Middle East, Asia, and Africa without depleting their own armies. In contrast, to assist the Israelis in the Yom Kippur War in 1973, the U.S. had to seriously deplete its NATO forces as well as its home arsenal.

The United States currently maintains an armed force of 2.1 million, compared to 4.5 million for the Soviet Union (see table 14-1). But the U.S. may not be able to maintain current manpower levels under the "all volunteer" concept—that is, without the draft.

The Soviet Union spends about 15 percent of its gross national product on defense, compared to 5 percent for the United States. (However, since the GNP of the United States is larger than that of the Soviet Union, the ratio of Soviet to

Table 14–1   Balance of Forces U.S. and U.S.S.R.

Strategic Nuclear Forces	U.S.	U.S.S.R.
ICBM (Intercontinental ballistic missiles)	1,054	1,618
SLBM (Submarine-launched ballistic missiles)	656	740
Submarines, strategic	41	43
Bombers, strategic	419	226
Total Armed Forces (millions)	2.1	4.5
Army		
Divisions	16	167 [a]
Deployment	5 Europe	31 Eastern Europe
	1 S. Korea	63 Europe and U.S.S.R.
	10 U.S.	28 southern U.S.S.R.
		45 Chinese border
Tanks (all types)	4,000	15,000
Marines [b]		
Division	3	—
Aircraft	500	—
Air Force		
Combat aircraft	5,500	5,300
Navy		
Major surface-combat ships	177	221
Attack submarines	73	245
Aircraft carriers	13 [c]	1 [d]
Aircraft	2,000	750 [d]

Sources: Institute for Strategic Studies, *The Military Balance 1975* (London: Institute for Strategic Studies, 1975); updated from *The Budget of the United States Government 1977.*

[a] At full strength, Soviet combat divisions include 8,000 to 10,000 men, compared to 10,000 to 14,000 men in full-strength U.S. combat divisions.

[b] U.S.S.R. "Naval Infantry" is organized in brigades and assigned to fleets; they have no separate air support units.

[c] U.S. carriers include the new nuclear-powered *Enterprise* and *Nimitz* at 76,000 tons capable of carrying 140 combat aircraft.

[d] The Soviet Navy relies primarily on missile-carrying cruisers rather than aircraft carriers; only one 40,000-ton carrier has been put in operation; most Soviet naval aircraft are shore-based.

U.S. defense spending is closer to two to one, rather than three to one.) If current trends in defense spending continue in both nations, eventually the Soviets will gain superiority in all aspects of war-making power. To maintain a reasonable balance of forces, the U.S. must either increase its defense spending or achieve some agreement with the Soviet Union that would limit both strategic and conventional arms.

NOTES

1. Hans Morgenthau, *Politics among Nations* (New York: Knopf, 1960), p. 27.
2. Quincy Wright, *A Study of War* (Chicago: University of Chicago Press, 1942), pp. 641–46.
3. Frederick H. Hartman, *The Relations of Nations*, 4th ed. (New York: Macmillan, 1973), p. 12.
4. Terms used in Article X of the Covenant of the League of Nations.
5. These moves included (1) the establishment of Communist governments in Eastern European nations in violation of wartime agreements at Yalta and Potsdam to support "democratic" governments "broadly representative" of all factions; (2) military support of the Communist takeover of Czechoslovakia in 1948; (3) the breakup of a four-power control commission that was to govern the occupation of Germany and the sealing off of the Soviet sector of East Germany; (4) a military blockade of Berlin in 1948 designed to oust American, British, and French occupation authorities; (5) Soviet military support for armed Communist troops in Greece and Turkey; (6) the continued maintenance of a large Soviet army in Eastern Europe threatening the security of Western European nations.

DISCUSSION QUESTIONS

1. Define *sovereignty* and discuss the role it plays in international politics. Describe the nature of international law.
2. Giving specific examples of each type of system, compare and evaluate the relative effectiveness of a balance of power system, collective security, and regional security. Include in your discussion a description of the organization of the United Nations.
3. Discuss the following components of the current United States policy of *deterrence*: assured destruction deterrence; the "triad"; damage limitation; credible first-strike capability.
4. Describe the balance of terror ("MAD") and identify the factors that pose a threat to the stability of this balance, as well as those factors that act as stabilizing elements.

5. Discuss the SALT I ABM treaty and offensive arms agreement. What did each side gain from the SALT I agreement? What effect did the agreement have on damage limitation efforts? What role does satellite reconnaissance play in the SALT agreement? Describe some of the factors that have complicated SALT II.

6. In the context of either the Vietnam War or the Middle East crises of 1956 (Suez Canal), 1967 (Six Day War), and 1973 (Yom Kippur War), discuss the concept of "mini balances of power." What is the danger of superpower intervention in local wars?

7. Discuss why "total victory" is no longer a realistic object of war and why conventional war is a more likely possibility than nuclear war in today's world. Why must the superpowers maintain conventional weapons as well as nuclear weapons? Discuss the current balance of U.S. and U.S.S.R. forces. Why is it difficult to make an overall estimate of their relative strength?

SUGGESTED READINGS

Congressional Quarterly, *U.S. Defense Policy* (Washington, D.C.: Congressional Quarterly, Inc., 1978).

Council on Foreign Relations, *Nuclear Weapons and World Politics* (New York: McGraw-Hill, 1977).

John E. Endicott and Roy W. Stafford, *American Defense Policy* (Baltimore: Johns Hopkins Press, 1977).

Colin S. Gray, *The Soviet-American Arms Race* (Lexington, Mass.: Lexington Books, 1976).

Jerome H. Kahan, *Security in the Nuclear Age* (Washington, D.C.: Brookings, 1977).

Appendix
Social Indicators

Increasingly, public officials are turning to social scientists to ask questions about the effectiveness of ongoing and proposed programs: What is that program doing? Why do we need it? What does it cost? The answers they receive are not yet consistently good ones, but the need for systematic social science research is now widely recognized.

Many social scientists have advocated the development of a set of indicators to show social progress (or retrogression) over time. They have urged the preparation of an annual "Social Report" designed to assess the social conditions of the nation. Most Americans can agree on the values of a healthy, well-educated, adequately housed, and affluent population, even if they cannot agree on public policies to achieve these values. Perhaps a general assessment of the nation's progress toward these goals would be helpful in an overall evaluation of the effectiveness of public policy. At least, that is the idea behind this "social indicators" movement. *Social indicators* are defined simply as quantitative data that serve as measures of socially important conditions in a society.

In 1977 the U.S. Department of Commerce published *Social Indicators 1976*. (This was the second such report ever made by the federal government; the first was *Social Indicators 1973*.) In this report, the federal government acknowledged that:

many aspects of our lives, particularly their qualitative features, are not adequately reflected in the available statistics. In addition, those aspects which involve complex interactions among a variety of factors cannot be expressed at all in terms of simple descriptive statistics. Still other aspects, such as our newly emerged concerns with environmental quality and the energy crisis, are not reflected in established statistical series relating to individual behavior or well-being. It has also been necessary to exercise considerable judgment in selecting from the enormous body of available data those data that are presented here. In this process, much detail has been buried in aggregate figures or omitted entirely. Thus the descriptive information contained in this report is no substitute for the insights and interpretations of our social analysts, commentators, and critics. But if statistical data do not tell the whole story, they do provide much of the factual "warp and woof" with which a comprehensive

435

picture of our condition as a society may be woven. In short, a critical examination of the report should provide a factual basis for independent assessments of our current social conditions and the directions in which we appear to be evolving as a society. These assessments, reflecting the different perspectives of individual readers and analysts, may help to provide awareness of both the problems and opportunities which are present in our society. The report does not provide such an assessment— that is up to the reader.

We have selected just a few of these "social indicators" to encourage students to assess current social conditions for themselves and to observe the directions of social change in America. We do not comment about whether these measures are "good" or "bad." As social scientists, however, we should have the best available information on topics of concern.

Figure A   College Enrollment of Persons 18 to 24 Years Old, by Sex and Race, for Selected Years: 1955–1975

Source: U.S. Department of Commerce, *Social Indicators, 1976* (Washington, D.C.: Government Printing Office, 1977).

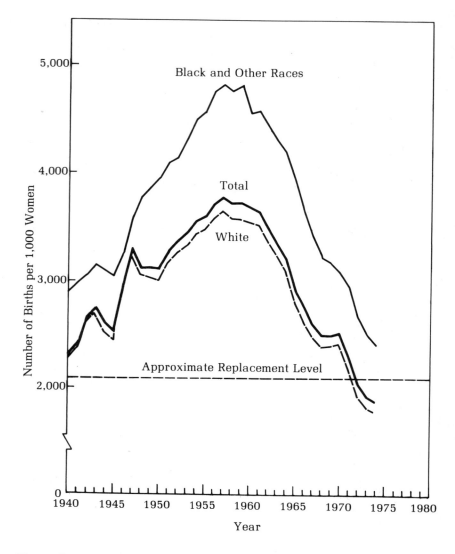

Figure B   Fertility Rates by Race: 1940–1974
Source: U.S. Department of Commerce, *Social Indicators 1976* (Washington, D.C.: Government Printing Office, 1977).

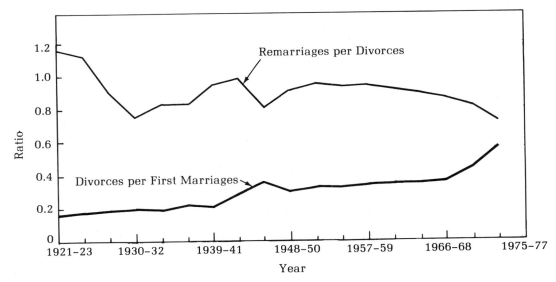

Figure C First Marriages, Divorces, and Remarriages of Women:
3-Year Averages, 1921–1923 to 1972–1974

Source: U.S. Department of Commerce, *Social Indicators 1976* (Washington,
D.C.: Government Printing Office, 1977).

Figure D Ratio of Number of Divorces to Number of First Marriages
and of Number of Remarriages to Number of Divorces of Women:
3-Year Averages, 1921–1923 to 1972–1974

Source: U.S. Department of Commerce, *Social Indicators 1976* (Washington,
D.C.: Government Printing Office, 1977).

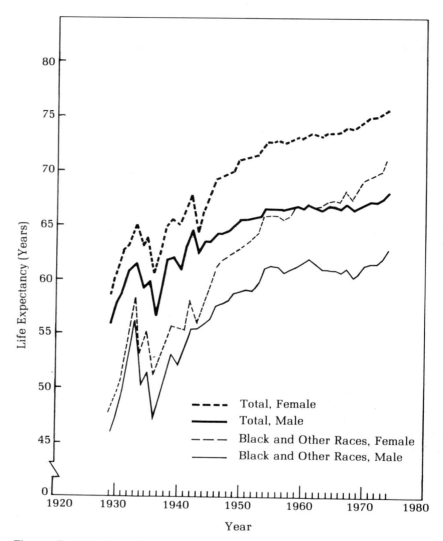

Figure E   Life Expectancy at Birth by Sex and Race: 1929–1974
Source: U.S. Department of Commerce, *Social Indicators 1976* (Washington, D.C.: Government Printing Office, 1977).

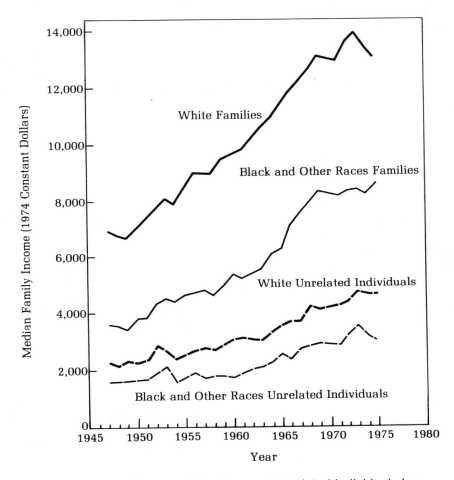

Figure F Median Income of Families and Unrelated Individuals by Race: 1947–1975

Source: U.S. Department of Commerce, *Social Indicators 1976* (Washington, D.C.: Government Printing Office, 1977).

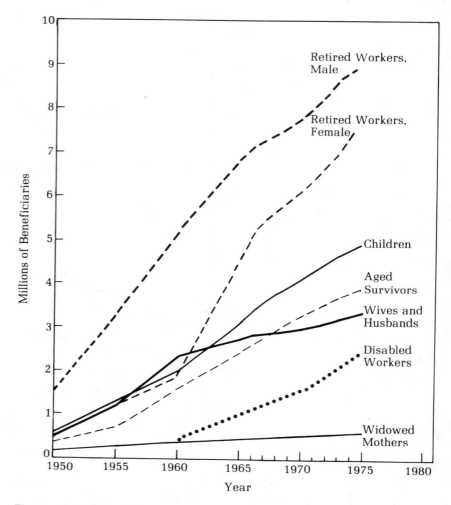

Figure G Persons Receiving OASDHI Benefits by Type of Recipient: 1950–1975

Source: U.S. Department of Commerce, *Social Indicators 1976* (Washington, D.C.: Government Printing Office, 1977).

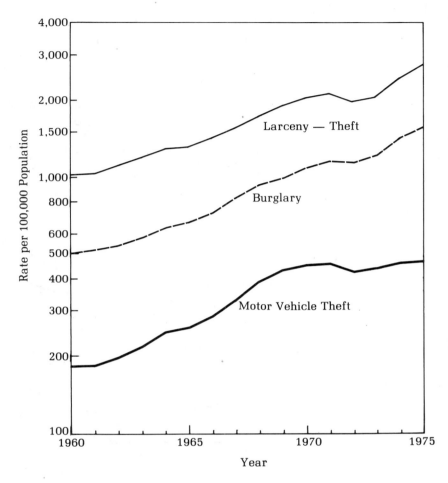

Figure H   Property Crime by Type: 1960–1975
Source: U.S. Department of Commerce, *Social Indicators 1976* (Washington, D.C.: Government Printing Office, 1977).

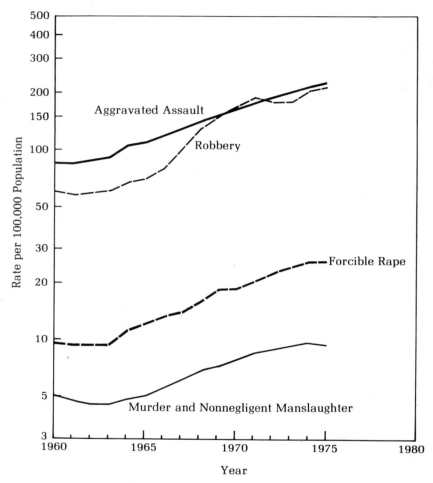

Figure I   Violent Crime by Type: 1960–1975
Source: U.S. Department of Commerce, *Social Indicators 1976* (Washington, D.C.: Government Printing Office, 1977).

Table A   Marital Happiness: 1973–1975

	1973		1974		1975	
Response	*No.*	*%*	*No.*	*%*	*No.*	*%*
Very happy	727	67.8	732	69.1	671	67.4
Pretty happy	317	29.6	290	27.4	297	29.8
Not too happy	28	2.6	37	3.5	27	2.7
Don't know or no answer	4	(X)	6	(X)	7	(X)
Not applicable[a]	428	(X)	419	(X)	488	(X)
Total	1,072	100.0	1,059	100.0	995	100.0

X Not applicable.

[a]Persons in the survey who were not married were not asked this question.

Source: National Opinion Research Center (NORC), University of Chicago, *National Data Program for the Social Sciences, Code Book for the Spring 19--, General Social Survey* (1973, 1974, and 1975). Copyright by NORC. Used by permission.

Table B Occupations of Employed Persons by Sex and Race: 1960 and 1975

Occupation	Total		White		Black and Other Races		Male		Female	
	No. (Thousands)	% of Total	No. (Thousands)	% of Total	No. (Thousands)	% of Total	No. (Thousands)	% of Total	No. (Thousands)	% of Total
1960										
All workers	65,778	100.0	58,850	100.0	6,927	100.0	43,904	100.0	21,874	100.0
Professional, technical, and kindred workers	7,469	11.4	7,138	12.1	331	4.8	4,766	10.9	2,703	12.4
Managers, officials, and proprietors	7,067	10.7	6,889	11.7	178	2.6	5,968	13.6	1,099	5.0
Clerical and kindred workers	9,762	14.8	9,259	15.7	503	7.3	3,145	7.2	6,617	30.3
Sales workers	4,224	6.4	4,123	7.0	101	1.5	2,544	5.8	1,680	7.7
Craftsmen and foremen	8,554	13.0	8,139	13.8	415	6.0	8,332	19.0	222	1.0
Operatives	11,950	18.2	10,536	17.9	1,414	20.4	8,617	19.6	3,333	15.2
Nonfarm laborers	3,553	5.4	2,602	4.4	951	13.7	3,471	7.9	82	.4
Private household workers	1,973	3.0	991	1.7	982	14.2	30	.1	1,943	8.9
Service workers, except private household	6,050	9.2	4,836	8.2	1,214	17.5	2,814	6.4	3,236	14.8
Farmers and farm managers	2,776	4.2	2,557	4.3	219	3.2	2,667	6.1	109	.5
Farm laborers and foremen	2,400	3.3	1,778	3.0	622	9.0	1,552	3.9	848	3.2
1975										
All workers	84,783	100.0	75,713	100.0	9,070	100.0	51,230	100.0	33,553	100.0
Professional, technical, and kindred workers	12,748	15.0	11,711	15.5	1,037	11.4	7,481	14.6	5,267	15.7
Managers, officials, and proprietors	8,891	10.5	8,493	11.2	398	4.4	7,162	14.0	1,729	5.2
Clerical and kindred workers	15,128	17.8	13,705	18.1	1,423	15.7	3,355	6.5	11,773	35.1

	Total		White		Black and Other Races		Male		Female	
Sales workers	5,460	6.4	5,218	6.9	242	2.7	3,137	6.1	2,323	6.3
Craftsmen and foremen	10,972	12.9	10,177	13.4	795	8.8	10,472	20.4	501	1.5
Operatives	12,856	15.2	11,042	14.6	1,814	20.0	8,971	17.5	3,885	11.6
Nonfarm laborers	4,134	4.9	3,349	4.4	785	8.7	3,777	7.4	357	1.1
Private household workers	1,171	1.4	728	1.0	443	4.9	30	.1	1,141	3.4
Service workers, except private household	10,486	12.4	8,590	11.3	1,896	20.9	4,370	8.5	6,116	18.2
Farmers and farm managers	1,593	1.9	1,538	2.0	56	.6	1,492	2.9	102	.3
Farm laborers and foremen	1,343	1.6	1,162	1.5	181	2.0	985	1.9	358	1.1

Average Annual % of Change, 1960 to 1975	Total	White	Black and Other Races	Male	Female
Professional, technical, and kindred workers	3.6	3.4	6.6	3.7	3.3
Managers, officials, and proprietors	-.2	-.5	1.8	.4	.2
Clerical and kindred workers	3.0	2.4	8.4	-.1	4.8
Sales workers	-	-.1	1.2	.3	-.8
Craftsmen and foremen	-.1	-.4	2.8	1.4	.5
Operatives	-3.0	-3.3	-.4	-2.1	-3.6
Nonfarm laborers	-.5	-	-5.0	-.5	.7
Private household workers	-1.6	-.7	-9.3	-	-5.5
Service workers, except private household	3.2	3.1	3.4	2.1	3.4
Farmers and farm managers	-2.3	-2.3	-2.6	-3.2	-.2
Farm laborers and foremen	-1.7	-1.5	-7.0	-2.0	-2.1

- Represents zero.

Source: U.S. Department of Labor, Employment and Training Report of the President, 1976.

Table C Socioeconomic Characteristics of the White, Black, and Spanish-Origin Population: 1975

Characteristic	White	Black	Spanish Origin	Characteristic	White	Black	Spanish Origin[a]
Age				**Labor Force Status**			
Total population (thousands)	182,500	23,785	11,202	Persons, 16 years and over (thousands)	133,501	15,541	6,724[c]
Percentage	100.0	100.0	100.0[b]	In civilian labor force (thousands)	82,084	9,123	4,024
Under 18 years	30.5	40.0	44.3	Percentage	61.5	58.7	59.8
18 to 64 years	58.9	52.7	52.1	Employed (percentage)	53.7	44.0	47.1
65 years and over	10.5	7.2	3.6	Unemployed (percentage)	7.8	14.7	12.7
Type of Residence							
Total	100.0	100.0	100.0[b]				
Metropolitan areas	66.8	75.2	81.4[b]	**Occupation of Employed Civilian Workers**			
Central cities	25.2	58.1	49.2[b]	Total employed, 16 years and over (thousands)	75,713	7,782	3,510[c]
Suburbs	41.6	17.1	32.1[b]	White-collar workers	51.7	30.8	33.0
Nonmetropolitan areas	33.2	24.8	18.6[b]	Blue-collar workers	32.4	39.3	46.7
				Service workers	12.3	27.3	16.8
Education				Farm workers	3.6	2.7	3.5
20 to 24 Years Old							
Total (thousands)	104,065	11,096	4,762				
Percentage	100.0	100.0	100.0				
Less than 4 years of high school	35.5	57.5	62.1				
4 years of high school	37.3	27.0	22.9				
Some college	27.2	15.5	15.0				

Family Income in 1974

25 Years and Over

Total (thousands)	15,883	2,162	992
Percentage	100.0	100.0	100.0
Less than 4 years of high school	14.0	28.3	40.6
4 years of high school	43.3	45.0	37.8
Some college	42.7	26.7	21.6

Size of Family

Percentage	100.0	100.0	100.0
Two persons	38.5	29.4	23.2
Three persons	21.6	22.7	22.5
Four persons	19.9	17.8	20.5
Five persons or more	20.0	30.1	33.8

Family Income in 1974

Total families (thousands)	49,451	5,498	2,477
Less than $5,000	11.1	31.5	21.6
$5,000 to $9,999	21.9	30.0	31.1
$10,000 to $14,999	25.1	19.1	24.3
$15,000 or more	42.1	19.4	23.1
Median family income (dollars)	13,356	7,808	9,559

Persons Below Poverty Level in 1974

Families with male head	5.5	16.6	16.6
Families with female head	27.6	55.9	53.2
Male unrelated individuals	18.3	29.9	29.0
Female unrelated individuals	26.5	51.9	40.7

[a] Persons of Spanish origin may be of any race.
[b] Based on March 1974 Current Population Survey.
[c] Unadjusted data for March 1975.

Source: U.S. Department of Commerce, Bureau of the Census, *Current Population Reports*, Series P-20, no. 292, March 1975.

Table D GNP and Personal Income, by Type of Income, 1950–1975

Period[a]	GNP (Billions)	Personal Income Total (Billions)	Wage and Salary Disbursements (Billions)	Social Insurance and Related Payments Amount (Billions)	% of Personal Income	Public Assistance and Related Payments Amount (Billions)	% of Personal Income	Other Income Total (Billions)	% of Personal Income	Social Insurance[b] (Billions)
1950	$ 286.2	$ 226.1	$ 147.0	$ 7.0	3.1	$ 2.3	1.0	$ 72.7	32.2	$ 2.9
1955	399.3	308.8	211.7	13.1	4.2	2.5	.8	86.7	28.1	5.2
1960	506.0	399.7	271.9	23.9	6.0	3.3	.8	109.9	27.5	9.3
1961	523.3	415.0	279.5	27.4	6.6	3.4	.8	114.4	27.6	9.7
1962	563.8	440.7	298.0	28.6	6.5	3.5	.8	120.9	27.4	10.3
1963	594.7	463.1	313.4	30.2	6.5	3.7	.8	127.6	27.6	11.8
1964	635.7	495.7	336.1	31.6	6.4	3.9	.8	136.7	27.6	12.6
1965	688.1	537.0	362.0	34.2	6.4	4.1	.8	150.0	27.9	13.3
1966	753.0	584.9	398.4	37.7	6.4	4.4	.8	162.2	27.7	17.8
1967	796.3	626.6	427.5	44.4	7.1	5.1	.8	170.2	27.2	20.6
1968	868.5	685.2	469.5	50.6	7.4	5.9	.9	182.0	26.6	22.8
1969	935.5	745.8	514.6	55.4	7.4	6.9	.9	195.2	26.2	26.3
1970	982.4	801.3	546.5	65.4	8.2	9.5	1.2	207.9	25.9	28.0
1971	1,063.4	859.1	579.4	76.3	8.9	11.8	1.4	222.4	25.9	30.8
1972	1,171.1	942.5	633.8	84.3	8.9	13.0	1.4	245.6	26.1	34.2
1973	1,306.3	1,054.3	701.0	97.7	9.3	13.5	1.3	284.3	27.0	42.2
1974	1,406.9	1,154.7	763.6	114.6	9.9	17.5	1.5	306.4	26.5	47.4
1975	1,498.9	1,245.9	801.6	142.3	11.4	20.8	1.7	331.0	26.6	49.8

[a] Before 1960, data are for the 48 States and the District of Columbia; beginning 1960, data include Alaska and Hawaii.

[b] Amount of personal contribution paid out of other income.

Source: U.S. Department of Health, Education, and Welfare, Social Security Administration, *Social Security Bulletin*, April 1976.

Table E Attitudes toward Spending on National Priority Items: 1973-1976

Item	1973 Total Replies	1973 % Too Much	1973 % Too Little	1974 Total Replies	1974 % Too Much	1974 % Too Little	1975 Total Replies	1975 % Too Much	1975 % Too Little	1976 Total Replies	1976 % Too Much	1976 % Too Little
Protecting nation's health	1,445	4.8	63.0	1,426	4.7	66.2	1,425	5.3	65.2	1,441	5.1	62.6
Halting rising crime rate	1,405	5.0	68.8	1,405	5.1	70.2	1,400	5.8	69.6	1,413	8.4	69.3
Dealing with drug addiction	1,399	6.4	70.3	1,396	6.9	63.5	1,370	9.0	59.6	1,390	8.1	63.0
Protecting environment	1,413	7.9	64.8	1,378	8.3	63.2	1,398	10.3	56.9	1,425	9.8	57.4
Improving nation's education system	1,434	9.4	51.2	1,418	8.9	52.7	1,420	11.8	51.3	1,449	9.7	51.8
Solving big-city problems	1,319	14.0	54.8	1,258	12.9	58.5	1,241	14.1	56.2	1,318	22.1	48.3
Improving conditions of blacks	1,402	23.1	34.8	1,379	22.2	33.1	1,372	26.0	29.2	1,392	27.2	29.4
Military, armaments, defense	1,407	40.3	11.9	1,379	33.3	18.1	1,387	33.2	17.8	1,395	29.2	25.8
Social welfare	1,432	53.8	20.7	1,422	43.8	23.1	1,405	45.2	24.7	1,429	62.6	13.9
Space exploration	1,432	61.4	7.8	1,427	63.4	8.0	1,425	60.8	7.7	1,459	61.9	9.4
Foreign aid	1,421	74.3	4.4	1,422	78.7	3.2	1,416	76.8	5.7	1,438	78.3	3.1

Note: Remaining percentages (not shown) cover respondents who think we are spending "about the right amount" on the specified area. Persons reporting "don't know" or not answering were not included in the calculations of the percentages shown.

Source: National Opinion Research Center (NORC), University of Chicago. *National Data Program for the Social Sciences, Code Book for the Spring 19––, General Social Survey* (1973, 1974, 1975, and 1976). Copyright by NORC. Used by permission.

Table F   Consumer Price Indexes: 1940–1976

Period	All Items	All Items less Medical Care	Medical Care	Food	Apparel and Upkeep	Housing	Trans-por-tation	Personal Care	Reading and Recrea-tion	Other Goods and Services	All Services
1940	42.0	(NA)	36.8	35.2	42.8	52.4	42.7	40.2	46.1	48.3	43.6
1945	53.0	(NA)	42.1	50.7	61.5	59.1	47.8	55.1	62.4	56.9	48.7
1950	72.1	(NA)	53.7	74.5	79.0	72.8	68.2	68.3	74.4	69.9	58.9
1955	80.2	(NA)	64.8	81.6	84.1	82.3	77.4	77.9	76.7	79.8	70.5
1960	88.7	89.4	79.1	88.0	89.6	90.2	89.6	90.1	87.3	87.8	83.8
1961	89.6	90.3	81.4	89.1	90.4	90.9	90.6	90.6	89.3	88.5	85.2
1962	90.6	91.2	83.5	89.9	90.9	91.7	92.5	92.2	91.3	89.1	86.2
1963	91.7	92.3	85.6	91.2	91.9	92.7	93.0	93.4	92.8	90.6	88.5
1964	92.9	93.5	87.3	92.4	92.7	93.8	94.3	94.5	95.0	92.0	90.2
1965	94.5	94.9	89.5	94.4	93.7	94.9	95.9	95.2	95.9	94.2	92.2
1966	97.2	97.7	93.4	99.1	96.1	97.2	97.2	97.1	97.5	97.2	95.8
1967	100.0	100.0	100.0	100.0	100.0	100.0	100.0	100.0	100.0	100.0	100.0
1968	104.2	104.1	106.1	103.6	105.4	104.2	103.2	104.2	104.7	104.6	105.2
1969	109.8	109.7	113.4	108.9	111.5	110.8	107.2	109.3	108.7	109.1	112.5
1970	116.3	116.1	120.6	114.9	116.1	118.9	112.7	113.2	113.4	116.0	121.6
1971	121.3	120.9	128.4	118.4	119.8	124.3	118.6	116.8	119.3	120.9	128.4
1972	125.3	124.9	132.5	123.5	122.3	129.2	119.9	119.8	122.8	125.5	133.3
1973	133.1	132.9	137.7	141.4	126.8	135.0	123.8	125.2	125.9	129.0	139.1
1974	147.7	147.7	150.5	161.7	136.2	150.6	137.7	137.3	133.8	137.2	152.0
1975	161.2	160.9	168.6	175.4	142.3	166.8	150.6	150.7	144.4	147.4	166.6
1976	169.2	168.4	182.6	179.9	146.8	175.6	163.5	158.9	150.3	152.9	178.4

Note: Index: 1967–100; yearly data are annual averages.

Source: U.S. Department of Health, Education, and Welfare, Social Security Administration. *Social Security Bulletin.* April 1976.

Table G Persons below the Poverty Level, by Age, 1966–1974

	Number (Millions)						Poverty Rate (%)					
	All Persons	Under 14	14–21 Years	22–44 Years	45–64 Years	65 Years and Over	All Persons	Under 14	14–21 Years	22–44 Years	45–64 Years	65 and Over
1966	28.5	10.0	3.8	5.3	4.3	5.1	14.7	17.9	14.3	9.8	11.0	28.5
1967	27.8	9.4	3.9	4.9	4.2	5.4	14.2	16.9	14.2	9.1	10.4	29.5
1968	25.4	8.7	3.7	4.6	3.8	4.6	12.8	15.8	13.1	8.2	9.4	25.0
1969	24.3	8.0	3.5	4.3	3.7	4.8	12.1	14.7	12.2	7.7	8.9	25.3
1970	25.5	8.5	3.7	4.8	3.8	4.7	12.6	15.7	12.6	8.3	9.0	24.5
1971[a]	25.6	8.4	4.0	5.1	3.8	4.3	12.5	15.9	13.2	8.5	9.1	21.6
1972	24.5	8.1	4.0	5.0	3.7	3.7	11.9	15.7	12.8	8.2	8.6	18.6
1973	23.0	7.5	3.9	4.7	3.5	3.4	11.1	15.0	12.2	7.6	8.1	16.3
1974	23.4	7.9	4.0	4.9	3.4	3.1	11.2	16.0	12.3	7.7	7.9	14.6
1975	25.9	8.6	4.6	5.7	3.7	3.3	12.3	17.8	14.1	8.8	8.6	15.3

Note: Excludes inmates of institutions and members of Armed Forces residing in barracks.

[a] Beginning with March 1972 Current Population Survey, data based on 1970 census population controls.

Source: U.S. Department of Commerce, Bureau of the Census, *Current Population Reports*, Series P-60, nos. 95, 98, and 102.

Table H Persons below the Poverty Level by Region and Race of Family Head: 1967–1975.

| | Number of Persons (Millions) | | | | | | Poverty Rate (%) | | | | | |
| | North and West | | | South | | | North and West | | | South | | |
	All Races	White	Black and Other Races	All Races	White	Black and Other Races	All Races	White	Black and Other Races	All Races	White	Black and Other Races
1967	14.8	11.7	2.8	13.0	7.2	5.7	10.8	9.4	27.3	22.1	15.3	50.1
1968	13.3	10.7	2.3	12.1	6.7	5.3	9.5	8.5	21.8	20.4	14.0	46.7
1969	13.1	10.5	2.3	11.2	6.2	4.9	9.5	8.3	22.2	18.3	12.6	41.0
1970	14.0	11.4	2.4	11.5	6.1	5.3	10.0	8.9	22.8	18.5	12.4	42.7
1971[a]	14.4	11.5	2.6	11.2	6.3	4.8	10.2	9.0	24.2	17.5	12.2	40.0
1972	13.5	10.2	2.9	10.9	6.0	4.8	9.6	8.0	26.2	16.9	11.5	39.8
1973	12.9	9.7	2.9	10.1	5.4	4.5	9.1	7.6	26.0	15.3	10.3	36.3
1974	13.1	9.9	2.8	10.3	5.9	4.4	9.2	7.7	25.2	15.4	10.8	34.9
1975	14.8	11.5	2.8	11.1	6.2	4.7	10.4	9.0	25.2	16.2	11.4	36.6

Note: Excludes inmates of institutions and members of Armed Forces residing in barracks.

[a] Beginning with the March 1972 Current Population Survey, data based on 1970 census population controls.

Source: U.S. Department of Commerce, Bureau of the Census, *Current Population Reports*, Series P-60, nos. 86, 98, and 102.

Table I Loss of Life by Violent Causes: 1940–1973

	Homicide	Suicide	Motor Vehicle Accidents	Other Accidents		Homicide	Suicide	Motor Vehicle Accidents	Other Accidents
1940	6.3	14.3	26.2	46.9	1957	4.9	9.6	24.1	29.3
1941	6.0	12.7	29.8	45.2	1958	4.9	10.5	22.5	27.3
1942	5.9	11.8	21.0	48.8	1959	5.1	10.5	22.8	27.1
1943	5.1	10.0	17.6	53.6	1960	5.2	10.6	22.5	27.4
1944	5.1	9.6	18.2	50.6	1961	5.2	10.5	22.1	26.1
1945	5.8	10.7	21.1	47.6	1962	5.4	11.0	23.1	26.6
1946	6.4	11.1	23.8	43.2	1963	5.5	11.3	24.3	26.6
1947	6.1	11.1	22.8	43.0	1964	5.7	11.0	25.8	26.3
1948	6.0	10.8	22.1	41.2	1965	6.2	11.4	26.6	26.8
1949	5.5	11.0	21.4	35.9	1966	6.7	11.1	28.3	27.3
1950	5.4	11.0	23.3	34.2	1967	7.7	11.1	27.8	27.0
1951	5.0	10.0	24.6	34.8	1968	8.2	11.0	28.4	26.7
1952	5.4	9.7	25.0	33.8	1969	8.6	11.3	28.5	26.8
1953	5.1	9.8	24.8	32.4	1970	9.1	11.8	27.4	26.3
1954	5.1	9.9	23.0	30.1	1971	10.0	11.9	26.6	25.3
1955	4.8	9.9	24.6	29.7	1972	10.3	12.1	27.0	25.0
1956	5.0	9.7	25.2	29.2	1973	10.5	12.0	26.4	25.3

Note: Deaths per 100,000 population adjusted to the age distribution of the 1940 population.

Source: U.S. Department of Health, Education, and Welfare. Public Health Service. National Center for Health Statistics, unpublished data.

Table J   Evaluations of Life in the United States by Selected Characteristics of Respondents

	% Who Think Life in the United States Is Getting:			Ratio, Worse/ Better
	Better	Staying Same	Worse	
Sex				
Male	20	44	36	1.8
Female	14	51	35	2.6
Age				
18 to 24 years old	24	45	31	1.3
25 to 34 years old	15	44	41	2.7
35 to 44 years old	16	50	34	2.1
45 to 54 years old	14	54	32	2.3
55 to 64 years old	20	42	38	1.9
65 years and over	13	52	35	2.8
Educational Attainment				
Eighth grade or less	12	55	33	2.9
Some high school, no diploma	11	52	37	3.3
High school diploma	17	47	36	2.1
Some college, no degree	22	42	36	1.6
College degree(s)	27	38	35	1.3
Race				
White	17	47	36	2.2
Black	17	50	33	1.9
Income				
Less than $3,000	12	52	36	3.0
$3,000 to $4,999	13	49	38	2.9
$5,000 to $6,999	15	50	35	2.3
$7,000 to $9,999	17	47	36	2.1
$10,000 to $11,999	16	47	37	2.4
$12,000 to $16,999	20	48	32	1.6
$17,000 or more	24	41	35	1.4
Size of Community				
Central cities	13	36	51	4.0
Large cities	20	42	38	1.9
Suburbs	21	44	35	1.7
Small cities and towns	16	51	33	2.0
Rural areas	15	53	32	2.2
Total responding	17	47	36	2.1

Source: Adapted from Table 8–3 in *The Quality of American Life: Perceptions, Evaluations, and Satisfactions,* by Angus Campbell, Philip E. Converse, and Willard L. Rodgers. © 1976 by Russell Sage Foundation, New York.

Index